AMERICAN INSECURITY AND
THE ORIGINS OF VULNERABILITY

American Insecurity and the Origins of Vulnerability

RUSS CASTRONOVO

PRINCETON UNIVERSITY PRESS
PRINCETON & OXFORD

Copyright © 2023 by Princeton University Press

Princeton University Press is committed to the protection of copyright and the intellectual property our authors entrust to us. Copyright promotes the progress and integrity of knowledge. Thank you for supporting free speech and the global exchange of ideas by purchasing an authorized edition of this book. If you wish to reproduce or distribute any part of it in any form, please obtain permission.

Requests for permission to reproduce material from this work should be sent to permissions@press.princeton.edu

Published by Princeton University Press
41 William Street, Princeton, New Jersey 08540
99 Banbury Road, Oxford OX2 6JX

press.princeton.edu

All Rights Reserved

Library of Congress Cataloging-in-Publication Data

Names: Castronovo, Russ, 1965– author.
Title: American insecurity and the origins of vulnerability / Russ Castronovo.
Description: Princeton : Princeton University Press, 2023. | Includes bibliographical references and index.
Identifiers: LCCN 2022057540 (print) | LCCN 2022057541 (ebook) | ISBN 9780691249858 (paperback) | ISBN 9780691249841 (hardback) | ISBN 9780691249872 (ebook)
Subjects: LCSH: Security (Psychology) in literature. | American literature—19th century—History and criticism. | American literature—18th century—History and criticism. | Security (Psychology)—United States—History. | Racism—United States—History. | Fear of crime—United States—History. | Public safety—United States—History. | BISAC: LITERARY CRITICISM / Subjects & Themes / Politics | POLITICAL SCIENCE / Privacy & Surveillance (see also SOCIAL SCIENCE / Privacy & Surveillance)
Classification: LCC PS217.S43 C37 2023 (print) | LCC PS217.S43 (ebook) | DDC 810.9/353—dc23/eng/20230515
LC record available at https://lccn.loc.gov/2022057540
LC ebook record available at https://lccn.loc.gov/2022057541

British Library Cataloging-in-Publication Data is available

Editorial: Anne Savarese & James Collier
Production Editorial: Ali Parrington
Jacket/Cover Design: Drohan DiSanto
Production: Lauren Reese
Publicity: William Pagdatoon

This book has been composed in Arno

10 9 8 7 6 5 4 3 2 1

For Maya, Julian, Leslie

CONTENTS

List of Illustrations   ix

Introduction: *Homo Securus* and the Story of Insecurity   1

PART I: CONTRADICTIONS AND CONTOURS

1 The Contradictions of Security in Thirteen Propositions   19

2 The Contours of Security across Nine Historical *Récits*   55

PART II: INFORMATION, AESTHETICS, POPULATION

3 Security and the Technologies of Liberalism: From James Fenimore Cooper to the NSA   81

4 Terror and the Informational Sublime: Data and Gothic Storytelling   115

5 Jeffersonian Trembling: White Nationalism and the Racial Origins of National Security   153

6 Creating White Insecurity: From David Walker's *Appeal* to the *Liberia Herald*   193

Epilogue: What Comes after Security?   229

Acknowledgments   237
Notes   241
Works Cited   259
Index   283

ILLUSTRATIONS

3.1. Frontispiece to *The Pioneers* — 105
4.1. Shannon's theory of sending information as a message — 136
4.2. Weaver's emendation to Shannon's account — 137
4.3. A "gothic theory of communication" — 140
4.4. Screenshot showing electronic advisory about malware — 150
5.1. Henan Howlett, "Plan of a Gradual Emancipation" — 171
5.2. Benjamin Silliman, "Some of the Causes of National Anxiety" — 179
6.1. Adriano Balbi, "Balance Politique du Globe en 1828" — 222
6.2. "Colony of Liberia, on the West Coast of Africa" — 226

INTRODUCTION

Homo Securus and the Story of Insecurity

SECURITY OFTEN GETS told as a tale of lost innocence. In the version of this story presented by C. Vann Woodward, a towering figure in Southern history and winner of the Pulitzer Prize, Americans throughout much of their history have enjoyed the good fortune of "a national disposition to look upon security as a natural right" (6). For close to two hundred years, "nature's gift of three vast bodies of water"—the Atlantic, the Pacific, and the once frozen Arctic Ocean—protected the United States from "any other power that might constitute a serious menace to its safety" (2). Thomas Paine had perceived as much in 1776 when he observed in a bluster of exceptionalism that "no country on the globe is so happily situated" as the independent states of America. If not by divine arrangement, then the geographical luck of the draw had relieved the white inhabitants of North America of the affective need to worry about security. That era seemed to have come to a close by World War II and certainly by 1960 when Woodward made this pronouncement in the pages of the *American Historical Review* not long after the United States and the Soviet Union each had demonstrated a capacity to launch ICBMs that could cross oceans in a matter of minutes. President George H. W. Bush would belatedly reach a similar conclusion, announcing in 2002 that "oceans no longer matter when it comes to making us safe" (qtd. in I. Young 10). But for much of its earlier history, from late in the War of 1812 when British soldiers invaded Washington, D.C., and set fire to the White House to December 1941 when Japanese planes bombed the U.S. naval base in the Hawaii Territory, the United States had enjoyed "free security," comfortably relying on the "bounty of nature" (Woodward 2) to save it from costly military expenditures and onerous taxes that burdened European powers preparing for national defense.[1]

That innocence was lost again most recently on September 11, 2001. Making direct reference to Woodward's essay a half century earlier, the military historian John Lewis Gaddis in *Surprise, Security, and the American Experience* (2004) remarked that the terrorist attacks of 9/11 shattered "the assumption of safety that had long since become . . . part of what it meant to be an American" (10). Speaking in the grandiose terms suited for a grand narrative, Gaddis describes this "national security crisis" as a "national identity crisis as well" (10). September 11 came as a shock to much of the world, but Gaddis believes that the breach of national security should not have been a blow to historical consciousness. Even though the burning of the White House in 1814 constitutes a "barely remembered violation of homeland security," U.S. continental expansion throughout the nineteenth century and internationalism can be viewed as elements of a "grand strategy" for securing territorial borders that shifted and adapted in response to changing geopolitical conditions (12, 14). This perspective helps bring into focus the tenets of unilateralism, preemption, and hegemony that have guided much of U.S. foreign policy in the twenty-first century, but it fails to explain why this innocence about security is repeatedly lost only to be reasserted and remade so frequently.

The confusion stems from the concept of national security itself, which tends to assume the nation's internal stability and domestic integrity in the first place. Security by this thinking encompasses the state's interaction with foreign powers through diplomacy, armaments, espionage, new technologies, population management, and information gathering that fall under its purview. When security first emerged as a core principle of governance for Thomas Hobbes, the immediate context was the internal strife of the English Civil War, but today and since World War II security refers predominantly to external threats.[2] Security gets grounded in national identity, an "us" unified against the potential threat posed by "them," that ignores zones of the homeland that are constantly being enumerated, tracked, and surveilled, in short, securitized. What conceptual elements of security become newly available for examination once the cloak of the national is removed? Security clearly has national significance, but this orientation has also meant its other components from the affective to the philosophical and from the biopolitical to the speculative are construed as having lesser importance. National security entails discussions of policy and military strategy, but security—without the buffer of a state-supported adjective—appears as an aesthetic and affective concern whose dimensions are at once as expansive as the sublime and as narrow as individual personal privacy. Even momentarily stripping away the "national" modifier forces security to stand on its own, as it were, and allows more direct examination of its effects upon social feelings and political sensations.

The curious aspect of national security is that it almost always involves an international context whether the danger appears as the specter of terrorist cells associated with foreign entities such as ISIS and Al-Qaeda or as the "debounding of uncontrollable risks" (Beck, "Terrorist Threat" 41) created by ecological and financial crises that pay no attention to borders. Even though global warming is a planetary concern, "the national security implications of climate change" are laden with ominous consequences that "exacerbate existing stressors, contributing to poverty, environmental degradation, and political instability, providing enabling environments for terrorist activity abroad" ("National Security Implications" 3).[3] Troll farms and keyboard armies sponsored by autocratic states such as Russia, Iran, and North Korea pose a threat to the security of democratic elections. Spreading misinformation and stoking partisan divisions fall well short of a coup d'état, a strategy that the CIA pursued in Latin America for decades. Yet the dangers of cyberterrorism are unrelenting: what such plots lack in the drama or suddenness of a military overthrow is made up by the burden of an ever-present awareness of the electronic infrastructure's vulnerability to such attacks. Inflated worries about election security and voter fraud, recent chimeras of the American right wing, have become a regular feature of the political landscape—and not without international help.[4]

In the face of such continuous emergencies, "the state is back, and for the old Hobbesian reason—the provision of security" (Beck, "Terrorist Threat" 47). In making this point, the sociologist of risk Ulrich Beck nonetheless asserts that ensuring safety from terrorism and other threats requires transnational solutions. Such bifocal vision is rare, as the tendency across disciplines has been to focus security outward in ways that overlook interior zones such as internal colonialism on the frontier, domestic tensions surrounding race, even the interiority of whiteness. The international tenor of security discourse ignores a long history of American insecurity in which threat is always located within. The friend/enemy distinction, so important to Carl Schmitt's understanding of the political state, operates most forcefully at home. In U.S. contexts, the rise of the carceral state reflects the degree to which security takes shape as an internal project. Racialized links between the modern-day prison system and plantation slavery and its legacies of Jim Crow are as much a matter of affect as policy and law. Feelings of racial resentment and vulnerability, simmering since the seventeenth century, that Michelle Alexander has identified among whites concerned about loss of status have proven an ample reservoir of fear, more than enough to justify the mass incarceration of millions in the name of public safety. Locking up Black people in cages, no less than the summary executions of Black men, women, and children in public parks, in their own homes, during traffic stops, while jogging, and more, is really about the deprivation of security for an entire population, the denial, in Ta-Nehisi Coates's words, of "the right to secure and govern our own bodies" (8).

Concrete policy discussions as well as theoretical treatments of security suffer from a critical hyperopia, an inclination to take the nation as an already coherent actor whose security imperatives play out primarily in a global theater. Such farsightedness during the Cold War perhaps explains why Woodward mentioned the slave patrols of the plantation South only in passing, as an ancillary consideration in comparison to the momentous affairs of statecraft on the world stage. "The southern constabulary that patrolled the slaves was organized on military lines" and thus "was concerned with a domestic police problem," hardly a national security matter in Woodward's view (4). Like the ideology of "free land" that drove expansionism and supposedly eased class tensions in packed seaboard cities, the belief in "free security" saved the United States from having to waste resources and manpower as European countries did. Yet as subsequent chapters in this book show, enslaved people and free persons of color were perceived as chronic sources of instability that demanded an urgent infrastructural fix that took shape as the American Colonization Society. While that problem festered, white people and especially white nationalists reported feeling paralyzed by their fears for the future of the United States. Yet rather than rely solely on the anguished musings of white people—surely an overrepresented genre in the scholarly archive—in ways that might make this study complicit in their colonizing logic, *American Insecurity* looks to the archives of nineteenth-century Black periodical and pamphlet culture to reinterpret the data and algorithms used to construe the Black population itself as an untamable source of bioinsecurity.

For now, though, the point is that two common assumptions about security stand in need of correction: first, that only recently has security become a defining feature about such fundamental issues as safety, privacy, and whiteness; and second, that when security concerns finally did make an impression upon American consciousness, the scope remained primarily strategic and international in character. This latter point bears more commentary. While "no nation, not even the most powerful, can ensure its national security by itself" (Beck, "Terrorist Threat" 48), it is no less true that the idea of nation still sets the horizon for how security is imagined. National security all too often presumes a sense of united purpose within the homeland. In its most insistent manifestations, security asserts a coherent sense of national identity that can become indistinguishable from nationalism itself. After all, who among "us" does not want to take precautions against terrorism, identity theft, biological pathogens, or any of the threats that provide a rationale for policing, border security, cybersecurity, and other safety measures? "We" all do—this answer, however true, smooths over the contradictions, divisions, and conflicts that arise from implementations of security, which, following Schmitt, are always decisive.[5] Schmitt's essential opposition between friend and enemy implies an external other, yet the crisis that security creates by unavoidably generating anxiety, fear, and uncertainty—in a word, insecurity—returns as the repressed, coming back home as a constitutive feature of the political world and the subjects that populate it. So, while security in the classic form of realist political science identifies people against whom precautions must be taken (e.g., Islamic terrorists, Chinese hackers, Russian honeypots, U.S. military forces acting under the Bush Doctrine of unilateralism), the more nuanced approach described here argues that security has become effectively deterritorialized to encompass the contingency of freedom and the uncertainty of the future.

Such safety concerns, in both their vagueness and pervasiveness, install security as an everyday phenomenon. In contrast to a singular moment like the Cuban Missile Crisis or a supposedly one-time breach of the levees in New Orleans, crisis has readily become a permanent feature of governance because, as this book shows, it was that way all along. The "state of emergency" that, according to Walter Benjamin, "is not the exception but the rule" (*Illuminations* 257), describes not a temporary declaration of martial law or related seizure of powers but rather the normative condition of a society that perceives risk everywhere and at every moment.[6] The suspension of the law that defines the state of emergency arises when security is thought to be in crisis, when the constitutional order, territorial sovereignty, or public safety suddenly appears to be shaky and insecure.[7] Of course, though, the idea of what counts as *sudden* is relative, a judgment call. It is easy to see how a sovereign entity like a president or a congress might make this determination, but it is also enacted by a wide swath of actors with varying degrees of power: settler colonialists, property owners, white nationalists, humanists, and, perhaps most acutely, citizens with respect to their neighbors as well as their own selves. Just because swift authoritative action may establish a "temporary" state of emergency does not mean that it is going to disappear any time soon. The crisis that makes necessary and justifies extraordinary security measures, even and especially those that suspend legal norms, may seem "absolutely unthinkable for the law" (Agamben, *State of Exception* 51). Yet, as Agamben explains, this "unthinkable thing . . . must not be allowed to slip away at any cost" (51) lest the investments, both real and psychic, that the state and its subjects have in security be thrown into question. From the perspective of the state, "there is no end to prevention," according to the spymaster in Joseph Conrad's novel of anarchist bombing, *The Secret Agent* (1907). Operation Enduring Freedom and Operation Infinite Justice, as U.S. counterterrorism efforts in the early twenty-first century were officially called, represent nothing less than the condensation of a logic that had made security continuous. At the risk of relying on academic shorthand, the dialectical slash within in/security marks the Janus-faced character of a fundamental political desire that promotes uncertainty as well as assurance, vulnerability alongside feelings of safety. It is, above all, a way of gesturing at a still visible scar on the political body that necessitates more critical observation.

Maintaining constant security awareness is draining. In financial terms alone, the United States, "driven by Americans' own material, ideological, and ontopolitical insecurities" (George 34), spends as much as all other countries combined on national defense.[8] Psychic and existential costs are much harder to calculate, but affective economies must invest heavily in "the ontology of insecurity within the constitution of the political" (Ahmed, "Affective Economies" 132). In other words, security regularly takes a toll on states and their subjects in requiring and then eating up a steady stream of material, intellectual, and emotional resources—but it could not be any other way since terror, not to mention less intense forms of disquietude and uncertainty, is structurally necessary to travel checkpoints, national defense, cybersecurity, and other precautions designed to ensure social stability. The state as both an institutional and affective formation ensures safety, but its position is beset by contradictions: on the one hand, people turn to the state for assurance against the threat of exceptional violence such as terrorism; on the other, the state monopolizes public safety in ways that can feed consternation for its subjects.

An abiding level of dread is found at the origins of the polis. If "biopolitics is at least as old as the sovereign exception" that Agamben traces back to the ancient world (*Homo Sacer* 6), then so too is security. Where the Greeks located the state of exception in *homo sacer*, "a life that could be killed" (86), by the seventeenth century this vulnerability widened to encompass potentially everyone trapped under conditions where the war of all against all or *bellum omnium contra omnes*, as Hobbes memorably put it, represents the brutal fact of human existence. To the fundamental categories central to modern politics—public/private, right/left, absolutism/democracy—that define for Agamben the "biopolitical horizon" (4), it is important to add security/insecurity.[9] Moreover, Agamben's observation that these distinctions "have been steadily dissolving, to the point of entering today into a real zone of indistinction" (4) just as aptly applies to security societies that spawn and require insecurity. This slippage between "real insecurity and illusory security" (158) is for Carlo Galli a function of global politics while the "shuttle between security and insecurity [that] marks the exceptional citizens of the US security state" (2) is for Inderpal Grewal a function of neoliberalism, but it would be a mistake to conclude that an older style of liberalism associated with the colonizing and plantation societies of the eighteenth and nineteenth centuries did not play an equal, if not greater, role in putting the state subject on constant edge. Rather than see the twinning and twining of security and insecurity about one another as a contemporary development, it is crucial to recognize how the contractual promise of safety and the affective state of fear have fed off one another for centuries. To chalk this dialectic up to modern surveillance society or the steady ravages of neoliberalism is to risk accepting the bargains, trade-offs, and other arrangements of convenience that predate and continue to buttress the creation of an identity I call *homo securus*.

If *homo sacer* simply meant "a life that could be killed," I build on that concept to propose *homo securus* as a life that could be first secured and then securitized. This political figure is already present in Hobbes, Schmitt, and Agamben; it is just a matter of connecting the dots to reveal the outline or, better yet, the profile of the subject who seeks protection and promises to obey. Schmitt's commentary on the Leviathan, composed in 1938 as a certain chill descended upon his relationship to the Nazi party, equated the lack of a strong, unified state to the Hobbesian state of nature.[10] People overcome a "'pre-political' condition of insecurity" only when "the accumulated anguish of individuals who fear for their lives brings a new power into the picture: the leviathan" (Schmitt, *Leviathan* 33, 46). This decision marks the moment when it is possible to proclaim that "a new secular God has emerged: Security" (Neocleous, "Securitati Perpetuae" 25). The first dots to connect are those that make security dependent upon the state, a conclusion that Schmitt shapes into the axiom, *extra civitatem nulla securitas*, literally, no security outside the city (48). This principle connects to the next dot when the state confronts a security crisis and responds by suspending the law and declaring a state of emergency. From here it is easy to get to the next point: as the danger to public safety becomes routine and as the exception also becomes the rule, "an unprecedented generalization of the paradigm of security" gets installed "as the normal technique of government" (Agamben, *State of Exception* 14) whereby everyone becomes a subject of security: *homo securus*.[11] Once decided, the security crisis "must not be allowed to slip at any cost" (51). *Homo securus* accepts this charge by watching for anything out of the ordinary, taking precautions, and exercising and consenting to surveillance, but perhaps the most important action is simply a set of affective responses: tremble as Thomas Jefferson did when contemplating the future of a multiracial society; experience the sublime when confronted with the floods of information described by writers as diverse as Charles Brockden Brown, Claude Shannon, and Maurice Lee; discern how liberalism requires fear, horror, and vulnerability as political theorists Judith Shklar, Elisabeth Anker, and Wendy Brown do.

While the decisive lines in this connect-the-dots sketch are provided by the state, there is plenty of shading to *homo securus* that involves noninstitutional elements of life wrapped up with aesthetics, culture, and affect. This identity at once scorns vulnerability as an unwelcome exposure to risk and embraces it as a necessary condition for preparedness. If, in traditional and masculinist terms, the political subject "establishes its agency by vanquishing vulnerability," as Judith Butler has suggested ("Rethinking" 24), it is also the case that feeling threatened and exposed can provide ongoing justifications for a continuous culture of security. Butler thus seeks a different rendering of vulnerability that discovers the possibility of resistance at moments "when we find ourselves radically unsupported under conditions of precarity or under explicit conditions of threat" (19). From Jefferson to David Walker, the American versions of *homo securus* that most concern me in the pages that follow exhibit deep affective attachments to the very insecurity that they seek to mitigate and control. This book is therefore not a study of the history of surveillance, wiretapping, security legislation, or the erosion of privacy and other constitutional rights, though many excellent books exist on these topics.[12] Nor does it pretend to lay out a step-by-step account of how national security has grown to become an indispensable multibillion-dollar undertaking. Instead, it offers a critical look that stretches to emotional and aesthetic zones beyond as well as below the state, which is where literature comes into play as both an object of study and an analytic tool for examining security.

If *homo securus* represents an abstraction and if security can seem an impersonal force, the project undertaken here demonstrates the critical work that cultural analysis, including literary and historical reading in combination with political theory and philosophy, can do in rendering this abstraction in material and embodied terms. Security secures nothing if not itself, which is to say that, as a political principle closely bound up with sovereignty and governance, security protects the order that justifies its existence. It does so not by eradicating vulnerability but by managing it, even prizing it at times. When Apollo in William Cowper's 1791 translation of *The Iliad* exhorts the Trojans to remember that the Greeks, "like yourselves, are vulnerable flesh" (I.605), the god's phrasing underscores how the state of vulnerability is almost always a passive one in which bodies or other matter await physical injury. Although notions of vulnerability later accrued figurative and psychological dimensions, its physical substrate remains in force, evident in the Latin *vulnerābilis* to signify wounding and the German *Verwundbarkeit*, which translates as "woundability."[13] Today, even the emotional virtue of "making oneself vulnerable" preserves the sense of passivity by syntactically implying the vulnerable self as the recipient of one's actions.

In kind, this book offers a vulnerable reading that is at once an examination of state-sponsored defenselessness and other forms of vulnerability and an encounter with texts that make us so fearful and uncertain that we beseech others to provide security and keep us safe. Yet, as a critical orientation, vulnerability can also facilitate a certain receptiveness to competing interpretations and discordant understandings. Feeling exposed means that one is potentially exposed to multiple readings, including new ways of seeing and making sense of a world that is structured by security. Collisions with the aesthetic help seed this attitude of openness and susceptibility to alternative meanings: as Marianne Hirsch has suggested, vulnerability prepares "a radical openness toward surprising possibilities" that enables creative and imaginative thinking (81). In contrast, striving for invulnerability requires "a defensiveness that shuts down debates and silences dissent" (81), effects that are toxic to the cultivation of democratic culture. "Vulnerability ought not to be identified exclusively with passivity," writes Butler (*Force* 192)—and, indeed, as a mode of reading, it has the potential to activate critique.

A vulnerable reading commits us to questioning forms of passivity that are hardwired into the relationship between *homo securus* and the state. It shares little with those who have a vested interest in using insecurity to maintain the normalcy and everydayness of the state of emergency. Contrast this view with Secretary of State Donald Rumsfeld's take on "the emerging security environment" that he detailed in an essay for *Foreign Affairs* in 2002. He argued for massive increases in national defense spending by using the sort of asymmetrical comparison that is a staple of homespun rhetoric. "It's like dealing with burglars: You cannot possibly know who wants to break into your home or when," he explains. The cautious homeowner installs a deadbolt and then moves on to an alarm system. But that's not enough: you have stop crime before it gets to your home and so you "patrol the neighborhood and keep bad guys off the streets." He wraps up the analogy with a jokesy understatement: "And you know that a big German Shepherd doesn't hurt, either." Well, it's the same for national defense, he suggests, because the military's job is not to prepare to fight any one country but rather to be ready to battle them all and, even more importantly, to intercept threats from anywhere, including nonstate actors. "We need to examine our vulnerabilities," Rumsfeld concludes, not just so that we can be ready but so that we feel the motivation, the ontological need, to ramp up the security state like never before. Vulnerabilities thus prove strategic, an affective resource that is the precondition for all the other expenditures of military hardware, data collection, surveillance technologies, and predictive algorithms that get poured into security. In contrast, the vulnerable readings proposed here are devoted to interrogating the fictions and theories that established insecurity as a political raison d'être in the first place.

A fanciful but no less gritty or ironic example illustrates how vulnerable reading practices intersect with security. Department 17 of the Central Intelligence Agency, as imagined by James Grady in the spy thriller *Six Days of the Condor* (1974), is obviously a state intelligence agency, but its purview is culture and aesthetics. Working out of a nondescript front known as the American Literary Historical Society, Joe Turner and his fellow intelligence experts "keep track of all espionage and related acts recorded in literature" (16). But it would be a disservice to call the society a front since its activities really are historical and literary! Turner and his colleagues read literature in order to discover potential insights about insecurity, exercising formidable interdisciplinary vigilance over scenarios and ideas that affect Americans' feelings of safety and stability. The fact that the society's intellectual resources have been applied to "volumes dating as far back as James Fenimore Cooper" (16) provides a precedent for this project since *American Insecurity* turns to *The Pioneers* for its first extended vulnerable reading. This fortuitous coincidence aside, the conviction that cultural texts can illuminate the concept of security in new and surprising ways deepens the belief that both academic and everyday readers of books, images, and other forms of media have much to contribute to understanding how we think and feel about security. In the film version directed by Sydney Pollack and starring Robert Redford, *Three Days of the Condor* (1975), Joe Turner puzzles his superiors who cannot figure out how a low-level analyst with few tactical skills manages to evade attempts at assassination. Turner's modest self-assessment offers no insight either: "I'm not a field agent, I just read books." It turns out that reading books is an underappreciated analytical skill for understanding security and surveillance.

> CIVILIAN: Where did he learn evasive moves?
> CIA DEPUTY DIRECTOR: He . . . reads.
> CIVILIAN #2: What in the hell's *that* mean?
> CIA DEPUTY: No. You don't understand. He reads . . . everything. (50)

At this point the screenplay directs that "Civilian is about to protest again" but is cut off. What if he were not interrupted? What if the audience heard a provocation about the capacity of reading to destabilize security? Reading everything, like collecting all the data, as we will see in the following chapters, soon creates a security crisis of a different scale.

This book is an effort to break down the concept of security by investigating its American origins and the structures of state as well as the structures of feeling that flow from what philosophers posit as the impetus to form a political community in the first place. The question is not whether people need security since risk, as Ulrich Beck contends, represents a defining feature of modernity. Rather, the goal is to examine how security provides an organizing principle for collective life in ways that both enhance freedom and limit it. While admittedly reading less than "everything" but still endeavoring to be attentive to a range of novels, tracts, pamphlets, and newspapers, including the complete run of *Freedom's Journal*, in conjunction with contemporary critical theory about media, biopolitics, and affect, I look at how security's generative capacity to provide a foundation for art and culture, as Hobbes proposed in *Leviathan*, is matched only by its capacity to incite fear and promote terror.

———

This book is organized into two parts. Part 1, "Contradictions and Contours," provides a two-phase setup to the overall argument, first, by laying out in chapter 1 a series of axioms about security and insecurity and, second, by pulling together and examining a constellation of historical moments in chapter 2 that as a whole exemplify how those propositions have been put into practice. The diversity of these snapshots arrayed from 1755 to 1837 with respect to tone and scale does not lend itself to any single narrative. Accordingly, part 2, "Information, Aesthetics, Population," burrows into instances of fear and racial terror across different modes from the gothic to the arithmetical and statistical. The chapters in this section adhere to a rough chronological arc, beginning with Cooper's *The Pioneers*, set in 1793–94, moving to Charles Brockden Brown's *Wieland* (1798), and then concluding with two chapters on white nationalism and Black protest in newspapers and pamphlets during the 1820s–1830s. Although plenty of reason exists to critique unbroken temporal sequencing (more on that in a moment), the importance of telling a story about security should not be underestimated when private security experts, government officials, and information brokers so often try to write that story of security for others. "When you're living in fear, it's easy to let others make security decisions for you," writes the security technologist Bruce Schneier (*Beyond Fear* 8). Fear and security are not diametrically opposed, however: the justification of everything from national defense to password protection rests on an acute and at times exaggerated sense of vulnerability.

Security emerges as the original motivation behind human beings' desire for political community in the political fairy tale that philosophy tells of the social contract and sovereignty. If the concept of security takes shape as a story, it is crucial to examine the narratives that it sets in motion as well as those that it forecloses. The story's beginning usually runs something like this: "Once upon a time, individuals living in the state of nature got so fed up with unceasing predation and uncertainty that they banded together for protection and—." At this point the story takes any number of decisive turns to justify absolute sovereignty, limited monarchy, or rule by "we, the people" as the best guarantor of public safety. This book complicates the story by supplying a counternarrative that views security not as the remedy for fear and anxiety or even insecurity but as their source. I thus posit the "origins of vulnerability" as part of this book's title to imply a different set of political beginnings for security as "one of the paradigmatic 'great words' of the modern state" (Arends 263). But not only the state: in ways that precede as well as exceed official governmental structures, terror and similar forms of vulnerability appear as both the cause and effect of thinking about security. In the chapters that follow, then, security thus also becomes paradigmatic for thinking about the frontier, zones of racial interiority, sublime infoscapes, and other spaces where the concept is frayed and at times thoroughly unraveled by the contradictions it creates.

If the mode of analysis here is literary critical and historical, the interventions are philosophical, aesthetic, and political theoretical. Locke on human understanding, Kant and Schiller on the sublime, and Hannah Arendt on freedom are as important to these pages as are the novels of gothic terror and frontier romance by Brocken Brown and Fenimore Cooper. With this interdisciplinary mix, I join recent discussions of security and terror by Inderpal Grewal, Paul Amar, Andrew Lakoff, Joseph Masco, Jasbir Puar, and Erica Edwards, among others. Writing in the wake of the most significant security lapse since World War II, the "shocking display of American vulnerability" (Masco 10) of September 11, these critics suggest the importance of understanding the leviathan that is the modern security state. Its power became manifest, for Grewal, after 9/11 in the appearance of "security moms" and other neoliberal citizens who themselves take on the state's policing and surveillance functions. From the establishment of the national security state in 1947 described by Masco to military interventions in Iraq, as Edwards shows, the security apparatus enlisted—often literally so in the armed forces or cabinet positions— Black women to support the ideologies of counterterror. Along similar lines, Puar stresses how the incorporation of queer and minority subjects into the security state reinforces "the ascendancy of whiteness" (27). The imperative behind making "state of exception discourses" an ongoing feature of public and private life, after all, is to ensure "the preservation of a way of life and those privileged to live it" (9). While Amar's focus in *The Security Archipelago* is on the Global South and Masco's *Theater of Operations* contends that U.S. security has become planetary in scope, these and other studies of the topic concentrate on contemporary moments, especially in their arguments that late twentieth- and twenty-first-century configurations of security represent an unprecedented development and expansion, a "new psychic infrastructure ... a new kind of security culture" (Masco 8), of leviathanic power. I do not disagree with these assessments: who could ignore the ubiquity of surveillance cameras or the everydayness of checkpoints, scans, and dual-factor authentication?[14] Nonetheless, the deliberate historical turn of *American Insecurity* to literary and cultural aspects of the eighteenth and nineteenth centuries is driven by the contention that security has always named an unstable concept, no less at war with than enamored by the feelings of vulnerability and other effects it creates. The point is not simply that a security crisis has been around for a long time, at least since justifications for the social contract, but that recognizing the essential tension of in/security can provide openings for questioning its hold on political desires today. Looking at this fault line reminds us that the justifications for security are not set in stone.

While loosely knitted together by the linear sequencing of literary history, the chapters in part 2 can better be described as anachronic time loops.[15] Samuel Taylor Coleridge disparaged the "anachronic mixture" of Ben Johnson's *Sejanus His Fall* to describe how the dramatist's Roman characters strutted about with "James-and-Charles-the-First zeal" (181). But where Coleridge found the mismatch between first-century Rome and Renaissance England to be "amusing" (181), indicative in his view of Johnson's lesser status compared to Shakespeare, the looping approach at times adopted here sets up a critical conversation between past and present. It is a conjunction that does not always obey the niceties of chronology; instead, the goal is to conjoin different slices of literary and cultural history in an effort to defamiliarize contemporary understandings of security that have come to be accepted as so many faits accomplis. A penumbra of information surveillance, racial antagonism, and terror after 9/11 thus hangs over these examinations, as debates surrounding constitutional notions of privacy, the algorithmic sorting of data, and the paranoid notion of a "white genocide" give a presentist edge to this project. However, the approach here is not to look to earlier crises in order to explain how we got to the security society of the twenty-first century. At one level, it is only too obvious that the past is prologue; at another, it is dangerous to assume that earlier encounters with security and terror are somehow quainter, less sophisticated versions of the contemporary state of emergency.

The hardly seamless fit between eighteenth- and nineteenth-century texts and present-day formations instead serves as provocation for thinking aslant about the conceptual encrustations that surround security. If the anachronic moment unfolds as "a strange kind of event whose relation to time is plural" (Nagel and Wood 9), it offers the possibility for thinking outside of "straight time" or strict senses of chronology that settle on a single conclusion. Such a counterchronological orientation disputes the maxim that "time is of the essence" in order to push back against essences, including the ones that see security as essential to both governance and human flourishing.[16] In this respect, then, this study relies less on the linearity of history that leads up to the present than on a series of time loops in which the origins of vulnerability overlap with the vulnerabilities of our contemporary moment. The two are hardly identical, and, indeed, the degree of similarity between emergency then and emergency now is not the point. Rather, it is the doubling and redoubling of vulnerability that makes security a constant need and desire. U.S. culture has always been in a state of emergency, and with each new threat—Indian raid, slave rebellion, epidemic, missile attack, catastrophic storm, hacked election, and so on—the feeling of vulnerability never gets old.

Temporal enjambments that, for instance, present the gothic as a commentary on twentieth-century information theory or posit debates over colonization as an anticipatory critique of algorithmic thinking may court charges of anachronism. Such an indictment, attributed to the Annales school of history, deems anachronism "the worst of all sins, the sin that cannot be forgiven" (qtd. in Rancière 21). The trespass occurs not simply when events are put out of sequence but rather "when a present way of thinking is imposed upon the past" (de Grazia 13).[17] Yet the accusation of anachronism itself betrays an ideological investment in the reigning temporal order, especially versions that are committed to the notion that history, along with things like human knowledge, democracy, and technology, is always progressing. "Perception of anachronism," writes Jeremy Tambling, "comes from a society comparatively confident about its present" (9). From this perspective, then, if thinking about contemporary security through perspectives offered by much earlier meditations on the topic seems to run afoul of temporal regularities, the advantage is that this orientation can make us less sure about the extent to which security sets the horizon for political, social, and intimate life.

Since chronology involves (more than) dates and numbers, it might be useful to turn to a mathematician-philosopher and then a poet for some guidance. Henri Poincaré put pressure on the strict ordinal logic that allows us to start with an expression like $x+1$ and reason that if we know the value of x, then we can figure out $x+2$, $x+3$, and so on. He called this "reasoning by recurrence," a process he associated with a certain amount of intellectual freedom "for it enables us to leap over as many stages as we wish" (11). Next, the poet: Paul Valéry found inspiration in this idea, and he hypothesized that reasoning by recurrence encourages unexpected conjunctions, new combinations and "violent contrasts" (39).[18] By encouraging these collisions, one can "attain the power of shaking oneself free of any thought that has lasted too long" (39). Reading for time loops can set us free from hidebound thinking; Valéry's passion for temporal leaps will not set us free from security, even if we were to be so heedless to wish such a thing, but it can change how we think about the concept.

Part 2 of *American Insecurity* comprises chapters that attempt to move in such a direction. In chapter 3, Cooper's 1823 novel provides an opportunity to examine how the twin origins of privacy and property provide something of a dubious legal and philosophical backstory to the collection of aggregate data by the National Security Agency (NSA) and other agencies. Chapter 4 extends this focus by using Brockden Brown's gothic tale to examine how the torrent of information scooped up by both humanistic and security endeavors intensifies doubt, uncertainty, and sensations of terror. In naming "Jeffersonian trembling" as a pathological national condition, chapter 5 seeks to diagnose the affective and biopolitical conditions that fuel feelings of white aggrievement. The final chapter explores the connections among data and national security by considering the accounting and enumeration of Black life by advocates of colonization as well as their fierce opponents, including James Forten and David Walker. A brief coda provides a conclusion by asking, with help from Herman Melville, what comes after security? New security measures are being implemented and updated all the time (your password must now contain at least one non-alphanumeric character, your laptop now stays in your bag at the TSA checkpoint, you no longer need show to proof of vaccination to enter), but the set of affects and attitudes created by insecurity continues to look familiar.

Becoming less comfortable with a value like privacy in debates over surveillance, as the looping and overlapping of Cooper and the NSA in chapter 3 suggest, may help enliven resistance to liberal models of governance. Or, to take a different example, becoming less assured about the insights and uses of political economy, as the temporal collisions in chapter 6 insinuate, can reveal how mortality functions as a security mechanism. In all, the anachronic approach here puts contemporary security in a different time in an effort "to think otherwise" (Rancière 38) about this indispensable element of modern existence. Bolstered by this approach, the readings and interpretation in *American Insecurity* introduce the potential for stepping outside one's time to contest the seemingly logical progression of history that got us to no other place than the present which we inhabit.

PART I
Contradictions and Contours

1

The Contradictions of Security in Thirteen Propositions

ALTHOUGH SECURITY PROMISES protection from any number of modern threats from computer viruses to terrorism, it readily raises a host of conceptual, affective, and political problems. Installed on laptops, built into the design architecture of public space, and institutionalized in the Department of Homeland Security and the National Security Agency, security measures seem to be everywhere and security awareness an around-the-clock obligation. Yet omnipresence is not the same as omnipotence, and certainly not all iterations of security are the same. So accustomed have people become to security that it often takes spectacular failures to remind us of its existence. Even just a potential breach of firewalls, borders, or other safety precautions can prove singularly productive in providing an urgent and ongoing rationale for security. Nonetheless, everyday reminders to update your password or to "place all metal objects in the bin" play an equally vital role by making the habits of security part of the background noise of social life. Security is thus both exceptional and ordinary, its continuing intrusion in our lives justified by its potential, however improbable, for failure. Without this interplay of acute vulnerability and a dull awareness of danger, security would soon seem superfluous, a tiresome encumbrance not worth the anxiety or resources it demands. Security, I argue, is a mode of governance and way of feeling that is always in tension with itself, at odds between its aims and its methods, its presuppositions and its effects.

Critical attentiveness to the contradictions of security jars with the self-evident status that the concept typically has across branches of knowledge. There is no more stable—or clichéd—use of the term than in Maslow's "hierarchy of needs," which establishes security as a foundation for the fullness of human experience without examining how this precondition rests on a jumble of contradictions. Other fields have not fared much better in their attempts to define security. Uses of the term are beset by "slovenly imprecision" (R. Walker 63); regrettably, the framework of security studies "is not seen as subject to debate," making the concept essentially "meaningless" (Krause and Williams ix); the "monopoly" that International Relations has "on the meanings of security" (Bigo and Tsoukala 6) impoverishes research and analysis by sidelining other approaches. Military-style realism tends to dominate discussions of security, which narrows the range of things that might be secured to states and borders and prevents interrogation of the topic itself.[1] At the same time, though, the predominance of defense concerns has widened the reach of nations' interest in security to encompass the climate and environment, even the heavens themselves. Hurricanes and earthquakes "have been brought into the same framework of 'security threat'" (Lakoff 247) while NASA's planetary defense against killer asteroids and near-Earth objects is considered "part of an official national security focus for the United States" (National Nuclear Security Administration). Even the humanitarian idea of "extended security" (Rothschild 57) that expands the focus from nation-states to individuals remains overwritten with the post–Cold War empiricism of International Relations. Within concerns such as computer security, financial security, food security, job security, election security, personal security, and emotional security, the core of "security" persists as a stable signifier without contradiction or question. Who, after all, would choose financial insecurity or would prefer to work on a computer network that did not keep private personal information safe? We know enough from *Deep Impact, Armageddon, Moonfall,* and other cinematic visions of planetary catastrophe that those who ignore cosmic threats do so at the peril of all humanity. When it comes to examining the origins and effects of security itself, however, the topic is hardly an unambiguous good or desired outcome, as the pursuit of security teeters uncomfortably close to the fear, insecurity, and terror that it seeks to allay.

For this reason, the following propositions are not intended to be straightforward but rather, as a whole as well as individually, laced with contradictions. Nonetheless, my argument throughout this book is that injecting complexity into otherwise under- or unexamined ideas and practices of security provides a fruitful means for thinking about threat and vulnerability. Each thesis at once offers a description of some aspect of security and introduces enough theoretical or historical context as to make something of a mess (a productive one, I hope) for defamiliarizing conventional notions about what keeps us safe. By establishing the contours of security across thirteen related theses, the cracks and contradictions within the concept of security become more evident. Neither definitive nor comprehensive, the sum total is instead meant to be suggestive and even a bit insouciant in an effort to move forward our thinking about a political principle and social precept that alternately forestalls and nourishes human striving. Just as rigid and unimaginative applications of Maslow's hierarchy of needs, with its emphasis on security, offer little insight into complex cultural situations or texts, approaches to security that get stuck in categorical and preconceived ideas fail to illuminate how freedom from risk and the desire for safety often limit the sum of political aspiration. Only by starting with this critique of security might both the foundation and horizon of political possibility extend beyond fear.

1. Security Is a Matter of Aesthetics

Feeling secure is an affective condition, one that is bound up negatively but also necessarily with anxiety, fear, and vulnerability. This subjective register opens out onto the philosophical zone of aesthetics, which is why Immanuel Kant, Edmund Burke, Friedrich Schiller, and also literary practitioners of the gothic such as Brockden Brown and theorists of emotion such as Sara Ahmed appear in the pages that follow. Instead of a loose synonym for "artistic" or "beautiful," aesthetics here more properly signifies a range of bodily sensations and corporeal affects, including the moments when people are overwhelmed by information, when they are struck dumb by shock and awe, when they are paralyzed with fear, when they are stopped in their tracks by an encounter with the sublime, and when they seek solidarity to hedge against risk and insecurity. Each moment resounds with the capacity to decenter the subject and breach both the physical and psychical protections that contribute to feelings of security and well-being. When or where these feelings might overtake us is anybody's guess: the importance of probability and predictiveness to security jars with the spontaneity and unpredictability inherent to aesthetic experience.[2]

Despite that security is inescapably an affective condition of feeling safe or unsafe, the topic is rarely viewed as an aesthetic matter and seldom is it that literature and other humanities fields are thought to contribute to the policy debates and scholarly discussions that it prompts.[3] Discussions of security have been dominated by the field of International Relations, studies of policing, and surveillance studies with an emphasis on social science particularly after 9/11. Drawing on Foucault's provocation that discipline makes discipline, critics have contended that scholarly approaches to security have disciplined those who would study the topic, ensuring that research abides professional divisions while relying on narrow definitions that seek to limit the term's "elasticity" (Hamilton 14) across national security, border security, financial security, social security, food security, network security, and so on.[4] Accepting national security as something separate from social security, to use Mark Neocleous's example, fulfills "the desire of the state to keep these things apart, to draw a veil over the unity of state power" (*Critique* 6). This line of argument, however, still keeps aesthetics on the sidelines by treating security only as a matter of state power in ways that are unattuned to the thoughts and feelings that people have about ideas and forms that, while bound up with the state, both precede and exceed it such as property, privacy, information, and race, to cite prominent examples from this book. The state has long been lodged at the front and center of security discourse, a tendency that favors diplomacy analysis, game theory, and probabilistic assessments of risk that orient discourse around facts and rationalistic assessments, not feelings and affect.

Rather than accept this division, I argue that the topic of security—how it makes us feel, how it contours ideas of privacy and property, how it affects our thinking about whiteness and race, how it so often serves as both the origin and endpoint of political community—cannot be left to policy investigations that fail to take up the full range of emotions from safety to terror. The appearance of *Critical Security Studies* in 1997 announced a shift away from Cold War perspectives dominated by superpowers and International Relations toward alternative approaches indebted to philosophy and political theory, feminist critique, public health, and environmental studies. Yet neither International Relations nor the field of critical security studies that emerged at the end of the twentieth century (see Krause and Williams; Peoples and Vaughan-Williams) is good at asking aesthetic questions. This oversight is understandable not only because researchers in these fields are instead concerned with constitutional, ethical, and technological challenges created by the governmental security state. For their part, cultural theorists interested in aesthetics have not asked very good questions about security. Not that literary critics, for example, haven't turned their attention to security, but when they have done so their focus has often been limited to the thematics of how ecological, terrorist, or other crises are represented. One prevailing approach takes shape as an appliqué that reads a novel or analyzes a film as an illustration of conclusions that theorists of security, surveillance, and biopolitics have already reached. As Johannes Voelz contends, "so far literary scholars have primarily offered readings of literary texts that illustrate and confirm the mappings of security mechanisms first articulated in other disciplines" ("Security Theory" 294). Foremost among these disciplines are International Relations, criminology, and political theory, which, while useful for understanding security as a matter of state, do not attend to all the zones of human activity that have become subject to securitization.[5] The military and the police constitute only the most recognizable elements of national security, but credit card fraud, computer hacking, and identity theft signal the extent to which security has expanded to encompass financial, epistemological, and even ontological concerns. Given the presence of security in every crook and recess of modern life via regimes of surveillance that have morphed into dataveillance, political theory by itself seems inadequate for grappling with security. But literary interpretation and theory, in limiting itself to representations of policing or state control, has claimed not much more than a subordinate and tertiary position with respect to security discourse. What if "instead of taking literature to reflect a set of problems and mechanisms first articulated in security theory," as Voelz suggests (295), cultural theorists took aesthetics as a provocation for asking fundamental questions about the project of security that shapes information, health, technology, media, and just about every facet of contemporary life? While not a response to all these questions, this book does make the case that any answer needs to grapple with the problem of why security makes us feel so unsafe.

2. Security Depends on Fear

No impetus for security exists without an active sense of fear. The homeowner who imagines burglars breaking through a kitchen window is impelled by fear to install an electronic security system. The investor worried about financial uncertainty and market downturns can create a portfolio that relies on financial securities to reduce risk—although recent history has shown that low-risk holdings such as mortgage-backed securities can turn out to be high-risk gambles in which billions of dollars' worth of homes, retirement accounts, and other assets evaporate overnight. The nation put on edge by fears of foreign aggression can heighten military preparedness and weapons security, though, of course, strategies of deterrence increase insecurity for other powers that feel they must now compete in an arms race. National security in this context relies on the apocalyptic capacity to imagine the ultimate insecurity of nuclear war. In each case, security requires imaginings of theft, catastrophic loss, and annihilation: the origin of security is fear. It is no doubt worthwhile mentioning that fearful imaginings can be well-founded and that apprehensions, like paranoia, are frequently grounded in reality. Malware and ransomware are worth taking seriously just as food security, climate security, and what the United Nations terms "human security" demand international attention and global action.[6] Yet in contrast to experts who see "living in a state of constant fear" as the antithesis of security (Schneier, *Beyond Fear* 9), fear is better recognized as a necessary precondition of security and, what's more, the source of its continuing justification.

Contradictory it may seem, then, that fear also provides pleasure. In *Elements of Law* (1640), a book that is as much an incipient study of psychology as a political treatise, Thomas Hobbes catalogues the "passions of the mind," which for the most part is a straightforward task of defining emotions such as lust and indignation. But then he comes to an attitude that defies easy categorization: "Other passions there be, but they want names," and foremost among them for Hobbes is the mixture of fright and pleasure. He provides an example—one that Schiller will repeat in laying out the somatic response to the sublime (see chapter 4)—of a storm-tossed ship observed from the safety of the shore. What to name the passion in which

> men take pleasure to behold from the shore the danger of them that are at sea in a tempest, or in fight, or from a safe castle to behold two armies charge one another in the field? It is certainly in the whole sum joy, else men would never flock to such a spectacle. Nevertheless there is in it both joy and grief. For as there is novelty and remembrance of own security present, which is delight; so is there also pity, which is grief. But the delight is so far predominant, that men usually are content in such a case to be spectators of the misery of their friends. (*Elements of Law*)

Schiller, like Kant before him, would have no difficulty identifying this jumble of passions as the sublime. The word "sublime" was certainly in use during Hobbes's day: his contemporary John Milton in *Paradise Lost* described Adam whose "Eye sublime declar'd / Absolute rule," poetic phrasing that surely would have appealed to the political theorist whose *Leviathan* (1651) justified the sovereign's authority over the populace. Much in Hobbes's scenario seems to fit the contours of the sublime, especially as it relates to security. Spectacle entails a secure location: witnesses to the battle in the distance are not caught between warring forces and observers of the doomed boat stand with feet safely planted on the ground. The important difference is that Hobbes, unlike later theorists of the sublime, makes no room for either release or transcendence. And that is precisely the political point: the Leviathan offers no respite from fear and, what's more, depends upon its ever-present existence, whether through the punitive scepter of the sovereign or the dim but ineradicable suspicion of what life in the state of nature would look like without security. It thus becomes necessary to supplement the conclusion reached in the previous paragraph: security not only has its origin in fear but requires its constant and continuous presence—the dull ache of anxiety, the steady throb of uncertainty, the paranoia that cannot be allayed—in the background.

Scratch the surface of people's feelings about the security that the sovereign provides, Hobbes suggests, and the "continuall feare" (*Leviathan* 186) that is humanity's true share comes to light. "Without other security, than . . . their own strength" (186), individuals would use up all their energy defending their persons from harm and their possessions from predation, leaving nothing for the creation of a common culture. Out of fear comes the security without which there would be "no account of Time, no Arts, no Letters, no Society" (186). Too much fear becomes disabling, but knowledge of its existence proves that security is at once requisite to human flourishing and that it can never be relaxed. For Hobbes, "fear does not betray the individual; it is his completion. It is not the antithesis of civilization but its fulfillment" (Robin 32). Hence the contentment, "joy," and "pleasure" that Hobbes discerns in fear. Fear emerges as the mainstay of social order and then provides ongoing and compelling justification for political subjects to strive in common, often against others, for the purposes of security.[7]

3. Security Generates Insecurity, Which Creates a Pressing Need for Security, Which, in Turn Generates . . . and So On

"We are frequently in most danger when we deem ourselves most safe," says the protagonist of Charles Brockden Brown's *Memoirs of Carwin* (279). The statement represents more than the unwelcome but somewhat obvious insight that harm can overtake us unawares. His words also imply that in deeming ourselves safe, we expose ourselves to danger. The Shakespearean variant comes from the goddess Hecate in *Macbeth*, as she plots the downfall of the murderer become king: "And you all know, security / Is mortals' chiefest enemy" (III.vi.33). The tragic contradiction stems from an irony intrinsic to the philology of security. If *securitas* is the state of being without care, then it also makes us careless, heedless of the dangers that abound. Does the fact that *securitas* now serves to name a company—Securitas—with 370,000 employees and a market capitalization of $4.3 billion mean that our cares can be effectively managed by some corporate entity, or does this relinquishing of responsibility to the transnational marketplace suggest cause for alarm?[8] "Security almost always works at cross-purposes because the concern for security is at bottom a concern to be without concern" (Hamilton 10), and this predicament intensifies the more secure that people in a society believe themselves to be. A utopia of complete security leads to its own dark counterimage: as John Hamilton contends, "Perfect security is purchased with mass carelessness.... The desire for total protection hands the individual over to totalitarian designs" (28–29). How can it be that the precondition and aim of political society also represent its undoing?

Headlines about the total reach of NSA surveillance make ordinary citizens wary of national security. Even before the revelations of Edward Snowden, popular imagination fed into the paranoia that government agencies meant to keep people safe actually pose a threat to individual liberty. From Alfred Hitchcock's *North by Northwest* (1959) to Sydney Pollack's *Three Days of the Condor* (1975) and from Francis Ford Coppola's *The Conversation* (1974) to Tony Scott's *Enemy of the State* (1998), film and literature often imply that security leaves a trail of personal and psychological destruction. The more one knows about security and surveillance, like security expert Harry Caul in *The Conversation* or CIA analyst Joe Turner in *Condor*, the more that person has to fear. These scenarios turn on the irony that insecurity is a by-product of an overweening and out-of-control security state. But insecurity is more than an unfortunate accident of security: it is instead structurally essential to the logic and continuing deployment of security.

The propensity for security to unravel into its opposite creates a recursive feedback loop that becomes something of a conceptual straitjacket whose only outcome is more security. Examples proliferate across different domains from philosophy to political theory to international relations to infosec.[9] "Because 'security' is bound into a dependent relation with 'insecurity,' it can never escape it: it must continue to produce images of 'insecurity' in order to retain meaning," writes Anthony Burke (20). The surveillance and defense mechanisms associated with national security wind up producing greater uncertainty and instability: in Masco's formulation, "counterterror becomes terror becomes counterterror" (194). Moreover, it is a relation that is routinely directed against others and weaponized, as one's security necessitates the insecurity of others. Security thus becomes both a justification and an apology for racism in which white security depends on increasing the risk, precarity, and vulnerability experienced by populations of color. Here, Ruth Wilson Gilmore's definition of racism as "group-differentiated vulnerability to premature death" (*Golden Gulag* 28) exposes the brutal consequences of expanding the carceral state to secure both the social order and profits at the expense of communities of color. Its most lethal form is the conviction that "our" way of life, indeed life itself, depends on "their" death (A. Burke 6; Berki 31–32). This existential conundrum provides the underlying principle of détente that John Herz in 1950 described as the "security dilemma" of international politics. Perceiving itself threatened by a rival power, a nation seeks to increase security, but those efforts incite insecurity in the adversary, which responds by taking countermeasures, and that in turn heightens the initial feeling of insecurity, thus requiring another round of security preparations, and so "the vicious circle of security and power accumulation is on" (Herz 157). When the bid for security involves having more nuclear warheads than one's opponent, a dangerous game that both the United States and the Soviet Union played during the Cold War, it is hard not to see how in/security endangers the continued existence of humanity.

The traditional focus of international relations in nation-states can obscure how policing, surveillance, dataveillance, and other security measures make people feel unsafe in their own skins. Since 9/11, "an insecure and destabilizing security" has become the global norm, threatening civil rights and life itself (Clough and Willse 7). Above all, security seeks to reproduce itself in the operations of "modern liberal rule," which "secures to secure" (Dillon, *Biopolitics of Security* 28). This tautology, echoed by Dillon's claims that security can be seen as "governing to govern" (*Biopolitics of Security* 28) and "ordering to order" (*Politics of Security* 25), represents the linguistic equivalent of a feedback loop. In generating insecurity, security regenerates itself.

Understanding the relation of security to insecurity as a feedback loop accentuates that security is preeminently a problem of information (more on this idea below). In simplest terms, the constant input of sensory and other types of information allows the mind (or a machine) to adjust its output based on the input it receives, which then, of course, changes the output coming its way. This cybernetic pattern explains why brains as well as computers have the capacity to perform ever-more sophisticated calculations about the nature of reality. But the feedback loop between security and insecurity introduces a decided note of ambivalence: just as hurricane safety shutters serve as reminders that catastrophic weather is a perennial seasonal risk, security reinforces and, in many cases, heightens the anxiety and apprehension we feel. Airport security reassures us about getting on a plane, but does it not also remind us about the remote possibility of hijacking and terrorism, indeed, worrying us much more than the statistical probability of such an unlikely event would warrant? Security may or may not prevent terrorism, but it certainly creates and amplifies the fear of terrorism.[10]

4. Terror Is an Effect of Security, Not Just Its Cause

The tendency of security to generate its opposite—insecurity—should remind us of the merging of antonyms that Freud describes in his classic essay on "that species of frightening" (*The Uncanny* 124) where the convergence of *heimlich* and *unheimlich* creates the uncanny. The rough parallel between in/security and *un/heimlich* is more than a structural similarity: both forms gravitate around affective experiences in which pleasurable and allaying sensations give way to "what evokes fear and dread" (123). Freud begins with a bit of fanfare by drawing attention to the aesthetic turn that his analysis takes. Psychoanalysts typically confine themselves to scientific questions, yet when it comes to deciphering how feelings of familiarity become disconcerting, Freud deems it necessary "to engage in aesthetic investigations" understood broadly, not as a discourse on beauty but as something that spans the gamut of feelings and "emotional impulses" (123). So, too, the first proposition here asserts that security is fundamentally an aesthetic matter. And on at least one level, the two revolve around the same emotional locus: the home and by extension the homeland. To be sure, Freud leaves behind concrete senses of home to talk about versions of the *unheimlich* coursing with repressed libidinal energies that are attached to the womb, the genitals, and the doubled self. But at the start, he compiles examples of its usage, pulling a line from Georg Gottfried Gervinus: "*Die Heimlichkeit der Heimath zerstören*, 'To destroy the tranquility of the homeland'" (127). In the uncanny, the familiar becomes frightening and the home a space of gothic horror. Poe's "The Fall of the House of Usher" plays upon these feelings expertly, as does Brown's *Wieland* where a series of killings and attempted murders all take place at home. Efforts to protect the homeland share in this dynamic, but the American security apparatus actively becomes a source of the terror it seeks to fight.

Rushed into law forty-five days after the destruction of the World Trade Center, the USA PATRIOT Act illustrates how security emerges as a response to terror. Homeland security as a whole represents a massive outlay of resources, not the least of which is the mobilization of people's fear, that ritualistically returns to the attacks of September 11, 2001. Terror does more than justify this vast expansion of government surveillance powers; it marshals both legislative and popular support for continued and increased spending on counterterrorism. If "Americans want more homeland security than they need," as one political scientist claims (Friedman 77), the idea of terror has proven singularly effective in feeding this miscalculated desire. Critical assessments of this "overreaction" (Friedman 86) have ample merit, as a look at costs (homeland security increased more than fivefold from 2000 to 2009, from $12 billion to $66 billion), civil rights concerns, and disputes about the overall effectiveness of counterterrorism suggests. From the ACLU to intelligence analysts at the Rand Corporation and the Cato Institute, organizations across the political spectrum have added to these objections.

It might be worthwhile to upend such criticism, however, by advancing a competing proposition: security measures are assuredly a response to terror, but security creates terror as well. While this claim clearly builds on the previous two theses about fear and insecurity, it also makes a more specific point that, paradoxically, involves the indiscriminate nature of terror. Terror may strike anywhere: that is one of the reasons why it is terrifying. In response, vigilance directs suspicion at every quarter in ways that make security not just a targeted response to specific threats but an outlook on the world as a whole. Rationally, however, we know there is no need to be afraid of darkness. So averred Locke in arguing instead that intense light causes distress; in contrast, our faculty of sight is "unharmed" by obscurity (*Essay* 90). But when Edmund Burke encountered this passage, he dissented from "Mr. Locke's opinion, that darkness is not naturally an idea of terror" because "in utter darkness, it is impossible to know in what degree of safety we stand" (130). This obscure logic—obscure because it is mired in the obscurity of unknowing—explains why, as examples in this book show, those seeking security define their target as nothing less than all. Destroy every single pest, as settlers on James Fenimore Cooper's frontier do, their mania an allusion to genocidal practices directed at Indigenous people. Retrieve every single scrap of intelligence, as the NSA's mantra of "collect it all" advises, no matter that innocent people's data gets scooped up in the haul. For all its laser-like targeting, homeland and other forms of security mentioned here roll out campaigns that make no distinctions. Their scattershot approach—literally this is how settler colonialists in Cooper's *The Pioneers* hunt—rests on the indeterminacy of a security agenda that targets all members of a population.

At the same time, however, the terror that security creates often ricochets to self-identity. Whereas security countermeasures indiscriminately project terror at "them," its particular thrust bounces back onto "us." Connections between home invasion and homeland invasion date back as far as Mary Rowlandson's account of an attack during King Philip's War and remain vivid in *The Purge* movie franchise in which the true danger comes not from roving bands of vigilantes but from state-of-the-art home security systems that fail, we might say, without fail. The fallout shelters that American suburbanites installed in basements and backyards during the 1950s brought home the existential dread of nuclear war. The "panic rooms" and "safe rooms" added to exclusive residences give tangible form to the vague fears of home invasion. "Us" has become a bigger target than "them": the multibillion-dollar global security strategy of the United States, aided by media coverage and politicians' rhetoric that exaggerates the threat of terrorism, is responsible for deepening a national "psychology of insecurity" (Brightman 9) that views the world as a scary place. If "security takes the form and promise of a metaphysical discourse . . . that makes the possibility of the world possible" (A. Burke 3), its corresponding effect is to incite constant and enduring terror with thoughts of how fragile that world must be, how vulnerable we are at each and every moment.

5. Security Requires Information, and Yet There Is Never Enough Information; There Is Only Too Much

The task of identifying dangers and calculating risk depends on having sufficient information to resolve the uncertainties that make for insecure futures. The more information, the better: computer algorithms, sophisticated probabilistic analysis, and the exponential increase in global information storage capacity in the digital age have stretched this pursuit to an unimaginable extent. Big data, in the parlance of tech gurus, relies on the three Vs: volume, velocity, variety. (The post-truth era associated with disinformation, "alternative facts," and the scourge of "fake news" has prompted suggestions about adding "veracity" and "value" to the list.) Although industry observers emphasize the positive potential of these attributes, some facets of information have at least an equal potential to generate insecurity. Velocity, for instance, increases the flow of data to allow for the faster delivery of knowledge and quicker response times, but the speed of information can also threaten the stability and continuity of a regime in an era of revolutionary ferment. Long before the era of big data, Loyalist adherents to the British Crown discerned the necessity of slowing the pace of public information and stemming the American patriots' propaganda. Preserving the imperial administrative state required concerted attention to information security, and, as Loyalists in the 1770s soon realized, they needed to take measures to offset the steady outpouring of satire and other forms of public expression destabilizing British control.[11] Two hundred and fifty years later, the unchecked velocity of (dis)information helped incite a mob of right-wing rioters to attempt a coup on January 6, 2021, by storming the U.S. Capitol. The actual content of the conspiracies and lies about a stolen election were only as important as the speed at which they spread on QAnon, Parler, and Twitter.

The volume of information places an infinite amount of data within reach of our keyboards, but the superabundance of information also stokes affective unease. Acquiring more information about an impending or imagined danger, whether in the shape of an approaching storm system or rumors of a terrorist attack, is traditionally seen as essential to citizen safety and national security. Too little information jeopardizes the ability to mount an effective response and meet the threat before it fully materializes. But too much information presents a corollary problem, generating insecurity from a gargantuan data set that can never be fully processed or understood. "So heavy [had] the tactical volume" of intelligence become that by the time David Kahn published his monumental *The Codebreakers* in 1967, he expressed amazement that the United States had to convert aircraft carriers and other warships into data-collecting vessels (672). The burden of finding enough physical storage is one thing, but remaining composed in the face of too many scenarios and too much intel is another, one that presents cognitive hurdles to the intelligence community attempting to track and make meaning out of the vast volume of data it amasses. The problem of textual superabundance, as Maurice Lee suggests, has long been an occupational hazard for readers and critics.

Again, however, the conundrum is not particular to the era of supercomputing. With the advent of statistics and political economy in the eighteenth century, the mass amount of biopolitical information that came to be studied as a "population" indicated both the range of the state's resources and the forms of life that could overrun society's capacity for order. While a voluminous amount of data offers the opportunity to discern patterns and tendencies, it also has the potential to flood the senses to the point where sorting, organizing, and classifying become impossible. "Patterns, ratios, indexes, whole maps of information. . . . This is our sweetness and light. It's a fuckall wonder," writes Don DeLillo (14). Swapping out "information" for Matthew Arnold's humanistic culture as the source of "sweetness and light," DeLillo registers the aesthetic quality of information.[12] The irony, of course, is that information has become so omnipresent and massive that it lacks all the delicacy and restorative power that Arnold associated with culture in its battle with anarchy. Instead, it frequently assumes sublime proportions, whether it is the "zettabytes and yottabytes of information" vacuumed up and stored by the NSA (Gray 4) or the infinite behaviors, preferences, and interests tracked—and predicted—by the algorithms of social media behemoths.

Security's demand for information is insatiable. Yet efforts to gather and interpret more and more information create the problem of not knowing how to store or what to do with all this information. How does one act upon information when there is a glut, when there is so much that patterns can be discerned everywhere and nowhere? Consider the everyday imperative that confronts us in the security line at the airport, on the subway platform, in employee breakrooms, and other spaces: "if you see something, say something."[13] This signage often includes a second injunction: to "report suspicious activity." Sighted people are always seeing something. What would it mean to take this directive at its word and begin compiling a list of all that we observe at the bus stop or metro station—shopping bags, vermin, trash, backpacks, faces, everything including petals on a wet, black bough? The result would be an unending accumulation whose sheer extent dwarfs the significance of one unattended backpack; the significance of information is overwhelmed by its ubiquity. Even more disruptive is the possibility that people might see and report other things such as crumbling roads and bridges, homelessness, or signs of environmental devastation and climate change (Masco 28). The desire to process all that we know, all that we do not know, and, to paraphrase former secretary of defense Rumsfeld, all the unknowns we do not know, is outmatched by our cognitive inability to do so. Seeing something and saying something makes security awareness a constant activity that forcefully reminds us of its impossibility.

It is not just that there exists an infinite amount of "something" to see and report. What to do with this trove of data once it is collected? Human communication ordinarily depends on the ephemerality of its utterance. If spoken sentences did not disappear, "their accumulation would very quickly lead to uncontrolled complexity, that is, chaos. Just imagine the noise that would result if spoken words did not fade away but remained audible!" muses the philosopher of systems theory, Niklas Luhmann ("How Can the Mind" 379). Yet advances in global information storage capacity have realized Luhmann's fanciful scenario in at least one sense. No email, no text, no digital trace fades away, and yet the chaos that comes with aggregating all this stuff remains. With so much information in storage or transactional form, it should not be surprising that what former CIA director Michael Hayden called "digital exhaust" leaks from GPS and other apps that we use (Gray 25). Recent security breaches have exposed how vulnerable information from the personal and private to the top secret is to theft. Perhaps, then, "vulnerability" should be added to the list of Vs associated with information: if so, the lesson is not merely that information is vulnerable to hacking, espionage, or loss; rather the surprising takeaway is that people are vulnerable to information, which has the potential to feed uncertainty, to overwhelm our capacities, and to heighten insecurity. The sense of vulnerability that necessarily accompanies "if you see something, say something" feeds into a "logic of vigilantism" that "has securitized the domestic sphere of home and nation" (Grewal 121). Unlike the first DHS advertisements to "report suspicious activity" that featured an abandoned bag in a train car or beneath a stadium bleacher, later spots promoting public vigilance no longer made mention of specific threats because the potentiality of threat had become omnipresent. "The formlessness of a threat only encourages its production," writes R. Guy Emerson (634) in a study of security PSAs that also draws on interviews with commuters. Subway riders and train passengers, according to this study, exercise vigilance only intermittently and provisionally. Yet security consciousness is an unending feature of the social contract in general and, as we will see in part 2, a specific feature of an American system built on settler colonialism and slavery. At core, the mantra to observe and process all information demands vigilance over every possible entry point, every out-of-place detail, in a word, everything. Under the imperative to "say something," domestic and international spheres have been rendered indistinct to the extent that it becomes possible to speak of home(land) invasion. Such vigilance, of course, is not unrelated to the cruel parody of community that is vigilantism.

Yet the idea of "care" that is inherent to the ancient notion of *se-cura* also seeds the possibility for an alternative ethics of understanding that views vulnerability as a shared condition.[14] Feminist theorists have suggested that vulnerability might not be rejected or denied but mobilized as a form of agency.[15] The "reawakening solidarity" (*Risk* 125) that Ulrich Beck associates with risk society emanates from a wider recognition that unending security alerts, public safety advisories, and even news and information itself distribute anxiety across everyday life. Instead of repressing insecurity with tight-lipped stoicism or denial, we should consider, as the next proposition does, that the collective acknowledgment of vulnerability is first and foremost an expression of collectivity.

6. Security Is Both a Threat to and Condition of Collective Striving

Confronted with imminent danger, people sometimes do the extraordinary by banding together instead of falling upon one another. Insecurity "mobilizes political solidarity among emerging communities unified by no more than threat," an enabling potential that Voelz aligns with the fictive qualities of literature that are especially suited for imagining action and agency in the face of uncertainty (*Poetics* 7; see also 23–30). While American fantasies of self-reliant individualism and hardy independence often stunt this sensibility, fire brigades materialize out of nothing, search parties spring up in an instant, and wagons get circled for common defense. As the latter scenario implies, however, the collectivity that rises up to meet danger frequently takes on racialized overtones.

Insecurity may spur collective agency, but it is harder to envision how security—with its tight controls, borders, surveillance, amassing of data, stigmatization of others—can do the same. In *Emergency Politics*, political theorist Bonnie Honig asks what sort of thinking might recuperate genuine democratic possibility from a regime of sovereignty that justifies its use of emergency powers as necessary for law and order. Paul Downes undertakes a similar endeavor by zeroing in on Hobbes as the prototypical theorist of sovereignty and wondering how sovereignty might be retooled for democratic purposes. Because Hobbes locates the promise of collective safety in the power of the monarch, these reevaluations introduce some variability to the key asset that the sovereign offers and that the populace so desperately wants: security. If obedience is tendered in exchange for security, this contractual logic also creates an obligation for the sovereign or state to make good on its promises. The sovereign's grip upon security is not absolutely fixed; the security that people receive from the state "postulates popular subscription to sovereign power" (Honig xv). Unlike the state's monopoly on force that Max Weber described, the hold on security may be fairly tight but it is never totally secure.

In the state of emergency that has become the norm, which Walter Benjamin first expressed as a defining feature of modernity, insecurity is held at bay by an exceptional display of power and control that has become routine. Even so, the ongoing need for extraordinary security measures constantly replenishes a deep reservoir of insecurity. As I write these pages under the formally declared state of emergency that obtains in Wisconsin and many other states and nations during the coronavirus pandemic of 2020–22, face coverings, bottles of hand sanitizer, and practices of social distancing offer protection against airborne contagion while also spreading an immeasurable amount of frustration and feelings of vulnerability. Several of these propositions up to this point describe affective states that discourage, if not outright foreclose, decision making and action; not for nothing do characters in gothic novels recount being struck mute by terror just as enthusiasts of the sublime report feeling paralyzed by a fearsome magnitude. Yet action and agency are not wholly foreclosed. While the state or other sovereign guarantor of security offers nothing like a contract between equals, it nonetheless remains the case that governance preserves the idea, however faint or buried in memory, that the people at some people sought security. Security thus persists as a site of ambivalence and conceptual struggle. Honig's bid to "de-exceptionalize the emergency" (xviii) adopts a questioning sensibility that refuses to accept that the extraordinary nature of an emergency necessarily places contemporary political arrangements beyond interrogation. Security may be a pressing and even paramount need, but that urgency need not always override the awareness that people can do things with security even as it so clearly does things—tracking, surveillance, sorting, identifying—to them.

Two far-flung literary examples, connected by the crosscurrents of utopia and dystopia, illustrate the collective aspirations wrapped up with security. In the imagining of countercommunities from Fenimore Cooper's *The Crater* (1847) to the apocalyptic novels of the twenty-first century, security is not just a basic need but a topic of active debate and discussion. The adventurers in Cooper's South Seas haven continually make improvements to their defenses and redefine who is or is not included. Their efforts entail "a registry of the entire population" (*Crater* 326) or a census that Cooper lays out in a table sorting people by sex, age, marital status, and vocation. While the safety of this Pacific colony rests on a people populous enough to defend themselves, its stability requires that the population not grow too large with "careless infusions of new members" (326). Sadly, the settlers remain united in their understanding of who their protections are meant to keep out, namely, the archipelago's indigenous inhabitants. The band of survivors after a global pandemic in Emily St. John Mandel's *Station Eleven* (2014) ponders similar questions. Achieving a fragile security is a collective performance for the living, which seems appropriate for a novel about a traveling Shakespeare troupe that caravans across the landscape in the wake of civilization's collapse. Where *The Crater* restricts security to a white settler population, Mandel's novel opens onto a notion of human security that is not limited by a sense of ethnos or nationalism. The fiction is instructive: in an era of climate change and other planetary threats, protecting people's "survival, livelihood and dignity," to cite the United Nations Trust Fund for Human Security, demands a collective performance for the living.

Within the challenge that critical security studies mounts against International Relations, the proposition that security constitutes not a national but a widely shared "public good" creates expectations for inclusiveness and democratic governance. Ian Loader and Neil Walker recognize that security, unlike feelings of fraternity or conviviality, "is not a constitutively other-regarding sentiment," but they also ask: what if people "may become educated in the virtues of security altruism" that views the safety of others as a "good in its own right" ("Necessary Virtues" 187–88)? To be fair, Loader and Walker do not pose this idea as a question, but I frame it as such because the "right of people to live in freedom and dignity, free from poverty and despair," to invoke once more the language of the United Nations ("Resolution"), is not only elusive but also contingent and insufficient even among those who advocate for it. As the Resolution of the General Assembly reads, "Human security does not replace State security."

7. Security May Be a Precondition of Freedom, but It Is Also the Case That Freedom Generates and Extends the Need for Security

The standard story goes like this: the fragility of freedom, threatened by any number of bad actors from one's neighbors to an intrusive state, requires security as a bulwark of protection. Hobbes and other theorists of the social contract, including the framers of the Constitution, laid out the terms by which timorous citizens cede some portion (for Hobbes, it would be the lion's share) of their liberties in exchange for security. At an extreme inflection point after the attacks of September 11, 2001, freedom itself was construed as something that needed to be secured.[16] Such thinking is hardly new: "The political thinkers of the seventeenth and eighteenth centuries . . . more often than not identified political freedom with security," writes Arendt (149). It's a story beset by complications: the false assumption that each of the parties agreeing to the social contract has equal standing sets up a power differential between a sovereign authority and citizens. The notable irony ensues that citizens seek protection from the same entity that they fear jeopardizes freedom: the state. This contradiction has led more than one theorist to view security as a protection racket (Dillon, *Biopolitics of Security* 32; Tilly 170) in which a sovereign power seeds uncertainty and incites fear in citizens who then reach out to that same power in hopes of exchanging some of their precious liberty for safety. Security is an offer that citizens cannot refuse: "Governments are in the business of selling protection," writes Charles Tilly, "whether the people want it or not" (175). What sovereign power really defends are its own defenses; what it really secures is its own security power. The standard story thus invites suspicion, which, however, does not make it any less true.

People got far less than they bargained for when they agreed to the social contract. The initial inequity that is baked into this arrangement has tremendous consequences in creating an imbalance between freedom and security. In Arendt's reading, "the guaranty of security" that "made freedom possible" (149) diminished the political significance of freedom. In effect, security depoliticized freedom, as "the word 'freedom' now designated a quintessence of activities which occurred outside the political realm" (149). As freedom was split off from the political, the need for security wormed its way into other zones, coming to envelop pursuits and strivings that, at least with respect to the tight framework of Arendt's ideas of what counts as politics, would seem beyond the purview of the state or other sovereign authority. To phrase this argument in a contemporary theoretical idiom, what Arendt is mourning is the aggressive evolution of politics into biopolitics.

In a remarkable passage anticipating Michel Foucault's account of biopolitics as governance that endeavors "to ensure, sustain, and multiply life, to put this life in order" (*History of Sexuality* 138), Arendt writes that government "was now considered to be the appointed protector not so much of freedom as of the *life process*, the interests of society and its individuals. Security remained the decisive criterion . . . a security which should permit an undisturbed development of the life process of society as a whole. This life process is not bound up with freedom but follows its own inherent necessity; and it can be called free only in the sense that we speak of a freely flowing stream" (150; my emphasis). Were Arendt merely describing biopolitics avant la lettre, her comments would still excite interest. But the full significance of her thinking about security and freedom hinges on her critique of the notion that security is supposed to prevent disturbances, implicitly stabilizing freedom and making life safe. Without security, freedom would be too risky and tumultuous—or so believe those authorities, institutions, and forces invested in order and governance. Her metaphor is telling, as the free flow of water occurs simply because of the immutable laws of gravity, not because the water has debated, decided, or agreed in common to pursue a certain course which, at any rate, does not constitute a course of action. This freedom flows unimpeded but is hardly a political sense of freedom. In short, security overtakes politics. At its most extreme, this worldview treats freedom itself as a security concern. As opposed to a freedom that has been securitized in this manner, Arendt favors a political sense of freedom whose dependence on action troubles the order that security would establish. Rooted in the contingency of action and the openness of possibility, political freedom poses a challenge to security's need for fixability and predictability.

But every challenge to order is also an opportunity, in this case, to push for the extension of security to everything that the "life process" entails. In Foucault's cynical appraisal, "freedom is nothing else but the correlative of the deployment of apparatuses of security" (*Security* 48). Instead of the familiar tradeoff whereby the extension of security diminishes liberty, Foucault collapses the two with a more insidious reading: freedom generates and extends the need for security. In lectures at the Collège de France, Foucault pinpoints this idea as a technology of liberalism, which continuously manufactures freedom, not as part of an emancipatory project but as the mainstay of nineteenth-century biopower.[17] The constant production of freedom requires constant security both to protect it from encroachment and, more importantly, to keep it in hand through regulation, monitoring, and surveillance. Liberalism arouses freedom ("Le libéralisme . . . la suscite" [Foucault, *Naissance de la Biopolitique* 66]) in order to keep tabs on it. Foucault's question is not "'how much liberty are we willing to sacrifice to security?'" but rather whether "the liberal project of 'liberty' is in fact a project of security" (Neocleous, *Critique* 13). Biopolitics marks off and then seeks to regulate an expansive domain by governing life itself. If "life is thus a permanent security problem for biopolitics" and if "the governance of life" constitutes "a continuous emergency" (Dillon, *Biopolitics of Security* 80, 151), this uncertainty provides both the excuse and justification to enact endless surveillance, statistical reporting, and other security measures over a population.

To push back against this situation in which liberty serves as the delivery mechanism of increased security, one could do no better than to take up the title of Arendt's essay that I have been drawing on here: "What Is Freedom?" The answer to her question requires a sensibility that aligns freedom with politics, not security. Only in the zone of shared striving and action does freedom appear, and because this setting is neither the inner project of self-governance nor a private life sheltered from the public sphere, contingency is its defining characteristic. The ancient notion of *securitas*, in contrast, guards against accident and the vicissitudes of public life; in etymological terms, *se-cura* is to be without care or concern. Security offers "the promise of a world without events," a continuous form of living "unbroken by surprise" (Masco 41) to the point where the contingency of what may happen in the future has already been delimited. The modern technology of biopolitics stultifies life itself, employing statistics, algorithms, and other countable forms of knowledge that make human behavior and desires not only predictable but also commodifiable. The overriding contradiction becomes that while security provides stability for freedom, it is also the case that "measures of security work toward a growing depoliticization of society" (Agamben, "Security and Terror" 3).

In light of these constraints, might we wonder if political freedom requires not security but insecurity as its essential ground? When people are secure, writes John Hamilton in his reading of Nietzsche, they are sapped of the desire to act and easily settle into a "paralysis, which traps life itself into a stable form, secure but lifeless" (245). But when they feel insecure, they take action, which for Arendt is the entry point to "a politically organized world" (148) that embraces uncertainty over prediction and spontaneity over planning and protection. It thus becomes necessary to upend my original proposition in this section by attaching a new corollary: *Security may be a precondition of freedom, but it is also the case that political freedom cannot exist without insecurity.*

8. Security Is Almost Always Security From

In a classic contribution to the political theory of liberalism, Isaiah Berlin cut a distinction between positive liberty (freedom to) and negative liberty (freedom from). Where the liberal tradition prioritizes *freedom from* interference and coercion, the *freedom to* associated with positive liberty more readily implies a politics of autonomy and independence. Despite the fact that liberty and security are intertwined concepts, it does not make ready sense to seek a corresponding distinction between *security to* and *security from*. There often seems to be only *security from*: people turn to numerous entities from insurance companies and financial investment firms to private contractors and governments to find safeguards against risk, contingency, and uncertainty. The historical example of American colonization that predominates the latter half of this book illustrates the lengths that white Americans went to in order to achieve security from the ever-present fear of slave insurrection. Today, fearful liberty of the sort described above aspires to be vigilant about terrorism while also voicing suspicions about government overreach and excessive surveillance that the threat demands. But it is also the case that many conservatives as well as libertarians regard the current imbalance between hyperactive security and the retreat of liberty as acceptable because only those with something to hide would insist on privacy. Within the security regimes of Western democracies, "freedom from fear," according to Anastassia Tsoukala, "does not refer any more to civil rights and liberties but legitimates the very restriction of these civil rights and liberties" (622). Such contentions make it well worth wondering the extent to which the desire for security *from* treats political freedom itself as a threat.

The sum of such contradictory logic may be the political desire to achieve security from freedom. Open-ended and performative, the experience of freedom that Arendt cherishes relies on and even invites unpredictability via actions that are never assured of a telos or outcome. As Judith Butler puts it in a slightly different context, "our political unknowingness" is "also the condition of action itself" (*Bodies* 241). The radical contingency that Arendt takes as the fundamental condition of freedom is viewed by Butler as the antifoundational ground of political possibility: despite this difference, the convergence is a critical orientation in which it is impossible to predict—and thus control or determine in advance—the outcome of people's actions. Such uncertainty can make freedom appear to some as an unwelcome proposition, at odds with the foresight and preparedness that constitute the hallmarks of security.

From this perspective, it bears asking: who among us is willing to forgo security from potential risk and harm for the unknowingness of freedom? Confirmation of what we already know can be deeply reassuring. While it may be easy to lambaste those who lack the confidence to embrace the chanciness of political action, few people today seem willing to watch a news channel or visit an internet forum where the political orientation, left or right, has not been scripted in advance. Even fewer are willing to exercise the foolhardiness to disable security software when we hop on the internet, the recklessness to sink all our retirement savings in risky securities promising improbably high returns, or the imprudence to deactivate other security precautions such as smoke detectors or safety seat belts.

Perhaps, it may be argued, these safety measures are not properly political, but the promise of *security from* that informs everyday actions is wrapped up with older meanings that touch upon the practice of freedom. Within *asphaleia*, the Greek word for security, the verb *sphallô* (to err, trip, or fall) sits at its center (Arends 267; Dillon, *Politics of Security* 124; Lennon, *Passwords* 6). The condition of *a-sphaeleia* thus implies stability or safety that prevents one from falling or being overthrown, much in the way that *sphallô* in *The Iliad* figures in the context of wrestling (Dillon, *Politics of Security* 124). In *The Odyssey*, *asphales* appears in the context of Mount Olympus, "the abode of the gods that stands fast forever" (6.42), secure and impenetrable. While an aversion to falling is understandable, taken to various extremes it can discourage us from not just tightrope walking to mountain climbing but everyday activities like walking or standing up. As a political principle, *asphaleia* or security itself can prove crippling: yes, it secures the ground for the enjoyment of freedom, but also "it can release us altogether from the burden of freedom itself" (Dillon, *Politics of Security* 30).

With so much energy devoted to the negative security of *security from*, it becomes difficult to flesh out a positive sense of *security to*. (As an incidental example, typing "security from . . ." into Google's web browser yields sharper, more appropriate predictive results than entering "security to" as a search term.) This incommensurability shows how hard it is to orient security around the contingency and unknowingness that are necessary to freedom. The paucity of possibility that surrounds *security to* exemplifies how inimical security can be to politics and action.

9. Security Aims to Domesticate and Tame Time

The mood and mode of security are anticipatory, directed at predicting behavior and avoiding future events. Preventing conflict requires that one look "before the danger cometh . . . for his security against that other in the time to come," as Hobbes advises in *The Elements of Law*. For Hobbes, our equality with others spurs discord and ceaseless competition, creating an anarchic setting lacking a sovereign authority who can provide order. *Leviathan*, of course, responds to this power vacuum by identifying anticipation as a critical faculty of governance. Originating in "feare of oppression," anticipation relies on a mixture of "force" and "wiles" (*Leviathan* 184) that enables one person to outflank and achieve mastery over others. Hobbes's seventeenth century also saw the rise of security in the market sense of financial instruments, and by the

1820s and 1830s the credit-based economies of the plantation South offered vast potential for speculation in securities. The coordination of finance and security hinges on speculation *about* and *in* the future, betting on what is going to happen and investing in possible outcomes. Speculation "seeks to secure a fickle future, tame uncertainty, and insure against disaster," objectives that align financial stability with national interest (de Goede, *Speculative Security* xxix).[18] Today, in addition to stock securities, technologies of anticipation take shape as algorithms, probability studies, and biostatistical projections. Despite the difference between Hobbesian cunning and mass data sets that enhance the predictive capacities of Wall Street, Google, and the NSA, the desired outcome is the same: to anticipate and therefore control the future by removing any and all contingency from the unfolding of political and social life.[19]

From policing and counterterrorism to online shopping and social media, the future points to a temporal terrain over which governments and corporations exert dominion. The ambit of security is chronopolitical. In the U.S. government's own words, surveillance and the collection of metadata serve as "a targeted way to find the terrorists tomorrow" before they act (qtd. in Gray 45). In military parlance, such measures constitute "forward deterrence" (Martin 262) designed to predict and preempt threats. In the operations of corporate capitalism, assembling and sifting through unimaginable amounts of information goes beyond anticipating consumer behavior to forming and creating it in advance. The raw data that Amazon, Nike, and other corporations collect becomes a commodity that is sold and traded in "markets for future behavior" (Zuboff 10). Both the military and corporate sector do more than predict behavior; they preempt choice and action, whether it is by stopping a terrorist attack before it happens or by creating a need for a product before we even think to desire it.

The Leviathan is about governmentality in addition to governance, and the predictive and preemptive capacities associated with surveillance and security facilitate this extension of power and control to life itself. What Antoinette Rouvroy calls "data behaviourism" ("The End(s) of Critique" 143) enables governments and other entities to predict people's attitudes and potential actions with incredible efficiency by allowing analysts to bypass individual psychology or intention to focus solely on aggregate statistical data. The "pre-emptive character of algorithmic governmentality" (Rouvroy, "The End(s) of Critique" 155) represents an attack on the tenses of human life by ordaining what will happen and negating the conditional of what could happen.[20]

While surveillance today increasingly operates hand in glove with corporate efforts to amass big data, the aim to limit future contingency, not to mention the contingency of the future itself, is an essential feature of security that exists independently of computer technologies. Literary, historical, and philosophical materials reveal how security relies on chronopolitical strategies that govern behavior and action in the future. These strategies include broad narratives about the evolution of private property and accounts of the sublime as well as the more specific operations of surveillance and computation. Brockden Brown, who will appear in these pages as something of a media theorist, describes how the secrecy of the Illuminati brotherhood rests on full disclosure and total surveillance. "Confessions of the past are required, because they are an earnest of the future character and conduct," the mysterious Ludloe informs his protégé, Carwin (*Memoirs* 282). The financial metaphor of "an earnest," used as a noun, refers to an initial down payment "for the purpose of securing a bargain or contract" (*OED*), that is, earnest money. By extending this surety to encompass the past, present, and future, Brown's master manipulator seeks to dissipate the doubt and diminish the risk that is an inevitable feature of social relationships. Ludloe and Carwin are players in a risk society where the calculation of risk aims "to discipline the future" (Mythen 14); the endeavor constitutes nothing less than the ambition to govern thought and action today as well as tomorrow. Preempting possible futures, most keenly those that anticipated the violence of Black rebellion, became a national priority amid the severe racial inequality and racial torture at the heart of U.S. society during Brown's era and beyond. From Benjamin Franklin's calculations about exponential population growth to Jefferson's reflections on the political economy of slave society, biopolitical assessments served as fodder for projections about how to avert that fateful moment when the delicate balance between a supposedly shrinking white majority and a fast-increasing Black minority would be forever overturned. National security in the nineteenth century was already fixated on possible racial futures to ensure that they never came to pass.

    The future is a scary temporal place, yet its vagueness and open-endedness also give security unlimited range for expansion and continual rationale for its existence. "The futurity of fear" (Ahmed, *Cultural Politics of Emotion* 65) represents an opportunity to amplify the sway of biopower and to acquire more information; security is always heavily invested in a futures market whose stock and trade is affect. Its chronopolitical mandate stretches to biblical proportions, as Milton well knew. Satan, the brightest of the angels, may have been booted from heaven, but his banishment to "bottomless perdition" (*PL* I.47) requires constant scrutiny. (Yet, of course, the flip side is also true for Milton, who saw human freedom as an ongoing project.) Once the victory over the infernal host is complete, "the policing of hell thereafter nonetheless calls for an eternity of low intensity operation," as Dillon puts it (*Biopolitics of Security* 26). In the end, it is contingency itself, embodied in the conspiracy of Chaos and Chance ("Chance governs all" [*PL* II.910]) that unlocks the gates of hell. Yet, the strange thing is that Milton's God does not seem all that perturbed by this second rebellion. After all, God in his omniscience knows that "no barrs of Hell, nor all the chains" can detain Satan forever—which means that God also knows that security measures will need to be in place forever. (As a security measure, Adam and Eve's capacity for free will proves woefully inadequate in this regard.) Because the future is unbounded and infinite, security remains incomplete and therefore unending.

10. Security Can Be Profitable, but It Is Insecurity That Is Truly Lucrative

The "war on terror," like all wars, has been good for the bottom line of defense contractors. With the rise of private military contractors, security itself has become a commodity that governments and corporations now outsource and purchase on the free market. "No one knows how many billions of dollars slosh around" (McFate 2) in the world of private security. The estimated $7 trillion that the Pentagon has spent on private defense contractors since 9/11, amounting to roughly half of the Department of Defense's overall budget (Knickmeyer), represents only a slice of the overall picture, as governments, regimes, oil companies, mining operations, and even NGOs outsource security. Blackwater USA (now renamed Academi), whose employees opened fire on a public square in Baghdad and killed seventeen civilians and wounded twenty more, is perhaps the most recognizable of the hundreds of private military companies that operate around the globe. These entities are not ragtag guns for hire of the sort mythologized in *The Magnificent Seven* but more akin to "heavily armed multinational corporations" (McFate 2). According to Blackwater's founder, "We are trying to do for the national security apparatus what FedEx did for the Postal Service" ("America's Private Sector Army"). Speed, efficiency, and privatization, not to mention a lack of public accountability, are presented as the alternative to a lumbering government agency, and the U.S. State Department bought into this promise by paying over $300 million to Blackwater. Not surprisingly, the bid to make national defense cheaper and more competitive through the use of private security contractors has ballooned costs while exposing people to increased "surveillance, martial policing, detention, and killing" (Paik 72).

This specific example of military contracting, however, does not capture the total extent to which capitalism as a system thrives on insecurity. Storms, pirates, and mutinies had long exposed oceangoing ventures to risk. The innovation of the nineteenth century, as Jonathan Levy argues, was to commodify that risk with the creation of financial instruments such as insurance to control for accidents and other contingencies. "The spread of capitalism had brought the insecurity of the sea to the land," but instead of discouraging economic growth, this expansion emboldened risk-takers and investors who saw opportunities to profit from "an era of pervasive insecurity" (Levy 2). In particular, the slave trade as a staple of maritime commerce invited speculative risk-taking, which demanded risk-management, and which led to insecurity in turn.[21] Bonds, insurance, stocks, mortgage-backed securities, and futures markets became a means not simply of taking precautions against risk but, more importantly, investing *in* uncertainty. Will Antonio's argosy in *The Merchant of Venice* return safe to port, its hold laden with goods that will fetch handsome returns? Or are his ships at the bottom of the sea? Stock markets capitalize upon this unknowingness, transforming insecurity into speculative commodities that can be traded, sold, and resold. Will the credit advanced to Southern planters be repaid with interest, or will insects and drought destroy this season's cash crops? Starting in the 1820s, a robust secondary market in the sale of mortgages held on enslaved persons—slave-backed securities—made this speculation an attractive one for European investors. Such financial instruments seemed scrubbed of racial contexts, and investors who traded in the derivative market in slave mortgages "escaped the risk inherent in owning an individual slave, who might die, run away, or become rebellious" (Baptist, "Toxic Debt" 82). Rates of return seemingly increased each quarter until they didn't: in a world where loans, securities, and inflated bank currency rested on enslaved persons put up as collateral, "[white] men bought just to sell again," in the words of one Depression-era economic historian, setting off "an epidemic of reckless speculation" (Sparks 237).

While security seeks to domesticate and tame time (per the previous proposition), it is also the case that the uncertainties inherent to capitalism offer new opportunities for speculation and growth. The idea that the future could be commodified in a "futures market"—derivative contracts that lock in the price of securities or commodities now for trading at a later date—neatly expresses how capitalism extends its reach to tomorrow. "The generative insecurity and radical uncertainty of capitalism" (Levy 18) have created at various times a brisk trade in derivatives, the easy availability of securities backed by subprime mortgages, and the gambler's rush of buying on margin to enable the purchase of more securities without having the necessary cash on hand. Each transaction embodies risk in commodified form: these investments may be risky, but such is the condition for the possibility of gain.

11. The Ultimate Goal of Security Is to Leave Nothing to the Imagination (or to Interpretation)

At first glance, this thesis runs counter to the previous thesis about the volume, velocity, variety, and vulnerability of information. After all, raw data—especially when there is a mountain of it—requires interpretation and analysis to be useful in determining a course of action. But the ultimate goal of security is to leave nothing to the imagination, which, as we know, is the child of fear and anxiety. In striving for "the predictability and repetitiveness that are the endless propensities of the state" (Rothschild 89), security consciousness seeks to tame the imagination of its worst fears. Care and concern would evaporate if only we could fulfill the etymological meaning of *securitas* and become care-less, which, of course, leaves us in a complicated spot since being without cares is indistinguishable from being careless (Hamilton 10–12). As security predicts and manages future contingency, it also eases our penchant for imagining all that could go wrong. Total security would thus negate the need for interpretation in the first place.

Interpretation thrives wherever there is uncertainty: the meaning of poems, the gist of a film's unexpected final twist, the significance of conflicting data, the intentions of an enemy. National security is especially intolerant of uncertainty. Did Saddam Hussein's Iraq possess biological and chemical weapons? Intelligence analysts were unsure, and this uncertainty, above and beyond the actuality of any threat, drove U.S. foreign and military policy. At a Pentagon briefing of February 12, 2002, Rumsfeld famously expressed the view that terrorist plots, especially those that could not yet be imagined, presented the gravest threat to national security. Responding to a reporter's question about Iraq's willingness "to supply terrorists with weapons of mass destruction," the secretary of defense framed the role of U.S. intelligence as identifying and removing uncertainty. Making a distinction among three categories of knowledge from "things we know we know" to "we know there are some things we do not know," and, finally, to things "that we don't know that we don't know," Rumsfeld suggested that this last category, so wide open to the imagination and interpretation, was especially vexing. "If one looks throughout the history of our country and other free countries," he continued, it is the category of "unknown unknowns" that frustrates the intelligence community ("Defense Department Briefing"). Does his statement express inadvertent envy of unfree countries, where security is total and totalitarian, that are not troubled by the undecidability of interpretation?[22] Neel Ahuja contends that the Iraq War represented "a fully theorized war using uncertainty against uncertainty" (149) in which the hawks urging U.S. military intervention mobilized uncertainty about the existence and extent of weapons of mass destruction in an effort to contain the larger geopolitical uncertainties that instability in the Middle East posed to Western interests. The U.S. military response illustrates how "uncertainty thus marks both the incitement to and the practice of security" (Ahuja 148). In literally combating uncertainty, security strives to interpret uncertainty in just one way by making a unilateral determination about what uncertainty means. The goal is to be certain about what uncertainty means— and what matter of intervention it dictates. Rather than entertaining a range of interpretations, which would only create more uncertainty about which interpretation is the right one, security seeks to tamp down on contingency and undecidability.

Information can be conceptualized as a probabilistic function of uncertainty. This proposition constitutes the core of mathematician Claude Shannon's development of information theory in the mid-twentieth century defining information in terms of all the possible messages that may be sent. I will have more to say about Shannon in the chapters that follow, but for now the key takeaway is that his theory spurred an interest in algorithmic computation to measure "the amount of freedom of choice we have in constructing messages" (Shannon and Weaver 13). Freedom, of course, has some weighty connotations, which, though perhaps not intended by Shannon, reveal how the calculation of uncertainty echoes with political significance. Algorithms manage and make sense of these possibilities, and in the societal realm such calculations serve as powerful tools for managing and making sense of people as data points, going so far as to predict and determine behavior. What Rouvroy calls "algorithmic governmentality" corresponds to "the decline of *interpretation*" ("The End(s) of Critique" 151): rather than merely imagining all that may happen, security often endeavors to take the next step and leave no doubt about what uncertainty means by allowing for just one predetermined reality. Security hates surprises.

This logic, as Cooper showed in his portrait of frontier security that is the subject of chapter 3, accrues genocidal overtones. Killing all the members of a "feathered tribe" (*The Pioneers* 246) makes interpretation superfluous. Likewise, the plan to exile all free people of color through the project of colonization (chapters 5 and 6) would supposedly unburden the white imagination of its obsessive fixation with the possibility of a Black uprising. The nineteenth century, it seems, had its own algorithms of governmentality, blunt instruments that met the biopolitical uncertainty posed by subject populations with approaches designed to leave no room for either nuance or ambiguity.

Yet we must also remember that aesthetic artifacts from that period and earlier are nothing if not imaginative texts. In fictions of the frontier, the property that security was thought to secure is seen to be on the run, fleeting, its clear title and possession always murky. The gothic imagination churned up a different set of existential doubts about the obscurity of Enlightenment communication networks. So, too, a fevered racial imagination proved ripe terrain for oratory and addresses that gave voice to white anguish over the specter of Black population increase. No matter how intolerant of uncertainty and interpretation that security might make us, the aesthetic register persists. And, of course, the inescapable contradiction, as CIA agent Joe Turner in *Six Days of the Condor* learns from his work combing through American literature, is that these imaginative fictions become the target of and generate the need for security.

12. Security Safeguards Whiteness

The emotional content of security is lodged in specific historical locations—white bodies and white minds. In similar fashion, the material apparatus of security is lodged in specific institutional locations that are sworn to protect white lives and white-owned property. Most encompassing of all, the conceptual apparatus behind security justifies its unequal distribution that extends the protections of privacy to some while exposing others to "stop and frisk," racial profiling, and state surveillance.[23] These emotional, institutional, and conceptual aspects of security accompanied practices of settler colonialism that seized Indigenous lands to convert the "wilderness" into "property" so that it could be improved, cultivated, and made profitable by another form of human "property." Likewise, financial security correlates to white economic advantage: in the nineteenth century, securities indexed to mortgages held on the bodies of enslaved people insulated white investment capital from risk. But with rampant speculation in slave securities, the bubble burst—but even then, those suffering the most brutal consequences were the people sold away from their homes and families. Today, it is not just that security protects property; rather, security itself has become property that can be bought and sold in such commodified forms as private policing and gated communities. These "new enclosures" (A. Crawford 111) provide a protective circle around accretions of class privilege that are intertwined with whiteness.

The same practices that secured white hegemony bred the fear and insecurity that made such attempted domination seem so precarious. Surveying tracts of wilderness secured property rights for settlers, but disputed land claims on the frontier created an affective surplus of trepidation over potential Indian attack. Even though "a successful frontier policy was supposed to make 'frontier people' feel secure" (Spero 7), the rapacity and fraud behind such land grabs as the Walking Purchase soon led to violence that left colonists feeling unsettled, often literally so. (An agreement of 1737 between Pennsylvania settlers and the Delaware people, the Walking Purchase stipulated that property lines would be extended by the distance that a person could walk in a day and half. From the outset, the Delaware complained of fraud when the whites ran instead of walked and, by some reports, continued after sunset.)[24] A collective sense of whiteness first emerged with the frontier security crisis created by the encroachments of settler colonialism. The constant dread of Indian attack gave birth to whiteness as a vulnerable identity; only with the terror of frontier warfare did whiteness become a shared point of identification. And yet, as Peter Silver argues in his history of Indigenous/settler violence during the eighteenth century, this sensibility was less "a racial self-identification" than an expression of "an overall opposition between Indian and European interests" coupled with a recognition of "the suffering of the great bulk of ordinary rural Europeans at Indians' hands" (xxi).[25] When white settler owners on the frontier used words like "naked," "open," and "exposed" to describe their situation on the frontier (Spero 7), their visceral language captured an acute sense of vulnerability. Yet the historian's editorializing here that white settlers showed "individual bravery and strength in the face of warfare" (115–16) can read like a romantic recuperation of whiteness.

When settler colonialism carved out land as property that the system of slavery, as Cheryl Harris has argued, extended to whiteness itself, it also created a form of matter that was alienable, subject to seizure, and susceptible to loss and flight. Whiteness needed securing, and legal ideas of private property proved more than adequate to the task. Property ownership allowed white people to enjoy privacy whereas others who lacked property or who were viewed as property themselves routinely had their privacy violated in the name of security. Not only did property ownership fail to provide protections to Black people, but as the nationwide campaign of African colonization in the early nineteenth century revealed, property ownership exposed free people of color to invasive restrictions. The town watch and the slave patrol, both forerunners of the modern police force, relied on technologies of "racializing surveillance" (Browne 16) to uphold white safety by monitoring and targeting Black people. After the Civil War, Ida B. Wells-Barnett's investigative journalism documented instances where Black property ownership stoked white resentment and the false accusations that fueled lynching.

Perceptions of an endangered white identity have routinely outstripped the actuality of any threat. Security precautions no doubt protected white people on the frontier as well as the plantation from some of the effects created by their own brutality toward others. But the true target was not a target at all but a beneficiary: security's role in safeguarding whiteness consisted largely in allaying the fears fueled by a gothic racial imagination. This state of vulnerability appears as a pathological symptom that I call "Jeffersonian trembling," a recurrent attitude obsessed with the potential likelihood of an impending racial cataclysm. The feedback loop between security and insecurity is nowhere more evident than in this particular racial conjunction, as white apprehensions over the biopolitical potential of Black and Indigenous people drove a security apparatus whose operations and very existence depended on the insecurities it struggled to allay. The project of white security, we might say, required Nat Turner as much as Thomas Jefferson. Where else would authorities in Southern port cities have gotten the idea to seize copies of Walker's *Appeal to the Colored Citizens of the World* as a necessary security precaution? Then again, did not beliefs such as the postmaster general's opinion of 1802 that "employing negroes, or people of color, in transporting the mails" constituted a security risk (*American State Papers* 1:27) already suggest the radical potential of Black print circulation for Walker and others to see? Just as likely, though, Walker found all the provocation he needed to sow white insecurity when he encountered the palpable anxiety within certain passages of Jefferson's *Notes on the State of Virginia*, not to mention the Declaration of Independence. Walker's pamphlet picks up on Jefferson's racial insecurity to instill apprehension among whites who "think they have us so well secured in our wretchedness" (82). In heightening the feedback loop between security and insecurity, Walker discerned how the project of safeguarding whiteness routinely puts white people on edge.

The misplaced sensitiveness that whiteness is under imminent attack illustrates that emotions have real effects even when they do not correspond to some objective reality. Securing whiteness frequently entails offloading insecurity onto others; expressed in still sharper terms, whiteness puts others at risk. "White emotional well-being is produced in part by the ritualized entertainments of the security state, which hinge on the regularized death of black people," writes Kyla Schuller in the context of Black Lives Matter (2). From zoning restrictions that increase the proximity of poor neighborhoods and communities of color to environmental hazards to the disproportionate rates of death during public health crises, Covid-19 being only the most recent example, official institutions and habits of indifference have combined to fulfill Foucault's maxim that biopower functions "to make live and let die" (*"Society"* 241). While it is undoubtedly true that individual white people bear the culpability for these effects, the security apparatuses that overlap so completely with whiteness represent a normative mode of seeing and structuring the world. If "whiteness is an orientation that puts certain things within reach" and functions as a form of "public *comfort by allowing bodies to extend into spaces that have already taken their shape*" (Ahmed, "Phenomenology" 154, 158), the historical and literary sources studied in this book examine how that space became coextensive with the idea of "America" itself. Imperiled by the growth of the Black population (or so believed many nineteenth-century white observers across political, religious, and academic spheres), the white population was thought to be facing an existential crisis. In reaction, the movement to colonize Africa with free people of color and manumitted persons explicitly presented itself as an urgent national security measure. White nationalism would shoulder the burden of preserving what historian Alexander Saxton called "the white republic." At the same time, the colonization movement redirected risk onto the bodies of Black migrants, who suffered high rates of mortality in the U.S.-backed colony of Liberia. If whiteness can be understood as a phenomenological experience of entitlement in space, as Ahmed contends, then the coordinates of that space are frequently set—and enlarged—by the emotional, institutional, and conceptual apparatuses of national racial security.

13. Security Muddles Agency

At first glance, security would seem to be all about pinpointing subjects and establishing their identities. Measures like Face ID and bank account PINs protect us and our property; others such as the biometrics of gait recognition target us. Even metadata such as the cell phone location that is not supposed to reveal anything about who we are provides ample clues to confirm personal identity.[26]

Identity, however, is not the same thing as agency. People are identified all the time, but by what or whom? Who are the agents that are doing the work of establishing identity? Satellites locate and identify targets, drones execute intelligence (and human targets), and search cookies help build a profile of our interests and desires. Passwords and dual-factor identification confirm the users of computer systems. Algorithms create consumer subjects with a biography built on statistical data, browsing habits, and assumed biopolitical markers. Where does agency exist across this dispersal of impersonality? The indeterminacy of agency that surrounds security reveals its tendency to confuse identity rather than confirm it. Security can be an emotional property of the subject, as when a person feels safe and protected. Yet talk of security generally obscures agency. Used to describe a policy or an overriding interest, security as an abstract value hovers in the air, seemingly without attachment to the institutions or people that might implement it. People do not enact security; instead, it is exercised over them by apparatuses that seem to have a life of their own. A woman who identifies as a "security mom" may exercise low-level watchfulness over perceived outsiders and also keep tabs on her husband and teenage children through surveillance apps, but, according to Grewal, she more likely suffers "the insecurity produced by the neoliberal securitization of everyday life" (129), which is to say that her motherly hypervigilance is the by-product of a system of economic governance that has left her feeling powerless. Even the workplace or retail store warning that a manager is going to "call security" conjures up an impersonal proxy force that will "escort" you from the premises despite lacking any decision-making power of its own. The language of critical theory exemplifies this tendency with formulations that at times seem to grant agency to security itself: "security . . . tries to work within reality" (Foucault, *Security* 47); "security addresses itself" (Hole 133); "security impresses itself upon us" (Dillon, *Politics of Security* 16). I share this tendency, and more than one of the axioms here, including this concluding thirteenth one, present security itself as an agent.

This attribution of agency to an abstract noun is not particular to security; political theorists speak of "democracy" and poets of "love" in ways that invest these abstractions with a volition and motive all their own. But the case of security, while not exceptional in this regard, carries undue significance because its expression in such reified form occludes the intentions of all of us who seek safety, especially in alternative forms that do not purchase well-being and protection at the expense of others or of our own freedoms.

It would perhaps have been hard to predict that the origin story of security would turn out this way by muting and muddling human agency. The social contract begins with people's conscious decision to band together in the interest of shared protection and collective safety. The Constitution's performative utterance that "we, the people" unite to "secure the Blessings of Liberty" stands as an exemplar of this origin story. But after that auspicious beginning, the document's authors did not have much to say about the concept. It appears twice in the amendments, once as a privacy protection against search and seizure (Amend. IV) and once more to outfit with guns a "well-regulated militia" necessary to "a free State" (Amend. II). In the body of the Constitution, it comes up in the context of financial securities and also in describing intellectual property rights. The cognate term "safety" appears but once, stipulating the circumstances when "public Safety may require" the suspension of habeas corpus (Art. I, sec. 9). Protection receives a trio of mentions in the presidential oath of office (Art. II), the promise of defense against foreign invasion or "domestic Violence" (Art. IV, sec. 4), and the guarantee of "equal protection" (Amend. XIV). The unlikely outbreak of domestic unrest implied, of course, the persistent threat of slave insurrection. Article IV concludes with a security preauthorization ready for implementation should widespread "violence" be the manifestation of Black people's agency. The debtor's revolt of 1786–87, known as Shays' Rebellion, suggested that the possibility of domestic turbulence was not as remote as many would have liked to have believed. This white uprising in western Massachusetts gave backers of the Constitution ready fodder in the debates over ratification, and the document that was adopted is described today by legal scholars as a "security constitution." As such, the Constitution "provides clear guidance on the issue of responsibility for homeland security" by spelling out the federal government's charge to finance and manage the "war on terrorism" (Mazzone 29). According to the language of Article IV, known as the Protection Clause, the "United States . . . shall protect each of them [the individual states] against invasion" and also when necessary "against domestic Violence." The obligation to protect, neatly expressed by the use of "shall," specifies the government's duty to act in the name of stability and order. Insofar as the people have agency, it would seem in contrast that popular action is the contingency that security tries to control.

So far, security, safety, and protection in the Constitution provide little support for agency and, indeed, the purpose often seems to be to guard against others exercising its revolutionary or rebellious potential. The Fourteenth Amendment, however, does offer some clarity to the tangle of agency by recognizing that the people implicitly alluded to in Article IV in terms of their capacity for insurrection and violence can now act as citizens. Nevertheless, the guarantee here remains indebted to the negative idea of "security from," in this case, from the governmental violation of individual rights.

This final proposition thus accentuates how any positive sense of "security to" define and assert agency remains elusive, sensed and desired but just out of sight.

2

The Contours of Security across Nine Historical *Récits*

THE TWENTY-FIRST CENTURY has been dubbed the "Age of Security" as well as the "age of the algorithm" (Voelz, *Poetics* 1; Mbembe, "Thoughts on the Planetary"). Algorithms enhance security in ways that brute force and surveillance never could by processing caches of data immense enough to allow for probabilistic predictions that would seem to render human decision making and action nugatory. Following on the heels of the Atomic Age and Information Age, these twin announcements might have seemed only a matter of time, a historical endpoint that had been predetermined by the march of technological innovation and its capacity for catastrophe. In similar fashion, we are told that now "every day is Security Awareness Day" and that we are also living in an "Age of Insecurity" (Neocleous, *Critique* 3; "Securitati Perpetuae" 3), making us perhaps wonder what filled our consciousness when we were not worried about the fragile protections offered by the mutually assured destruction of the Cold War or the vulnerability of computer passwords and the personal information that they safeguard. The so-called Ages of History, of course, did not have to lead to the ubiquity of security consciousness or the unease that it instills as a type of collateral political and psychic damage. Yet it did, and the rest of this book offers a literary, cultural, and historical explanation of how security became an ascendant political value that often overrides democracy, if not politics, itself. The trajectory is hardly a straight one, and the eddies where the imperatives of security get stuck, exposed, or otherwise momentarily destabilized represent opportunities to think about alternative imaginings of security. Looking at episodes where security became ossified in reaction to uncertainty and fear can provide a glimpse of what possibilities might have been available before those consolidations occurred.

The *récits* that follow complement the propositions laid out in the previous chapter but not in a one-to-one way. While some of these sketches directly illustrate a claim such as "security depends on fear," most of the foregoing axioms hover in the background of these brief histories. Several are nestled together, overlapping in ways that reveal how the contradictions inherent to the concept and practices of security complicate any effort to derive a narrative with clear victors and antagonists that offers unambiguous takeaways. Security represents more than a constrictive force just as it surely falls short of providing forms of safety and protection that do not also increase anxiety or feelings of vulnerability. The progression is loosely chronological, yet this unfolding represents a constellation less concerned with notions of causality that requires "telling the sequence of events like the beads of a rosary" (Benjamin, *Illuminations* 263) than with setting out key nodal points from the historical and literary past that continue to animate how people every day understand and negotiate security.

1755: The Opposition of Liberty and Safety

The defining moment within the cultural history of American security is awash with the bloodshed of frontier violence. During a dispute with the colonial governor of Pennsylvania about who would provide border security to white settlers, Benjamin Franklin first framed the issue in terms of an opposition that has since been invoked countless times: "Those who would give up *essential Liberty*, to purchase a little *temporary Safety*, DESERVE neither *Liberty* nor *Safety*" (*Historical Review* 289). Balancing the need for protection with the desire for political freedom, Franklin would seem to have come down squarely on the side of liberty by casting safety as merely a "temporary" fix. His conclusion has appealed to generations of subsequent commentators such as Franklin D. Roosevelt, who invoked Franklin's words in his "Four Freedoms" speech of 1941 that pledged to defend democracy against the rising tide of European fascism. Appeals to this hallmark formula of liberty/security have been subject to distortion, as when one lawmaker misremembered the original in ways that provided a convenient defense of neoliberal values: "Very simply—and I'm paraphrasing here—but Ben Franklin essentially said at one point, those who would trade privacy for a bit of security deserve neither privacy nor security" ("Ben Franklin's Famous"). It was probably Franklin himself who was the first to recycle his formulation two decades later when political tensions in the British colonies of North America were boiling over. This familiar contrast between liberty and security continues to frame debates about terrorism, sovereignty, immigration, borders, and dataveillance, but the circumstances of its initial utterance suggest that the opposition was never clear-cut. When Franklin minimized the fleeting value of safety in contrast to the inviolable nature of liberty, he was trying to resolve an uncertainty with respect to how the theoretical notion of the social contract between a sovereign power and its subjects was being played out on the ground in America. His argument would rely on an emergent structure of feeling rooted in whiteness as a defense against the violence created by settler colonialism.

Framing his ideas with a loose mix of Lockean liberalism as well as Hobbesian notions of a unitary sovereign body, Franklin assessed the exposed situation of the North American colonies. Even after the clash with this particular governor had passed, Franklin continued to chide those in England who viewed Americans' security interests as a provincial matter by asserting that the colonies instead represented the first line of defense for the British empire. If "the inhabitants of that frontier" are "attack'd," it is the "whole body" that suffers harm (*Interest*). The ravages of the Seven Years' War, which saw the combined forces of the French and Native tribes threatening white settlements in the Ohio Valley, made it dire to remind policymakers in Britain about the urgency of the Crown upholding its responsibility to provide security to all the appendages of the social body. Appealing to liberal principles of economic exchange as the basis for just governance, Franklin declared, "Where the frontier people owe and pay obedience, there they have a right look for protection" (*Interest*). The assertion countered the tendency among some back in England to view the war effort as conducted solely on behalf of the colonies. Franklin reminded the Crown of its obligations to the social contract: faithful subjects who consent to the sovereign's rule deserve something in return, in this case, security. The terms had not changed since the mythic moment when individuals first ceded their natural liberties to the state in order to acquire protection for life and property.

Franklin here seems to be cribbing from the final paragraph of *Leviathan* where Hobbes states that his entire purpose has been "to set before mens eyes the mutuall Relation between Protection and Obedience" (728). Two hundred years later, Carl Schmitt would condense this insight into a statement of Cartesian simplicity: "*protego ergo obligo* is the *cogito ergo sum* of the state" (*Concept of the Political* 52). The principle of "protection, therefore obedience," however, is not quite the same as either Hobbes's or Franklin's rendering.[1] Minor differences in temporal sequencing carry some not unweighty political implications. In the context of colonial defense, Americans demonstrate obedience first so that they then may claim security as a state-guaranteed right. In Schmitt's view, however, state protections precede obedience; that is, the people's duty to obey is an obligation created by and owed to the state. If Hobbes sets up a "mutuall Relation" where both sovereign and subject are co-present, Franklin slants the social contract toward the priority of the people while Schmitt emphasizes the precedence of the state. The first implies a dispersal of popular power, the second consolidates the authoritarian sway of the state by making security the fundamental component of the state's reason for existence. In Franklin's understanding, security is already infused with democratic potential, but, for Schmitt, the justification for authoritarianism is immanent to the concept: the contrast could not be starker. The stakes of this theoretical debate would be clarified when the outbreak of frontier hostilities gave Franklin the opportunity to insert "liberty" into the relation between obedience and protection.

Raids by Delaware and Shawnee Indians along Penn's Creek in the Susquehanna Valley in fall 1755 put this arrangement to the test. Disturbed by white encroachments into the backcountry, the Indigenous combatants had attacked farms, killing more than a dozen people while taking almost as many captive. Scared but also irate, settlers loaded a wagon with the dead and dumped the scalped bodies of their murdered neighbors on the steps of the statehouse (later to be renamed Independence Hall). Such "corpse displays" (Silver 77) mobilized gruesome spectacle to stage an affective appeal for frontier defense. Yet the battle lines were never neatly drawn: while the conflict initially flared up between white settlers and Lenape inhabitants, the animosities quickly spilled over into an already existing power struggle between the colonial governor of Pennsylvania, Robert Hunter Morris, and the Assembly. The practical matter of frontier security was soon enveloped by a political tussle over the proper balance of democratic authority, freedom, and security. Then again, the issue was never all that lofty considering that the accusations and recriminations from each side arose from a tax dispute. Liberty might have been "essential," but an unavoidable question remained: who was going to pay the costs of frontier security?

Franklin pitted "essential liberty" against "temporary safety" when the crisis of Pennsylvania border security spilled over into a battle of words and principles with the governor. He charged the governor with heightening Philadelphians' fears by feeding rumors of an imminent attack from French troops stationed at Fort Duquesne and their Native allies. Unverified reports circulated that 1,500 French regulars and hundreds of Delawares and Shawnees had closed to within 80 miles of the province's capital city. Painting a scene with "the Indians now engaged in laying waste the Country, and butchering the Inhabitants," Morris implied that a band of peace-loving Quakers in the Assembly were hardly to be entrusted with providing protections for the frontier. This bluster of paranoia accomplished little besides creating "Circumstances of Alarm and Terror," as Franklin and the five other assemblymen put in their response to the governor (*Historical Review* 277). They alleged that the crisis was artificial, a false panic orchestrated by the colonial governor in an attempt to make the Pennsylvania General Assembly appear weak and unsuited to managing frontier defenses and ensuring public safety. What had annoyed the governor, however, was the Assembly's proposal to tax the Penn heirs back in England, who held proprietary claims upon the vast tracts that white settlers had begun farming. If the Assembly had its way, the bill for security, including money for troops and weapons, would be paid with tax revenues now flowing to England. American colonists, by Franklin's estimation, had already paid their share through obedience and defending the outer edge of the empire with their lives.

In the dispute over funding frontier security, Governor Morris sought to use the crisis to undercut the colony's democratic power, placing the blame back on the Assembly, declaring that its members "were to be considered *public Enemies*" (Franklin, *Historical Review* 278) for dragging their feet when it came to allocating money for the protection of the backcountry. Franklin at this point reiterated the objection that neither the governor nor the Penn proprietors were fulfilling the terms of an implied contract: Pennsylvanians were enhancing the coffers of absentee landlords who had "formally refused to bear any Part of our yearly heavy Expences" associated with military expenditures. Out of time-honored duty, colonists had surrendered the "immense Advantages" arising from their "cultivating and maintaining Friendship with the Indians" but received insufficient protection in return. It was, according to the governor's critics, his botched negotiations with the Delawares and Shawnees that had forfeited such amity and encouraged these tribes to ally with the French instead. In this view, not only was the governor playing political games with white people's safety, but his incompetent policies had fueled the animosities that made the frontier an unsafe zone.

Whatever the governor's (mis)characterizations, Morris rightly discerned the conflict over security as a struggle over whether democratic or authoritarian power best guarantees the people's safety. He thus cast Franklin's tactic as "a very extraordinary measure, as the people will be thereby taught to depend upon an Assembly for what they should only receive from the Government" (qtd. in Lemay, *Life* 3:475–76). Should "the people" seek security from their elected representatives? Or was an appointed—not elected—government the better custodian of public welfare? The governor had his answer, but Franklin persisted in viewing Morris's position as dangerous to both security and liberty.

Security, because it inevitably involves questions about competing forms of sovereign power, is always beset by ambivalence, perceived at once as protection for and a danger to the people's liberty. Franklin and his colleagues expressed frustration that the governor had rejected the Assembly's proposal out of hand, leaving them unable to "raise no Money for the King's Service, and Relief or Security of our Country, till we fortunately hit on" the exact language that the governor would accept (Pennsylvania Assembly). This guessing game delayed sending military aid to backcountry settlers, but, for Franklin, the real blow was to popular legislative authority. For his part, Morris was untroubled by the uncertainty his arbitrariness had created, writing of Franklin's scheming to entrust the people's safety to the Assembly, "if it is not criminal I am sure it ought to be so" (Lemay, *Life* 3:475–76).

Franklin saw through the governor's alarmist theatrics. "A provincial Dictator he wanted to be constituted" (*Historical Review* 278), as Franklin summed up the power grab that he alleged was the governor's true motivation. In portraying the democratically elected Assembly (though, of course, this was a democracy severely limited by racial status, property qualifications, and gender) as ineffective, Morris was asserting that a singular authority—himself as the Crown-appointed governor—could better ensure the security of the colony's inhabitants. In reality, however, it was the governor, acting in collusion with absentee landowners, who had consistently undermined Assembly measures to make allocations for the defense of frontier settlements. In a letter sent to Governor Morris, the Assembly asserted that it took seriously the need for *"further Security"* along an *"extended Frontier, settled by scattered single Families at two or three Miles Distance"* and would have done much "to secure them from the insidious Attacks of small Parties of *skulking Murderers*" (290) had not the governor himself vetoed the security provisions. The trenchant response of the Assembly framed the disagreement as part of a larger crisis over the issue whether citizens, by freely exercising "the just Rights of Freemen," have the liberty to "defend themselves" (289) or whether they should temporarily relinquish this responsibility to others. Years after when Franklin wrote a history of the Pennsylvania colony, he celebrated the Assembly's language (which, of course, he had written himself) as a perfect expression of the people's sovereignty: "There is not in any Volume ... a Passage to be found better worth the Veneration of Freemen, than this, 'Those who would give up *essential Liberty*, to purchase a little *temporary Safety*, DESERVE neither *Liberty* nor *Safety*'" (289).

The crisp phrasing of Franklin's formula makes it easy to understand its rapid political canonization. But the curiousness of its rhetoric often goes unremarked: it functions as an anticipatory admonition—a rebuke—of anyone who errs by judging the transitoriness of "safety" as permanent and its "little" consequence as something more significant. The sentence features a bit of parataxis that speeds past an expected conjunction that might connect the two clauses ("Those who do *x* thus deserve *y*"). The effect is to make the capitalized decree all the more absolute and forceful, authorizing a sovereign who establishes a state of exception around "those who" make this miscalculation. The sovereign determines who does or does not "DESERVE" security, but who occupies this deciding role? Neither the governor nor the Assembly, the sovereign implied by Franklin's maxim is something like the abstract political logic of security itself. Still more curious and ironic, then, is that this move that establishes security as "being at the same time within and outside of the juridical order," as Didier Bigo puts it in a helpful gloss on Agamben ("Globalized (In)security" 33), is expressed within a principled statement about people's liberty. While "essential Liberty" overrides "temporary Safety" at the level of manifest historical content, it is also the case that the logic of the exception latent within Franklin's proposition works at cross-purposes to this conclusion by illustrating how security is external to the measures it would implement. In other words, Franklin's recounting of colonial legislative history not only anticipates Agamben's contention that "measures of security ... are irreconcilable with democracy" ("Security and Terror" 3) but also reveals that people's cherishing of liberty along with the steps taken to protect it are regularly decided through anti-democratic means.

These inherent contradictions to the conjunction of liberty/safety were projected outward in racialized violence that by the mid-eighteenth century had come to constitute a defining feature of an American landscape impacted by settler colonialism. Franklin's reference to *"skulking Murderers"* injects a lethal racial component into the equation by targeting people that his public letter on behalf of the Assembly had spoken of in terms of "Friendship."[2] As the colonial legislature was squaring off with the governor, Franklin was also sending tips to settlers about using dogs to track, corner, and maul Native Americans. Best to have the dogs tied up before setting them to attack their human quarry since it will make them "fresher and fiercer." Keep the dogs tightly leashed, but let them loose when the tracking party comes to "thick Woods and Suspicious Places" where enemies may be hiding (Franklin to Read, *Papers* 6:235). If one thrust of Franklin's prescription is to stigmatize "those who" do not qualify for liberty, his graphic advice here underscores how security for some people entails the intentional production of insecurity for others.

1751, 1776, and a Brief History of Indigenous Security

The famous opposition between liberty and safety requires a prologue, a postscript, and an altogether different account of origins.

In 1751, Franklin published *Observations Concerning the Increase of Mankind*, a tract whose insight into the "peopling of countries" stands as among the earliest works to connect security to biopolitical questions of population.[3] Connecting the longevity and vitality of the British empire to "the increase of her people" (*Observations*) residing in colonial possessions, he warned that a failure to guarantee Lockean protections could jeopardize imperial hegemony and give an advantage to other occupying powers such as France. When governance fails to ensure security for people and their property, population ebbs, draining the reservoir of popular biopower. A combination of "bad government and insecure property," especially in the form of excessive taxation, encourages outmigration, diminishing a nation and its people. Even more worrisome in Franklin's mind were the policies of transatlantic slavery, which he believed had skewed the ratio of Blacks to whites in the British West Indies while also enervating white slave owners and their families—that is, their *white* offspring—whose reproductive capacity suffers in turn. He ended his reflections with a panoramic view of world population sorted by race and geography. Seeing other continents inhabited by darker races, Franklin asserted that America could shine forth, so brightly that extraterrestrials on Venus and Mars might notice the illumination, as a haven for whiteness in the world. The best hope for "increasing the lovely White and Red" lies in America, provided that "all Blacks and Tawneys" be excluded (10). Franklin's argument relies on a set of implicit contractual associations: an increase in the number of white people will boost imperial prowess, but if these subjects feel insecure about their property or their own persons, then the link between population and security will be severely strained. Yet who exactly might be included under this social arrangement remained ambiguous. Did "lovely white and red" reserve beauty as exclusively a property of white people, or does "lovely" also apply to the continent's Indigenous inhabitants?

As the political crisis between the colonies and the Crown intensified, Franklin believed that the delicate balance of liberty/safety was at risk from imperial administrative overreach. When England tried to bring its American subjects back within the fold by offering a plan for reconciliation, Franklin wondered outright whether Americans would be better off risking "the Hazards and Mischiefs of War" than accepting the diminishment of their historic rights ("Objections" 498). He underscored the point by quoting the language he had used twenty years earlier: "They who can give up essential Liberty to obtain a little temporary Safety, deserve neither Liberty nor Safety" (498). While the changes to the original wording and emphasis are minor, the historical context had altered in subtle but meaningful ways. In 1755, the complaint had targeted a colonial governor's attempts to barter away the people's self-rule for the promise of security; now twenty years later, the formula received a fresh application directed not at an aggrandizing governor but at timorous compatriots who might be tempted to exchange reduced autonomy for the opportunity to patch things up with their mother country.

In 1776, one year after Franklin had retrofitted the opposition of liberty and safety to urge unified dissent, Jefferson blamed England for deliberately sowing insecurity in the American colonies. According to the argument laid out by the Declaration of Independence, the Crown had shown its lack of interest in promoting Americans' "future security," specifically by limiting their biopower. Jefferson charged that the king "has endeavored to prevent the population of these States" by restricting immigration, refusing to open new lands to settlement, and hampering efforts to naturalize non-British subjects. Population for Jefferson was wrapped up with security much as it had been for Franklin: the racial ratios that secured white hegemony in a world of slaveholding, yellow fever and smallpox, land-grabbing, and imperial warfare waged by the French and their allies always required more bodies for the militia as well as the plow. Advocates of colonial security—which Jefferson would reconceive as the security of "independent States"—must keep watch over the future by ensuring the continual replenishment and, if possible, increase of the white population. Unless conditions were favorable for producing future generations, any people's hold on permanence seemed at risk, and none more than that of a people whose notions of trade, ownership, cultivation, and liberty encouraged the diminution of others.

Last among the list of twenty-seven grievances spelled out by the Declaration is the accusation that King George III "has endeavoured to bring on the inhabitants of our frontiers, the merciless Indian Savages" and incite domestic unrest. Rhetorically, this accusation supplies the Declaration's coup de grâce by contending that the people's contractual obligation to obey had become null and void not simply with the monarch's failure to protect but with his intentional sowing of racial insecurity among white Americans. From Jefferson's perspective, these actions threatened to return America to a veritable state of nature where constant and indiscriminate warfare reigned. His grievance protests the exceptional nature of such racialized violence by highlighting the implicit differences between the supposedly "civilized" character of European military campaigns and the lawlessness of Native tribes "whose known rule of warfare, is an undistinguished destruction of all ages, sexes and conditions." Jefferson perceives how the state of exception functions as a weapon: Indian violence is a rule without rule that, with encouragement from the Crown, is now encroaching on white settlements. Ever since the Royal Proclamation of 1763 prohibiting settlements west of the Appalachians, quasi-official policy had relied on and even encouraged the threat of Indian violence to enforce this decree.[4] Jefferson's allegation represents the final piece of evidence in the Declaration's argument about the urgency of Americans taking resolute steps to "throw off such Government, and to provide new Guards for their future security." The temporal marker of the "future" adds an affective dimension to the legalistic case by advocating independence as the only solution for dispelling anxiety and apprehension about the uncertainties to come. Having not just failed to provide safety but also actively destabilizing the American frontier of the empire, British sovereign power, according to the case laid out in the Declaration, had reneged on its contractual obligations to provide security to its subjects.

It would be a grave mistake to assume that the signatories to the Declaration of Independence were the only ones concerned about "future security" or that they meant it in the same way as did the land's original inhabitants. In 1742, elders of the Iroquois Confederacy, also known as the Six Nations, met with the Pennsylvania governor (George Thomas) to revisit provisions of a 1736 treaty that had never been fulfilled. The governor's report to the Assembly stated that these tribal representatives also came with another purpose: to ensure the "future Security" (Thomson 41) of peace in the backcountry, which the Walking Treaty and other incursions on Indigenous lands had rendered increasingly fragile. "Future security" signified differently to the Iroquois

Confederacy than to Jefferson and his band of rebels: "in case of a Rupture with the *French*" (Thomson 41) and amid the power struggle between European nations being played out in America, the Six Nations, as relayed by the governor, were seeking security *with* their neighbors.

Native diplomacy was not about acquiescence, however. In their complaint to the Penn family that claimed ownership over most of the province, the Iroquois "treated the Proprietors with a great deal of Freedom, remonstrated against the Injustice that was done them, and declared their Resolution of maintaining the Possession of their Lands by Force of Arms" (Thomson 42). The appeal for peace and safety could start to look like a warning or even a threat. Unease about the relations between the "lovely white and red," to recall Franklin's locution, was long-standing, generating more than enough suspicion to imbue the anticipatory nature of security with an affective surplus of uncertainty. The gap between open warfare and interracial peace underscored the contingency of the future. In contrast to the desire expressed in the Declaration for "future security" that guides events toward a single advantageous outcome, the treaty negotiations revealed how Indigenous diplomats attempted to convey a sense of security that recognized the variables of shifting alliances and double dealing.

Centuries before the Declaration presented its version of security, the Haudenosaunee peoples (composed of the Cayuga, Mohawk, Oneida, Onondaga, Seneca, and later the Tuscarora nations) created what political scientist Neta Crawford calls "a well-functioning security regime" (346). The alliance helped the tribes withstand the "exogenous shocks posed by the Europeans' arrival" (346) including epidemics, war, dispossession of lands, and environmental devastation. With few exceptions, information about the origin and function of the Iroquois Constitution is not always adequately presented in Western sources, but, thanks to the efforts of the Seneca archaeologist, museum director, and folklorist Arthur Caswell Parker more than one hundred years ago, ancient notions of Indigenous security start to come into focus. In his *The Constitution of the Five Nations* (1916), Parker recounts how through the efforts of Dekanahwideh ("Heavenly Messenger"), warring nations agreed to a pact of mutual protection. Combining diplomacy with a persuasive symbology, Dekanahwideh pointed to a bundle of arrows tied together with deer sinew to illustrate unity, gestured to the eagle as a sign of watchfulness, and described a Tree of Peace atop which an eagle perched. Their pledge ratified a symbolic vision: "We therefore bind ourselves together by taking hold of each other's hands and forming a circle so strong that if a tree shall fall prostrate upon it, it could neither shake nor break it, and thus our people and our grandchildren shall remain in the circle in security, peace and happiness" (Parker 102). While it is unclear to me whether Skarehhehsegowah, the great tree signifying peace, is fully distinct from the tree that may fall upon the circle, the possibility of their similarity suggests that even if amity fails, collective security remains intact. This idea resonates with what the Iroquois elders expressed in 1742 in their meeting with the Pennsylvania governor: security *as* contingency not against contingency. In weaving contingency into the fabric of security, Indigenous people did more than prepare themselves for survivance in the face of instability and change; they calculated how the capacity to thrive in the future depended on accepting the uncertainty of that future. In this respect, the origin story of the Iroquois Confederacy represents an alternative to the fear and endless aggression that characterize the Hobbesian state of nature. What if instead of Hobbes's "'war of all against all' paradigm," as Crawford asks (347), Iroquois history provided a counterethos that underwrote the concept of security?

Spring and Fall 1775

Some people outside of Boston seemed ready to consent to the trade-off that Franklin had disparaged by exchanging their liberties for the safety offered by British soldiers. In a 1775 letter, the selectmen of Plymouth County wrote General Thomas Gage that they had learned that their neighbors in Scituate and Marshfield had beseeched the military governor of Massachusetts to send "a detachment of his Majesty's troops, for the security and protection of themselves and properties" ("To His Excellency"). In times when the stationing of soldiers in and around Boston represented a sore point, the circumstances for requesting an increased military presence would had to have been exceptional. And so perhaps it seemed to those who made the appeal to Gage: rumors that a "Negroe plot has lately been discovered" appeared in multiple newspapers along the eastern seaboard, including the *Maryland Journal and the Baltimore Advertiser* of March 13, 1775, the same issue that featured on its first page the news about colonial landowners imploring the British high command for increased security. According to the report, first appearing in the *New-York Journal* and then republished verbatim in nearly a dozen other papers, the insurrectionary plot entailed an alarming cross-racial alliance in which Black rebels had pledged to "convey ammunition to the Indians." The *Maryland Journal*'s next issue recirculated a similar unverified report from Long Island of a slave "conspiracy . . . to destroy the white people" ("New-York, March 16"). It is, however, more likely that the individuals who sought Gage's protection harbored Loyalist sympathies and feared becoming targets of the radicals' patriotic zeal. Whatever the case, the selectmen were adamant that their neighbors' "fears . . . were entirely groundless" and "existed but in their imagination." Yet the misrepresentation to Gage was serious because the invented security crisis served as a pretense to declare a false state of emergency and to send more troops into the countryside.

Similar stories involving stolen gunpowder, arson, and a Black-Indian alliance, as Robert Parkinson demonstrates (78–97), appeared with some frequency in the lead-up to the battles at Lexington Green and Concord Bridge. According to bits of historical lore collected in the nineteenth century, the initial response in some neighboring towns to the revolutionary commotion of April 19, 1775, fueled suspicions of a rebellion by free Blacks, enslaved persons, and Indigenous allies (Parkinson 79). Three days later but still too soon for the news about this opening skirmish in the war for independence to have arrived in Williamsburg, the *Virginia Gazette* printed a copy of a letter sent by the mayor and Common Council to Lord Dunmore, destined to be the last colonial governor of Virginia, that took issue with the decision to remove munitions used to equip the militia and that were necessary for "the protection and security of the country . . . in cases of invasions and insurrections" ("Williamsburg, April 22"). While history tends to associate colonial militias with the virtuous minutemen who quickly mustered at Lexington and Concord, they more routinely functioned, in the words of Philip Deloria, as "violent paramilitary forces organized to kill Indian people and take their lands." Across the South, militias broadened their operations by functioning as the forerunners of slave patrols. Despite the impression that militias responded at a moment's notice only in the event of a crisis, the cruel realities of slavery and settler colonialism made every day a state of emergency.

The Williamsburg city leaders explained that their consternation flowed "from various reports at present prevailing in different parts of the country, [and] we have too much reason to believe that some wicked and designing persons have instilled the most diabolical notions into the minds of our slaves, and therefore the utmost attention to our internal security is become the more necessary." Information heightens insecurity, no matter the possibility that the scare could be either real or imagined. Parkinson in *The Common Cause: Creating Race and Nation in the American Revolution* also draws on this passage from the *Virginia Gazette* but skims past the phrase "we have too much reason to believe." I think that this omission is understandable: it does not enhance the meaning and likely muddles it. But the confusion reveals that the affective aesthetics of security can easily overcome the rational discourse of security. On the one hand, the town authorities seem to be saying that they have a surfeit of information indicating that "internal security" needs to be ramped up; on the other, so rational are these men that they scarce believe such stories. In the end, it did not matter which sense prevailed because both were correct, which is to say that the emotional register of vulnerability proved every bit as potent and actionable as the real thing.

While nonwhite people in the colonies presented a heightened security risk at the moment of open rebellion in spring 1775, Franklin later that fall found assurance by returning to ideas about population he had first raised in his pamphlet on "the increase of mankind." Biopower was clearly on the Americans' side: in a letter of October 3, 1775, to Joseph Priestley, Franklin put the British losses at Bunker Hill into the larger context of American reproductive power. He told the famed English chemist and natural philosopher that a mutual friend of theirs might want to reconsider his tendency to underestimate both the patriots' resolve and resources: "Britain, at the expence of three millions, has killed 150 Yankies this campaign, which is £20,000 a head.... During the same time 60,000 children have been born in America. From these *data* his mathematical head will easily calculate the time and expence necessary to kill us all, and conquer our whole territory" (Franklin to Priestley). Franklin connected population data to state security even before the American colonies formally declared their status as independent states. Political arithmetic backs up this impudent challenge: with a little calculation, any blockhead can conclude that the population constitutes a formidable military resource. Yet the cheeky mention of killing every American cannot escape a residue of ambivalence that seems at once to allude to and repress the genocidal practices waged against Indigenous peoples throughout the seventeenth and eighteenth centuries.

1798: Internal Enemies

The passage of the Alien and Sedition Acts in 1798 showed that the tensions between liberty and safety had not eased with national independence. Described by one historian as the "internal security program of the Federalist Party" (Smith 94), these measures clamped down on potential dissent while regulating the entry and movements of foreign nationals in the United States.

"The Federalists were so interested in providing for the security of the state," wrote James Morton Smith in his exhaustive 1956 history, "that they were willing to run the risk of suppressing the liberties of the individual" (147). Talk of individual liberty may have been more an artefact of 1950s consensus liberalism just as Smith's description of the Naturalization Law of 1798 as "a system of national surveillance" (34) seems to register the aftershocks of McCarthyism. Nevertheless, the partisan divisions of the 1790s between Federalists and Democrat-Republicans had set the stage for clamping down on civil liberties. Even before the John Adams administration signed the bills into law, George Washington made security a central theme of his 1796 farewell address. He began by stressing the need to ensure "security from external danger" but then shifted to domestic matters to warn that homegrown animosities and distrust, especially the rise of political factionalism, threatened "the secure and tranquil enjoyment of the rights of person and property." The outgoing president recommended that the best insurance for an orderly transition of power lay in a sovereign governmental authority strong enough to match the robustness of public freedoms. At this moment when Washington calls for "a government of as much vigor" as necessary to provide political stability, he introduces a subtle but radical revision to the Franklinian prescription. Instead of opposing liberty to safety, he folds one into the other by speaking of "the perfect security of liberty." Under British colonial rule during the 1750s, liberty, in Franklin's view, required protection from the encroachments of the imperial state, but Washington's phrasing now implied that liberty had grown so fragile as to need security itself. This logic explains why the Alien and Sedition Acts, first proposed during Washington's administration, had the president's support. It also explains why Democratic-Republicans opposed the legislation so vociferously, alleging, not without reason and accuracy, that the debate revolved around the invented and imagined dangers of foreign-backed conspiracies. Nothing proved so useful as a false state of emergency in justifying the development of a security apparatus.

Enforcement of the Alien and Sedition Acts ensnared more people and resulted in more prosecutions than historians have generally believed. New research puts the number of defendants at 126 (well beyond the dozen or so thought to have been the case) and increases the number of court cases from 14 to 51 (Bird 7).[5] One of the most high-profile and quarrelsome figures caught up in this surveillance net was Matthew Lyon, congressman from Vermont and the first person to be tried for sedition under the new law. His arrest indicated the willingness of Federalist officials to go beyond Fisher Ames's recommendation in a 1798 letter that "the government must display its power *in terrorem*" (247), that is, issuing a legal threat but without resorting to prosecution. Lyon's offense lay in words that to opponents' ears sounded like "the trumpet for sedition" (247), a clarion call for Jacobin anarcho-democracy that threatened to overturn the political order. According to the indictment, Lyon had first sought "to stir up sedition" by making a speech that harangued and mocked the Adams presidency for its "unbounded thirst for ridiculous pomp, foolish adulation, and selfish avarice" (Wharton 333). Next, Lyon read from a letter by Joel Barlow, a poet and ardent supporter of the French Revolution, that expressed wonderment that Congress had not issued "an order to send him [Adams] to a mad house" after the president appeared to be taking his political cues from Edmund Burke's reactionary *Reflections on the Revolution in France* (334). As it turned out, however, Lyon was the one who was sent away to an institution, specifically a sixteen- by twelve-foot-long jail cell with a privy in the corner that, in his words, "affords a stench about equal to the Philadelphia docks in the month of August" (341). His sentence coincided with his reelection campaign, making Lyon the first—but not the last—political figure to run for office from prison.[6]

It probably did not help Lyon's case that back in January 1798 he had spat tobacco juice into Roger Griswold's face, who responded two weeks later by caning Lyon with a stick of hickory. Both incidents occurred on the floor of the House of Representatives. At the time, the House vote to expel him fell short of the necessary two-thirds majority. Nor did it help that Lyon had recently started his own newspaper with the title, *The Scourge of Aristocracy and Repository of Important Political Truths*. But the most serious obstacles he faced came from the indictment that charged him with three counts of violating the Sedition Act. Section two of the act made it culpable for anyone to "excite ... the hatred of the good people of the United States" against their government (Wharton 337). The grand jury heard evidence that Lyon's public criticism of the president amounted to an illegal action made "with force and arms" (Smith 230), a reference to the legal notion of *vi et armis* indicating an injurious trespass against another person or their property. The presiding judge, Supreme Court Justice William Paterson, inveighed against sedition as a matter of national security: "Ah licentiousness! thou bane of republics, and more to be dreaded than hosts of external foes" (qtd. in Bird 90). Victory over Britain a generation earlier and national independence had done nothing to alleviate and perhaps only exacerbated domestic insecurity. In further instructions to the circuit court, Paterson advised jurors that if they were at all sympathetic to the defendant, they would do well to remember "the intention and wickedness" (Wharton 340) of Lyon's actions.[7] An hour later, the jury returned the verdict of guilty.

1798 Redux

Two days after July 4, 1798, John Adams signed legislation that would become the second part of the surveillance bundle otherwise known as the Alien and Sedition Acts. For the record, the legislation seemed to some fully consistent with the Constitution's control over security. When the Massachusetts legislature in February 1799 passed a resolution in support of new federal powers to apprehend suspected "internal as well as external foes" (qtd. in Mazzone 55n), it appealed to the Protection Clause of Article IV. The Act Respecting Alien Enemies gave the president the authority to seize and deport all male citizens of any nation at war with or having made "any invasion or predatory incursion" of the United States. Such persons are "liable to be apprehended, restrained, secured and removed, as alien enemies." This exact language provided the precedent for and is cited in Presidential Proclamation 2525 in which Franklin Roosevelt declared all Japanese inhabitants of the United States, including Japanese American citizens, to be alien enemies. Two months later, again building on the Alien Enemies Act of 1798, Roosevelt issued Executive Order 9066 for ostensible security reasons to provide "every possible protection against espionage and against sabotage," resulting in the incarceration of 120,000 people of Japanese ancestry.

Included among the documents archived in the Japanese Internment and Relocation Files at the University of Hawaii-Manoa are letters that so-called concerned citizens sent to the secretary of war about their Nisei neighbors. Urging a "thorough search" of "alien homes," one correspondent advised, "We are at war and business as usual cannot and must not be condoned especially in a vital theater of operations such as Hawaii.... Some say 'It can't happen here.' But others say it actually is happening here" (Heater). Never mind that the creation of internment camps on U.S. soil that Sinclair Lewis's *It Can't Happen Here* (1935) speculated about was indeed happening here, the letter writer called for a system of racialized surveillance and a thorough census of the territory's Japanese population. Two weeks later he received a response from the assistant secretary of war that offered the different view that evacuation of Japanese persons "would do more to impair the security of the Islands than enhance it" (McCloy) because of their importance to the wartime economy.[8] Nevertheless, the assistant secretary did write that he considered the suggestion to gather biopolitical information about all Japanese households in Hawaii to be a good idea that would provide "helpful" intelligence.

The notion of national security that underpins the Alien Enemies Act would be trotted out once more, this time in defense of Donald Trump's controversial Muslim Ban that prohibited the entry of individuals, who, because they come from putatively "terrorist nations," pose a "security or public-safety threat" (Executive Order 13769) to the United States. To those who questioned its legality, a former aide from the Reagan White House held that the Muslim Ban stood on "the Alien Enemies Act of 1798, signed into law by John Adams. It is still on the books this minute" (Kirell).

1816

Apprehensions of a Black-Indigenous alliance did not disappear with the fading of Revolutionary-era rumors of Black conspiracies to supply Native Americans with powder and ammunition. Similar fears were reignited by proposals to establish an internal colony for free Black people. Reverend Robert Finley, founder of the colonization movement to send U.S. Blacks to Africa, opposed this domestic solution, arguing that whites would be courting danger by promoting "an independent settlement of people who were once our slaves" in new territories acquired through the Louisiana Purchase. His *Thoughts on the Colonization of Free Blacks* (1816) warned that such persons "might be cause of dread lest they should occasionally combine with our Indian neighbors" (6). His short pamphlet had an outsized influence in shifting the conversation around colonization so that Black resettlement on the west coast of Africa, much as the British were doing in Sierra Leone, seemed like the more prudent course. Finley would be dead within a year, but his views lived on and shortly after publication of his pamphlet, the American Colonization Society formed in 1817 to advocate for what William Lloyd Garrison derided as an "expulsive crusade" (30).

White distress over a potential union of Blacks and Native tribes made "proposed black colonies in North America" appear as "threats to national security" (Mills 9). Whites in early American society had long eyed both groups with suspicion, but what had caused the nightmarish scenario of a Black-Indigenous liberating force to flash into view was, ironically, the implementation of Jefferson's bold plan to protect the continent from European encroachments. The treaty signed with Napoleon in 1803 stated that all military installations would be ceded to the United States and further stipulated that all French and Spanish troops "shall be embarked as soon as possible" (National Archives). As early as the 1780s, Jefferson had pondered the possibility of colonization, and the Louisiana Purchase seemed ideal for realizing his "conviction that the United States would function best as an all-white nation" (Levine, *Dislocating* 28). What was a coup in terms of international security, however, opened the door to domestic insecurity by encouraging plans to establish Black colonies in the U.S. backyard.[9] Yes, Finley acknowledged, it would certainly be cheaper and easier to "form a colony of free blacks in our own wild lands," but the security risk was too great. Founding a settlement for free persons of color in North America would continually destabilize slavery by affording an exemplar of Black sovereignty. Secret communications would flow from across this new border, making it easy to "send information to those who remain in slavery, so as to make them uneasy in their servitude" (7). In short, an independent Black population abutting the homeland would be a perpetual source of white insecurity.

In asking the question, "What shall we do with the free people of color?" Finley revealed that the only acceptable answer was one that met the necessary condition in which "we should have nothing to fear." The dream of total security was also the dream of complete whiteness.

1825

The Mother Bethel African Methodist Episcopal Church in Philadelphia was the scene of a racist attack involving a biological agent. As close to a thousand worshippers crowded into the church at Sixth Street near Lombard, white men "with segars in their mouths" tried to enter the service (*Daily National Intelligencer*). Reports varied, setting the number of young and apparently well-dressed young men demanding admission at between two and several more. Not until they stopped smoking were they allowed in at which point they began yelling "vengeance against the negroes." Meanwhile they either tossed in the air or placed in the heating stove a packet of cayenne pepper mixed with salt and "brimstone" or sulfur (*National Advocate*). After the contents of this crude bioweapon suffused the air, churchgoers felt suffocated and soon rushed to the exits. Pews were overturned while "women screamed and the men clamoured." In the panic that ensued, one woman was trampled to death while others received broken bones from jumping out of windows. "The whole congregation were seized with terror," according to newspapers that called for the apprehension and punishment of the assailants.

What had fueled the white ruffians' desire for vengeance? Racism was not hard to come by in pre–Civil War Philadelphia, which had a growing population of free persons of color and persons who had escaped slavery. Likewise, there was nothing original about Americans calling for retribution against people whom they were already persecuting. But the terrorist attack at the Bethel Church featured something more than a spectacular outburst of racism; it disclosed how white insecurities stemmed from biopolitical anxieties involving projected increases of the Black population. The size of the Black congregation increased with each telling: the *National Advocate* estimated the assembly at 800 to 1,000 persons; the *National Gazette* counted "a multitude of 1500 people"; that number swelled to over 2,000 people in the pages of the *Daily National Intelligencer*. The supporting role that the *National Gazette*, with the anti-Black agenda of its editor, Mordecai Noah, played in contributing to this fevered accounting offers clues about how ideas of race, population, and national homogeneity fed into security concerns.

The future of the United States as a country reserved for Franklin's "lovely white" was hardly at risk from a crowded AME church. Yet the sight of Black people in Northern cities made white people jittery, who reacted to their own feelings of racial vulnerability by projecting terror outward. While the cayenne pepper attack seems to have been an isolated instance, the 1820s and 1830s were decades that witnessed the constant presence of a white security apparatus in the form of the colonization mission to transport and exile Black Americans, especially free people of color, to Africa. What befell the migrants upon arrival was population management at its most cruel, as tropical fevers tore through the colony. Opponents of Liberian colonization later seized upon the chance to interview one disillusioned exile, pressing him for mortality figures: "Were the emigrants taken sick after their arrival? . . . How many of them—how soon—what number died? . . . What proportion of the colonists die in this process of seasoning. . . . Do the grave-yards at Liberia look as though there were frequent deaths?" (*Examination* 8). In the end, it may not have been altogether inconvenient or less than fortuitous that colonization proved for many to be a veritable death sentence. As David Walker accurately perceived, white people were intent on "colonizing us. . . . more through apprehension than humanity" (56).

1827

Soliciting subscriptions in support of the first African American newspaper, an agent for *Freedom's Journal* visited New Haven, Connecticut, in July 1827. He was favorably received by prominent members of the Black community, who called for a public meeting so that the agent could lay out the prospects and purpose of this landmark publishing venture begun by John Brown Russwurm and Samuel E. Cornish earlier that year. The next morning, the correspondent for *Freedom's Journal* "had the honour of an introduction to the Rev. Dr. D. of Yale College," whom the newspaper's agent esteemed "as a man of superior intellect" that "the most casual observer would immediately select . . . from a hundred others" ("To the Senior Editor" 86). In the letter he sent to the New York editorial offices of *Freedom's Journal* describing the interview, the agent explained that he made this assessment of Dr. D. "according to my notions of craniology" and then added "not Dr. Spurzheim's" in order to distance himself from the racist conclusions that many drew from this pseudoscience (86).

The nod to and quick dismissal of the noted phrenologist is a tip-off, however, that the correspondent treats the entire encounter with skepticism and ironic reserve. His comment that Dr. D. possesses formidable reasoning powers seems dubious upon mention that this professor of mathematics also serves as vice president of the American Colonization Society (ACS). These details help identify Dr. D. as Jeremiah Day, president of Yale College for nearly thirty years.[10] Despite their best efforts to overcome Day's reticence, the *Freedom's Journal* agent and his host do not succeed in getting Day to join their conversation about colonization. "Mathematicians, are men who say but little; such was the case of Dr. D," writes the agent (86). They leave the matter at that, and the interview concludes amicably enough. But in a second installment of this dispatch from New Haven that appeared in the next week's issue, the anonymous correspondent, perhaps the editor Russwurm himself, declared, "I deem it high time that our friends, in different parts of the Union, should know the truth of the matter—we are all, to a man, opposed, in every shape, to the Colonization Society" (86).[11]

The visit to Yale revealed how academic authority combined with the social power of whiteness to establish the ACS as a preeminent security apparatus in the antebellum era. As a mathematician and ardent supporter of colonization, Day embodied the coordination of institutional authority and political arithmetic that treated Blackness as a biopolitical problem of security. His Yale colleague, Dr. Benjamin Silliman, joined these efforts, using his university training to illustrate how Black population increase was chief among "Some of the Causes of National Anxiety," as the title of his contribution to the leading colonizationist journal of the day put it. The argument for colonization relied on numbers and counting: if the census data showing that the Black population of the United States was increasing at a geometric ratio was accurate, then Blacks would one day overwhelm white inhabitants across entire regions of the United States. For anyone who did not see the demographic evidence as a matter of national security, the lesson of Saint-Domingue should serve as a cautionary tale.

1837

A man climbs to the top of a church steeple and looks about him, his gaze tracking various human subjects scurrying through the streets of Boston below. The unnamed narrator pursues this activity until a thunderstorm nearly chases him from his aerie. Such is the plot of Nathaniel Hawthorne's "Sights from a Steeple" from *Twice-Told Tales* (1837), itself more of a sketch than a tale. His gaze wanders over the local militia, a funeral procession, the busy activity at the wharf, and a young gentleman who meets up with two women "arrayed for a summer ramble" (43), but his observations do not result in the close correlation of surveillance, security, and power that readers familiar with two of Hawthorne's more notorious snoopers, Roger Chillingworth and Miles Coverdale, might expect. He strives for but does not achieve panoptic knowledge. He muses that the smoke from kitchen chimneys might "betray in smoking whispers" their inhabitants' secrets and momentarily imagines that his position would allow him to see how "guilt is entering into hearts" of criminals (43, 46). "But none of these things are possible," and, in fact, his experience leaves him feeling "powerless" (43, 47). He seeks interior knowledge, wondering if the young gentleman is plagued by debt, infatuated and in love, melancholic, or simply overcome by the summer heat. He does not and cannot know, but the lack of certitude does not trouble him. He rather enjoys the contingency of what may happen; he indulges in the imagination, inventing and then abandoning the seeds of storylines for the characters he observes.

His gaze takes in the bustle of clerks and merchants at the warehouses on the wharf. Had Hawthorne's narrator attained a still broader and transatlantic perspective on the networked workings of political economy, he might have discerned what Jessica Lepler calls "the many panics of 1837." By summer of that year, mortgages, stocks, paper money, and financial investments suffered devastating market devaluation. Various forms of collateral—the cotton crop, cheap western lands, enslaved persons—put up as security rapidly lost value as well. The financial instruments meant to insure against risk accelerated the crisis. Banks and creditors were caught in the economic undertow, struggling to keep their reserves and reputations afloat, but none were made as vulnerable by the crash as "securitized people" (Lepler 166), that is, enslaved persons upon whom mortgages were held. The slave population, valued at more than $1 billion, constituted the "the biggest pool of collateral in the United States" (Baptist, *Half* 245), and starting in the late 1820s, the mortgages held upon these persons were bundled together and then divvied up as purchasable securities in financial markets. When creditors called in their debt, as happens in the opening chapter of Harriet Beecher Stowe's *Uncle Tom's Cabin*, the human collateral that had securitized that debt experienced firsthand how security could create vulnerability. Hawthorne's narrator sees none of this distress, and there is little temptation in the narrator to read the gathering storm as an omen of financial panic or other impending national cataclysm.

What he does see from his panoptic perch, however, is the possibility of experiencing the power of oversight as well as his own impregnability in ways that invite contingency rather than protect against it. These historical episodes of security conclude with "Sights from a Steeple" because the sketch illustrates the capacity of "security to" that appears only as minor chords in the chapters of *American Insecurity* that follow. Hawthorne's narrator, his aesthetic sensibilities awakened by his secure position aloft, contemplates alternate perspectives and alternative fates. Since "slight differences are scarcely perceptible from a church-spire," he is able to take pleasure in confusing the militia with a "battalion of schoolboys" that mimic their drilling (45, 47). Looking at the merchants at the harbor who, to his mind, are "wasting the summer afternoon in labor and anxiety" (44), he fantasizes about an existence of beachside leisure for these individuals. So, too, he wonders about a different future for himself. True, the darkening sky looks as "gloomy as an author's prospects," yet he glimpses an unexpected possibility when "the glory of another world" seems to be clearing on the horizon (47–48). The pages that follow share this impulse in wondering what other worlds of security might become visible.

PART II
Information, Aesthetics, Population

3

Security and the Technologies of Liberalism

FROM JAMES FENIMORE COOPER TO THE NSA

BENJAMIN FRANKLIN'S PROTOTYPICAL conjunction of liberty and security emerged from the bloodshed of colonial settler violence along the Pennsylvania frontier during the Seven Years' War. This imperial conflict between global powers later provided James Fenimore Cooper with the historical setting for his second novel in the Leatherstocking Tales, *The Last of the Mohicans*, which follows a white scout and his Delaware companions in skirmishes with the French and their Native allies. Improbably enough, though, it is a different Benjamin—Walter Benjamin—who discerned how American fictions of the frontier set the pattern for narratives of surveillance and security that remain in force today. The continuous observation and vigilance that make the detective novel an emblem of urban modernity have their origin in "the *savannah* and *forest* of Fenimore Cooper," according to a 1937 article, "Paris, *mythe moderne*," that Benjamin included in *The Arcades Project* (439). The detective is the hunter transposed to the city; the flâneur is kin to the forest tracker. How else could Alexandre Dumas's *Les Mohicans de Paris*—a work "where the title says all" (439) in Benjamin's estimation—resonate with French readers? The plenitude of clues in the wilderness "where every broken branch signifies a worry or a hope, where every tree trunk hides an enemy rifle or the bow of an invisible and silent avenger" (439) anticipates the skill set necessary for urban survival. The ubiquity of danger reappears in the detective novel as the watchfulness that treats every character as a suspect also creates an environment of distrust whose latest incarnation is the routine paranoia of "See Something, Say

Something" campaigns that ask people to scan the ordinary features of modern life for signs of potential terror.

Benjamin turned next to Balzac to intensify this conjunction of frontier warfare and urban existence, citing a passage from *A Harlot High and Low* that relocates "that poetry of terror which the stratagems of enemy tribes at war create in the heart of the forests of America, and of which Cooper has made such good use" (442) to the streets of Paris. The wilderness scout, the detective, the flâneur all exercise a constant watchfulness that sees threat everywhere. Whether focusing on forests or crowds, their surveillance is born out of the insecurity that senses the potential of danger all around, lurking behind every tree or hidden in the anonymity of a crowded boulevard. It is for Balzac "that poetry of terror," after all, which carries an affective charge that makes every forest sign, including "a beaver's dam, a rock, a buffalo skin, a motionless canoe, a branch drooping over the water" (442) into a potential clue that demands the same vigilance that the detective and the flâneur deploy in their urban milieu.

"The American security myth," writes Susan Faludi, is fueled by anxious visions of a national community besieged by savages and heathens (*Terror Dream* 262). Attuned to historical echoes embedded in the September 11 attacks, Faludi looks back to seventeenth-century colonists' ever-present fear of Indian attack as "our original 'war on terror'" ("America's Guardian Myths"). She draws a line from Mary Rowlandson to Mohamed Atta, one of the 9/11 hijackers, to explain the defensive psychological posture that forms in reaction to the awareness that the homeland is always under threat. Peril is everywhere in the uncanny safety of the homeland, as Freud has helped us to discern. Influenced by vestiges of the myth-and-symbol school of American Studies, Faludi's cultural analysis, though updated with insights about the prominent role that gender plays in this story, profoundly misses seeing that the true terrorists were white settlers who invaded Indigenous lands and destroyed tribal communities. To claim that "our ancestors had already fought a war on terror, a very long war, and we have lived with its scars ever since" (208) is at once to recognize frontier violence as an enduring structure of feeling and to misrecognize four centuries of aggression against Native peoples as an injury against a small band of white settlers. Armed with media representations from the captivity narrative to the Hollywood western, "our [white] ancestors" conveniently forgot their genocidal violence by fabricating histories of their own victimization instead.

According to the philosophical origin story of the social contract, people, fed up with the constant risk and uncertainty suffered in the state of nature, become political subjects by vesting sovereign power in an authority that provides for their security. The vastness of America offered something like geographic proof of this hypothesis, explaining why philosophers like "Locke and Rousseau themselves could not help lapsing into the empirical mood when they looked across the Atlantic," as Louis Hartz put it decades ago in *The Liberal Tradition in America* (61).[1] Meanwhile, eighteenth-century colonial officials likened the frontier to a Hobbesian state of nature and openly mused that civilized people degenerated into lawlessness with prolonged time in the barren wilds.[2] With his novels of a white hunter traipsing through the forests, Cooper deepened these connections in ways that cast the crisis of frontier security into highly racialized and gendered terms. Yet by rendering the mythic state of nature as the literal setting of his novels, Cooper's fictions of wilderness and waste, perhaps unexpectedly, denaturalize the conceptual rationale for security. Locating security at the scene of frontier warfare is really about the dread of what may be concealed behind a forest tree at each and every moment, as passages in Benjamin's *The Arcades Project* suggest. "Early American settlers dwelled in a state of perpetual insecurity, in what they repeatedly described as an experience of 'terror,'" writes Faludi (*Terror Dream* 211). Terror in this case is an affective response that displaces the violence of settler colonialism even as it gestures, not unproductively, to a long historical arc connecting surveillance mechanisms adopted in the wake of 9/11 to much earlier emanations of frontier security.[3]

While it is evident enough that the Leatherstocking Tales fuel this myth, the novels offer an occasion to develop a critical understanding of how white notions of property, privacy, and propriety create the affective and ideological armature that justifies security as a necessary value. Modern ideas of detection and surveillance that Benjamin traced back to frontier novels are wrapped up with ideas of property and privacy—one guaranteeing the other—that are carved out of the fabled state of nature that Cooper makes literal as the American wilderness.[4] White colonists, who protested inadequate border defenses provided by colonial governments during the historical era that sets the eighteenth-century stage for *The Last of the Mohicans*, often felt that they had been abandoned to a perpetual state of war (Spero 117–18). The state of nature is often conceptualized abstractly as a realm of "*perfect freedom*" and "*perfect equality*" (Locke, *Second Treatise* 8, 10) that precedes political society, yet the downside of total equality is that "there is no superiority or jurisdiction of one over another" (9), no sovereign authority to adjudicate disputes or mete out justice. Cooper's setting provides the opportunity to measure this political abstraction as falling somewhere between historical actuality and historical fiction. In his long life across the five novels in the Leatherstocking series, Natty Bumppo strains to understand the proprietary forms that he associates, often with disdain, with whiteness and civilization. In *The Deerslayer*, where readers encounter Natty at his youngest, Hawkeye opines that "it's more a pale-face than a red-skin gift to be prying into other people's secrets" and that only in garrison towns are people eager to "learn their neighbor's secrets" (217). And, as an old man in *The Prairie*, he contrasts the openness of tribal communities with the suspicious ways of white squatters who zealously keep their property—in this case a young woman whom they intend to traffic in sexualized slavery—out of public view. By all accounts, the author identified with his hero's jealous regard for privacy: on his deathbed Cooper "insisted . . . that his wife and children protect his life and his papers from outsiders" (W. Franklin xii).

My interest extends beyond and at times rather far afield from these thematic consistencies found in an American author whose status in scholarly circles and college classrooms is likely waning. Cooper may be falling out of critical fashion—and if indeed that's the case, we need not mourn—yet he remains useful because issues of privacy and property that his work wrestled with are bound up with our data futures. His novels, especially *The Pioneers* (1823), establishes an organizing pattern for security logics that are operative across both intimate spaces and the political philosophy of liberalism, interior lives and land surveys, private closets as well as environmental expanse and wastelands. Across these sites, what I call the "ancient technologies of liberalism" come into play by imagining fictive states of nature that explain and justify the need for security. "We should read liberalism less as a philosophy of liberty and more as a *technique of security*," writes Neocleous (*Critique* 31). This provocative insight that theories of social contract talk a good game about liberty while also implementing security is incisive, but the antagonism between liberty and security is perhaps overstated. Under liberalism, the freedom to amass property requires and legitimizes the use of security so that claimants can hold onto their property and take advantage of the privacy it affords. More recent technologies come into play as well, specifically tools of surveillance and data collection, that link an overaggressive security apparatus to diminished senses of privacy. This chapter puts together temporal contexts of Enlightenment philosophizing about the state of nature, novelistic renditions of the nineteenth-century wilderness, and twenty-first-century warnings about surveillance technologies in an effort to upend the usual pattern of cause-and-effect that makes security seem unavoidable and necessary. Whether as a reaction to recent attacks or as a precaution taken against potential threats in the future, security, we commonly believe, is a response to terror. But what the random violence waged to protect property on the frontier allows us to recognize is that terror is, in fact, instilled by security. Terror, in other words, is an effect of security, not its cause.

New and Ancient Technologies of Liberalism

How and why has security become a prerequisite of both political liberty and social life? The tendency to bemoan the ubiquity of electronic surveillance, dataveillance, biometric tracking, and other forms of securitization emerges from our dwindling capacity to imagine private spaces that would be immune to the combination of corporate and government overreach. The right to privacy further eroded after the attacks of September 11, which "led the NSA to put the entire planet under surveillance" (Schneier, *Data and Goliath* 63). As the U.S. Supreme Court ruling in *Carpenter v. United States* (2018) demonstrated, government surveillance often works hand in glove with data brokers that track, collect, store, and sell personal and private information. Government agencies are effectively using privately held corporations to "outsource the surveillance state" (*New York Times*, "Government Uses"). For every revelation that telecommunications giants have been sharing information with data collection agencies such as the NSA, there exists the small but still palpable hope that these disclosures can energize a vigorous defense of privacy in the face of technologies of surveillance and security that have become ever more invasive and omnipresent. Defenders of civil liberties have kept a close eye on court cases such as *Carpenter* in addition to *ACLU v. Clapper* (2015), which found that the bulk collection of telephone metadata constituted "an unprecedented contraction of the privacy expectations of all Americans" (74). Metadata, despite its supposed anonymity, still provides a surprisingly granular view of individuals: whose phone but yours leaves a certain address at roughly the same time five mornings a week to travel the same route to arrive at the same office complex? If privacy names a zone that should remain free of snooping, the sheer scope of Stellarwind and other NSA surveillance programs that mine financial records, email, and phone logs raises significant concerns that the space of privacy has been contracted to a pinpoint.

Surveillance encompasses more than a government apparatus just as security represents more than a global network of cellular towers, a web of CCTV cameras maintained across office lobbies, parking garages, and storefronts, or a fleet of drones whose cameras can "zoom in and read a milk carton from 60,000 feet" (Electronic Freedom Foundation).[5] While these devices and gadgets are daunting enough, they pale in comparison to the ancient technologies of liberalism that first made it possible to conceive culture as a state of security. Fictions about the state of nature, like those appearing in Locke's *Second Treatise of Government* or Cooper's *The Pioneers*, mobilize ideas about wilderness and wasteland in order to conceptualize private property as the literal ground for individual privacy and liberty. Although Cooper's state of nature is much more local and geographic than what Locke had in mind, the securitization of property and persons remains a particular point of anxiety for each. The worry that property is always capable of being seized, alienated, or left to rot, that it is essentially never secure, provides justification enough for surveillance and other security measures to operate continuously and without end.

In the context of much-publicized exposures of top-secret government surveillance programs, the modest victories that some see in these court decisions such as *Carpenter* have revitalized efforts to imagine zones of culture that might or should be legally impervious to securitization. The hope is that a robust defense of individual privacy, often described as the "right to be let alone" following the paradigm Samuel D. Warren and Louis D. Brandeis laid out in an 1890 *Harvard Law Review* article (193), can beat back the surveillance overreaches of the security state. For an assortment of unlikely bedfellows—internet freedom fighters, liberal protectors of free speech, libertarians worried about the specter of unchecked government power, conservatives devoted to preserving traditional notions of individual autonomy, and left-leaning critics wary of biopolitical metrics—privacy remains an evocative political resource.

Ultimately, though, the reliance on privacy cannot be distinguished from the logic of property, both of which hinge upon the concept of security. Across the political theory of liberalism, surveys of territory, and fictions of the frontier, the imagining of land as empty space allows security to appear as an organic development in the history of civil society. Or, more precisely, the insecurity that constantly looms in the state of nature, what political philosophers describe as the "liberalism of fear" (Shklar) and the "liberalism of horror" (Anker), impels individuals to bond together for safety and protection. Political society thus might be better described as "risk society," according to Ulrich Beck, a social and political formation that emerges from the "*hazards and insecurities induced and introduced by modernization itself*" (*Risk* 21). The shared vulnerability experienced in the state of nature and risk society, along with "the *commonality of anxiety*" (49) it encourages, recalls the affective underpinnings of social contract theory. Acting out of fear and anxiety, people determine to leave the state of nature, a hypothetical decision that represents a pivotal moment in the history of modernization. "The movement set in motion by the risk society," writes Beck, "is expressed in the statement: *I am afraid!*" (49). Is there some deep affective consonance between the origins of political society and the emergence of risk society? Political society forms, according to Locke, because people in the state of nature may be free, but they also inhabit an environment "full of fears and continual dangers" (*Second Treatise* 66). Reason provides the antidote to such affective distress, as people agree to unite for "the mutual preservation of their lives, liberties, and estates," all of which Locke groups under the name of "property" (66). The state they bring into existence guards against predation and piracy, allowing individuals, now become subjects and citizens, to amass property, which they eagerly do because the risk of losing that property along with the labor invested in it has been mitigated. Not unlike the security deposit that renters pay to reduce a landlord's risk, political subjects pay with their obedience to enjoy the security society that at once protects their property and limits their freedom.

As we saw with Franklin's stirring conjunction of liberty and security in the context of settler violence, white people turned to the colonial administrative state for the protection of life and property from the theoretical dangers in the state of nature that had become decidedly real on the frontier. Franklin placed a democratic spin on this appeal by disputing the idea that security would be best secured by sacrificing liberty to some feckless servant of the British imperium. Fantasies about the state of nature had no place in Franklin's focus on realpolitik: his account implicitly corrects the just-so story of political foundations by reminding his colleagues in the Assembly that the uninhabited wilds of America were peopled by Native tribes allied with the French. Despite the bloody evidence that Franklin invoked in making his case, the imagination of the wilderness as vacant, as a veritable *vacuum domicillium*, from Locke to Cooper combines with images of waste and wasteland to generate a narrative that makes tracking animals, clearing forests, laying down survey lines, and collecting all matter of aggregate data foundational to the project of peopling America. The range of these pursuits suggests that the difficulty of envisioning culture without security stems from the unavoidable fact that security is indistinguishable from the culture of liberalism itself and the notion of property that it upholds.

Before excavating liberalism's prehistoric investments in security, we may first observe how thoroughly security has wrapped itself around social life as a cache of data that can be mined, aggregated, even monetized. According to a report from the Technology and Liberty Program of the ACLU, in urban spaces such as Manhattan, "it is impossible to walk around the city without being recorded nearly every step of the way" (Stanley and Steinhardt). By 2004, a date now light years away in technological time, the infrastructure was already in place to record the average person's image three hundred times a day in metropolitan centers like London (Monahan 5). More recently in its 2018 decision in *Carpenter*, the Supreme Court observed that cell-site records for mobile phones "give the Government near perfect surveillance and allow it to travel back in time to retrace" a person's locations and movements. The erosion of privacy may have accelerated since Warren and Brandeis asserted the right to privacy, but even at the time of their writing more than a hundred years ago, the advent of photography and the ability to capture people's images without their consent were seen as a threat to self-possession. With a biblical flourish, Warren and Brandeis forewarned that "numerous mechanical devices threaten to make good the prediction that 'what is whispered in the closet shall be proclaimed from the house-tops'" (195). Few today would doubt that their prediction about surveillance has come to pass. Their invocation of Jesus's rebuke of the Pharisees not only anticipates a day of complete transparency, but, as the subsequent verse in the Gospel of Luke (12:5) puts it, such intrusions act to "forewarn you whom ye shall fear" by exerting an anticipatory power that identifies enemies and threats.

It would be a mistake to conclude, however, that any fundamental difference exists between government surveillance and social media applications that track our tastes, our workouts, or our sleep patterns, which we supply, often quite willingly, with biographical as well as biometric data. So, too, facial and gait recognition software threatens to "end privacy as we know it" by searching massive data sets to pinpoint identity (K. Hill). Commoditizing personal information is all about property ownership. The wilderness tracking that Benjamin saw as a precursor to the detective novel achieves totality in the digital tracking that telecommunications companies exercise over the internet. In each case, the aim is to assert property rights: as former Federal Communications chairman Tom Wheeler wrote in 2017 in opposition to proposed legislation that would allow internet service providers to sell personal information, "the digital tracks that a consumer leaves when using a network are the property of that consumer." Once the Republican-led Congress passed the bill, a consumer's privacy became corporate property.

Network companies indeed may be "selling something that doesn't belong to them," as Wheeler asserted, but within the logic of frontier surveillance, their skill and ability to track establishes and legitimates their proprietary rights to others' privacy. As WikiLeaks cofounder Julian Assange asserted, "Google and Facebook are in the same business as the U.S. government's National Security Agency. They collect a vast amount of information about people, store it, integrate it, and use it to predict individual and group behavior" (Assange). This accusation rests on Edward Snowden's disclosures in 2013 that the partnership between the NSA and telecommunications conglomerates such as AT&T, between the state and private enterprise, means that virtually every internet search, transaction, email, text, and keystroke can be recorded, logged, and assembled into patterns. Rather than speaking of a surveillance state, we need to think about what it means to live in what Assange calls "a surveillance society."[6] Whether described as isomorphic to society itself, an encompassing "political technology" (A. Burke), an indomitable "security fetishism" (Neocleous, *Critique*), or a multidisciplinary security *dispositif* (Bigo and Tsoukala), the near-total reach of security makes observers on both the right and left uneasy about the level of surveillance that society has achieved and the amount of mass data it stores.

There's no need to continue describing the ways that individual privacy seems virtually extinct, not the least because we welcome security into lives, whether out of fear or convenience, to track and predict our locations, our workouts, our consumer choices, our future goals and desires. As the CEO of Sun Microsystems declared at the dawn of the twenty-first century, "You have zero privacy anyway. Get over it" (qtd. in Schneier, *Data and Goliath* 4). Besides, it is likely that any mention of the latest surveillance technologies, at the time of this writing in 2022, are already obsolescent, superseded by newer tools and algorithms. But what remains consistently in force are the biopolitical technologies that view data, especially lots of it, as essential to the project of security. Even though personal identifiers are supposedly scrubbed from the cache of aggregate information, the secrets of individual private lives are less valuable than the bulk data that is used not merely to comprehend but also to anticipate the choices and habits of a data set that at an earlier time had made itself known with the announcement, "we, the people."

Call it a populace, the demos, or the commonwealth: this collective body was never left to its own devices. Security has always been intertwined with the social contract and the sovereignty exercised over or by the people. Security imperatives associated with liberalism may probe the inner spaces of personal identity, as David Rosen and Aaron Santesso assert in reading "surveillance and literature . . . as kindred practices" (10), but the larger power of security resides in ignoring the individual altogether and collecting metadata about mass populations. Instead of targeting specific individuals, the aim of security is random and, as the case of *The Pioneers* shows, often both reckless and destructive. Simultaneously taming and stoking fears about potential yet unspecified threats, security promises that not just anyone but everyone can be scooped up in a surveillance net. Liberalism feeds anxiety about terror, predation, and rapine so that the mass amounts of data collected by tech companies like Facebook and processed by government agencies like the NSA or other modern incarnations of Leviathan seem like sensible responses to the threat of social uncertainty. From at least Hobbes onward, liberalism "understands security to be the state's *raison d'être*" (Berman and Voelz 4).

Insecurity and fear prove productive: as Elisabeth Anker explains, "*Leviathan* capitalizes on the horrors of the state of nature to legitimate consent to a sovereign governing order" (796). But so also do gentler—that is, more liberal—versions of sovereignty rely on insecurity to legitimize the state. If "liberalism has only one overriding aim: to secure the political conditions that are necessary for the exercise of personal freedom" (Shklar 21), fear becomes the precondition of that freedom. Instead of being driven by some notion of the greater good or "*summum bonum* toward which all political agents should strive" (29), subjects are motivated by an aversion to the "*summum malum*" of death associated with Hobbesian nature.[7] Locke perceived how fear is lodged at the heart of the social contract: "if a Hobbist be asked why" people adhere to compacts, the response is that "the Leviathan will punish you if you do not" (*Essay* 38). In Judith Shklar's account, this "liberalism of fear" (30) also applies to the state itself and provides the affective justification for guarding against government overreach. The liberal subject's passion for limited government is born out of a fear of the state. Anker intensifies this rendering by describing how "the liberalism of horror" impels people to freely submit to an anti-democratic sovereign who provides protection. Or, in Franklin's terms, such people are indeed ready to purchase a bit of temporary safety by giving up their liberty.

But Franklin's history is off: it is not that individual liberty precedes security; instead fear makes liberty and security coincident. No one enjoys first liberty and then only later agrees to surrender some portion of that liberty for security. Instead, people become political subjects by accepting—or even encouraging—the concomitance of liberty and security: as Foucault writes, "There is no liberalism without a culture of danger" (*Birth of Biopolitics* 67). It's not just that liberal values such as individual freedom and privacy are articulated within the context of fear; rather, the state and other institutions of liberalism ramp up the threats to liberty in order to provide continuing justification for their efforts to secure liberty. "The motto of liberalism is 'Live dangerously,'" writes Foucault (*Birth of Biopolitics* 66). The injunction takes on biblical proportions: "The horsemen of the Apocalypse disappear and in their place everyday dangers appear, emerge, and spread everywhere" (66). The nonstop imagining of terrorist attack, contagion, and other sources of misfortune provides the rationale that validates liberal institutions, the most prominent of which is the state itself. The state does not do away with fear but instead exploits it in order to garner consent for the loss of freedom. Fear becomes the "constituting ground" (Anker 805) of politics, which justifies—retrospectively, of course—the sovereign power that promises security to its citizens. "The monster Leviathan becomes desirable" (805) because people so compulsively imagine anarchic alternatives.

Security today is the effect of an older set of assemblages, specifically the political theory of liberalism, which through the institution of property made security and society one and the same. If it seems impossible to remember a moment when people did not live within cultures of security, it is because the social world, as we have constructed it in philosophical terms, is unimaginable without security. Security is everywhere, not simply because of the reach of PRISM, STORMBREW, TARMAC, and other anagrammatic embodiments of the surveillance state that Snowden disclosed to journalist Glenn Greenwald and filmmaker Laura Poitras in *Citizenfour* (2014). Just as significantly, the desire for security is wrapped up in the genetic code of liberalism and its guarantees of privacy and property. Theorists as different as Hobbes and Locke had a name for what culture would look like without security: the state of nature, a wild zone, a theoretical extreme where no one can claim security for life or property, which, in Locke's thinking, are pretty much the same thing. At risk of being set upon by "a *lion* or a *tyger*, one of those wild savage beasts," not to mention the human malefactors bent on doing us harm, people can "have no society nor security" (Locke, *Essay* 11). This nervous logic also underwrites Alexander Hamilton's argument in the eighth essay of *The Federalist Papers* stating that without a federal constitution the former colonies will be effectively thrust back into a state of nature. The scenario that Hamilton paints is one of "plunder and devastation," "frequent war and constant apprehension," and in a nod to Locke's famous pairing, "the violent destruction of life and property" (67)—as though he were anticipating the doomsday visions of *The Road* (2009), *The Walking Dead* (2010–22), *The Purge* (2013), *San Andreas* (2015), *Mad Max: Fury Road* (2015), *Train to Busan* (2016), or any number of media scenarios in which the chaos of earthquake, reanimated corpses, and other cataclysms sets in motion a Lockean drama that presents society and security as pretty much the same thing. If, as Beck comments in the wake of 9/11, "the terrorist threat has made everyone into a disaster movie scriptwriter" ("Terrorist Threat" 46), it is because the narrative of vulnerability was already a feature of liberalism. That these fantasies of disaster encourage sequels, spin-offs, and remakes shows how security, by design, is never achieved but instead remains in constant peril and needs to be constantly produced by constantly imagining its imminent failure. Unlike older and less mobile forms of sovereignty, security is a "continuous and permanent" project (Foucault, *"Society"* 36). Never let your guard down, never take your eyes off the horizon, never relax or breathe a sigh of relief. For the hapless, expendable secondary characters of these films and television series who are stabbed, shot, crushed, bludgeoned, and eaten, the lesson about constant vigilance is never learned, requiring its repetition in the next cinematic disaster about a sudden, terrible irruption of the state of nature.

Even though Locke seeks to establish an alternative to a kneejerk social order—one that is not reactive to hobgoblins of "perpetual disorder and mischief, tumult, sedition and rebellion" (*Essay* 7)—his plan for government nonetheless requires these nightmarish scenarios, which, of course, are also fantasies of insecurity. The situation was particularly acute in the American wilderness where, if Locke were correct, the principle of equality might itself generate competition, aggressiveness, and widespread social instability. When everyone enjoys sovereignty, "for all being kings" and "every man his equal," the individual is alarmed to discover that "the enjoyment of the property he has in this state is very unsafe, very unsecure" (66). More practically for Hamilton, the citizens of a weak American confederacy were flirting with disaster by leaving their newly independent nation exposed to "perpetual menacings of danger" (69) posed by predatory foreign powers and internal squabbling. Dire predictions about "calamity," "constant apprehension," "continual danger," and other ominous signs of an impending devolution back to the state of nature are not scare tactics, according to *Federalist* #8, but a potential reality that had doomed other republics in the past and needed to be avoided now (68). In America, the course of human history threatened to reverse itself, and discord and despotism would again become "the natural course of things" unless steps were taken to preserve "our security" under which people agree to trade liberty for security in an effort to withstand the political entropy that is otherwise the natural order of things (68). Some sacrifice is necessary to ensure that predation and force are not allowed to reign or, as Hamilton puts it, "to be more safe, [people] at length become willing to run the risk of being less free" (67). From this perspective, people have no choice but to consent to security as a condition of their political survival.

Hamilton does more than rehash the opposition that Franklin had laid out, however. He significantly adds to the debate by discerning the affective components that accompany the liberty/security trade-off. No people can thrive in a state of vulnerability and unceasing worry. Hamilton's repetitions become crucial here, as he paints a picture of a citizenry made fragile by its own fears. "Constant apprehension" begets "constant preparation" for the worst. Living in "a state of continual danger" requires "continual effort and alarm." Exhausted by these political anxieties, people become incautious—they "run the risk"—and are guided by emotions. The result is that people become trapped in a paradox of their own making, opting to protect their liberties by adopting security measures that imperil the existence of those very liberties. Their choice is not a rational one but is instead impelled by an affective overinvestment in security and safety. When Hamilton first contributed this short essay to the *New York Packet* in the fall of 1787, the warning that the wolves from the state of nature were at America's door was designed to inspire support for a stronger federal union. Writing as "Publius," Hamilton drove home the argument for the Constitution. Only this ambitious plan to form a national union could allay feelings of vulnerability: the Constitution, in effect, would make the people safe from their own yearning for security.

The affective charge behind Hamilton's argument and others like it has had prolonged aftershocks. For critics such as Lauren Berlant and Louise Amoore, the feeling of being exposed to unpredictability, precarity, and risk is inextricable from the reassurance that security culture provides. Being "bound to a situation of profound threat," writes Berlant, "is, at the same time, profoundly confirming" (2). Feelings of insecurity confirm a repeatable notion of the everyday as a shared but fragile sensorium: people's "affective judgment on the look and feel of a place with which one is familiar is enlisted into security practice," writes Amoore (142). When we are all at risk, "we" can experience ourselves, however temporarily, as a collective entity. The script for "Protect Your Everyday," a series of public service announcements produced by the Department of Homeland Security for television, internet, and radio, takes shape as a free-verse ode to collective ordinariness in the face of an unnamed threat at once so familiar and so indistinct that it registers as uncanny. What is security? The answer is insecurity.

It's when you experience a moment of uncertainty.
Something you know shouldn't be there.
Or someone's behavior that doesn't seem quite right.
. . . .
It's not about paranoia.
Or being afraid.
It's about standing up and protecting our communities.
One detail at a time.
Because a lot of little details can become a pattern.
We.
We.
We.   (Department of Homeland Security, original formatting)

In the uncanny of surveillance society, the dialectical interplay of paranoia/protection, random details/patterns, and, above all, insecurity/security makes for an ongoing performance of anxiety and reassurance that never draws to a close.[8]

This governmental rhapsody about an ordinary "we" alternately protected and threatened by everyday life runs counter to an enhanced public sensibility. Although security and surveillance endeavor to safeguard the homeland, they do so in the name of privacy. Liberalism renders security in individual terms that are keyed to property and other forms of private accumulation. "The only way whereby any one divests himself of his natural liberty," writes Locke, is uniting with others "in a secure enjoyment of their properties, and a greater security against any, that are not of it" (*Essay* 52). On this side of the border, property is safe; on that side roam those aliens and renegades who exist outside and in opposition to political community. For the subject of liberalism, however, the threat is not only foreign but lodged closer to home in the form of an overzealous government ready to intrude upon individual freedoms. So, despite the collective determination to band together for mutual safety, the result of this decision reinforces the sanctity of individual privacy over any recognition of common vulnerability. Familiar debates that pit individual privacy against the overreach of national security thus lead to a conceptual dead end that fails to interrogate the idea of privacy itself. In the face of controversies over electronic eavesdropping and other forms of surveillance, defenders of civil liberties reaffirm the value of privacy without asking how the right for people, in the language of the Fourth Amendment, "to be secure in their houses, papers, and effects" upholds notions of possessive individualism. "The opposition between privacy and security," writes Clare Birchall, "positions the citizen as an individual first and foremost, for whom collectivity is envisaged and imagined by the securitised state" (28).[9] Privacy and security are linked by a dependent relation on the surveillance state as at once the protector of private property and the biggest threat to individual privacy. Anyone seeking an illustration of how these seemingly antagonistic tendencies reinforce one another need go no farther than the explanation offered by General Janet Alexander, head of the Domestic Surveillance Directorate: "We are often asked, 'What's more important—civil liberties or National Security?' It's a false question; it's a false choice. At the end of the day, there are no civil liberties without National Security" (Domestic Surveillance Directorate).

Justification for this view that collapses liberty into security appears in former secretary of homeland security Michael Chertoff's warning that "the rise of ungoverned space throughout the world" (54)—a resurgence of the social contract theorist's state of nature for the twenty-first century—is among the most pressing challenges to national security. Even though Chertoff and others make this point as part of a larger effort to scrap earlier paradigms of national security that have been outmoded by global terrorism, an older model grounded in liberalism and its neurotic concern for private property, as the next section suggests, continues to set the terms of the debate.

Privacy and Privies

Since the attacks of 9/11 there has been no shortage of feverish scenarios in which modern liberalism confuses and makes one and the same the imperatives of surveillance, security, and privacy. From its first sentence, Cory Doctorow's multi-award-winning novel *Little Brother* (2008) activates traditional concerns about civil liberties: "I'm a senior at Cesar Chavez High in San Francisco's sunny Mission district, and that makes me one of the most surveilled people in the world" (9). The crisis of this popular teen novel is set in motion after a terrorist strike on San Francisco's Bay Bridge cripples the Bay Area. The Department of Homeland Security swoops down on the city and rounds up thousands of civilians, including this high school student, the hero of Doctorow's nightmarish fantasy of the U.S. security state. The challenge for this seventeen-year-old is to reveal the black box sites, the waterboarding, and the extreme incursions upon privacy to which he and others are subjected. What unfolds is a story of hacking and encryption in which a photographed, fingerprinted, trailed, tracked, and surveilled high school student attempts to broadcast secret information while remaining anonymous.

Doctorow's spin in *Little Brother* on George Orwell's "big brother" began to look a bit more real by 2013 when Glenn Greenwald flew to Hong Kong to meet a private security contractor who wanted to leak classified information about the surveillance practices of the NSA. In *No Place to Hide: Edward Snowden, the NSA, and the U.S. Surveillance State*, Greenwald describes Snowden typing away on his laptop in a hotel room, head under the covers, to thwart security cameras that he feared could pick up passwords. Not unlike Doctorow's high school student, Snowden and eventually Greenwald worry about having their online presences tracked, their every keystroke recorded by the NSA, their accounts hacked by computers that can make a billion guesses per second at passwords. Squirreled away in Hong Kong, how can Snowden spill the government information he has stolen? It's one thing to steal state secrets; it's quite another to spread, disseminate, and propagate them.[10] Anyone can try to keep a secret. The real challenge is to make secret information public while preserving the right to privacy.

Informing global publics about the massive security apparatus operated by the U.S. and other governments is ultimately about safeguarding privacy. Snowden's disclosures of top-secret NSA documents, according to Greenwald, "have generated unprecedented worldwide interest in the menace of mass electronic surveillance and the value of privacy in the digital age" (*No Place to Hide* 2). If privacy has a value, is it something that only the subject of liberalism can value and enjoy? A few years ago, I saw Greenwald speak not far from the NSA's Bluffdale data repository where visitors are greeted with the sign, "Welcome to the Utah Data Center. If you have nothing to hide, you have nothing to fear." Greenwald rebutted the implicit proposition that electronic surveillance only affects the guilty—or should we say those who are not yet guilty?—by prioritizing "individual liberty" as the reason "why privacy matters" ("Edward Snowden"). The mission of the Utah Data Center is encapsulated by the Domestic Surveillance Directorate: "Defending Our Nation. Securing The Citizens," which in practical terms means that the computers at the Bluffdale site can vacuum up all the data and "monitor all networks that are vital to the Security of the Nation" (Domestic Surveillance Directorate). The evident tension in the motto between the possessive "Our Nation" that is both conjoined and opposed to the impersonal "The Citizens" indicates how the mission of national defense commits to security in a double sense. "Securing The Citizens" at once keeps people safe from danger and ensures that these same citizens do not pose a danger to the state. The rhetorical imprecision lays bare a disturbing precept of sovereignty: citizens need security, but along the way they themselves need to be secured.

In a world where citizens operate with the assumption that every nook and cranny are subject to surveillance, only "an act of conscience" can preserve "individual liberty" ("Edward Snowden"). The recourse to privacy here seems fully consistent with liberalism's underlying precepts of freedom and autonomous self-ownership. Doctorow's teen protagonist in *Little Brother* puts things a bit more, shall we say, prosaically:

> There's something really liberating about having some corner of your life that's *yours*, that no one gets to see except you. It's a little like nudity or taking a dump.... What if I decreed that from now on, every time you went to evacuate some solid waste, you'd have to do it in a glass room perched in the middle of Times Square, and you'd be buck naked.... It's not about doing something shameful. It's about doing something *private*. It's about your life belonging to you. (57)

The protagonist of *Little Brother* may be a millennial cyberguerrilla, but his language seems better suited both for a more infantile subject fixated on anality and for a more old-fashioned identity, the traditional subject of Lockean liberalism who values privacy. As Dominique Laporte proposes in *History of Shit* (1978), ideas about privacy, property, and propriety are all connected to waste. If, as Locke asserts, we all have property in ourselves, then Laporte's contribution in looking at the history of outhouses, latrines, and, of course, privies explains the obsessive need to keep that self and all its property hidden and private as an instinctive urge created by liberalism. Warren and Brandeis's emphasis on "what is whispered in the closet" as a matter of privacy also hearkens back to the history of the closet as *privé*, the implementation of the *cellas familiares* described by Laporte that relocated pit latrines to the private domestic space. As the depository for waste became conflated "with the site of *material accumulation*," state authorities began to require "that all *property owners* build these so-called private pits" (46). This development in "the privatization of waste" (29) touches upon the earthy origins of liberal privacy in ways that reveal why the concept is suffused by psychic attachments of such depth.

According to Freud, neurotics are preoccupied with "their special scatological practices, ceremonies, and so on, which they carefully keep secret," that is, concealed and private (*Three Essays* 187). Not for nothing does the toilet *topos* of Doctorow's example reappear across defenses of personal privacy. As one security technologist and also board member of the Electronic Freedom Foundation contends, the presupposition that you have no reason to complain about surveillance if you have nothing to hide breaks down when you "go to the bathroom[,] . . . sing in the shower," or engage in other intimate activities (Schneier, *Data and Goliath* 124). Bathrooms serve as the metonymic substitute for the legal abstraction of privacy. The neurotic diagnosed by Freud is not a singular case but the normative condition of the subject under liberalism, who, on the one hand, holds onto their property because it affords them privacy and, on the other, prizes privacy above all because it keeps their property safe. The scene of anal pleasure is not all that far removed from the political principles of liberalism: the toddler who "obstinately refuses to empty his bowels when he is put on the pot—that is, when his nurse wants him to"—is locked in a battle against "a restriction . . . upon his personal freedom" (Freud, "Character" 295). Freud's mention of the hired nurse of course imbues the setting with a heavy dose of fin-de-siècle bourgeois privilege, but at a deeper level the child's affective posture offers stout resistance to relinquishing what one possesses. Whether it is one's property or one's shit—and at core there is no difference between the two—liberalism says that we have the right to dispose of it as we wish. And likewise, whether the threat comes from a nurse telling us what to do or a government overreaching into our personal information and secrets, liberalism also says that we should resist the incursion as an assault on personal freedom.

In "Character and Anal Eroticism," Freud argues that children who once experienced "subsidiary pleasure" in "holding back their stool" mature into adults who are "especially *orderly, parsimonious* and *obstinate*" (294). Although Freud does not make the link to property, the *OED* does by reminding us that *parsimony* entails an inordinate reluctance to "part with money and other resources." Like the gold in fables that, as Freud suggests, is always associated with shit, property under liberalism is but a half step away from waste. Property affords the individual privacy so that bodily functions can be performed outside the public gaze. Property, along with the notion of privacy that it underwrites, emerges as the prophylaxis against surveillance even as it requires fences and other forms of security. But the trajectory here does not open up onto civil society or public life. For Locke, "every man has a *property* in his own *person*: this no body has any right to but himself" (*Second Treatise* 19). Doctorow and, to a certain extent, Greenwald tell us that we have to update this maxim for the electronic age so that the property we own in ourselves is effectively encrypted as private property. For these writers, only by asserting a right to private property can we withstand surveillance, whether it comes from high school administrators in a YA novel or the NSA. Above all, though, it is Freud who reveals how the Lockean maxim of having property in one's "own *person*" hinges on a dark and intimate obsession where the idea of "person" represents less an abstract entity than a body defined by its excretions.

Beyond creating the need for security, property also motivates us to consent to its presence in our lives. Security is part of a complex affective tangle wherein we both dread and invite surveillance. The tension is inherent to the social contract in which people come together in order to protect what the individual removes from the state of nature by claiming it as his. This version of the social contract faces a hurdle: "how should any one ever come to have a *property* in any thing. . . . how men might come to have a *property* in several parts of that which God gave to mankind in common" (*Second Treatise* 18)? How can the universal inheritance of humankind be privatized? Part of Locke's origin story of property goes like this: a hunter secures his right to a hare by hunting it. Significantly, his possession of said rabbit exists before he actually captures it and has it in his hands. Instead, pursuit of the rabbit makes it property; tracking the animal through the woods is enough to establish a claim upon it. "The hare that any one is hunting, is thought his who pursues her during the chase," explains Locke, because by having become quarry the rabbit can no longer be viewed as common (20). The hunter makes the rabbit into property because he has "employed so much *labour* . . . to find and pursue her," actions that effectively remove the rabbit from the state of nature and reconfigure it as potential property (20). Indeed, the rabbit is always already property. When the hunter discovers, tracks, and pursues the rabbit, he "hath *begun a property*" (20). He does not even have to catch it; for Locke, pursuit creates property.

Cooper's Waste Management

Locke's pursuit of the hare is reanimated at the outset of Cooper's *The Pioneers*, when settlers and hunters in the novel's famous opening scene disagree about the ownership of a fleeing deer. Locke, in fact, did not need Cooper to translate his chase scene of the hare to an American forest imaginary: he prefaced the example of how the labor of pursuing the rabbit creates the right of property by referencing the "law of reason [that] makes the deer the *Indian's* who hath killed it" (*Second Treatise* 20). More than a novel about the wilderness in Otsego County circa 1793–94, Cooper's treatment seeks to understand how the theoretical fiction of the state of nature sets in motion the activities of tracking, pursuit, and surveillance.[11] Whether his cognomen is Deerslayer, Pathfinder, or Hawkeye, the Leatherstocking displays a skill in tracking and asserting property rights to the deer and other animals that he pursues. As always seems to happen in the United States, multiple shots are fired while questions are asked later, creating uncertainty as to which shooter has fired the fatal bullet that brings down the deer. Even though Judge Marmaduke Temple hears Natty's dogs in pursuit of the deer, he still does not think that pursuit creates property in this instance because the hunted animal is crossing his own property and thus already within the domain of his possession. A debate ensues over these competing ideas of property, so the parties weigh the forensic evidence, counting the shots fired and matching up each with the bullets that are lodged in the animal's carcass. The matter is soon settled when it is determined the Judge's final shot, the one he claims to have bagged this magnificent buck, is actually lodged in the shoulder of one of the hunters. Injury, not pursuit, creates ownership. Or, better yet, landownership as the possession of property enables and, to some extent, allows wounding. The Judge accepts the evidence that he did not kill the deer but promptly forgets this finding, saying to his slave, "there is . . . a deer of *my* taking, that I will thank you to bring in" to the house (53; emphasis added). Any disagreement that Natty and the Judge have over the disposition of property is fundamentally a disagreement between white men over white notions of property that leaves no space for Indigenous understandings of the land.[12] Locke's meditation on property may begin with an Indian hunter, but when Cooper completes the story, only white men can debate the rightful ownership of the deer carcass.

Once Oliver Edwards reveals that he has been shot, the Judge as the shooter asserts his proprietorship, not just over the deer but over the situation itself, first inviting and then insisting that the wounded man accompany him back to his residence, the most prominent habitation for miles. Yes, the Judge is showing kindness and concern. But there is more at work here. He frames the issue as a matter of consent, which, for Locke, is the key concept that transports human beings out of nature and into a civilized state. "If thou wilt consent to dwell with us," then the wounded young hunter can live with the Judge and his family until he has fully recuperated—and perhaps even longer (39). While the Judge literally brings the injured hunter out of nature, let's not forget that what appears as a consensual matter is in actuality the threat of force realized as a gunshot wound. Nor should we think that the various shooters pursuing this deer are in the state of nature since Judge Temple owns this tract of land. Locke's question of "how should any one ever come to have a *property* in any thing" is answered by pursuit and surveillance. The mere thought of property—not property that is in hand but property that is on the run—generates the desire to secure it.

After losing his argument about the deer, the region's principal landowner reasserts his authority by distinguishing property from waste, or rather, by converting waste into property. The wounded hunter "is made of materials too precious to be wasted in the forest" and should be brought under the Judge's roof lest his education, manners, and noble bearing are left to rot in the wilderness (202). Edwards needs to be secured, not simply because he might sue for damages but also, in the Judge's reasoning, for his own sake. Again, Judge Temple is tapping into a Lockean logic, but he—or Cooper's narrator—is also adjusting the logic in midstream since both the dead deer and the Judge's land are simultaneously viewed as elements of the state of nature and as property. This doubleness is hardly accidental since, as Eric Cheyfitz notes, *The Pioneers* relies on the "fiction that Indians, like individuals, have always already operated within a system where the alienation of land is the norm; the fiction that all land everywhere is always already *property* and all people individuals" ("Savage Law" 125). Property provides security against waste: the "vacant places of *America*" need to be converted into property lest such uninhabited, uncultivated lands remain "waste land" (Locke, *Second Treatise* 23). Of course, though, the notion of uninhabited land was a violent fiction that justified settler colonial ambitions. The pressure to uphold and extend English land claims stands behind Locke's efforts to theorize how a common wilderness could be made private. As Barbara Arneil explains, "Locke's *Two Treatises* were a response to England's need, by virtue of its colonial aims in America, for a new definition of property" (18) that effectively dispossessed the land's original inhabitants by making it seem that Indigenous peoples never cultivated the ground beneath their feet, leaving them without legal ground (in Western eyes) to press their claims. In this respect, Locke's *Second Treatise* is more a fiction than Cooper's novel because it falsely imagines that Native Americans adhered to the same philosophy of liberalism that held land to be property in the first place.[13]

This fiction required the concept of *vacuum domicillium* to seize "land that is left wholly to nature, that hath no improvement of pasturage, tillage or planting" (Locke, *Second Treatise* 26) because it represents an affront to God who wants to see soil cultivated and made productive. "Waste," the word that Locke repeatedly uses to characterize such land, is ripe for the taking. And surely the pursuit of property is easier when the quarry are immovable tracts of wilderness and not a fleeing rabbit. As secretary to the Lords Proprietors of Carolina and secretary to the Council of Trade and Plantations, Locke had a vested interest in developing a theory in which "the individual in America need not have the consent of his fellows to appropriate property" (Arneil 137). His career in "waste management," as we might wish to call it, converted the vacant lands of the New World into potential property, provided such tracts could be cultivated and improved in ways recognizable to Europeans. Civilization demands that waste be made private and the surest way of accomplishing that goal is to define it as property.

What does all this talk of waste have to do with Edwards, who, as far as the Judge knows, may have mixed bloodlines? To the Judge, the young hunter looks like a piece of shit because he enjoys neither property nor the privacy that it affords. His natural "gifts," to use a term favored by Natty Bumppo throughout the Leatherstocking series, are soiled if they remain uncultivated.[14] Make no mistake: by ensuring that Edwards's talents do not go to waste, by seeking to improve the hunter and lodging him under his roof, the Judge is treating the youth as potential property—an operation he has already effected in more brutal terms by holding Aggy as a slave. Slavery manifests a theory of property ownership not inconsistent with liberalism's slippage between persons and land. Waste becomes property once it bears the imprint of labor and cultivation. In this way, then, bullet holes in the deer establish a right to ownership. Bullets, like the stakes driven home by surveyors or the lines gouged in a field by a settler's plow, ensure that potential property such as game and land do not go to waste. Just as the *Second Treatise* famously creates continuity between persons and property ("every man has a property in his own person"), rude and uncultivated foragers like Edwards run the risk of being viewed as a sort of living and breathing *vacuum domicillium*, which is to say, as human waste. Across the expanse of what Locke saw as "the wild woods and uncultivated waste of *America*" (24), a combination of surveillance and surveying secures the embodiments of wilderness, from Edwards to the land itself, against waste.

Sophisticated financial instruments secure vacant land as property in still deeper ways. In *A Guide in the Wilderness* (1810), William Cooper, the novelist's father who lent his name to the settlement he founded at Cooperstown, New York, detailed how the enterprising land speculator can use mortgages to provide security. "I have already settled more acres than any man in America," crowed Judge Cooper, a boast rephrased as a classical comparison by one admirer who wrote, "Leave to Caesar the boast of having destroyed two millions of men; let yours be that of having cut down two millions of trees" (W. Cooper 13). Judge Cooper, however, was more inclined to biblical comparison in assessing his role of "having been an instrument in reclaiming such large and fruitful tracts from the waste of the creation" (13). Although the title suggests a handbook of trails and tracking, *A Guide in the Wilderness* is less a compendium of forest wisdom than the story of a real estate developer's innovative wheeling and dealing on the New York frontier in the days after the Revolution. Instead of selling land outright to settlers, the astute speculator negotiates contracts that protect both settler and landlord. Through mortgages, writes Judge Cooper, "the settler sleeps in security" since he is assured of his possession while "the landlord has his security . . . in his mortgage deed" that lies in "the improved value of the land" (6, 11). Long before he became a model for Judge Temple, William Cooper had "reaped a national reputation as the consummate developer," according to Alan Taylor (75).

But in the end the financial equivalence of property and security proved unstable in more ways than one. Disputed land claims, market downturns, and seasonal environmental factors introduced unforeseen risks to the settlement at Cooperstown. *The Pioneers*, in fact, allowed Cooper to explore how "his father's possession [of such large tracts of land] began in a controversial tangle of conflicting property rights rather than in a state of nature" (Taylor 54). On December 22, 1809, an unknown assailant snuck up on Judge Cooper as he left a political meeting and coldcocked him, causing severe enough head trauma that he later died.[15]

Surveying and Surveillance

As *The Pioneers* translates Locke's story about the state of nature to the early American frontier in the 1790s, the novel illustrates how property sits at the origin of security and surveillance. More is at stake than the insight that people consent to surveillance so that they can secure their safety and property. The foundational scene in the political theory of liberalism reveals, for Cooper, how rabbits, deer, and other animals, including the human species, invite, beseech, and justify surveillance. *The Pioneers* provides an architectonic perspective that discloses how the concept of property establishes security and surveillance as settled notions, which, after all, seems only appropriate for a novel all about settler colonialism's destruction of the wilderness. If Judge Cooper strove to convert the waste of *vacuum domicillium* into property, his son expressed ambivalence by portraying how settlers were subjecting the land and its species to the waste of devastation. Complaining of white settlers' "wasty ways" is Natty's bitter refrain.

The bundling and consolidation of property, privacy, and security comes into view before Cooper's narrative even begins. The frontispiece to an early edition of the novel, a sort of a coat of arms designed for the American pioneer, presents a jumble of weapons and animal pelts that puts property on public display, all held in place by a veritable arsenal standing guard over the frontier settlement in the background (see figure 3.1). Through a notch in the hills, the scene opens on Lake Otsego and Cooperstown in the distance. In an 1828 book devoted exclusively to the illustrations in Cooper's works, an admirer of his novels observed, "The tasteful manner in which the letters composing the title of the book are thrown on the smaller branches will not escape attention" (Hall). *The Pioneers* and weaponry are deeply intertwined by the visual pun that at once gestures to the "title" of the novel and the legal notion of "title" that guarantees property rights.[16] But not everything is secure in the illustration. Or, rather, the deer hide and bear pelt are suspended to a maple tree by a belt of American Indian wampum, a detail that the nineteenth-century curator of the book on Cooper illustrations does not mention. A visual metaphor, the wampum suggests how property rights absorb Indigenous land claims much as the apprehension of fugitive panthers, deer, and other property requires the bow, arrow, and tomahawk pictured here alongside the ax, carbine, and fishing trident. All these implements facilitate primitive accumulation but are also emblematic reminders of frontier warfare. The trophy that dangles from a length of wampum is pulled into the strife that pits collective tribal understandings of the land against settler claims of ownership under which the celebrated subject of liberalism is empowered as "an 'individual' . . . 'free' to alienate this land in a market economy" (Cheyfitz, "Savage Law" 112). The corollary to this statement is even more significant: just as there is no property without an individual to claim, pursue, and hold it, "there is no individuality without property, so inseparable are the two terms" (112). This definition, identification, and, above all, enactment of individualism illustrates how Locke's formulation that "every man has a property in his person" presents an origin story of "the individual" that rivals Foucault's account of subject formation in *Discipline and Punish*. Where Locke renders the idea of "man" as an effect of property relations, Foucault contends that the individual is a function of discipline and surveillance.

Perhaps, however, Locke's and Foucault's respective biographies of the individual are not in tension with one another but rather complementary. Within liberalism, the individual emerges as a rights-bearing subject because of property relations much as the individual is also brought into focus by surveillance within disciplinary society. Surveillance and property are functional equivalents. Human beings are not that different from either rabbits or deer.

TECHNOLOGIES OF LIBERALISM 105

FIGURE 3.1. Frontispiece to *The Pioneers*.

Each is the subject of pursuit because each can become property. The only difference is that humans seem to be unique when it comes to creating this property in their own persons. Pursuing a rabbit or tracking a deer, what Locke calls the process whereby an individual "hath *begun a property*," is in the end an effort to surveil and secure it. Likewise, the right to privacy, the "right of the people to be secure in their persons," in the language of the Fourth

Amendment, requires property that can be shuttered, locked, and barred "against unreasonable searches and seizures." Around the time of the amendment's ratification, Johnson's *Dictionary* defined the word *search* as an "Enquiry by looking into every suspected place . . . a pursuit" (qtd. in Gray 264). If we accept Rosen and Santesso's contention that security is both "a threat to our freedoms [and] . . . one of their guarantors," then it is also surely the case that any freedoms guaranteed by state surveillance are limited to privatized notions of liberty (244). Privacy makes no sense without property. But it is also the case that property begins in pursuit: along with any of the cognate activities from collecting to surveying to hunting to searching, pursuit and surveillance create the property that allows individuals to be private.

As the liminal space between the theoretical fiction of state of nature and the historical realities of settlement, the frontier connects property to surveillance via the material activity of surveying that establishes land claims and boundary markers for fence posts. From the Latin *videre* or "to see," surveying seems less active and intrusive than surveillance, a word that makes its way into French and then English from *vigilare* meaning to watch and, by extension, to watch *over* as in a vigil. The act of surveyance that came from *supervidere* and *surveeir* in the fourteenth century has connotations of spiritual or philosophical elevation that suggest contemplation and consideration. The word *surveillance*, in contrast, is politically charged from the get-go, coming into circulation with the Committees of Surveillance during the French Revolution. Although *surveillance* and *surveying* have different origins, the conceptual, administrative, and practical links between these activities, as Cooper shows, were being forged on the frontiers of the early republic. More than one founding father, including Washington and Jefferson, were land surveyors while another, Hamilton, worked as a lawyer to sort out the disputed land claims to the Otsego Patent held by William Cooper.

Set in 1793, *The Pioneers* follows on the heels of the Land Ordinance of 1785 that put into effect the surveying of virgin land as federal practice. Specifying that the secretary of war would have a role in the operations of surveyors and geographers, the Land Ordinance of 1785 established a grid over the landscape, so that nature could become territory and territory could divvied up into townships and salable lots. In his younger days, when he was known by the appellation Deerslayer, Natty rails against surveyors, but his accusation that they "lead the way to waste and destruction" lacks the subtlety to see that the point of surveying is to reclaim wasteland as property (*Deerslayer* 222). As a prototype for the federal survey devised by Jefferson, the Land Ordinance of

1785 represented a new technology that the world had never seen. Although it drew on the Roman system of land division known as centuriation (which makes sense given the founding fathers' interest in all things Roman as they established their *novus ordo seclorum*), the Land Ordinance departed from that ancient precedent by not altering its survey lines for anything. The American survey proceeded with a "complete disregard of the terrain," sweeping up the entirety of a landscape into "as complete an occupancy of [the federal government's] territories as possible" (H. Johnson 21). By not stopping for mountain ranges or other geographic features, the Land Ordinance was "continuous not only in concept but in practice over thousands of square miles—the most uninterrupted cadastral system in the world" (30).[17] As a prototype of modern surveillance, the continuous nature of the survey makes it possible to "collect it all," amassing the variegated environment itself into a data set that can be broken down into repeatable and salable patterns.

Shoot Everyone

No matter the array of different forms of security—the Lockean contract, mortgages, fence posts, and smooth-bore rifles like the one favored by the Judge—insecurity persists as part of the social landscape. Property always seems to wriggle away; even after property is pursued, surveilled, surveyed, and marked with legal title, it remains hard to pin down. In *The Pioneers*, everyone wants to secure the deer that is bounding away, but what remains under contention are the methods of securing this escaping property. Natty accuses his adversary of sloppiness, stating Judge Temple has used a gun loaded with multiple pieces of buckshot whereas Natty has used a rifle that fires a single ball. "A body never knows where his lead will fly, when he pulls the trigger of one of them uncertain fire-arms," as the woodsman reproves the Judge (25). Such methods anticipate the logic of mass data collection. No need to aim or have a specific target. Shoot everywhere by shooting at nothing in particular. Fire at everything becomes find everything. Or, in terms of the personal motto of General Keith Alexander, head of the NSA, "Collect it all."[18] Not surprisingly, one NSA program for scooping up mass data goes by the codename BOUNDLESS INFORMANT.

Such directives have long been programmed into the precepts of liberalism. *The Pioneers* exemplifies how total is the aim to secure property by recounting deer hunts, bass seining, and pigeon shoots. The pursuit of venison, fish, and fowl suggests a global effort at dominion that encompasses earth, water, and sky. When the people of Templeton fish or shoot, their goal is to catch all the fish in the lake or decimate the entire flock that flies overhead. Caught up in these indiscriminate practices is the wounded hunter, Edwards. By contrast, Natty brags of his skill in tracking prey and taking it in a single shot, a talent he displays on multiple occasions. His precise aim suits a Lockean landscape of pursuing a hare, deer, or other singular quarry, but such techniques are inadequate where game is plentiful, suspects potentially everywhere—and data superabundant. While the reach of technologies that enable the state "to collect, store, monitor, and analyze all electronic communication by all people around the globe" (Greenwald, *No Place to Hide* 94) is difficult to fathom, the justification for surveillance depends upon links between security and terror that we might begin to parse here with Cooper's help.

Associations between surveying and surveillance and between territory and terror converge in extraordinary fashion during a tavern scene in *The Pioneers* when Natty and the Judge debate property rights. Natty complains that a settler's fence has impeded his pursuit of a "fine buck" that he considered already his property because he was pursuing it: "Now I want to know who is to pay me for that deer," he protests (161). No wonder that Natty's frontier bonhomie disappears when he learns that Marmaduke Temple, who holds title to the land, is surveying his extensive tract so that it can be plotted, parceled, and sold off to settlers. The word *fence*, geographers remind us, derives from *defense* (H. Johnson 158). For his part, the Judge sees no conflict between fleeing and fenced property because he believes that "a vigilant magistrate" can prevent overhunting (160). Before too long, Natty finds himself accused by just such a magistrate for killing a deer out of season, while the Judge receives a surveillance report from the magistrate that "we have kept a watchful eye" on Natty, because suspicions are afloat that he is secretly mining coal on the Judge's property (321). Judge Temple relies on surveillance to enforce claims of ownership created by surveyors. But this discussion of property is only an interlude in the larger tavern conversation about French Jacobins and the Reign of Terror, as the drinkers discuss tidings that the king and queen have been guillotined. The historical backdrop of the French Revolution reminds readers that the echoes between surveillance and surveying are shadowed by a deeper homology between terror and territory. "To control a territory is to exercise terror; to challenge territorial extent is to exercise terror," writes geographer Stuart Elden (xxx). In light of these associations, it is worth asking how accidental the Judge's shooting of the young hunter is. Although the Judge has not specifically targeted Edwards, such latitude is, after all, the point of sovereign power. His property rights allow him to fire nearly at random when the deer crosses onto his property. Within the nascent culture of security on the frontier, randomness ensures that Edwards's wounding is no accident. Temple may be on the other side of the political aisle from "the Jacobins of France," but his methods are not entirely dissimilar from those of the revolutionaries under which "hundreds of... inhabitants, who are royalists in their sentiments, are shot at a time" (161). Terror, like security, depends upon *not* taking specific aim. Being able to act at random, to discharge a weapon broadly or to gather communications by the terabyte, is both the privilege and sign of sovereignty enacted under settler colonialism.

This power to act indiscriminately is one outcome of the dialectic that unites security and insecurity. Security is not a response to terror; terror is instead an effect of security. Unlike Natty who can blow the head off a turkey at a hundred yards, sovereign terror has no target. Shoot all the aristocrats. Scoop up all the fish in the lake. Shoot all the pigeons in the sky. Cut down millions of trees, as Cooper's father boasted. Terror is a total approach that relies on a mass calculus. By presiding over a settlement that deploys security methods with such zeal and scope, the conservatively minded Judge Temple comes to resemble the French Revolutionaries and their Committees of Surveillance that he abhors. Modern security has no use for an old man like Natty whose ability to single out the lone pigeon or spear fish one at a time, skills that befit the nickname Hawkeye, reveals nothing so much as his irrelevance to the reconsolidated order of property that emerges at end of the novel and has continued into our own era of "suspicionless mass surveillance" (Greenwald, *No Place to Hide* 251).

Terror is Americanized when an immense flock of passenger pigeons, now extinct, flies over the settlement and the townspeople enlist every weapon imaginable in a scene of tragicomic civil defense. Bows, arrows, sticks, poles, and "every species of fire-arms, from the French ducking-gun with a barrel near six feet in length, to the common horseman's pistol," not to mention a cannon loaded with bird shot, are fired without any real aim (244). Braced by Cooper's allusions to the martial fanfare of the Fourth of July, the pigeon hunt confirms that this is a sovereign people whose claims extend from the earth to the heavens above. An insistence on liberal property rights justifies the slaughter: "If you had to sow *your* wheat twice, and three times," a farmer complains to Natty, you would not mind this massacre of the bird population (244). There are no specific targets because everything that moves is already a target. The slaughter is random but hardly accidental: "I see nothing but eyes, in every direction, as the innocent sufferers turn their heads in terror. Full one-half of those that have fallen are yet alive," the Judge comments as he looks on a field littered with bleeding pigeons (250). By firing arbitrarily, randomly, and indiscriminately into the "immense masses," the townspeople cause game to rain down upon the earth, catching up "innocent sufferers" in the carnage (246). Of course, there is no way to distinguish a guilty pigeon from an innocent one, but that is precisely the point here.

The problem of pigeons is a biopolitical one. Beyond number, the birds at once present an opportunity (for sport) and pose a threat (to agriculture) because of their limitless population. Reference to the flocks of "the feathered tribe" (246) makes clear that the allegory of security and property protection resounds with genocidal implications. The closing episode of Natty's career in *The Prairie* (1827) erases any doubt that Indigenous people threaten security because of their multitude. Targeting his enemy du jour, Natty, now an octogenarian, pronounces that "the Siouxes are a numberless and bloody race." Even worse in Lockean terms, the Sioux offend against civilization by letting the "deep and alluvial soils" of the prairies go to waste by making only halfhearted and "imperfect" attempts at agriculture. Their encampment "bore the appearance of having been tenanted longer than its occupants had originally intended," and their unsettled state suggests that they are ready to return to a nomadic lifestyle and leave behind a vacant landscape to be filled by others. Any but not all doubts: the Sioux chief portrays the threat of settler colonialism by comparing the "countless numbers to the flights of migratory birds in the season of blossoms" to white settlers pushing westward. Are swarms of white people as much of a menace as other populations? The task of security remains whether the confrontation is with a mass of data, a flock of birds, or a horde of people: in each case a scattershot approach, not individualized targeting, is the response. Even in shooting but one deer without any real aim, Judge Temple proves that the coordination of pursuit and property draws unintended victims into the net of injury.

So many pigeons are shot, covering "the very ground with the fluttering victims" (246), that the townspeople do not pause to collect the birds, letting property go to waste. Too much property creates waste; as Natty looks on a fish haul that has netted an overabundance of bass, he rejects the offer to take a fish home with him, saying, "I eat of no man's wasty ways" (265). He utters this same critique now during the pigeon hunt, telling the Judge that such wastefulness has no limit. Waste undoes the notion of property by erasing the evidence of labor and cultivation. The Leatherstocking disdains such clumsy sport, and, on this occasion, he adds to his mythic stature by downing a pigeon with a single shot. His careful tracking and precise aim entail a skill set that seems a quaint vestige of older modes in comparison to the categorical methods of "the new surveillance" that are used, for instance, to drug test all employees or screen all passengers. In "the maximum security society" that is also "a *suspicious* society in which every one is suspected" (Marx), ever-closer and more intimate scrutiny—DNA analysis among the most obvious—works in tandem with methods that rely on the collection of bulk data. The coincidence of the settlers' haphazard approach and Natty's eagle-eyed targeting in *The Pioneers* does more than indicate the total dimensions of frontier security. The simultaneous deployment of distant and targeted surveillance practices also suggests that the newness of "new surveillance" is as old as the fears for privacy and property that underwrite liberalism.

Which is to say that for all his disgust with settlers' wasteful methods, Natty still believes in property and the need to secure it. Despite views of Natty as a critic of those who would fence in nature, the backwoodsman, more often than not, upholds the precepts of liberalism. Natty prizes property more than anyone because of the privacy that it affords. A series of ingenious locks and latches secures his hut, and he denies entrance to all the townspeople, including the sheriff who comes with a search warrant of the premises. Resisting the court order, the hunter refuses to allow the magistrate to enter his cabin, stating that such "wasty ways" (356) are unwelcome. The worry is not that the sheriff will seize foodstuffs, deerskins, or the rest of Natty's stuff; he defies the officer of the law in order to prevent his privacy from going to waste. His objection to the "wasty ways" of state security and surveillance rests on the liberal insistence that any trespass upon an individual's property depletes his store of privacy.[19]

Privacy allows Natty to keep his shit out of public view. But because he does not actually own the land upon which his cabin stands, because he lacks property rights, privacy is hard to come by. So instead Natty buries his shit, which in this case is a friendship from the colonial past that he would rather keep secreted. The waste that Natty has kept secret in a cave, in the bowels of the earth, comes to light when old Major Effingham is revealed to the sheriff and posse commitatus pursuing the Leatherstocking. Frail and prone to mental wandering, Effingham now bears all the signs of decrepitude brought on by "the decay of nature" (437). The unreconstructed British Loyalist is human waste in this new American society. Out of a sense of delicacy and respect, Natty "could not bear to exhibit to the world" (441) this adherent to the monarchical past who is now without property. The liberal subject, according to Laporte's *History of Shit*, "never reconciles himself to his 'remnant of earth' and will go to great lengths to conceal it" (76). Even though the former British colonial officer "was the rightful proprietor of this very soil on which we stand" (437), his present condition offers him no protection from a state-authorized search. The very fact that Natty is hiding something in his cabin and nearby caverns creates the suspicion necessary to put him under surveillance. Only when Major Effingham is recognized as the rightful owner of these wilderness estates, which, the Judge quickly points out, have "multiplied, by the times and my industry, a hundred-fold in value" (440), does the old man gain the ability to enter a room, close the door, and shut out the world. Used up and stuck in the past, the former landowner does not regain his place in his society. What he does reacquire is the property that allows him to retire in private.

Nothing to Hide

The strenuous defense of privacy in *The Pioneers* echoes the Fourth Amendment's guarantee that the people have the right to be secure in their "houses, papers, and effects," and, we might add, their emails, web searches, and viewing habits. Greenwald draws on this amendment to underscore the relevance of Snowden's revelations. As a matter of basic human rights, "the desire for privacy is shared by us all as an essential, not ancillary, part of what it means to be human. We all instinctively understand that the private realm is where we can act, think, speak, write, experiment, and choose how to be, away from the judgmental eyes of others. Privacy is a core condition of being a free person" (*No Place to Hide* 172). Legal scholars assert as well that privacy sits at the core of people's distinct individuality.[20] This stirring plea for the existential importance of privacy is impossible without a notion of private property. Even as private life is held up as the limit to searching and surveillance, this defense has little to say about the public life of citizens. If all that security protects is a diminished autonomy and a limited sense of agency, it seems worthwhile asking whether policing, antiterror campaigns, and other safeguards confuse the matter by portraying public life itself as risky, dangerous activity. In our pursuit of security, have we mistaken the social and political contraction that results in a narrowed sphere of activity and human relation for the affordances of the social contract? The fetishization of privacy comes at the expense of the fragile vitality of the public sphere.

Then again, Cooper makes it difficult to romanticize public life since Natty's longest public appearance comes when he is placed in the stocks, a spectacle for all to see. This humiliation follows Natty across the Mississippi River in *The Prairie*, as years later he remembers when he was "laid neck and heels by the law, and held up as a spectacle for the women and boys of a wasteful settlement to point their fingers at!" In light of such abuses, we can understand why, for Greenwald, "privacy is essential to human freedom and happiness for reasons that are rarely discussed but instinctively understood by most people" (*No Place to Hide* 173). Yet such notions of liberal privacy legitimate a political aphasia, the point where discussion stops, the threshold where people like Natty appear at their front doors with rifles in hand. Perhaps this critique is injudicious, too harsh. After all, the liberal hero—or, is it the hero of liberalism?—falls back on notions of property and privacy to counter the very techniques of securitization and surveillance without which there would be no property in the first place. Greenwald and other civil liberties advocates invest privacy with an innate power that protects the intimate spaces where citizens experiment, "test boundaries," and "explore new ways of thinking and being" (174). Such a defense of privacy, however, will only be robust if it can be distinguished from what liberalism upholds as the right to private property. Privacy needs to be articulated in terms of public life rather than assumed automatically as a fundamental but ultimately inexpressible dimension of the human. In no small part because of its deep reliance on concepts of property and waste, privacy is perhaps an inadequate concept for thinking about rights. In place of the right to privacy, critics have proposed an alternative capacity framed around a more elusive right to secrecy and opacity that rejects an individualized notion of politics for one based on communication and shared knowledge.[21] Taking a stand against surveillance and security entails thinking about a wider array of rights than privacy.

Yet jettisoning privacy altogether may prove difficult, as it has long been recognized as "the realm where creativity, dissent, and challenges to orthodoxy germinate" (Greenwald, *No Place to Hide* 174). As a function of property, privacy gives birth to the construct known as the liberal individual who comes into existence alongside the subject of surveillance. Who better to watch, survey, and surveil than the person who insists on privacy? In a culture of security whose early incarnations are portrayed in Cooper's *The Pioneers*, this question can be applied to every random individual, who, in the end, may be nothing other than one of a billion data points that can be assembled into an infinite cache of information used to predict—and preempt—human behavior.

Even when there is nothing to hide, the project of security is overwhelmed by all the data that is in the open. What needs to be reckoned with are not simply infinite individual pieces of data but the connections that can be traced and the patterns that can be discerned among them. While entire forests can be leveled and passenger pigeons rendered extinct in the world of *The Pioneers* and beyond, bits of knowledge about human motivations, behaviors, and expression are inexhaustible, part of an "informational sublime" that challenges comprehension. How does one convey knowledge about entities and forms so large that they defy expression? This self-reflexive question adds a new dimension to terror, one that shifts our focus on security from external scenes of settler colonialism to gothic settings where every whisper, misplaced letter, and chain of communication fits into a larger story, indeed, a story so large that it cannot be told. This impossible storytelling is the subject of the next chapter.

4

Terror and the Informational Sublime

DATA AND GOTHIC STORYTELLING

SECURITY IS JEOPARDIZED when there is too much. Too much what? The previous chapter identified this excess as aggregate forms of life. Axes and guns helped settlers exert control over wild expanses of land and endless flocks of birds viewed as an object of sport. These tools literally cut down the population of nonhuman life forms by the million. Via the murderous allegories of the frontier, the biopolitical implications of clear-cutting and massacre extended to settler colonialism's treatment of Indigenous people. Whether it is "millions of pigeons [that] . . . extended from mountain to mountain in one solid blue mass" in *The Pioneers* (249) or "the sublimity connected with vastness" (1) of the primordial forest seen in the opening sentence of *The Pathfinder*, these aggregate forms can still be broken down into comprehensible and usable units. Every family in Templeton that snaps the head off of a dying bird can have pigeon pie for supper and the "broad and seemingly interminable carpet of foliage" (*Pathfinder* 3) furnishes firewood for the scout and his expedition. All these utilitarian activities associated with settler colonialism tame emanations of the sublime by making it less immense, less teeming with life.

This chapter considers how unmanageable excess in the form of information creates apprehension and fear. The security effort to gather intelligence frequently results in too much information, precipitating an encounter with the terror of the sublime. Behind the perception of superabundant trees, pigeons, and especially data is a dull but unnerving awareness that not everything can be assimilated, that the mass is too overwhelming to be disaggregated, that the flood will swamp any human effort to understand it. In modern terms, the

NSA's informal motto "collect it all" fuels doubt and epistemological uncertainty since what is a person to do with this "all" should it somehow be amassed? The impossible task of contemporary security is to comprehend and find patterns within the boundless amount of data gleaned from every email, cell phone call, wire transfer, and web search. While this brush with the infinite relies on the supercomputer and the microprocessor, the affective condition of being so overawed that cognition and reason are derailed is not merely a technological matter. It is also shaped by an aesthetic crucible, specifically the disorienting, terrifying, subject-splitting encounter with the sublime. Which is to say that what we currently think about contemporary security is just as much a matter of what we *feel* about security. And, what's more, what we often feel about security is, contradictorily, a profound sense of insecurity. To understand why ever more sophisticated technologies of security unhinge us, it is necessary to start closer to the beginning of the story of how, with the rise of bourgeois print culture, information assumes sublime proportions.

Storytelling is itself compromised by information. Surveying the periodical press and other "instruments in fully developed capitalism" of his day, Walter Benjamin postulated that the ready availability of information in modern society eclipses older narrative forms associated with collective experience (*Illuminations* 88). The ascendancy of print capitalism, emblematized by the daily newspaper, both speeds and widens the flow of information, which "proves incompatible with the spirit of storytelling" (89). In Benjamin's view, information creates a crisis in narrative because it promises to convey intelligence without the aid of narrative; self-evident and containing no mystery, information makes storytelling disposable, a quaint practice from a bygone time. Benjamin contrasts the stolidly ordinary nature of information with "the miraculous" (89) once found in ancient texts. Unlike the marvelous happenings of epics that remain shrouded in mystery, information is stuck in the realm of the plausible and thus "lays claim to prompt verifiability. The prime requirement is that it appear 'understandable in itself'" (89). Benjamin's attention to how information has no patience for the aesthetic qualities of storytelling does not consider the sublime aspect of information as an always expanding set, the volume of the whole piling up. While each individual piece of information may be intuitively "understandable," information as an aggregate frustrates the desire for narrative coherence. Why the friction between storytelling and information matters to security is that defense and national security experts grapple with a remarkably similar version of this problem, which is fundamentally an aesthetic one: as security requires more and more intel, it inevitably creates the conditions of its narrative impossibility. Too much information has an inverse effect on narrative: too little story.

Too Much Information, Too Little Story

How to process in narrative form the unimaginable haul of information that is collected and stored by the NSA and other government agencies? The director of the RAND Corporation's Center for Global Risk and Security, Gregory Treverton, asserts, "Intelligence ultimately is storytelling" (4). Such a statement might tempt us to conclude that people who work with and think about narratives, not the least of whom would be literary critics and other humanities types, have more to contribute to understanding the war on terror than previously thought. Treverton offers this dictum to explain how the game of national intelligence has fundamentally changed ever since relatively stable models of interpretation associated with the Cold War gave way to the uncertainties of global terrorism. The problem today is that coherent stories with discernible actors can no longer be told. At a time when the United States spends more than $40 billion per year on counterterrorism and counterintelligence, the challenge has not been to collect enough information; instead as government agencies around the world struggle with a glut of information, the task is to assemble the data hauled in by surveillance operations into usable narratives that can inform foreign policy approaches and guide future interventions both at home and abroad. In *Intelligence for an Age of Terror* (2009), Treverton observes that whereas it had once been possible to narrate stories about state actors, nonstate actors such as Al-Qaeda present something of a black box for storytelling and interpretation. Nation-states are knowable by their geopolitical boundaries, their governments composed of human agents who can be identified by their position in a bureaucratic hierarchy. Intelligence analysts can generate classified reports profiling key players in the Kremlin, for instance. As a literary critic might put it, state actors observe at least some of the classical unities outlined in Aristotle's *Poetics*. Nonstate actors, in contrast, pose more of a cypher, belonging to networks, not nations.

Al Qaeda, ISIS, and other amorphous networks with no overriding national loyalties stymie attempts to develop coherent, unified stories about the digital communications, transactions, and online recruiting efforts of terrorist organizations. Double agents may have switched sides during the Cold War, but those defections could be narrated with twists appropriate to the spy novel of international intrigue. Recognizable stories can be told about Soviet-era spies, but terrorists who dissolve into the ether of networks defy conventional forms of narration. "There is no comparable story for nonstates which come in many sizes and shapes," writes Treverton (4), nor do those stories adhere to familiar unities of place and action. Nonstate actors are essentially un-narratable. According to contemporary intelligence analysts like Treverton, we now live in a world where experts struggle to tell stories about networks of extremists with the same confidence and certitude that once characterized intelligence briefings about shake-ups and power plays in an era of detente. Whereas intelligence about foreign states is characterized by too little information, nonstates emit too much information for analysts to organize and understand. Unlike secrets about the inner workings of a Cold War state such as the former Soviet Union that were traditionally hard to come by, information about terrorists and other transnational targets is potentially everywhere, in plain sight but hidden in the massive volume of cell phone calls, web searches, wire transfers, and keystrokes logged by the NSA and other intelligence-gathering agencies. Nonstates, in essence, are characterized by an abundance of information but a paucity of story.

Compounding the difficulties of telling stories about decentralized terrorist networks, states have determined that they must also keep tabs on the millions of their own citizens. While experts such as Michael Chertoff, former secretary of homeland security, fret over the "rise of ungoverned space," it is worthwhile remembering that Chertoff coauthored the USA PATRIOT Act, giving surveillance agencies broad latitude to gather information about the U.S. domestic population. "In an age of terror," writes Treverton, governments "all face the need to collect more information about their inhabitants" (2). It is not just that yet another inexhaustible supply of communication needs to be monitored but also that the raw data has to be made into patterns and narrated in order to attain the status of useful intelligence. Chertoff's recommendation that security agencies be empowered with "as many tools as possible to be applied overseas and at home" (61–62) heightens the problem: how is one to process the countless text messages, billions of emails, and ceaseless activities of bot accounts? Such immense data sets would seem to cry out for ever more capacious and sophisticated surveillance tools to collect and sort information, but the unimaginable expanse of information is itself the problem. As Matthew Potolsky neatly suggests, "big data has replaced Big Brother," leaving intelligence experts, security analysts, and other storytellers "drowning in seas of information that not even most sophisticated algorithms can sort" (xvii). The crisis is at core affective and aesthetic, as the surfeit of information appears as a source of sublime terror.

Security and surveillance always seek more only to find that there can never be enough. "At present, U.S. collection produces too much data," according to Treverton. "The sheer volume of the data, or 'take,' from collection, just from intelligence's own secret sources, threatens to overwhelm the processing of it" (9). Intelligence gathering, in effect, creates its own knowledge deficits. Criminologists who view security as a "'thick' public good" (Loader and Walker, *Civilizing Security* 4) recognize that security often becomes an obsession that can never achieve its task of controlling for every possibility. Knowing that there is always more to know, the project of security confronts "an infinite and ever-disappearing horizon of possibility" (84) that, ironically, makes security a source of apprehension and doubt. As a security apparatus tracks more and more things—letters in the eighteenth and nineteenth centuries, telephone calls and wireless transmissions in the twentieth, digital footprints and biometric data in the twenty-first—it gives rise to a dizzying awareness that there are an infinite number of things to keep tabs on.[1] "The more it knows, the less it knows," writes Michael Dillon in *Biopolitics of Security* (39). The coordination of observation, data, and reason surely provides increased knowledge about the world and ourselves, but the catch is that the mission to produce, assemble, and, most importantly for my purposes here, understand and convey information results in anxious awareness that this mission can never cease. Security can do no other than generate insecurity.

Faced with the prospect of too much data and too little story, analysts—security officers as well as scholars—begin to confront information as a sort of sublime overload. Even proponents of surveillance and data collection admit that security exists "as a condition beyond our grasp that appears endlessly to require more 'security measures'" (Loader and Walker, *Civilizing Security* 84). The infinite amount of data that overwhelms our capacities represents more than just a symptom of contemporary intelligence gathering. It also suggests a problem of perception, cognition, and imagination that tracks back to eighteenth-century theories of the sublime and forward to the future of contemporary security and surveillance. Information is more than a technical matter. It is also a philosophical and aesthetic problem, whose unsettled and expansive dimensions indicate that the human need for security cannot be solved by more data, sharper cameras, or faster computers. Long before the accumulation of massive data sets, thinkers such as Edmund Burke, Immanuel Kant, Friedrich Schiller, and John Locke thought about the connections between infinite amounts of information and terror only to discover obscurity and darkness hovering at the fringes of the human desire to know and communicate. The concept they applied to that which staggers our comprehension is the sublime, an affective state often associated with inexpressible terror and fright but also with exhilaration and transcendence. Rather than parse the differences between Burke's sublime and the Kantian sublime, or even between Schiller's very different takes in two similarly titled essays, "Of the Sublime" and "On the Sublime," here I register how security in its drive to amass information and anticipate dangers comes to resemble a sublime pursuit.

Yet viewing security as a sublime experience does not mean that people encountering avalanches of information attain a commanding perspective of some "absolute totality" (Kant 88). The sublime coordinates of security—being overwhelmed by data, being struck dumb by infinite points of connection, being confronted by the limits of one's own comprehension—do not ultimately generate feelings of transcendence.[2] Appreciating the sublime dimensions of security and surveillance, however, does help bring into critical focus an aesthetic substrate that frequently goes unnoticed in either International Relations or critical security studies. Even though security analysts acknowledge that narrative and storytelling are needed to make sense of a massive volume of intelligence, they do not often think about the aesthetic—and why that may matter. Only by considering the corporeal sensorium that is the aesthetic can we begin to understand why security so often makes people feel powerless.

The Aesthetics of Information Overload

How sublime it is to conceive of a colossal, unending stream of sensory information, and yet "the terrible uncertainty" (E. Burke 58) of such a thing rattles our faculties. The idea of complete and instant access to limitless information at once appears as the realization of enlightenment knowledge and "the frightful" (Schiller, "Of the Sublime"), an aesthetics of totality and terror that Burke identified as "the ruling principle of the sublime" (54). Just talking about the sublime poses problems. "That task would be infinite," muses Burke, as he embarks on the daunting mission of conducting *A Philosophical Enquiry into the Origin of Our Ideas of the Sublime and Beautiful* (4). Such tension is constitutive of an *informational sublime* in which the amassing of knowledge promises unbounded comprehension while also threatening "a moment of linguistic and cognitive breakdown" (McCarthy 548) inextricable from the impossible burden of knowing so much. Coming in and out of focus, defying human reason but broadening the imagination, the informational sublime denotes an aesthetic zone in which the political rationale for security is always shadowed by sensations of terror.

The sheer idea of information—whose status as an uncountable noun hints at its lambent potential for expanse—carries an affective charge that takes its toll on our equanimity. Maurice Lee's inventive formulation that "grammar notwithstanding, information is a gerund" (16) reinforces that idea that information, by virtue of its ongoingness, its essential and inescapable incompleteness, fosters unease, distress, paranoia. Surely, people act upon pieces of information all the time, but it is also the case that information, not so much in small bits or even large data sets but as a total concept, acts on us in ways that erode our affective poise. "Information is not an ontological Thing but rather something that happens to communication," writes Lee (16). This sensibility that information generates an aesthetic stimulus in us, however, is hardly the usual way of understanding information. By the twentieth century, information became aligned with a "rational mathematical calculus" that imparts stability to definitions of the concept (Geoghegan 173). In treating overloads of information as sublime, this chapter toys with anachronism by temporarily forgetting that the word *information* did not accrue its modern meanings associated with "discrete, serial patterns amenable to statistical description, measurable in terms of binary digits" (Geoghegan 174) until well after the aesthetic interest in the sublime peaked in the eighteenth and nineteenth centuries. Yet this temporal mismatch also suggests that the break between archaic and modern notions of information is not as decisive as it might seem. Data that conceivably runs on forever proves captivating not in itself but because it awakens our imaginative capacity to envisage such vastness. "Infinity has a tendency to fill the mind with that sort of delightful horror," in Burke's estimation, that arises when our senses prove inadequate to comprehending a seemingly limitless phenomenon. A dizzying rush of unboundedness ensues when "the imagination meets no check" in considering an endless series. This feeling lingers even after the physical cause of this stimulus wanes or is removed: "the objects about us still seem to whirl" (E. Burke 67).

The Kantian subject brings a bit of order to this maelstrom of pleasure and horror. The *Critique of Judgement* postulates that in contrast to beauty, which depends on external stimulus from flowers and such, we make the sublime a function of our own subjectivity, as we seek "the sublime merely in ourselves and in our attitude of thought" (84). When we confront some incomprehensible magnitude or innumerable quantity, a sort of two-step process ensues in which our imagination runs to infinity and then reason cleans up the scene by employing math to comprehend it. How sublime is the mind that can ponder a question as eternal as the number of stars in the heavens! Or, per a contemporary variant, how sublime must it be to cull an endless stream of raw data from global telecommunications! Information might not appear sublime—after all, colloquial usage often aligns it with basic, straightforward stuff—but its superabundance can prove dizzying.

What Kant termed the "mathematical sublime" outstrips sense and provokes a vertiginous encounter of the mind with its own capacity to contemplate infinity. From this perspective, what keeps security experts up at night is that data abundance and information overload appear as threats in their own right, taxing to the extreme any meager human ability to assemble, process, and, most crucially, tell a coherent story about an expanse of information so incomprehensible that it can only be understood as sublime. Kant makes the crucial distinction that it is not the colossal object that is astonishing; rather it is our own mind coming to grips with the inadequacy of our senses, as we try to imagine some staggering infinity, that is sublime. We do not find pleasure in some object just because it is immense, but we do find "[a satisfaction] in the extension of the imagination by itself" to apprehend "*what is great beyond all comparison*" (Kant 86–87). Unlike the experience of the beautiful that leads to "*restful* contemplation" (85), the sublime unnerves the rational person. Stupefied by excess with no end in sight, "the feeling is one of *on and on*, of being lost," as aphasia sets in and the subject becomes "speechless" (Weiskel 26, 30). More profound and soul-crushing than the discovery of any specific threat hidden in emails or other data, the terror of intelligence gathering lies precisely in the challenge of imagining all communications that may be captured as well as the incalculable connections they create. A glut of information carries the overpowering force of the sublime, but it differs from philosophical accounts in one crucial respect. Kant's subject achieves "a state of mind" that becomes "compatible" and "comfortable" (95) with sublime magnitudes, but the intelligence expert finds no such cognitive haven. Infinite amounts of data imbue security with the terror of the sublime, but it is the sublime without release or enlightenment.

The crisis is narratological: how can experts armed with sophisticated algorithms, let alone ordinary human beings, detect a terrorist plot when there are so many details but no single story? The dilemma that the sublime poses for storytelling did not seem to ruffle Kant, who averred that the contemplation of magnitude and infinity produces satisfaction "that is universally communicable"

(87). Others are not so sure. Doubt that aesthetic experience provides a gateway to shared sensibilities has stoked criticism of Kant's idealism. Beneath the intoxicating ether of a universal aesthetic often lies an all-too-real zone of social domination. In addition to critics who take direct issue with Kant, the eclectic group assembled in this chapter—intelligence experts, media and information theorists, and an American gothic novelist from the 1790s—variously wonder whether information, especially when there is a lot of it, can be truly communicated. As anyone who has struggled through Kant's *Critique of Judgement* knows, aesthetic experience is difficult enough to parse; now try to imagine communicating the overwhelming aspect of sublimity that takes the form of a data set so vast and capacious as to be indescribable. Communication is always a matter of security—and no more so than when the impossible project is to describe an encounter with a cache of information that appears sublime.

The sublime only "works" if assurances of ultimate security and safety mitigate the terror and fear that it inspires. This, at least, is Kant's view of the human subject who experiences the sublime not directly but in mediated fashion, filtered through the mind's capacity to imagine an overawing plenitude. Acting like the guardrail on a scenic overlook, the human mind transforms a potentially paralyzing moment into a reassuring cognitive experience. As a physical sensation, the sublime is a "paroxysm . . . manifested by a kind of shudder" that leads to a "joyous state" (Schiller, "On the Sublime"). The excess that the senses are unable to process—the "sight of a distant infinity" ("On the Sublime") such as an ocean vastness or some immeasurable height—is rendered pleasing by the human capacity for thought that converts a supercharged sensuous experience into an accord of aesthetic judgment. It is, however, a less famous essay, Schiller's "Of the Sublime" (not to be confused with his "On the Sublime"), that addresses how such rapturous excess becomes a matter of security. Schiller's *topos* for the sublime is a shipwreck seen from the safety of the shore. Those aboard the doomed vessel, in contrast, are "little disposed to pronounce this aesthetic judgment over" the scene since they are in its terrifying midst. The spectators on land also feel terror, but their feelings are elevated to the sublime since they are only experiencing the disaster by proxy, as it were. "We must find ourselves in security, if the frightful is to please us," he stipulates ("Of the Sublime").

A particularly—but not exceptionally—American example helps clarify the vulnerable position of the subject who distills rapture from the terror of the sublime. Finding the view atop Virginia's Natural Bridge exquisitely "painful and intolerable" (*Notes* 263), Jefferson felt crushed by the experience, falling involuntarily to his knees. He proclaimed this geological wonder "the most sublime of Nature's works," but other than this gush of Romantic emotion, he deemed the overall sensation "really indescribable!" succumbing to the incommunicability that characterizes the intensity of the sublime (24–25). Jefferson's experience echoes Schiller's contention that "physical security" provides "reassurance to our sensuousness," restoring our feelings of well-being that have been assaulted by the sublime. Against this purely physical sense of safety, Schiller identifies a second disposition, "moral security," keyed to an individual's conviction of their own righteousness. Fortified by "the consciousness of our guiltlessness," the morally secure person never feels that sublime peril—in this case, death and eternal judgment—applies to them. But, as we will see in the subsequent chapter, the brutality and sinfulness of American slavery eroded Jefferson's moral security and that of the colonizationists who followed in his wake.

Jefferson only regained his bearings back below on the canyon floor from where the view of this rock formation now became "delightful in an equal extreme" (*Notes* 25). Jefferson's calculation that the stream flowing beneath the Natural Bridge could power a watermill completed the transposition of an arresting aesthetic experience into a pleasing object of capitalist speculation. Sublimity inheres not in such natural phenomena themselves but in our contemplation of "shapeless mountain masses piled in wild disorder upon one other with their pyramids of ice, or the gloomy, raging sea" (Kant 95). Like Jefferson, we can only exercise the aesthetic discernment necessary to apprehend the sublime if we are positioned at its edges. Terror is disabling: "He who fears can form no judgement about the Sublime in nature . . . it is impossible to find satisfaction in a terror that is seriously felt" (Kant 100). Unmediated contact with the sublime incapacitates the viewer. With some distance or protection, however, the observer can indulge in the sort of reflection that provides pleasure—how thrilling to see "volcanoes in all the violence of their destruction" or the "lofty waterfall of a mighty river" (100)—but only when the subject is assured that any danger is minimal. (Thanks to drone video footage, one can watch streams of lava without risk or remain totally dry while watching a tsunami strike the coast.) The sublime must be experienced from a zone of safety otherwise the threat is too imminent to be intellectual. "Provided only that we are in security," writes Kant, can we feel safe enough to ponder sights of colossal power in ways that elevate the soul.[3]

Mountain crags, rushing torrents, and other sublime features of the earth's landscape can be viewed from safe distances, but what has been called the "digital sublime" (Mosco) of cyberspace allows for no such buffer. The annihilation of time and space promised by the digital extends the limitless reach of governments and corporations into public space and private lives. Geography plays a role in the digital sublime but only through its negation and overcoming. Whereas Kant, Jefferson, and Schiller each invoke Romantic landscapes, assertions about the transcendence of political borders and geography within cyberspace make the digital sublime an experience of awe and terror with no refuge. Alarm rather than elation accompanies predictions that the internet will usher in an age of zero privacy where all human behavior becomes data and is commodified. For those who herald "computer communication as the logical continuation of Enlightenment rationality" (Mosco 91), it is worth remembering that security and surveillance fit nicely into ideas of progress, as Foucault proposed. The Latin maxim *sapere aude* (dare to know!) that kicks off Kant's "What Is Enlightenment?" might also be seen as the motto of a security state that strives for infinite knowledge.

Unspeakable Terror

What if information leads not to illumination but to obscurity? If "intelligence ultimately is storytelling," it remains a question what mode of storytelling might be in play.

The gothic, a mode obsessed with secret intelligence acquired through whispers, glances, misdirected letters, long-lost manuscripts, and unpredictable encounters with print culture, transposes the informational sublime to narrative form. Often corrupted, frequently deficient, and always lacking transparency, these media stoke an impossible desire to know more, driving characters to incur greater risks and propelling readers to turn page after page. The sublime is an "overglutted sign" (Mishra 19) whose manifestation in gothic fiction stages a confrontation with excess and superabundance that induces a terrible but inexpressible crisis of subjectivity. Within "gothic sublimity" (Mishra), the subject crushed by an excess of information achieves neither exaltation nor epiphany in the end. Gothic sublimity instead represents a "version of the sublime utterly without transcendence" (Morris 306). Knowledge is at once promised and withheld by the mainstays of gothic fiction—secrets and surveillance—that make for emotionally charged storytelling suffused with terror and suspense. Affective intensity reaches such depths that gothic novels routinely resound with "the despair of the incommunicable" in ways that recall the sublime's tendency to leave the subject speechless (Sedgwick

18). If readers, according to Eve Kosofsky Sedgwick, "can predict" the gothic novel's "contents with unnerving certainty" (9), what is certain is that this perilous environment jeopardizes the security of information at every turn.

Creepy dungeons, supernatural events, and other stock features of the gothic novel produce unease, but at bottom it is information that frightens. Even though gothic tales routinely reveal some "unutterable" or "unspeakable" terror, Charles Brockden Brown's *Wieland; or the Transformation, an American Tale* (1798), as we will see in more detail, is strangely prolix when it comes to the topics of information, communication, and media. The hero of *Arthur Mervyn* speaks for many of Brown's characters when he says, "it was impossible to be incommunicative" (391). Kindred narrators such as Clara Wieland or Constantia Dudley in *Ormond* struggle to convey their surprise when they are rendered speechless by any number of instances of gothic horror. Brown's characters pore over other people's diaries, discover hidden letters, consult translations, scan newspapers, and become fixated by cultish religious tracts. As is typical for the gothic, scenes of doubling and repetition transform the lack of verifiable information into its opposite, namely an excess of information that characters and readers alike struggle to assimilate and understand.

Since the publication of Brown's *Wieland*, the fortunes and future of the American novel have been wrapped up with the gothic. "Until the gothic had been discovered, the serious American novel could not begin; and as long as that novel lasts, the gothic cannot die," wrote Leslie Fiedler (143), as though the gothic were itself some un-killable supernatural entity. Completed in short order during the spring and summer of 1798, *Wieland* fit a print landscape flooded by gothic titles coming from Europe. Quickly following with *Ormond; or, the Secret Witness* and *Edgar Huntly; or, Memoirs of a Sleep-Walker*, both in 1799, and then the two-part publication of *Arthur Mervyn; or, Memoirs of the Year 1793*, Brown made sizable contributions to the "outpouring of flamboyant Gothic fiction in the 1790s" (Watts xv). Swept up into this "vogue for the gothic" on both sides of the Atlantic (Roberts 29), Brown used novelistic form to engage philosophical anxieties about whether supposedly free individuals could trust in the rationality of an enlightened age or even their own perceptions. Heavily influenced by the currency of Locke's ideas in America, the "pervasive rationalism of his day" (Ringe 3) met its undoing in Brown's gothic fiction that exposed readers to characters paralyzed by what they see, hear, and, most crucially, read. Readers in the early United States did not need Freud to appreciate the capacity of literature to expose the mind's subterranean recesses. The horrors of live burial or immurement in dank dungeons, as in

Sedgwick's reading, are a recurrent gothic symptom of stories embedded within stories. Brown Americanized the gothic, transposing its features not merely to New World locales but also to frontiersmen, immigrant exiles, and other New World subjects. As early as 1815, a commentator appreciated that Brown "discard[ed] the hacknied machinery of castles, banditti and ghosts" associated with the European productions of Ann Radcliffe and Horace Walpole in favor of exploring a "mysterious" interior zone (Dunlap 12).

Writing and print culture seemed to Brown equally obscure and treacherous terrain.[4] Although Brown produced no formal or systematic study of information and its transmission, his gothic novels, above all *Wieland*, imply that every medium of communication, from public records such as newspapers and court transcripts to the human voice itself, is proximate to terror. Even the sentimental novels he wrote after the 1790s, which portray characters whose motivations and desires are transparent, insinuate that any and all information makes people vulnerable to fear and deception. Brown's recognition that each communicative act has the potential to bring subjects to the brink of terror is more than an uncanny anticipation of the epistemological crises that emerged with the advent of information age. Instead, I make the stronger—and provocatively anachronistic—claim that the gothic offers a competing account of information theory that casts doubts on the intelligibility of any and all communication. In commenting on messages, transmitters, and noise, Brown's intervention is not technical but aesthetic and humanistic: why does the communication of information make human beings feel unsafe and insecure?

Simple and straightforward acts of communication unhinge listeners and readers in *Wieland*, which is overburdened with letter writing, scenes of textual exegesis, and "vocalic surplus" (Sizemore 95). Notices in newspapers create fears of pursuit. Court proceedings are doled out bit by bit lest immediate and full disclosure overwhelm the recipient. One-word commands such as "hold!" incite extreme terror. Religious texts sear the soul instead of providing solace. Even silence is viewed as a type of aural communication that amounts to deception. "Brown's work has few peers in its almost obsessive attention to speaking, hearing, reading, and writing," summarizes Michael Gilmore (646). After tripping over a corpse that he will soon dispose of in fitting gothic fashion by carrying the murder victim to the cellar for a quick and clandestine burial, Arthur Mervyn sputters, "How to communicate my thoughts . . . I knew not" (84). The impossible desire to express the unspeakable and incommunicable aligns with the genre's conventions.

What is more surprising is that a rational, serious, and dry setting—that is to say, a secular temple devoted to textual scholarship and humanistic interpretation—can provoke terror. Consider a communicative scene where gentlemen scholars debate the wording of a classical text and failing to agree, they return to the original source. The task seems simple enough: hunt up the original, check the text, and resolve the discrepancy. But in the world of *Wieland* the endeavor soon turns gothic when the search throws the fundamentals of humanities inquiry—verifiability, rationalism, empiricism—into doubt. The novel sets out a scene that might be familiar to any academic. The novel describes a group of humanities scholars who enjoy a sort of endless sabbatical, discussing classical rhetoric and ancient texts without any care to labor or precarity. Clara Wieland describes her brother's rustic seminar in superlative terms: "no spot on the globe enjoyed equal security and liberty" as this secluded academy on her family's estate (35). Two more mentions of "security" quickly follow, but the delicate balancing of security and liberty that Franklin and Hamilton presented as a political tipping point is upset by what seems like innocuous and, if you will, boring humanities scholarship.[5] Theodore Wieland "was diligent in settling and restoring purity of the text. For this end, he collected all the editions and commentaries that could be procured, and employed months of severe study in exploring and comparing them" (23). Information becomes an obsession. The author in question is Cicero, an emblematic figure of virtue for a new nation that saw itself as a republic. "Brown's invocation of classical rhetoric as one of the binding forces of this little community of colonial gentry" (Rowe 30) applies more broadly to an American nation that measured itself against the standard of Roman republicanism. Neoclassical humanism in this context constitutes more than an academic exercise; it is also the basis for political authority. That authority depends on data collection, however quaint and scholarly, tracking down all citations and amassing textual variants.

Although Theodore Wieland is more an analog humanist than a digital one, his activities reflect a concern for security consistent with the drive to procure, gather, and compare information. His dutiful attention to the "purity of the text" at once strives to safeguard some intrinsic meaning and entails consulting variants and "commentaries" beyond the text.[6] What happens next is completely accidental but also a direct outcome of trying to aggregate information about Cicero's writings. Wieland's intense devotion to secular humanism, itself an ironic echo of his father's religious fanaticism that ends in spontaneous human combustion, leads to a prolonged chain of unreliable but still strangely authoritative communications. His "psychological fall from devoted father and pious classicist to homicidal lunatic" (Cahill 192) originates from textual inconsistencies in addition to mental ones. Trying to resolve a disagreement about Cicero, Wieland returns to the summerhouse for a book when a servant meets him with a letter describing a waterfall, which leads to talk of another letter describing another waterfall. The goal seems to be a cross-referencing of the sublime, comparing a European cataract with an American one. Wieland's search, jumping from "variant corrupt texts, to disputed quotation . . . to suddenly interpolated letter, to disputed recollection of the letter's contents" (Looby 165), ends in a disorienting sonic experience. Sublimity goes from merely being the content of communication to its medium when a disembodied voice commands Wieland and Pleyel to desist in their investigations. Awesome, mysterious, and unknowable, this voice produces "a thrilling, and not unpleasing solemnity" (32), not so much for what it says as for the attention it draws to communication itself as an always corrupted endeavor.

To be clear, the Latin volume Wieland is reading is hardly gothic, but, then again, the strange and unpredictable chain from Ciceronian rhetoric to biloquial utterance suggests that any text, simply by virtue of its communicative properties, leads to places unknown. His sister Clara recounts how debate over a fine point in classical rhetoric introduces the possibility of "misquotation" (28), prompting Wieland to return to his pastoral think tank for the book. But instead, he meets up with a letter that then has him retracing his steps to the temple promontory where he encounters an "auricular deception" (32). The information carried across this communication chain is raw and disparate, and it offers neither accord nor resolution about either Cicero or waterfalls. Instead from within the "bosom of security and luxury" (35) of the Wieland family's demesne, this information sets in motion a complex affective response that is expressly linked to both gothic storytelling and, in Clara's words, "that terror which is pleasing" (42). The original source should settle the matter of "misquotation." Comparison of multiple texts should help determine aesthetic judgments about sublime splendor. But in *Wieland* philology fails, spectacularly so. When Wieland and his friend Pleyel question the authority of the mysterious voice, the reply from the void insists that the news (about the death of a noblewoman across the ocean) is "from a source that cannot fail" (41). Neither can the volume of Cicero fail—until it does. Not unlike the unimpeachable textual authority that Wieland wants to summon but never does, the source behind this information remains incomplete, hidden, and suspect.[7]

A dearth of information in *Wieland* seems to pose a barrier to human understanding. Unreliable postal deliveries, impassable rivers, and other infrastructural obstacles in the early United States impeded basic communications. Brown, however, suggests something different: the problem of information is immanently conceptual, not just historical. Viewed as a proto-theorist of information, Brown questions the security of knowledge within Paine's vaunted "age of reason." His novels assess "the rise of an early information society" characterized by rapid transformations in which information appears "too shifting and unstable to be encompassed by print sources" (Margolis 344–45). Brown reverses an enduring and influential trajectory of historical interpretation that views public print communications as paving the way for the expansion of commerce, the diffusion of knowledge, and the progressive broadening of political liberty.[8] By falling out of step with this narrative, *Wieland* opens a path for a suspicious rereading of one of the signature texts of Enlightenment rationality, John Locke's *Essay Concerning Human Understanding* (1690).

Named by *The Guardian* as one of the hundred best nonfiction books of all time, Locke's *Essay* "could hardly be more topical today" (McCrum) when reason seems in short supply and empirical knowledge about election results and global temperatures has been actively dismissed by heads of state. And it was just as topical in Brown's day, as *Wieland*, a novel whose "primary assumption is vintage Locke" (Fliegelman 237), cautions against dangerous conclusions that may be derived from faulty sensory data—like taking a counterfeited voice to be the real thing or reading written words as the truth. Even as *The Guardian* wants to hold onto Locke as a beacon in our contemporary darkness, the gothic gloom that tints the informational sublime in Brown's novel retroactively unsettles Locke's ideas about cognition. Indeed, as Locke reflects on his frequent use of the word *idea* in the *Essay*, he explains its use as a substitute for a variety of words, including "phantasm" (20), to refer to whatever may be in people's minds.

For Locke, the question to ask about phantasmatic ideas is "how they come into the mind" in the first place (*Essay* 20). By a mixture of accident and deceit: Brown's answer to Locke's query reveals the extent to which information and communication frustrate Enlightenment rationality—despite that the expansion of print has been generally regarded as integral to the advancement of humanist knowledge and governmental transparency. Writing, print, and speech are precisely the problem in *Wieland*. "Let us then suppose the mind to be, as we say, white paper, void of all characters, without any ideas:—How comes it to be furnished?" runs Locke's famous image of the unimprinted mind (68). This pristine state never exists: it is not just that this white sheet is soon scrawled over with ideas and superstition but also that in Brown's world, papers are routinely misplaced, forgotten, secreted away, or, even worse, read without authorization or our consent. So, while readers have often noted Lockean accents in Brown's oeuvre, the reverse proposition that gothic suggestions worm their way into Lockean reason has rarely been entertained.

The *tabula rasa* might be better described as a *tabula tenebris*, its darkness a barrier to enlightenment. Locke's treatment of human understanding has obscure corners enough to insinuate that this magisterial monument to reason is also obsessed with its others, crowded with madmen, centaurs, changelings, and the "chimeras of men's brains" (447). Beneath the treatise lies a set of elusive tendencies that defy understanding; the rational subject that Locke describes seems at times trapped in its own gothic narrative. This assertion might be met with skepticism: the many associations between light and moral and intellectual illumination are more than figurative, as the *Essay Concerning Human Understanding* also draws on Newtonian physics to describe the particles that give light its material essence. Light, we might say, floods Locke's text in its goal of making the mind intelligible to itself. For all this clarity and optimism, he nonetheless is forced to admit that the mind is a "dark room." Even if our capacity for reflection opens the windows of understanding so that "light is let into this dark room" (116), the discomfiting possibility remains that the understanding hides secrets from itself. Locke tries to put a good face on this situation, averring that no matter what "keeps us so much in the dark to ourselves," we can find enough agreement about sounds and words to communicate our ideas to one another with some degree of confidence. But might not an incipient gothic effect be felt in the double negation that follows: "For, methinks, the understanding is not much unlike a closet wholly shut from light, with only some little openings left, to let in external visible resemblances, or ideas of things without: which, would they but stay there, and lie so orderly as to be found upon occasion, it would very much resemble the understanding of a man, in reference to all objects of sight, and the ideas of them" (116)? The *topos* of the dark closet and dark room, so common in the gothic, here appears an internal feature of our own mental landscape. What's more, once we attempt to move from thinking about simple ideas to complex ones, "we fall presently into darkness and obscurity" (232). The subject of Lockean rationalism seems beset by the psychic perils that also bedevil gothic heroes and heroines.

Stability reenters the picture with the long chapter "Of Power" in which Locke asserts that the human capacity for judgment rescues us from this darkness. It is not a divine force that lets light come into existence but the understanding. Locke writes, "Liberty is a power to act or not to act, according as the mind directs" (208); our mental sovereignty exercises command over liberty so that it becomes an internal and individual possession. Liberty, in essence, is not free but subject to the human mind and its capacity for judgment. This attitude requires that understanding precede liberty: the alternative, in Locke's estimation, "seems to me to place liberty in a state of darkness, wherein we can neither see nor say anything of it" (208). Lacking the light of thought and reflection, "no agent" is "allowed capable of liberty" (208). Not until Book III, "Of Words," does Locke spell out the consequences of incapable agents—persons impaired or acting duplicitously—who are also exercising liberty. Individuals who employ liberty prior to understanding create a crisis in signification, disrupting the fragile linguistic accords by which people communicate ideas to one another. There is no way, Locke asserts, for any person to convey what is "within his own breast, invisible and hidden from others" (204), without the use of words to externalize those thoughts and feelings. But because of the "inviolable liberty" we each have in selecting words to express our ideas, the danger emerges that words will be perverted, introducing "obscurity and confusion into whenever we make them [words] stand for anything but those ideas we have in our own minds" (309).

The Lockean subject, to invoke Siân Silyn Roberts, may be more accurately described as a "gothic subject." Locke's "defensive stance against any mode of thinking that undermines the principles of self-enclosure and internal coherency" associated with Enlightenment subjectivity proves vulnerable to gothic suggestions entering the mind "through the portal of the senses" (Roberts 13). For Brown, the senses seem especially at risk from print and writing. In the genteel society of philosopher-farmers depicted in *Wieland*, a servant can bring a letter at any moment or a newspaper can catch the unsuspecting eye. Sunny predictions about the American Enlightenment of 1750–1820 in which "widespread publication of ideas of correct ideas [would] make all of the difference in human history" (Ferguson 87) bump up against Brown's rude reminders that gothic messages can intrude without warning upon even the most idyllic scene.

The problem is not the familiar epistemological one about the limits of sensory perception; instead, an excess of textual stimuli and a glut of information vex—rather than facilitate—the project of human understanding. Whether one agrees that Brown's work displays "egregiously sloppy writing" or that "his prose carries the dispensations of print to extravagant lengths" (M. Gilmore 648), there is simply too much text in a book that is presented as though it were one single letter written by Clara Wieland. What's more, this epistolary performance that is coextensive with the novel itself makes mention upon mention of books sent from Germany, newspapers carried by ship captains, letters beset by "miscarriage" (37), and memoirs hidden in closets. If the central question of the novel is "how to establish the authority of information" (Levine, *Conspiracy* 27), then the surfeit of information that dwarfs the human capacity to sort, verify, interpret, and understand speech and written communication renders that question still more pressing and fraught. As a speculative anticipation of the gothic energies that haunt the underside of modern information theory, *Wieland* offers a peculiar history of the uncertainty and distortion that inevitably accompany enlightened, humanist communication.

A narrative about transatlantic print production and reception, the novel (which surely falls into the category of material that it scrutinizes) is filled with the suspicion that writing does more than convey intelligence, deepen knowledge, or simply provide news. Books and newspapers appeal to characters in ways that defy rational explanation. The history of the Wieland family takes a decisive turn when the paterfamilias encounters a book by an obscure religious sect. Not much of a reader, the elder Wieland "entertained no relish for books, and was wholly unconscious of any power they possessed to delight or instruct" (7). By chance, this volume that "had lain for years in a corner of his garret, half buried in dust and rubbish" (7), gets reactivated by no discernible logic or intention. Books are not about human agency. Brown's doomed characters do not consult texts because they want information or diversion. Instead, some inexplicable force draws them to the text. As the elder Wieland becomes a reader, he becomes a deranged symptom of transatlantic print culture: born in Saxony, migrating to London, attracted to an obscure book by an obscure French Protestant sect, and, finally, impelled to become a missionary spreading the Word of the gospel to the Indigenous peoples of North America, he becomes as combustible as the paper of the texts he reads. Not for nothing did Kant in "What Is Enlightenment?" cite falling back on "a book that thinks for me" as an example of self-imposed tutelage. In his first contact with a dormant book, Wieland *père* mistakes print culture as a genuine source of illumination. After reading this religious text for a while "he regretted the decline of light which obliged him for the present to close it" (8), a not-so-subtle indication that books may not be messengers of Enlightenment, after all.

No matter their dubious status, books, manuscripts, newspapers, and letters assuredly do provide information to Brown's characters that wander the transatlantic world and come variously to settle, hide, or reinvent themselves in

America. The source of that information may flow from God or it may spring from the deceptions of an unscrupulous ventriloquist—or, still yet, it may be immanent to print itself. Books, not the least of which are *Wieland* and the other specimens of Brown's corpus, regularly fail to provide illumination and, along with all the other vehicles such as letters and newspapers that provide intelligence, stand counterpoised to enlightenment. This tension cuts across Brown's dark take on communication in the eighteenth-century transatlantic world, and it also suggests why the informational sublime continues to pose a problem for security in our own age of terror. To allow these two temporally distinct idioms to bleed into one another is to begin to wonder what lies in the gothic cellar of information theory.

A Gothic Theory of Communication

Over lunch in the cafeteria of Bell Labs, the British mathematician Alan Turing (who had cracked "unbreakable" Nazi code) and the American mathematician Claude E. Shannon (who had written influential papers on cryptography) chatted about information overabundance. A core question that emerged from their conversations, as James Gleick has characterized it, was "how to measure all this *stuff*" (214). The stuff in question was information, but the possibility that it also could be noise complicated attempts to produce algorithms for understanding the information transmitted by wire, voice, or other media. Shannon's research on this problem earned him acclaim as "the father of information theory." His breakthrough applied principles of thermodynamics, especially entropy as a measure of uncertainty, to communication. Its potential for surveillance and secrecy was clear from the outset: calculating the range of possible messages that can be sent relies on similar principles as the effort "to track an airplane and to compute its probable future positions" (Shannon and Weaver 3). Such information, of course, would be of immense value to anyone programming a "guided missile" in pursuit of this airplane (3). That Shannon had preceded this paper with another, "A Mathematical Theory of Cryptography," suggests that connections between a secrecy system and an information system are closer than at first thought.[9]

In 1948, Shannon contributed two historic papers to the *Bell System Technical Journal* that presented the amount of information ("all this *stuff*") as a mathematical function—specifically, a logarithm—of all the possibilities that might exist for message. For a simple message that conveys either a "yes" or "no," like any system of binary code, he proposed that $H = \log_2 N$ where H is "the quantity of information" and N is "the number of possible states of the message" (Paulson 55).[10] As the "translator" of Shannon's theory, Warren Weaver acknowledged that people might get thrown by this equation: "It doubtless seems queer, when one first meets it, that information is defined as the *logarithm* of the number of choices" (Shannon and Weaver 10). This feeling of queerness intimates that the aesthetics of information are as significant as the mathematics. What exactly is disorienting about a logarithm? As an exponential function, a logarithm simply registers how information increases exponentially. But that simplicity belies a more complex affective state that must deal with the propensity of information to grow. The statistical approach to communication necessarily entails an aesthetic component that is wrapped up with the capacity of information to accumulate, to dwarf its users, and to become sublime.

By showing how massive amounts of information might be quantified, Shannon "single-handedly launched classical information theory" (Collins), pioneering developments that are now considered the foundation of modern communications essential to everything from email to cell phones. In the words of his recent biographers, "every email we have ever sent, every DVD and sound file we have ever played, and every Web page we have ever seen loaded bears a debt to Claude Shannon" (Soni and Goodman xii). Beginning with Weaver, who in 1964 collaborated with Shannon to publish *The Mathematical Theory of Communication*, writers have helpfully simplified Shannon's equations for non-specialists. I want to ask both how this translation of mathematical formulae to lay terms reveals some gothic undertones within information theory and, just as crucially, how *Wieland* might be repurposed as a significant commentary on the aesthetics of information that tends to get overlooked in discussions dominated by technological or policy matters.

Information theory tends to treat information as though it is clear and unadulterated at the outset, an attitude not unlike the manner in which Wieland *fils* trusts in the original of Cicero. According to this model, distortion only makes its way into the communication chain in the process of transmission when unwanted noise is added to the message. *The Mathematical Theory of Communication* lays out a linear schematic that tracks a message from its "information source" to its "receiver" and "destination." But a "noise source" not located on this trajectory, seemingly external to the system itself, interrupts and intrudes upon the message somewhere between the sender and recipient. Noise enters printed texts, telegraph messages, and faxes as typographical errors, smudges, creases, and the like. Radios pick up static and analog TV sets at one time were interrupted by random patterns called "snow." Today cell phone calls can sound eerie due to an echo effect in which callers hear their own voices, inviting plenty of internet speculation about whether this experience of audio discomfort means that someone is tapping into phones. All these effects are added to the message at later stages *after* it leaves the "information source" at the start of the chain. Brown's gothic novel, however, points to a concern of a different order: not only is a message never secure from tampering or what Weaver called "unwanted additions" (7), but it is also always potentially corrupted at its origin.

In the wake of deconstruction, the notion that sending a message, like any linguistic action, might be interrupted by noise from the start might be familiar enough to literary critics. From this vantage, the language that is most burdened by noise is also most enriched by it: literature. Building off Shannon as well as Paul de Man, William Paulson posits that the noise within a message constitutes its literariness. What others might ignore as noise, literary critics treat as "information" that "can bring us to more subtle forms of understanding, because it is the unexpected" (Paulson 99). Noise equates to nuance and complexity, revealing new possibilities of meaning that escape not just our intentions but also the more circumscribed range of meaning that abides social normativity. Perhaps I don't intend to be rude, but my tone gives offense. Perhaps I don't mean to confess my crime, but my words give me away. In the words of Carwin, "Who can betray me but myself" (281)? Hardly a deconstructionist, Weaver in translating Shannon's equations for lay readers felt compelled to acknowledge that noise may intrude upon messages in several ways. If given the opportunity, Weaver stated that he would amend Shannon's original schematic and relabel the "noise source" in figure 4.1 as "engineering

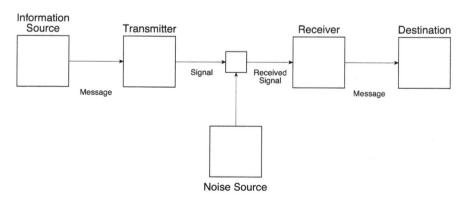

FIGURE 4.1. Shannon's theory of sending information as a message.

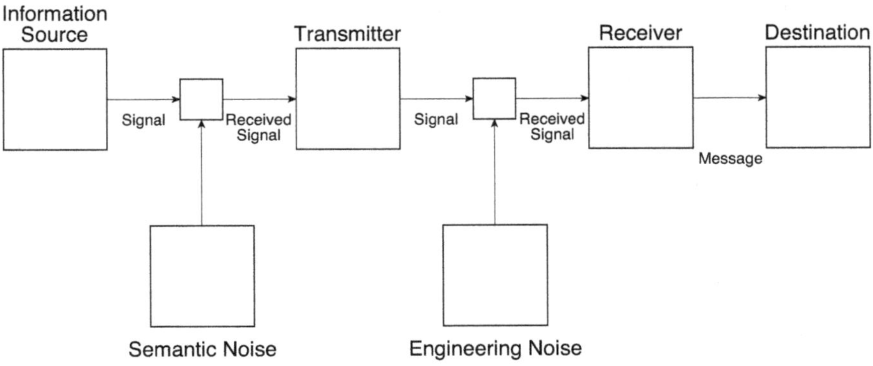

FIGURE 4.2. Weaver's emendation to Shannon's account.

noise" to allow for static or other distortion. Next, a new box, labeled "semantic noise," would be added to the diagram, placed between the information source and transmitter to register "the perturbations or distortions of meaning which are not intended by the source" (26) but nonetheless affect how the message is received, decoded, and understood at the other end of this communication chain.[11] (Taking up Weaver's cues, I offer figure 4.2 as an emendation of the initial schematic for a mathematical theory of communication.) Overall, though, Weaver adheres to the temporal lag that structures Shannon's theory of communication by proposing that semantic noise only comes into play *after* information leaves its source.

The gothic theory of communication that might be adduced from Brockden Brown is both shorter and less linear. Even though characters in *Wieland* hear voices and receive letters, the suspicion is that ultimately there may be no outside vectors that distort information because it is already corrupted at its source. Rather than a linear schematic moving along an orderly temporal progression (first a message is sent and then it is received), this representation suggests that communication is part of a media "environment" that is not easily tamed as are "logical systems of structures" (Mitchell 203). There's little rhyme and certainly no reason to how people communicate with books and other texts in Brown's world. Doing nothing in particular in his cluttered London flat, Wieland's father looks about the room and "his eye was attracted by a page of this book, which, by some accident, had been opened and placed full in his view" (8). Variations of this scene are repeated in the novel, as characters "glancing carelessly round" (183) suddenly and without reason fixate on private correspondence and diaries. The insistence on the passive in this account of reading suggests that human beings have little control over the information they seek. Even more disturbing, in *Memoirs of Carwin, the Biloquist*, the unfinished prequel to *Wieland*, Brown raises the possibility that it is not people who interpret books but rather books that interpret people. As Carwin gains access to the study of his Illuminati mentor, he considers that the "private book-cases contained" volumes that will penetrate the "impenetrable secrecy" that Ludloe otherwise maintains. Books "cannot fail of letting in some little light upon his secret thoughts." Books may be the message, but Ludloe—like all readers—becomes the information that is revealed. Carwin is as misguided a child of the Enlightenment as the elder Wieland: both trust too much in books as sources of illumination. The metaphor of light as understanding is, of course, faulty. Returning to the religious book that inspires Wieland, the phrase "seek and ye shall find" (8) jumps out at him, but it offers neither assurance nor guarantee about what might be found. Like Wieland, do we know what we will dredge up from our searches? Do we know what results, either actual or metaphysical, our searches will yield?

Clear answers are not readily forthcoming when information is perceived as sublime and communication as gothic. In *An Essay Concerning Human Understanding*, Locke hoped to set the "bounds between the enlightened and dark parts of things, between what is, and what is not comprehensible by us" (20), but the inhabitants of Brown's transatlantic world have little success in this regard. Clara initially seems inspired with a formidable supply of Lockean optimism in offering her tale as a contribution to human understanding: "If it be communicated to the world, it will inculcate the duty of avoiding deceit" (5). Her stipulation echoes Locke's advice to readers that people should give wide berth to the "dark parts of things" lest they "wander into those depths where they can find no sure footing" (20). But Clara proves to be a better student of Burke, who disputed "Mr. Locke's opinion, that darkness is not naturally an idea of terror" and saw empiricism as no match for the uncertainty that at every moment and in every direction surrounds us in darkness (30). The opposition between rationality and terror may be overstated. Nestled within the "darker implications of Locke's psychology" lies a mentality "stressed to its own limits" (Weiskel 14, 17) and bruised by its inability to grasp what is at the fringes of perception. Terror like Clara's is not the antithesis of the Lockean faith in reason but its inexorable—might we say "logical"?—result.

For Clara, it is precisely communication that creates uncertainty and erodes a sense of security. Seeking and finding in *Wieland* leads not to revelation but to distressing encounters with obscurity and noise. Clara retrieves a manuscript "which contained the most secret transactions of my life" and "this being secured," she is set to depart when she once again is plunged into "obscurity" and surrounded by a "darkness [that] suited the color of my thoughts" (177). Such incautious moves, precipitated by contact with writing and print, replay what seems to be a family pathology. After leaving Europe to evangelize among American Indian tribes, the elder Wieland proves too timid to venture into wilderness and never responds to the call of becoming a missionary. Nor does he become what we might call a trans-missionary since he never transmits the Word, insisting on complete seclusion in making his religious devotions. His prayer has no recipient other than God, who, as far as we know, does not reply, instilling doubt about whether his message ever reaches its destination. In a still more mysterious episode of transmission, Carwin, the biloquist, avers that he did not deceive Wieland into committing his horrible deeds. Carwin has no problem admitting when he has introduced "noise" to a message, for instance, inserting the false tidbit that the "Baroness de Stolberg is dead" (39) into the information he has gleaned from reading a letter left behind at the temple. In the case of the murders, however, Carwin repeatedly swears that he has played no part, leaving the conclusion that the deception is innate to Wieland's supposedly rational system of thought (or that some supernatural force indeed instructed him to commit these heinous acts).[12] Amid these extremities, information and noise become indistinguishable from one another.

Events in *Wieland* fit a theory of communication that muddles Shannon's linear diagram that tracks a message from its point of origin to its destination. A *gothic theory of communication* (as opposed to Shannon's mathematical theory of communication) gets rid of the outside "noise source" that interrupts the message in its transit from its source to its destination (see figure 4.3). But it does not do away with noise altogether and instead understands noise as part of the process from the get-go. No hard-and-fast distinction between "information source" and "noise source" can be made. Noise is always buried deep within information. In this gothic diagramming of information, no reason explains why people are drawn to texts. Seeking and finding hardly seem like intentional activities and, what's more, the implicit link between the two is rendered more doubtful than ever. "Some instinct induced me to lay my hand upon a newspaper" (119), says Pleyel in an effort to explain how he learns that Carwin is a hunted fugitive not to be trusted. This explanation explains nothing other than the fact that Pleyel is no more able to account for his textual attractions

FIGURE 4.3. A "gothic theory of communication."

than anyone else. In another scene of unaccountable textual attraction, Pleyel confesses that "my eye glanced almost spontaneously upon the paper" (115) of Clara's diary in a halfhearted attempt to exculpate snooping on his friend's innermost thoughts. His reward is a partial, hurried reading, making the diary the source of misinformation and conjecture about Clara's virtue. Reading here is not all that different from the invasion of privacy, the niceties of the Fourth Amendment neatly cast aside. Clara proves susceptible to the same condition: "What was it that suggested the design of perusing my father's manuscript?" she wonders (86), effectively repeating her parent's pathology in being drawn inexplicably to enigmatic texts.

A little bit of information goes a long way—not in providing any clarity but in fueling the search for more information, more seeking in the hopes of finding. Pleyel acknowledges that he "caught only parts of sentences" (115) when he spies over Clara's shoulder, which is more than enough to persuade him that more surveillance will enable him to understand the whole. And so he sneaks up to the summerhouse at midnight in order to listen in on Carwin and a woman, whom he assumes is Clara, having sex. In the darkness, "hearing was the only avenue to information" (125), but for Pleyel it suffices because this intelligence fits with what he has learned from transatlantic dispatches reprinted in the Philadelphia newspapers. The article he reads in the American press, reprinted from a British paper, impels more searching: "it occurred to me, that though the information I possessed was, in one sense, sufficient, yet if more could be obtained, more was desirable" (120). The news item about Carwin, even if authoritative and complete, nonetheless motivates a search for additional reports, whether to satisfy curiosity or supply corroboration. Yet adding more details, acquiring more data, and securing more intelligence fail to uncloud Locke's "dark parts of things" that limit human understanding.

A similar impulse seized Brown himself, who completed *Wieland* and then later began working on serial installments of *Memoirs of Carwin*, whose plot hinges on the mania for information. In his relationship with his shadowy benefactor, Carwin "must determine to disclose every fact in his history, and every secret of his heart . . . and must continue to communicate, at stated seasons, every new thought, and every new occurrence. . . . This confidence was to be absolutely limitless" (263). Critical self-examination becomes indistinguishable from gothic surveillance. Information is always in need of supplementation even when it is, as Pleyel declares about the newspaper story, "sufficient." To return to the biblical verse that animates Wieland's fanaticism, finding does not put an end to seeking. Instead, finding only drives more seeking.

The countermeasure to terror, especially when this sensation is provoked by some indistinct apprehension of the unknown, is often assumed to lie in the collection of more information. Enveloped by the darkness, we are "forced to pray for light" (E. Burke 30). With more data comes more knowledge, illuminating what had been obscure. But there is never enough information; there is only, paradoxically, too much information—and too much to process and too much to assemble into a coherent story. The more information Pleyel uncovers, the more horrified he is by the false proofs of Clara's sexual perfidy. The more evidence Clara receives from her senses, the more inarticulate she becomes. "My terror kept me mute," she says (128). She realizes the futility of enlightening her fellow humanist who is also her off-and-on love interest: "all my conversations and letters, affords me no security" (108) from Pleyel's suspicions. Her realization might diagnose the communication anxiety that pervades the novel as a whole. Prized volumes about Ciceronian rhetoric produce confusion. Misplaced letters enable deception. Voices confound hearers. Newspapers deepen distrust. In short, information affords no security and, in fact, imperils the sense of safety. The reasons, as we have seen, are several: the restless search for more information; the glut of data received but also its incompleteness; and, above all, the "noise" and uncertainty that are endemic to information.

Information is closely associated with uncertainty. In an effort to describe how such uncertainty might be measured, Shannon borrowed the concept of entropy from thermodynamics to calculate the amount of randomness and range of meanings that accompany any message. Uncertainty resides within all information as the possible number of messages that can be sent and received. When a message is predictable or known in advance, when there is no uncertainty, the message supplies no information. A helpful—and prototypically American—example that Gleick provides is the intel about British troop movements transmitted from the steeple of the Old North Church in Boston by the number of lanterns. In this simple scenario from 1775, two possible messages exist ("one if by land, two if by sea"), and this fundamental uncertainty is the precondition for communicating information. In contrast, "if only one message is possible, there is no uncertainty and thus no information" (Gleick 219). A courtroom where "only one answer is really conceivable" to the question, "Do you solemnly swear to tell the whole truth?" conveys "almost no new information—we could have guessed it beforehand" (Soni and Goodman 142).

A different and more complex scenario, say, trying to decode messages sent by a German enigma machine during World War II, has a much greater degree of entropy, but nonetheless the uncertainty is "still susceptible to statistical analysis," as Turing famously proved (Gleick 218). In this way, a mathematical theory of communication is also a theory of uncertainty.

When Weaver translated Shannon's research at Bell Labs, the explanation took shape as an analogy suited to the era's fantasies about gender and technology: "communication theory is just like a very proper and discreet girl accepting your telegram. She pays no attention to the meaning, whether it be sad, or joyous, or embarrassing. But she must be prepared to deal with all that come to her desk" (Shannon and Weaver 27). The expectation for a modern communication system is no different, and like this feminine embodiment of discretion, it "ought to try to deal with all possible messages" no matter the content—and certainly without gossiping about that content. Perhaps inspired by the unnamed telegraphist in Henry James's *In the Cage*, the girl's femininity makes her the perfect transmitter since her indifference ensures that no noise is added to the message. In contrast to what Weaver saw as the queerness of Shannon's algorithm, this "discreet girl"/communication system seems unfazed by the message's semantic meaning. The heroine of this brief example is in no way gothic since she exhibits neither trembling nor desire, remaining unruffled by unpredictability. Her passivity makes her the ideal conduit and nothing more. Neither excited nor paralyzed with fear, she is immune to the gothic problem of trying to communicate inexpressible terror.

But what if that girl is Clara Wieland? What if that girl is a "story-teller" who produces "enjoyably terrible and deliberately obscure pleasures" (Galluzzo 262) that take shape as the first gothic American novel? The aesthetic intensity of Clara's somatic responses to the information she receives, her trembling, her aphasia, and her despair, all challenge Shannon's presentation of "information as a probability function with no dimensions, no materiality. . . . It is a pattern, not a presence" (Hayles 18). That is, in place of a mathematical approach to communication, a mode for understanding communication as gothic is rooted in the suspicion that information is incomplete and unstable at its source and made less secure the more it accumulates and the more it becomes attached to particular embodiments. This decidedly eighteenth-century approach listens for the hints of queerness within communications systems that are typically ignored as so much noise. While Clara might not exhibit the equanimity and calm of the discreet office girl, she does share with her a profound insight about information: the content of the message ultimately is not as important as the otherwise unnoticeable contrivances and accords that enable communication in a presumably enlightened era.

The novel sets about violating the normative behaviors of human understanding in which "the understanding, like the eye, whilst it makes us see and perceive all other things, takes no notice of itself" (Locke, *Essay* 17). Clara is not so sure about this supposition since the media that inform her understanding are a constant source of *apprehension* in both senses of the word, as a feeling of misgiving and as the capacity to grasp an idea or concept. *Wieland* examines what happens when the understanding does, in fact, take notice of itself, insinuating a challenge to Locke's investigation of how the mind operates. The path is self-reflexive and dizzying, drawing attention away from the content of information toward the medium of its own conveyance. Media scholars such as Lisa Gitelman and Niklas Luhmann have suggested that communication depends on our *not* recognizing the media that facilitate communication. Built into our experience with media is a "structural amnesia" (Gitelman 7) that allows us to forget that communication requires an intervening medium such as a letter or a telephone.[13] Of mass media, Luhmann writes that "we have to observe their observing" in order to overcome the "transcendental illusion" (*Reality* 4) that allows them to appear as unfiltered reality. As N. Katherine Hayles points out, "the page from the *Bell Laboratories Journal* on which Shannon's equations are printed" remains a medium in spite of the fact that one effect of Shannon's work has been to sever information from its materially embodied forms (13). "The success of all media depends at some level on inattention or 'blindness' to the media technologies themselves," according to Gitelman (6). The trick, then, is to perceive what is invisible, to see the media that lies in our blind spot. But how can something "be made visible which must remain invisible to itself" (Luhmann, *Reality* 121)?

Any effort in this direction confronts what Luhmann calls "an injunctive paradox" (*Reality* 121) that prohibits the eye from seeing itself, that keeps us from observing how we observe. Luhmann is writing about mass media, and we should remember that gothic novels, no matter how popular they might have been in eighteenth-century America, are not produced or disseminated as radio or television are. Then again, Luhmann also remarks that the question of second-order observation arises independently of the mass media, as Locke's philosophical reflections at the outset of the *Essay Concerning Human Understanding* surely suggest.[14] He points to the Romantic fascination with "doppelgängers, twins, reflections" that "represent the transformation of identity into communication" (Luhmann, *Reality* 114). Plays and novels afford audiences the opportunity to witness how the secrets of identity are communicated via soliloquies, internal dialogues, and other contrivances. When that communication is simultaneously propelled and derailed by gothic twists, as it is in *Wieland*, the project of gathering information and knowledge, no more so than in pursuit of self-understanding, descends into terror. As Clara reflects on the mysterious aural communications that leave her trembling, she exclaims, "How had my ancient security vanished!" (56).

Whenever terror seizes Clara, she steps aside from the flow of her narrative to observe her own writing practices. Or, perhaps more accurately, each time that she pauses to think about the account she is writing and to observe her own observing, she is thrown into terror. She experiences this shock on at least three separate occasions. First, as she basks in her brother's humanist knowledge, assured that "the world would have accepted a treatise" on the Daemon of Socrates "from his hand," she breaks off and turns her narration to the present time and space of her own writing (45). "My blood is congealed: and my fingers are palsied," she exclaims. Having reached the moment when Carwin appears in her story, her trepidation ostensibly arises from remembering the fateful chain of events linked to the deceiver. But what stokes her initial interest in Carwin is the "sketch upon paper" (49) that she executes of his countenance and then stays up "half the night" (50) fantasizing about the portrait in her bedroom. Not the biloquist himself but the examination of the media she uses to represent him places her in the vertiginous position of trying, in Locke's terms, to enable her eye to observe itself. A second moment comes as she leads up to the discovery of her sister-in-law's murdered body. Her present writing anticipates the shock she is set to narrate: "my fingers are enervated . . . my language is faint" (135). Once more she is brought to the brink of an expressive abyss as she communicates "incommunicable sentiments" (135). In this state, she interrupts the flow of her narrative and warns her reader that "abruptnesses, and dark transitions" (135) will mar her account, which is itself an abrupt, if not a dark, transition. As Clara writes about her own writing, the action of the story is "displaced by the process of uttering itself," a recursive strategy that Mark Seltzer finds symptomatic of the novel's fixation with books (83). A note from Carwin warning that she is about to behold "a sight so horrible" (137) heightens her alarm, not for what it says but because its ink is still wet, suggesting that Carwin lingers nearby and is perhaps at that very moment of her reading creeping up behind her. Seized a third time by the mania of writing about her own writing, Clara announces that she will die when she puts down her pen and ends her story. "A few words more and I lay aside the pen for ever" (202), she declares, but like a true obsessive she goes on for three more chapters—and when is all done Brown himself goes on by providing a prequel from the biloquist's perspective in *Memoirs of Carwin*.

What is far from clear, however, is whether any of these endeavors of the eye to see itself, to write about writing, and to understand human understanding can provide clarity about ourselves. More likely, these efforts generate more noise and distortion, what Luhmann calls "irritations" (*Reality* 7), that are routinely folded into self-reproducing media systems. But not always. While "it is conventional to assume that humans can communicate," in strict actuality "humans cannot communicate; not even their brains can communicate" directly with one another since a medium is always required (Luhmann, "How Can the Mind" 371). Locke, too, had his doubts that the "thoughts of men's minds [might] be conveyed from one to another" and regrets that many ideas, especially ones with the potential to instruct or delight, frequently are "invisible and hidden from others" (*Essay* 304, 307). Worse still, these potentially enlightening ideas cannot be intuitively apprehended or immediately (read: without media) understood since thoughts cannot "of themselves be made to appear." Some other medium—air for vibration, language for words, ink for texts—is needed, but "when it [the mind] becomes visible, it becomes disruptive, just as the strong whoosh and whistle of the air inside a car traveling at high speed disrupts words of communication" (Luhmann, "How Can the Mind" 378). Clara Wieland experiences this disruption at her core when after writing about writing, she reflects, "I stand aside, as it were, from myself" (203). Should her claim be believed, which, after all, is itself interrupted by the subjunctive ("as it were") to mark its status as supposition? When it comes to communication media, standing aside is a fantasy. As Gitelman contends, getting "outside" (20) of media is practically, if not conceptually, impossible when the formulation of such an external account in Brown's world requires intense scrutiny of pens, paper, and other tools used for self-expression. The example Gitelman gives of such inescapable reflexivity is the impossible project of writing a history of the World Wide Web without resorting to the resources, archives, and links of the Web itself. Clara's example is similar but only more gothic: information about the self is always bound by the medium of its own existence.

This heady observation about the self does not pretend to pass as a metaphysical conclusion. It might better be taken as a materialist description of information and media. "However commonplace it is to think of information as separable from" or "uninformed by media" (Gitelman 7), the stuff that gets communicated is always determined by the mode of its communication.

Luhmann's assertion represents a radical condensation of this idea: "only communication can communicate" ("How Can the Mind" 371). The upshot of this sibylline pronouncement is that neither half-formed thoughts nor full-blown ideas can circulate without a medium. Yet any medium must also have enough transparency to allow us to forget that it is there. "Sentences that are thought and spoken are only parts of a process that disappear at the moment of their generation. They are constitutively unstable. Their accumulation would very quickly lead to uncontrolled complexity, that is, chaos. Just imagine the noise that would result if spoken words did not fade away but remained audible!" writes Luhmann ("How Can the Mind" 379). Biloquism in *Wieland* represents an eerie twist on this formulation: what if words appeared in two places at once, three, if you count their reappearance in Clara's letters, four if you count the novel, and so on? We misread if we dwell upon "content without attending to the medium that . . . communicates that content" and, in the process, shapes what can be thought and expressed (Gitelman 7). The gothic nature of Brown's novel draws unwanted attention to media that would otherwise remain invisible. Clara's narrative-as-letter refuses to let the noise fade away in its compulsive return to the medium of its own narration.

Wieland obsesses over authorship but not in the familiar sense of a specifically literary identity in the early United States. Instead, the fixation on authors and writing disallows the structural amnesia that is necessary to smooth communication. In thematic terms, Brown "attempts to make visible complex modes of communication" (Margolis 362). In terms of style, this refusal might explain Brown's verbal excess that "carries the dispensations of print to extravagant lengths" (M. Gilmore 648). It certainly explains Clara's many locutions about people being the "authors" of events, outcomes, and narratives. She identifies Carwin as "the author of this black conspiracy" (174) and later accuses him directly, "Thou art the author of these horrors!" (208). Attributions of authorship would seem to clear up the mystery by identifying a single malevolent agent as the guilty party. Yet assurances that the malefactor behind a conspiracy can be brought to light become uncertain in the next breath, as Clara acknowledges that the "relief" found when an "author is discovered or imagined" may, in fact, only be illusory. When she presses her uncle to learn why her brother languishes in a prison cell, he asks her, "Shall I make him the narrator of his own tale?" (149). The scenario is gothic in more ways than one: Wieland, the murderer, sits in a dark hole with the sole ambition of escaping to kill his sister while at the same time this odd estrangement from his own tale hints at an array of intervening institutions and media:

medical authorities such as her uncle, legal documents, signed confessions, and, of course, letters. Beyond simply the criminal court and the written text of her brother's confession, the screen or barrier between Wieland and his own narrative invites the darker possibility that human beings are always hidden from others. As a communications theorist, Brown deepens this gothic undercurrent by implying that the information we seek is hidden from not only others but ourselves.

A gothic theory of communication meets with at least one serious obstacle, however. From its first page, Luhmann's *The Reality of Mass Media* would seem to invalidate the untimely gambit of using Brown's novel to understand the sublime terror that comes with too much data and media information. "Unlike in the gothic novels of the eighteenth century" where readers encounter "someone secretly pulling strings behind the scenes," the system of modern media, Luhmann argues, is not orchestrated by nefarious villains cloaked in deceit and intrigue (1). Even though Brown's literary environment has its share of evildoers and conspirators, the real culprit is the distinctively aesthetic combination of pleasure and terror wrapped up in the recursive effort to understand human understanding. Who tells Wieland to murder his family? Who burns the paterfamilias to a crisp? In terms of media communication, "the answer to 'Who's behind it?' may also be 'Ourselves'" (Mitchell 221). If mass media, as Luhmann asserts, constitute a self-reproducing system that produces and then validates its own reality, no doubt producing "the headache endemic to recursive thinking" (Mitchell 215), then *Wieland* ruptures this system by reminding us of all the background noise, normally transparent protocols, and unforeseen accidents that we forget in communicating information.

~~Digital~~ Gothic Humanities: A Postscript

Not long after publishing *Wieland*, Brown would abandon the gothic in a conscious effort to communicate more easily with readers. He veered away from terror and sublimity (and their capacity to rupture self-reproducing systems of communication) in favor of sentimentality. Perhaps the gothic as method too much resembled exhumation, leading him to renounce dark schemes and shady characters for a world of light and transparency. After his brother complained about "the gloominess and out-of-nature incidents" in his novels, Brown promised, "I shall not fall hereafter into that strain" and set about "dropping the doleful tone and assuming a cheerful one" (qtd. in Ringe 433).

The immediate result was *Clara Howard; In a Series of Letters* (1801), an epistolary love story of frustrated desire that in the end is resolved with none of the entombments, murders, or other gothic scenes because the characters have no ulterior motives. The novel, William Dunlap suggested in 1822, features a "regular plan" (142) whose sensible grounding makes for a sort of anti-sublime. Heartfelt communication requires full disclosure and openness about the most cherished desires. The prefatory note to the correspondence that constitutes the novel promises, "The inclosed letters, which I have put into a regular series, contain all the information you wish. The pacquet is a precious one; you will find in it, a more lively and exact picture of my life, than is possible, by any other means, to communicate" (*CH* 3). Such devotion to full transparency governs the ensuing events, as the characters exchange information and share letters in order to untangle a messy love triangle. "She shall not be deceived" (*CH* 113), avows the male suitor, as he endeavors to discourage the unwanted affection of another woman. Meanwhile, writing to his true love, he yearns for a state of pure information free of interference or artifice: "I hope that this is the last letter I shall have occasion to write to you. The next time I shall address you, will be through no such wild and ambiguous medium" (*CH* 116). Lovers wish that they could be in the presence of their beloveds without delay and receive reassuring looks now as opposed to suffering the slowness of the mails for a reply. This desire for immediate and unmediated presence represents more than affective longing; it is best understood as a plea to remain untouched by the accidents of media in which newspapers fall by chance into people's hands, letters are forgotten in desks, and rumors unsettle the characters in the transatlantic world of *Clara Howard*. The novel as a whole yearns for a type of anti-gothic communication—critics have frequently considered it a botched attempt at a sentimental novel—that requires no search for hidden motives, no skepticism, in short, no information to be parsed or decoded. The fact that the heroine of *Clara Howard* shares her first name with the narrator of *Wieland* suggests the extent to which the heroine of Brown's 1801 sentimental novel is both the twin and alternative to the heroine who narrates his 1798 gothic tale. In effect, Clara finally lives up to the etymology of her name, *clarus*, meaning "bright" or "clear."

In my efforts as a humanities scholar, I sought more information about this seldom studied but often dismissed novel. But in the process had I become like Theodore Wieland consulting editions of Cicero? The information I received took on a dark and confusing aspect. For me, at least, things quickly became mysterious, paranoid, and obscure when I tried to use the methods of

Digital Humanities to access this work generally esteemed as "the weakest of all Brown's novels," a joyless example of "overwrought sentimentalism" (Watts 134). The goal here is not to launch a crusade to reevaluate *Clara Howard* so that it can take its place alongside *Wieland, Arthur Mervyn, Edgar Huntly,* and *Ormond*. Instead, my purpose is to relate one final episode about the misfortunes of seeking and finding information. I offer a bit of narrative that explains why the subtitle to this subsection strikes through the ~~digital~~ in order to signal how our interactions with data are less straightforward and more gothic than we might otherwise believe. If not coming completely full circle, the idea is to indulge in a bit of anachronism by using Brockden Brown's 1801 novel as a reflection on digital searching. The gambit entails a coda in the shape of a story of my own.

I first learned that Brown wrote an unsuccessful sentimental novel by analog means in reading Emory Elliott's 1994 introduction to *Wieland*, which mentions *Clara Howard; or the Enthusiasm of Love*. This racy subtitle—Leslie Fiedler's complaint that the book is a "sentimental novel without seduction" (152) notwithstanding—was appended after a pirated British edition appeared in 1807 with the title *Philip Stanley; or, the Enthusiasm of Love*. The texts are virtually identical save for the fact that the name of the male suitor at the center of the love triangle changes from Edward Hartley to Philip Stanley. The titles of subsequent American editions became something of a mash-up in *Clara Howard; or the Enthusiasm of Love* (editions and reprints published in 1827, 1857, 1859, 1887, 1963, and 1970), with Philip Stanley all the while remaining the hero. Not until 1986 was the confusion cleared up.[15] At this point, however, I did not know the full textual history, and had only the title given by Elliott, which I promptly sought to retrieve digitally. My search result yielded a link to a facsimile of the 1807 London edition. When I first tried to access this online source, my computer went into panic mode and sent me a code-red alert: "The site ahead contains malware. Attackers currently on exlibris might attempt to install dangerous programs on your Mac that steal or delete your information" (see figure 4.4). I panicked as well. Had my computer already been infected by malware? The advisory had an eighteenth-century ring to it not all that different from the disembodied warning that Wieland receives, "Stop, go no further. There is danger in your path" (31).

So, of course, I clicked on the link.

Before I explain what happened next, let's pause to consider the implications of the link that I didn't click on, the one leading "back to safety." Seeking and finding here poses a threat. Data is potentially dangerous; communication becomes contagion. Information on the next screen and quarantined by this

150   CHAPTER 4

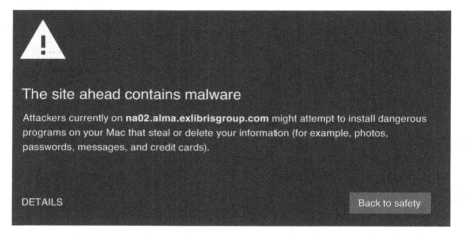

FIGURE 4.4. Screenshot showing electronic advisory about malware.

warning likely poses a hazard to the safety of privacy and personal information. The gothic peril to the self reappears as the loss of digital identity. This disclosure is hardly news for readers of *Wieland*, who learn that all communication, if it is to be successful, presumes a self that is porous, susceptible, even vulnerable. So, too, data, which might be better reconceived as *capta* (Drucker) that is pursued and secured, is a function of searching and surveillance. Whether as technophobia or as a terror that is more metaphysical, fear and loathing are affective accompaniments of all media. "The shock of new media is as old as the hills," writes W.J.T. Mitchell (211)—and, we might add, also as new as an eighteenth-century gothic novel.

What happened when I clicked on the link? Predictably enough, things got worse but not in the predictable way. Setting out to read to Brown's departure from the gothic, I read in digital form the first volume of *Philip Stanley*, a text that Mary Shelley, who knew a thing or two about the gothic, dismissed in her journal as "very stupid" (qtd. in Ringe 454). Just as I became embroiled in the plot, volume one of the digital facsimile came to an abrupt end and online access to volume two was nonexistent through my university library database. So, I resorted to an older method of seeking and finding. In the library stacks I located the bicentennial edition of the text and picked up where volume one left off with Philip, Clara, and Mary. But now a new character entered the plot, a guy named Edward Hartley and, like Philip, he was now writing to Clara and Mary. The love triangle became a love quadrangle. Would Clara bring everything out into the open and tell Edward about Philip? Would Mary, who now had a viable suitor in Edward, release Philip from his oath so that he would be free to wed Clara?

By now my mistake must be obvious. My initial dalliance with the digitally accessible text had led me to the pirated British version from 1807, which in its facsimile form had the aura of being the older—and hence more authentic and authoritative—text than the 1986 bicentennial edition. Intending to read *Clara Howard; or, the Enthusiasm of Love* by Charles Brockden Brown, I read *Philip Stanley; or, the Enthusiasm of Love*, also by Charles Brockden Brown. When I resumed with volume two in the form of the physical library copy, I encountered the original American form of Brown's character, Edward, before he became Philip in later editions. The mystery is easy enough to clear up on one level: too trusting of digital sources but also somewhat reckless in my own right, I practiced a method that was based on misreading. Brown's gothic tale *Wieland* is subtitled *The Transformation*, and my experience suggested that the doubling relationship between print and digital cultures also transforms the presumably stable and authoritative texts that we encounter.[16] Infinite repetition without end is also a hallmark of the sublime, according to Burke, who adds the disconcerting observation that the pleasure found in limitless copies also accounts for the affliction of "'madmen' who are unable to let go of an object, sound, remark that keeps repeating itself without end" (67). While we have long admitted to ourselves that all reading is misreading, it is tempting nonetheless to argue for the reverse corollary, namely, that all misreading is reading. What insight does misreading produce? What can fallacious methods reveal? In my case, reading had made me as vulnerable to error as any of the characters in *Wieland* who misread both the print information that surrounds them and the data provided by their senses.

The transformation of Edward Hartley into Philip Stanley suggests how a coherent identity of a forthright hero committed to full disclosure and transparency is tripped up by its own schismatic structure. In this scenario, however, the instability is not the psychological effect of Brown's use of the gothic. Rather, it is the textual effect of the ongoing transition of print culture into a digital one undertaken in the name of accessibility and exhaustiveness. Which is to say that open, transparent texts and methods can produce decidedly gothic effects.[17] To recall the letter from Edward Hartley or Philip Stanley or whatever his name may be, media are "wild and ambiguous." This claim is hardly a revelation for any inhabitant of a gothic mediascape: a rational intellect like Wieland proves susceptible to evil suggestions and a trusting soul like his sister Clara learns soon enough that a pen knife can serve as a weapon. Not unlike

Burke's "madmen" who experience "delightful horror" (67) in repetition, the gothic nature of communication shows that the effort to understand information, even amid scenarios predicated on complete revelation and emotional honesty, is always poised on a precipice of uncertainty. The excess inherent to the informational sublime generates insecurity because its superabundance remains unaccountable and elusive. While "the terrible uncertainty of the thing described" frequently proves overwhelming (E. Burke 58), it is also the case that uncertainty is necessary to description and, by extension, to communication itself. Communication requires uncertainty because without it there would be no compelling need to seek or find information in the first place. Uncertainty, for Luhmann, is something like the lifeblood of communication, renewing itself with "further information" by creating shocks that beg for explanation (*Reality* 54). In a situation of complete confidence and total knowledge, any message sent would be superfluous since the information it contained would already be known. Only with uncertainty is there the "freedom," to use Shannon's word (13), to choose from a range of potential messages.

In the end, what do we get by recognizing that knowledge in the humanities, digital or otherwise, rests on a gothic substratum of uncertainty? There's nothing in my account that says we should be paralyzed with fear by online archives, searchable databases, or algorithms that crunch texts. Instead, there's simply that age-old terror of trying to communicate and tell a story that will be intelligible to others when there is too much information and too much to tell.

5

Jeffersonian Trembling

WHITE NATIONALISM AND THE RACIAL ORIGINS OF NATIONAL SECURITY

WHITE PEOPLE CELEBRATING the Fourth of July enjoyed nothing more than imagining the providential day when free Blacks and emancipated persons would be sent back to Africa. In New England towns miles away from Black populations in New York or Philadelphia, to say nothing of those in the plantation South, orators in the 1820s and 1830s mounted church pulpits and lyceum rostrums and spoke longingly about the colonization of Africa by the exiles in the nation's midst. Independence Day doubled as "a virtual colonization holiday" (Sweet 260), a ready-made venue for endorsing plans designed to secure the blessings of liberty, but only for some, well into the future.[1] Along with their counterparts in the South advocating for the deportation of free people of color, colonizationists imagined themselves as humanitarians, people of good intentions who would combine census data with their love of Christ to offer a slow but, according to their projections, surely steady solution to the problem of American slavery while redeeming the African continent in the process. Their "unmingled benevolence to the coloured population of this land" lent passion and purity to the cause, as one ardent supporter put it (Reese v). Colonization enjoyed the millennial aura of hastening the end of slavery by peopling savage lands with Christianized African Americans.[2]

Doing the math each Fourth of July became something of a patriotic ritual for whites in the decades following the War of 1812. When Elisha Whittlesey addressed the Tallmadge Colonization Society on July 4, 1833, he made a claim about "the alarming increase of slaves" and backed up his concern by citing decennial censuses of Black population over the previous forty years: "in 1790, 697,697; in 1800, 896,849; in 1810, 1,191,364; in 1820, 1,538,128; and in 1830,

2,011,320" (9).[3] On this celebratory day, the topic shifted from the pursuit of happiness to the pursuit for racial security. Blackness seemed to be standing in the way of this goal, but for an optimistic subset of white nationalists who supported colonization, the problem had a mathematical solution that merged the pursuit of happiness with the quest for security. At a moment when many whites felt that their historic entitlement had become fragile, destined to vanish before the immutable laws of population increase, the concerted effort to engineer racial homogeneity through colonization promised to secure freedom in perpetuity. Even though the prospect of removing millions of Black people from the United States was never much more than a racist fantasy, white crusaders saw themselves as realists acting on biopolitical statistics and other forms of calculation to ensure a white racial destiny.

Statistics emerged at the end of the eighteenth century as the "study of the state," and both French (*statistique*) and German (*Statistik*) usages denoted the application of mathematical techniques to comprehending the voluminous data associated with the state and its subjects (*OED*). As "the state's knowledge of the state" per Foucault's gloss (*Security* 315), statistics enables the study of people as a population resource for war and labor. Yet such a resource also constitutes a security threat. Colonizationists obsessed over mathematical data: the ratio of whites to Blacks, birth rates, rates of incarceration and insanity, all of which seemed leading up to the nation being overrun by Blacks. "They are more than a sixth of our population," exclaimed Baxter Dickinson of Springfield, Massachusetts, in his July Fourth oration. "Their ratio of increase exceeds that of the whites. . . . who can look at it even in distant prospect without horror?" (17). For white nationalists, extrapolating population data and using statistics to make predictions often pointed to an impending racial nightmare.

Rational calculation, of course, is never as rational as it seems to be. In a state of emergency where security is viewed as critical, it is more appropriate to speak of "affective 'calculation,'" as Brian Massumi does in describing how indiscriminate threats become "indiscrimin*able*" (154, 157). When it came to counting up the millions of Black people in the United States, at times separating the free Black population from the enslaved and at other times lumping both together, the political arithmetic spawned contrasting affects. On the one hand, biopolitical calculations performed a function that is "massifying, that is directed not at man-as-body but at man-as-species" (Foucault, *"Society"* 243), offering security in the knowledge that a population has been accounted for. But, on the other, the figures generated *in*security merely by documenting the numerical existence, in the most fundamental sense of the word, of a people whose power exceeded the sum of individual bodies' potential. "The country is kept in perpetual alarm" by both the rhetoric and arithmetic of colonization, according to *The Liberator* ("Liberia Herald" 282). As we will see, David Walker and other Black activists associated with *Freedom's Journal* invoked these same population statistics to demonstrate the proportional strength, relative to the white republic, of the Black community.

Behind the triumphalism that imbued these Fourth of July orations and other patriotic endorsements of colonization, a pervasive sense of vulnerability impelled influential white men at all levels of government and social station to back plans for the settlement of Liberia by the so-called "surplus" Black population of the United States. Slave owners rallied around colonization out of "sheer terror," according to William Lloyd Garrison. "The increase of the free colored population disturbs the security of the planters," he explained in terms that cast racial anxiety as an affective debility (78). Meanwhile, for Northerners, the task, as Calvin Yale put it in his 1827 sermon to the Vermont Colonization Society, was to ensure "national safety" (10) lest Northern cities be inundated with Black criminals. So, although white Northerners came to the colonization crusade with different motives, like their Southern counterparts, they were ultimately trying to save themselves from Black population increase and a brewing race war that they feared the numbers tokened. At one level, the contrast between Southerners who turned to colonization as a means of preserving the slave system by exiling meddlesome free Blacks and Northerners who saw the movement as an initial step toward one day ending slavery could not have been greater, though the American Colonization Society (ACS) endeavored to downplay these regional differences of opinion. But at another level, each responded as nationalists, specifically white nationalists, who acted out of fear that their country would one day be swamped by Black population increase. Fundamentally, then, colonizationists relied on political arithmetic to predict and therefore avert a future racial catastrophe; their campaign operated as a prototypical discourse of national security, one that continues to set patterns for policing, immigration, and governance today.

The project of national security, I will argue, was beset by the affective intensities of "Jeffersonian trembling." No one was more afraid than Jefferson, who experienced an infamous case of trembling when he turned his eye to the arithmetic of Black population increase. "I tremble for my country when I reflect that God is just," he opined, because the United States seemed ill-equipped to handle the problem of growing Black biopower.[4] The phantasmatic notion that whiteness was somehow a vulnerable racial identity had been in play at least since Benjamin Franklin in *Observations Concerning the Increase of Mankind* (1751) reflected with some concern that "the negroes brought into the English Sugar Islands, have greatly diminish'd the Whites there" (7). This worry became full blown over the next two generations as Jefferson's guilt-ridden musings about race grew into a national security matter. In contrast to the "hardness" that Ahmed associates with the "the phenomenology of whiteness" (*Cultural Politics of Emotion* 4), Jefferson's quavering undermines this confident posture with an admission of vulnerability. Yet make no mistake, the claim of vulnerability also functioned as a strategy of security that, in this case, allowed an aggrieved majority to clamor for protection while justifying the state of exception that it necessitated. As a biopolitical mechanism, colonization fixated on the techniques of population that centered on "individuals belonging to the same species, living side by side," as in Foucault's description ("Omnes" 252)—except that "living side by side" was precisely the objection voiced by white nationalists. Foucault's ideas about population thus cannot account for the way that colonizationists literally counted up and segmented the national population, as they deployed racialized algorithms in an effort to reduce the numbers of free persons and Black people overall.

Despite the assertion that colonization "helped Americans throw off Jefferson's legacy in ideas about race" (Saillant 274) by promoting Liberia as a venture grounded in the virtues of liberalism and trade, the unease Jefferson felt lasted well into the nineteenth century as a psycho-political inheritance evident in anguished Fourth of July speeches about the dire need for Black expatriation.[5] The faith in market liberalism that John Saillant sees underpinning support for Liberian emigration may have superseded Enlightenment ideas held by Jefferson, but his affective misgivings were another legacy altogether. American colonizationists would experience an array of Jeffersonian symptoms, frequently employing the language of horror, apprehension, and, above all, trembling, as they confronted a Black population that had increased from nearly 700,000 in 1790 to over 1.5 million by 1820, according to federal census figures. These and other numbers appear all over ACS reports that sought to provide a practical solution to the moral problem that Jefferson had posed by sending African Americans to Liberia to become settler colonialists. Five years after its founding in 1817, the ACS established a colony on the west coast of Africa for repatriating free persons of color as well as enslaved persons manumitted by owners under the stipulation that they leave U.S. shores. More than 200 local chapters and auxiliary societies sprang up soon afterward (S. Young 99). (The ACS did not formally disband until 1964.)[6] Never more than a trickle, the approximately 10,000 to 13,000 free persons of color and emancipated slaves transported to Liberia represented less than 3 percent of the total Black population at the time.[7]

By gathering and then acting on census statistics and other biopolitical information, colonization functioned as an algorithm designed to manage the statistical risk that Black people were thought to pose to future national security. An algorithm in simplest terms is "a set of rules used in calculation and problem-solving" (*OED*), especially where colossal amounts of data are involved. Yet even the purest calculations grow sticky because algorithms "operate through the medium of culture"; algorithms are always attached to "imaginative grammars" that concentrate, refract, or otherwise distort the real phenomena to which they are applied (Finn 5, 41). When the problem to be solved was the population of Black people that the federal census began counting in 1790, the discourse of colonization provided a set of rules for dealing with the numbers. Members of the ACS used mathematical ratios of increase to make grim predictions about a future, which unless action were taken looked less white with each census. With rules that sort people into categories and predict their future behavior, algorithms answered the needs of racial governance.[8] Algorithms cooked up evidentiary support for white nationalism; colonization operated as a type "algorithmic governmentality," to use Antoinette Rouvroy's idea ("The End(s) of Critique" 144), that predicted the size of the Black population in order to prevent it from growing any larger. For white nationalists made uneasy by thoughts of Black millions, colonization offered a security mechanism for lumping those bodies into a single aggregate: a population. The data that white nationalists felt most pressed to predict was: how many Black people would be born, how many might be sent to Africa, and how many might die.

In response to census numbers that fueled ominous predictions about the fate of the white republic, the colonization movement drew on "algorithmic governmentality" as a way of handling the population data that was creating such despair about the national future. While nowhere as technologically sophisticated or powerful as neoliberal societies intent today on installing "a government of the social world that is based on the algorithmic processing of big data sets rather than on politics, law, and social norms" (Rouvroy, "Algorithmic Governmentality"), the early nineteenth-century United States, both North and South, found in the data set of population statistics predictive evidence that Blackness represented a growing national security crisis. Liberia in this framework represented not so much an actual place that received a few hundred American Blacks each year as an affective placeholder for removing uncertainty by removing Blacks themselves. Race may not figure explicitly into Rouvroy's description of algorithmic governmentality, but its potential to discriminate among the "indiscrimin*able*," to return to Massumi's language, should be clear. Biostatistical projections ensured that Blacks, especially free people of color, were easily "algorithmed," to adopt Katherine McKittrick's recent coinage, in no small part because algorithms derive from "a larger colonial and plantocratic logic" (103, 109).[9] The projected rates of Black population increase of enslaved persons and free persons of color changed the entire calculus of national security by shifting the biopolitical imperative from producing life to grappling with its unpredictability. For political economists the question had been, "Is there sufficient population? And the answer was: There is never enough" (Foucault, *Security* 344). Foucault's query meets with a totally different answer from white nationalists who, in effect, responded, "Yes, there is sufficient population—*unless there are too many*." Instead of targeting individual Black bodies, white nationalism read the latest data about Black people in toto as a threat. Different in scale from the surveillance techniques described by Simone Browne that overseers, patrollers, and other agents of slaveholding society employed, colonization represented a security algorithm for tackling a data problem that was the size of the Black population itself.

When it came to aggregating data about the Black population as a worrisome contingency for the future, the experience of information overload examined in the previous chapter was both abstract and intensely embodied as a threat to white hegemony. This chapter and the next track how principles of security organized around whiteness were undone through the concerted efforts of *Freedom's Journal*, Walker's *Appeal to the Colored Citizens of the World*, and other landmark achievements of Black print culture. The biopolitical concept of population that drove the racialization of security discourse ultimately rendered it unstable, as the figures and statistics fueling algorithmic governmentality gave Walker and others evidence of the potential power of Black collectivities. This arc concludes in the next chapter with an unexpected twist, however, as colonization discourse was partially stitched back together by none other than a former editor of *Freedom's Journal*, who in November 1829 landed in Monrovia, assumed the editorship of *Liberia Herald*, and began writing articles expressing optimism about the fortunes of transplanted Blacks in West Africa.

Statistics and the Probability of "Plots and Insurrections!"

Vulnerability provides the affective motivation for white nationalism. Fearful that an influx of immigrants, declining fertility rates among whites, and other demographic changes are endangering white people's status and privilege, white nationalists today see themselves threatened with dispossession and the loss of entitlement. As the marchers at the "Unite the Right" torchlit rally in Charlottesville, Virginia, in 2017 chanted, "You shall not replace us!" White nationalists deploy the loaded rhetoric of "white genocide" and "replacement theory" to voice their distress over a supposed surge of nonwhite peoples and a corresponding "decline" of the white population.[10] Despite the term's recent origins, particularly its simultaneous denial and appropriation of the Holocaust, the conceptual illogic of "white genocide" dates back to colonization and biopolitical anxieties over the chimera of Black population excess. In the late twentieth century against the backdrop of the civil rights movement, busing and school integration, affirmative action, and the loss of skilled labor jobs, white supremacists "built a movement around the idea of white dispossession, the notion that the country they believed had once been the sole property of white people was no longer only theirs" (Zeskind xvii). Their predecessors in the early nineteenth century had no real need to view themselves as victims since they were not a fringe group but men with access to the centers of power. Men like Henry Clay and John Randolph of Roanoke, along with ministers and orators who addressed Independence Day crowds, embraced white nationalism as defense against a future whose contingencies included Black insurgency, Black majorities, and Black rule. Their rhetoric drew support from local colonization societies, which provided the organization, membership, and access to print media for promoting whiteness as the guarantor of national security.

White nationalism corresponds to much of Ruth Wilson Gilmore's definition of racism as "the state-sanctioned and/or extra-legal production and exploitation of group-differentiated vulnerabilities to premature death, in distinct yet densely interconnected political geographies" ("Race and Globalization" 261). Yet it also draws on a complex affective disposition toward security that inflects Gilmore's definition a bit differently. Hence: white nationalism is the state-sanctioned and/or extra-legal production and promotion of *group-differentiated entitlement to security and belonging within a political geography deemed a rightful and historic homeland*. Even as white nationalism foists premature death onto others per Gilmore's definition, it claims vulnerability as its exclusive emotional entitlement. Reserving vulnerability for itself, nineteenth-century white nationalism used the fantasy of its own precariousness to police the contingencies it associated with other populations that it viewed as threats to its hegemony. "Whiteness," as Alexander Weheliye reminds us, "designates not actually existing groupings but a series of hierarchical power structures that apportion and delimit which members of the Homo sapiens species can lay claim to full human status" (19). As a prominent delivery vehicle for this ideology, colonization identified, enumerated, and, above all, targeted those who were denied the right to make this claim.

Buoyed by widely shared beliefs in the biblical and historical supremacy of "Anglo-Saxonism," to use Reginald Horsman's term, white nationalists fabricated more than enough pseudoscience, ethnology, and literature to convince themselves that American whiteness would lead to the "perfection of governmental institutions and world dominance" (9). Even so, the "popular sense of whiteness represented a hesitantly emerging consensus" (Roediger 7), one that remained riven by doubts about whether immigrants, particularly the Irish but also at times French, Spanish, and Italians, counted as white.[11] Far easier than confronting their own anxieties about the fluidity of white identity or nightmares about white dispossession, they instead eagerly anticipated the dispossession of others. Despite the consistent anti-Blackness of white nationalists then and now, significant differences exist between nineteenth-century supporters of African colonization and contemporary advocates of a white ethno-state who subscribe to "the great replacement" and other conspiracy theories. Unlike the fringe nature of hate groups and extremist websites today such as *The Daily Stormer*,[12] white nationalists in the nineteenth-century mainstream boasted their connections to the founding fathers, sat on the highest courts, and enjoyed access to major publications and platforms at reformist conventions. "What right, I demand, have the children of Africa to a homestead in the white man's country?" asked George Washington Parke Custis, step-grandson of the first president (Jay 109). But vulnerability did not mean retreating inward, as white nationalists beginning in the 1820s projected risk outward, effectively exporting insecurity and precarity onto Blacks. Yet despite the zeal for ensuring the United States as the rightful and future inheritance of white people, colonization could never allay the ever-present doubt that whites could not protect themselves from the surging potential of Black biopower.

Never a remotely practical undertaking given the distances, expense, and sheer numbers of people involved, the colonization scheme to outfit vessels and pack their hulls full of Black emigrants, whether somehow to undo or cruelly replay the trajectories of the Middle Passage, encouraged supporters to be punctilious about the math behind the enterprise. In sermons and Fourth of July addresses, speakers alternated between the lofty (and paradoxical) prospect of deporting Blacks in the name of liberty and more prosaic details by totaling up shipping costs, estimating natural rates of increase from reproduction and birth, and projecting the ratio of Blacks to whites ten, twenty, forty years in the future. For a tax of less than ten cents a person—that is, white people recognized as legal persons—the $140,000,000 needed to transport the entire free Black population to Africa could be raised. Baxter Dickinson made this pitch to the Auxiliary Colonization Society of Springfield, Massachusetts, on July 4, 1829: his vision of a white republic "destined within the compass of the passing century to embosom a white population of eighty millions" was certainly in reach but only if the variable of an unwelcome, fast-growing Black population was removed from the overall national equation (12).

For others, though, a racial apocalypse seemed just as mathematically imminent. Drawing on "one very simple arithmetical calculation," an 1823 report commissioned by the ACS concluded that since the size of the slave population "doubles in less than 20 years," in the span of sixty years the United States will become "a nation of slaves larger by 4,000,000 than the whole present white population" (*Seventh Annual Report* 90). The numbers fueled dire predictions: given that this extensive data set would total 12 million slaves by 1880, one could only guess at "how many plots must be detected, how many insurrections must be quelled. Plots and insurrections! These are words of terrour" (91). With racial violence liable to erupt anywhere and at any moment from now and into the future, uncertainty and contingency made "terrour" more terrifying still. In this context, political arithmetic was doubly affecting, relying on population data for predictive security while also fueling alarm about the extent of the Black population whose were numbers so large as to increase the probability of vengeance. So even though the census of 1820 showed that whites were actually increasing faster than either free people of color or the enslaved population, these fears persisted.[13] Black people may have been calculable, but the consternation they created among white nationalists was not.

As an incipient form of algorithmic governmentality, colonization obsessed over numbers, particularly those purportedly showing alarming rates of Black population increase, in an effort to guarantee continuing white supremacy for generations to come. Knowing the size of the Black population now would allow white Americans to forestall the future that those numbers seemingly foretold. Estimates about the ratio of Blacks to whites, especially figures showing that Blacks were destined to pull even with and one day overtake whites, utilized census data as part of an advance warning system. Yet biopolitical statistics involved more than prognosticating: colonizationists viewed population projections as the first step to preempting the future. "The strategy of algorithmic governmentality consists in either ensuring or preventing its [the future's] actualization," contends Rouvroy ("The End(s) of Critique" 157). White nationalists saw the future that they wanted so desperately to prevent, and their plan of action called for massive emigration and deportation that, in the end, sputtered without achieving any real success. Yet despite the obvious failures of colonization, the vulnerability that activated white nationalism continues to shape security as a fevered reaction to Blackness.

While the threat of slave insurrection might have been most pressing for Southerners who embraced colonization as a security measure, projections about what the U.S. population would look like in 1880 stretched insecurity across the better part of the century. This elongated horizon was crucial to aligning reformers and racists under the banner of white nationalism that the ACS offered. The July Fourth orators in New England town centers who urged a program of exile did not share the same immediate concerns as slave owners worried about regional Black numerical superiority, and yet censuses and other biostatistical information that foretold the eventual waning of racial hegemony made population data a matter of shared white vulnerability. White nationalists who advocated colonization set their task as dealing with the racial arithmetic of population data in order to detect "plots and insurrections!" before they could erupt. The question was not whether there would be a slave revolt: rather, it was a matter of how soon, how frequent, and how large. Statistically speaking, a population of millions was bound to have its revolutionaries and its cabals, and the goal for anxious observers was to figure out a practical strategy for governing and, most urgently, limiting the population so that it could be parsed, understood, and controlled before a "Toussaint, or a Spartacus, or an African Tecumseh" arose to establish "a black empire" (*Review* 19).[14] The possibility that even a single revolutionary could arise from a population of millions was as limitless as the population itself. White nationalism, from this perspective, sought to minimize contingency now and into the future by controlling the size of the Black population. Yet the racialization of security discourse ultimately instilled insecurity when it became apparent that the efforts of colonization could hardly keep pace with the increase of the free Black population alone.

Population represents "a kind of thick natural phenomenon" (Foucault, *Security* 71) that was absorbed within the science of government starting in the eighteenth century. When "a population cannot be transparent," when "the relation between the population and sovereign cannot simply be one of obedience," and when "the variables on which population depends" are moving and unfixed to the "extent that it [the population] escapes" (71) calculability and predictability, its density and variability becomes an unappeasable source of insecurity. In the context of nineteenth-century white nationalism and beyond, however, the Black population existed as a different sort of phenomenon, an alien phenomenon that required solutions on a scale as grand—and as impractical—as a deportation plan intended to operate for decades, perhaps as long as a half century, to accomplish its object. If nothing else, supporters of colonization knew how to be patient. Yet the compulsive attention to "the *present* annual increase" which "must be continually increasing" (*FJ*, "People of Colour" 9) made the task of securing a white homeland that much more urgent. The early Black press seized on these fears, as *Freedom's Journal* asked if colonization was anything other than "a sort of *safety valve*" for shipping off an excess population, which, coincidentally, was the same size as the number of free Blacks ("People of Colour" 9). Among people of African descent, colonization signaled an existential threat, an ongoing state of emergency that disrupted their communities, separated families, devalued Black-owned property, and forestalled the rights of citizenship.

In rehearsing this argument, I am of course drawing on the supporters of the American Colonization Society, which used virtually all available print resources—missionary reports, sailing captains' logs, firsthand testimonies, speeches and addresses, admonitions and newspapers editorials, travelers' impressions of West Africa, even poetry—to support its biopolitical agenda. Just as crucially, I have relied on opponents of the ACS, who combed through the pages of the organization's official publication, the *African Repository and Colonial Journal*, to question its population estimates, dispute its political principles, and, finally, protest its racialized approach to the internal security of the United States. This publication ran for the better part of a century, and in addition to making my way through annual reports of the ACS, I have followed the path of nineteenth-century critics of Liberian colonization such as James Forten, John Russwurm, Samuel Cornish, David Walker, Lydia Maria Child, William Jay, David Ruggles, and Garrison, who all did battle with the *African Repository*. "See how we are, through the medium of that periodical [the *African Repository*], abused and held up by the Americans, as the greatest nuisance to society, and throat-cutters in the world," protested Walker in his *Appeal* (78).

Being perceived as a source of perpetual insecurity, Walker realized, was not without its strategic advantages. As subsequent sections of this chapter and the next show, Walker and his compatriots assailed the political arithmetic and biopolitical maneuvering behind colonization, and often these writers' most effective strategy was to quote generously from ACS documents and then affix scathing commentaries of their own.[15] Scarce a week passed when *Freedom's Journal* did not reprint a column from the *African Repository*. And while many of these examples of colonizationist propaganda blended history and ethnology to depict the grandeur of early Black civilizations, *Freedom's Journal* just as regularly included original pieces by Black correspondents who viewed colonizationist schemes as "unrighteous and meddling" and avowed that "the free people of colour will never go to Africa" ("For the Freedom's Journal" 102).

Colonization as National Security

Despite the mathematical impossibility of expatriating an entire population, not to mention Black opposition to the plan in the first place, the white nationalist dream of racial security remained a prominent reform movement across the nineteenth century.[16] The ACS continued to operate well beyond the Civil War, maintaining offices at the Colonization Building on Pennsylvania Avenue in Washington, D.C., through Reconstruction. As late as 1878, the president of Girard College pushed for colonization, but since cost had proved an obstacle for so long, he now called on Blacks to fund their own deportations. After all, if these people were free, they could now be expected to pay their own way to Liberia. "The time has come to encourage a self-paying emigration, or an emigration at least partly self-paying," wrote William H. Allen (6). In keeping with the philanthropic mission of the ACS, he advanced this proposal on behalf of the "Americo-African republic" (Allen 11), arguing that increased settlement would address Liberian labor shortages and shore up defenses against native tribes. The solution to both problems was biopolitical: more bodies would be instrumental in bolstering the militia while also adding numbers to the agricultural force that could work the African soil. Yes, "Liberia has passed its infancy," but "it needs population" (Allen 5) to become economically viable and militarily self-sufficient. From this perspective, people of African descent who posed a security threat to the white republic embodied an untapped reservoir of biopower whose potential could be safely realized only in Africa. Although updated for the postslavery era, Allen's colonizationist argument falls back on the supposed beneficence of white nationalism:

sending formerly enslaved persons to Africa represented an effort to promote Black self-reliance, not white self-interest. Philanthropy should have its limits, of course. Lest do-gooders take their reformist energies too far, the United States should not be looking to annex the Liberian colony, which, by the way, had declared its status as an independent nation in 1847.[17]

Sending a few handfuls of exiles each year to Liberia made little dent in overall demographics. But at conceptual and affective levels, establishing a colony for American Blacks across the Atlantic on the west coast of Africa held out hope for a solution to the imminent threat to domestic tranquility that whites saw brewing amid the contradictions of a slaveholding republic. In this way, the ACS acted as a national security agency even though it never achieved official government status or anything near the level of appropriations it repeatedly requested from the federal government.[18] Petitions to Congress to fund Black colonization might not have netted much support, but the ACS gained testimonials and contributions from powerful, nationally prominent men such as Supreme Court Chief Justice John Marshall (a lifetime member of the ACS), George Washington's nephew and Supreme Court Justice, Bushrod Washington (ACS cofounder and president), Francis Scott Key (on the Board of Managers for the ACS), Massachusetts governor and later Harvard University president Edward Everett (an ACS attendee who believed colonization would civilize the African continent), and Speaker of the House of Representatives, secretary of state, and presidential candidate Henry Clay (vice president of the ACS and chairperson of its first meeting). Even though Clay failed to convince congressional colleagues to earmark federal dollars for this charitable undertaking, his involvement in the ACS, like that of other statesmen and jurists, indicates how the effort to count, manage, and surveil a Black population was deemed essential to public safety.[19] Despite the private status of the ACS, its public crusade made it akin to a nineteenth-century NGO whose mission encompassed nothing less than the armature of national security. Membership consisted of a "strange amalgam of racists and humanitarians" (James 31), who found common ground in viewing free people of color as lucky recipients of the opportunity to achieve equality elsewhere. By also including manumitted slaves as potential beneficiaries of their largesse, ACS members were able to construct the entire Black population as eventual objects of deportation.[20] Whether they backed colonization in order to make slaveholding more secure or to gradually promote abolition, Southerners and Northerners mobilized biostatistical information to offset the perception of racialized risk.

Efforts to regulate Black life intensified in the 1820s, a moment dubbed at the time as the Era of Good Feelings owing to a supposed ebbing of partisan politics. These years witnessed a multipronged campaign to restrict Black freedom and rights in virtually all aspects of everyday life: public transportation, voting, education, ability to purchase property, access to the mails, just to name a few of the repressive effects of what historian Gary Nash described as the rising Negrophobia of the era (224–27). States across the Northeast actively pursued the curtailment of African Americans' political rights in the first decades of the nineteenth century: New Jersey restricted the franchise to white men in 1807; New York mandated in 1811 that Black voters provide proof of their freedom; Connecticut amended its constitution in 1818 to effectively disenfranchise Blacks; New York stood by property qualifications for Blacks in its 1821 constitution even as it abolished the requirement for white voters; Rhode Island stripped Black inhabitants of the franchise in 1822. After New York adopted property qualifications limiting the franchise to only those African Americans who could prove that they owned $250 in property, "by 1826, only sixteen blacks in New York County were eligible to vote" (Harris 119). Leon Litwack in *North of Slavery* estimated that "by 1840, some 93% of the northern free Negro population lived in states which completely or practically excluded them from the right to vote" (75). Starting with the admission of Maine to the Union in 1819, every territory that gained statehood before the Civil War restricted the franchise to white men. The Naturalization Act of 1790 already had laid the groundwork at the federal level by recognizing whiteness in the language of officialdom by decreeing that "any alien, being a free white person" could apply for U.S. citizenship after two years of residence. Soon after in 1792 congressional measures "restricted militia enrollment to able-bodied white male citizens" (Litwack 31). The Era of Good Feelings, it seemed, permitted white Americans to feel good about their common ability to unite around a shared agenda of anti-Blackness.

In these contexts, a distinct technology emerged for dealing with Blacks not as people but as a population. State legislatures were not shy about denying nonwhite people individual rights; colonization ramped up racism by taking an entire population as its target. By aggregating Blacks under a single demographic category, colonization "responds to and creates the racial calculability of populations" (Kazanjian, *Colonizing Trick* 121), which is to say that for white nationalists, Liberia signified much more than an actual destination for a few dozen transportees each year. African colonization mapped out a notional geography of the future: based on the current size of the African

American population, how many would there be in ten or twenty years? The political arithmetic of population management lent itself more to psychosis than rationality: surely, some measure of reassurance lay in knowing exactly that "on the 1st of January, 1835, there were in the United States, 2,245,144 slaves" (Jay 7), yet this surety quickly gave way to the unassuageable insecurity presented by the sheer immensity of this figure itself. Knowing how many Blacks were in the United States created the fearsome burden of knowing just how many Blacks were in the United States.

This tally did not include free people of color, and the ACS, divided between Northern and Southern adherents, struggled unsuccessfully about whether to focus its attention exclusively on free persons or to extend its efforts to the enslaved. But from the start, security as a guiding principle seemed beyond question: attendees at the Washington, D.C., gathering that gave birth to the ACS explicitly described the "insecurity" posed by free persons and the necessity of "secur[ing]" slave property. White nationalists were keen to exile free people of African descent even though—but also precisely because—this strategy supposedly kept the slave system intact by removing a class of people thought to sow discord among their enslaved brethren. The ACS never resolved the contradiction that its efforts strengthened slavery as an institution by concentrating primarily on Blacks who were already free. Yet, for white Southerners, this feature was precisely the attraction of colonization, and Northern members of the ACS conceded that the organization should not interfere with slavery at all. This fundamental confusion about the aims of colonization stemmed from the intrinsic confusion of racial security: just thinking about the existence of a sizable Black population, free and enslaved, made whites insecure.

Five Hundred Thousand Strong: Counting Blackness

Identified and targeted as a security risk, how did Black people respond? For participants in the rapidly evolving Black print culture of the 1820s, highlighted by Samuel E. Cornish and John Brown Russwurm's founding of *Freedom's Journal*, the aggregation of Black lives without respect to class, education, or condition required a different sort of accounting.[21] Yet it would be a mistake to flatten early African American print culture into a simply reactive formation created to offset myths about Black crime, Black intellect, Black morality, and other aspersions that Cornish and Russwurm encountered every day in the pages of established newspapers such as the *New York Enquirer* and the

Morning Chronicle. Instead, as Frances Smith Foster argues, "African Americans developed a print culture as one means of creating and nurturing their own individual and communal agendas" (720). Early expressions of Black nationalism encompassed more than a mere counterimage of the era's white nationalism. "Nation" in this sense corresponded more closely with "'family' and 'religion' than with phenotype or legal status" (Foster 717).[22] The biblical snippet beneath the masthead of *Freedom's Journal*—"RIGHTEOUSNESS EXALTETH A NATION"—declares allegiance to a nation above and beyond official state institutions. The unquoted remainder of this verse from Proverbs 14:34, "but sin *is* a reproach to any people," supplied an implicit accusation against a slaveholding republic that the paper's readers and auditors, given their likely connection to the AME church and other religious societies, knew well. Then again, the editors' penchant for scolding Black New Yorkers for frequenting grog shops, indulging in dandyism, and engaging in public spectacles suggests that this implicit reproach included more than whites.

As this population came under the scrutiny of what Simone Browne describes as "racializing surveillance" (16), Black editors, newspaper correspondents, and pamphlet authors reexamined the political arithmetic that identified free people of color as a security risk.[23] Their calculations did not always allay concern; in fact, they often counted in ways that added to the sum of white fears. Drawing on the same census data referenced by colonizationists, these writers and their readers looked critically at the colonization movement and concluded that its security agenda promoted Black insecurity. The irresolvable question they posed emerged from the internal contradictions of colonization: did not the project of securitization promote insecurity? As the editors of *Freedom's Journal* asserted in their March 16, 1827, inaugural issue, "Daily slandered, we think that there ought to be some channel of communication between us and the public: through which a single voice may be heard, in defence of *five hundred thousand free people of color*" ("To Our Patrons").[24] The front-page address "To Our Patrons" underscored this point by remarking upon "the interesting fact that there are FIVE HUNDRED THOUSAND persons color" who would benefit from a paper dedicated to their cause. What seems like a simple parry—after all, Cornish and Russwurm described their motive for starting a newspaper as a defensive maneuver—also represented an effort toward reappraising the connections that political economy made between population and security. "Five hundred thousand" free people, not to ignore the more than two million enslaved persons whose plight would be addressed in subsequent issues, contained more than enough latent biopower, not just to make white people uneasy but also to manifest Black collectivity. Whether italicized or in all caps, what was the biopolitical significance of 500,000 people? A fraction of the 9.6 million inhabitants tabulated in the 1820 national census? A feeder of outsized prison and asylum populations, as white nationalists of the day alleged? A potential army, an "imperium in imperio," to invoke the language of Sutton Griggs's novel of conspiracy and vengeance that would appear at the century's end?[25]

Population statistics may have been immutable, but *Freedom's Journal* used its columns to draw different conclusions from the data. Consider Cornish and Russwurm's decision to reprint an essay by the prominent Black Philadelphian Russell Parrott in a July 1827 issue. Parrott's accounting in *Freedom's Journal* made the political arithmetic of five hundred thousand free Blacks indissociable from the two million enslaved in a system more terrible than "Gothic darkness." By Parrott's reckoning, the sheer presence of free people of color kept slaveholders and state militias in the South on continual edge. Why else would Virginia make manumission a crime, asked Parrott, unless the state feared adding to the numbers of free people in their midst? "With an overgrown black population . . . groaning under a cruel despotism," it was understandable that white nationalists would try to trim the excess. Eager to defuse the potential for slave insurrection—immediate abolition was of course out of the question—whites embraced colonization in search of a safe alternative. "The free black population have become a source of uneasiness to those who are determined to adhere a ruinous system," in Parrott's diagnosis. What seemed like purely a matter of demography became a crucible of affective intensity for whites.

Parrott vowed to keep fighting against colonization "until the safety and happiness of these states are placed upon a secure basis." This promise is perhaps unexpected: why did the essay switch from "the defence of *five hundred thousand free people of color*," a stance in line with Cornish and Russwurm's prospectus for a Black newspaper, to ensuring the stability of "these"—that is, slave—states? Why concern himself with slave state security? After expressing concern for the security of the South, Parrott pivoted to describe "an overgrown black population," a move calculated to sow alarm among the very states seeking reassurance about their security. The "safety and happiness" of white people was surely—and ironically—the priority for Parrott, and putting the interests of five hundred thousand Black people aside for a few moments would not create any jeopardy unless what came into view was an even larger Black mass, nearly three million strong. For white nationalists trying to solve the problem of racial insecurity, the arithmetic of Blackness represented an insoluble remainder. In searching for security, Parrott stumbles—no doubt an accident—upon "a source of uneasiness" in latent Black biopower that would not subside, not even with coerced expatriation to Africa. And even then, as subsequent contributions in *Freedom's Journal* would make clear, the mathematical hurdles to that proposed remedy remained insurmountable.

For their part, white nationalists rarely lost faith that they could square the circle and colonize millions of Blacks despite the fact that the ACS had no reasonable hope of keeping pace with the annual rate of increase. Henan Howlett claimed to have solved this intractable problem when he crunched the numbers in 1834 to show that the six-sevenths of the enslaved population could be manumitted and colonized in as quickly as thirty-two years. The case Howlett made in *An Address on Slavery, and Against Immediate Emancipation; with a Plan of Their Being Gradually Emancipated & Colonized* drew on census data to offset abolitionist mania. His calculations depended on the assumption that 657,142 enslaved persons—the one-seventh remainder—"*will voluntarily remain with their masters*" (14). He also assumed one-seventh of slaveholders would voluntarily free their slaves, 328,571 persons to be exact, without seeking any reimbursement for their losses. Next to this estimate of Southern magnanimity, Howlett noted parenthetically that the Union could count on the goodwill of slave owners "*(in all probability)*" (14). Mathematical probability, it seemed, was always a matter of moral probability. In just one year alone, then, the number of slaves needing transport, not to mention emancipation, would drop from over two million to 1,642,858. Most encouraging of all, Howlett's crude spreadsheet demonstrated that the perennial problem of population increase would become more manageable every year since in proportion there would be fewer Black women in the United States having children (see figure 5.1). His assumptions about the likely generosity of slave owners blinded him from seeing that the South had a vested financial interest in this increase even as it added to overall security concerns.

By the time Howlett published his pamphlet, Cornish and Russwurm had parted ways, *Freedom's Journal* folded under Russwurm's sole editorship, and Russwurm himself had left for Liberia. But David Ruggles, who had subsidized *Freedom's Journal* by purchasing running advertisements listing the butter, cider, sugar, and other items available at his grocery store, found the math in Howlett's pamphlet laughable. Ruggles's support of *Freedom's Journal* likely had given him a firsthand view of how Black print culture exposed the fallacies inherent in white efforts at population management. Perhaps, too, the

PLAN OF A GRADUAL EMANCIPATION.

The number of Slaves in the United States,	2,300,000
I allow one seventh part will voluntarily remain with their masters	657,142
One seventh of the Slave holders, (in all probability) will free their Slaves without a compensation. 328,571	1,642,858

2,300,000, produces, 69,000—free 80,000, annually.—years

It will take 32 years to free them, admitting the increase to be in proportion as 2,300,000—69,-000—1,642,858 80,000
49,285

The neat decrease for the first year, 30,714

EXPENSES.

80,000, freed annually for 31 years, amounts to	2,480,000
the 32d year there remains but	47,741
Slaves	2,527,741
Each Slave costs	300
	$758,322,300,00
Which will cost annually, -	23,697,571,87
The interest of that sum at 7 pr. ct.	1,658,830.00

year	number
1	1,612,143
2	1,580,507
3	1,548,022
4	1,514,462
5	1,479,895
6	1,444,291
7	1,407,619
8	1,369,847
9	1,330,898
10	1,290,824
11	1,248,548
12	1,206,004
13	1,162,484
14	1,127,319
15	1,081,138
16	1,033,572
17	984,579
18	934,116
19	882,139
20	818,603
21	773,461
22	716,664
23	658,163
24	597,907
25	535,884
26	472,160
27	406,324
28	338,513
29	268,668
30	196,728
31	122,625
32	47,741

1st. No Slave to receive their freedom over fifty-five years of age, unless the masters or, some charitable individual, or, society become responsible to the proper authorities for their maintainance.

2d. All those who do not wish to colonize, to be disposed of as follows : Those between 45 & 55 years of age to be employed, or, apprentic'd, for 3 years; to receive wages, or salary, deducting out 10 pr. ct. for the trouble & expence of the person so apprenticed, also as an inducement for such persons to employ them ; the half of which sum (after deducting the necessary expenses for clothing) to be paid over to the proper authorities, to liquidate the debt incurred by their emancipation.

3d. Those between 35 and 45 to be as article 2d. but to have 1 quarters schooling annually, (if wanting) which time will be deducted from their wages.

4th. Those between 21 and 35 to be as above and 5 months schooling, and pay accordingly.

5th. Those between 10 and 21 to be indentured, and to receive as others do under like circumstances, and to have 1 quarter's schooling every year until the end of their apprenticeship.

1st. If the plan of apprenticing is adopted it will save (at least) one third of the whole expence ; besides their education.

The expence will be - - - -	$505,548,200,00
The annual expence to the government	15,798,381,25
The interest annually - . - -	1,105,886,68
2nd. If 1 half colonizes the expence will be	631,935,350,00
Annual expence to the government - -	19,747,976,56
Annual Interest - - - - -	1,382,355,35

This plan in all probability will (most likely) go into operation.

FIGURE 5.1. Henan Howlett, "Plan of a Gradual Emancipation."

grocer's familiarity with accounts and columns of numbers made him a match for anyone using math to make an argument. At any rate, Ruggles found errors enough in Howlett's totals to compose a satire of colonization fantasies: "Mr. H's plan of gradual emancipation is a masterpiece. He shows mathematically, that the slaves in the U.S. can be colonized. Expences ONLY $758,322,500,00!" (47). So harebrained did Howlett's scheme appear to Ruggles that he challenged all comers to produce a better "burlesque" of colonization (48). Had Howlett marketed his plan as a farcical send-up of the ACS, his pamphlet would have been so wildly successful that "he might have realized an independent fortune from it" (48).

The Biopolitics of Increase

Today we encounter Parrott's irony and Ruggles's sarcasm midstream, as it were, in the moment that their rhetoric defied the security discourse that everywhere surrounded people of African descent. Jails, hospitals, churches, and schools have long cared for and controlled individuals. A population represents an altogether different technology of control, a modern idea created by political economic approaches to governance.[26] Foucault developed this account of "governmentality" in lectures he gave at the Collège de France from 1975 to 1979, which offer a sweeping overview from early Church doctrines about pastoral care to justifications of princely power in the Middle Ages to the physiocrats' interest in statistics and the science of the state.[27] Individuals were no doubt still being prodded, surveilled, and punished all the while during this unfolding of history, but a marshaling of energies around biopolitics witnessed the deployment, not of more chains or torture beds but of information and aggregate data to establish the population as a key node of governance. "The multiplicity of individuals is no longer pertinent, the population is," according to Foucault (*Security* 42). A population, unlike "the people," is eminently calculable. While sexologists and psychiatrists had no difficulties proliferating categories of individuals from A to Z, from "auto-monosexualists" to "zooerasts" (Foucault, *History of Sexuality* 43), the physiocrats expended their energies in counting and, most importantly, making projections about the undifferentiated mass of subjects as a whole. The population supplies the military with troops, manufactures goods, grows food for the nation, must be fed in turn, and increases the potential power of the state. And, without ever doing anything other than being born, living, reproducing, and dying, the population constitutes a large enough statistical pool to allow for predictions about people's behavior.

As a target of governance, the population represents a cache of data promising intelligence about everything from life spans and family size to food shortages and the likelihood of social unrest. The more information that can be gathered, the richer the sample, more exhaustive the census, and, most importantly, greater the potential of algorithmic governmentality to predict behaviors, assess risks, and preempt outcomes. The aim in developing the study of political economy, in the language of one prominent physiocrat, was to control for "une infinité de circonstances variables" (qtd. in Hewitt 631) by tamping down on contingency and steering the future toward a single desirable present. Approaching the problem of population as a matter of arithmetical information enabled authorities to comprehend and locate human behavior "within a series of probable events" (Foucault, *Security* 6). Like any moving target, the population represents "a multiplicity on the move" (126), an indeterminate set of behaviors that can be made more determinate if enough information can be assembled to identify patterns and statistical tendencies. Biopolitical governance forces people to live through statistics and other forms of political arithmetic that treat aggregate bodies as a national resource. The sovereign's power that consisted in "the right to take life and let live" evolved into biopower that mandated "the right to make live and let die" (Foucault, *"Society"* 241). It becomes necessary, however, to modify this formulation in the context of racialized security: colonization was preeminently about the "right" to make Blacks live *elsewhere*. As to letting them die, the high rates of mortality among emigrants to Liberia suggested that even passive but lethal solutions could be deemed not entirely a failure by supporters of colonization.

The population data that the federal government, reform societies, and city officials gathered about Blacks raised questions about the national future, all of which found their answer in support for colonization. What was the likelihood that indigent free persons would thieve or drain the scant funds of relief societies? What was the probability that Blacks would increase at a rate that one day would topple white supremacy? In both cases, white nationalists turned to the data, much of it faulty or cherrypicked to present worst-case scenarios, to make dire predictions about an impending racial cataclysm. Whether it was the ratio of Blacks to whites in the West Indies, police reports of Black crime, or physicians' evidence about disproportionate rates of insanity among free people of color, these varied registers all led to the same conclusion that the United States, maybe not today but certainly within a generation or two, would be swamped by the Black population in its midst. Black correspondents at times welcomed these anxious speculations. In its multipart series titled "People of Colour," *Freedom's Journal* admitted that the "Colonization Society has indeed made a beginning," but then swiftly asked "how long it will probably be before the institution can dispose of 30,000 blacks in a year, which is only the *present* annual increase." The question provided information enough for an ominous prediction: never.

The colonization algorithm in the first half of the nineteenth century may have been cruder than contemporary uses of analytics, but the scale was the same: how can a series of calculations about a population predict the contingencies of its behavior and, if necessary, preempt them?[28] From the first decennial federal census of 1790 to Howlett's plans for the steady reduction of Blacks, American biopolitical techniques created knowledge about millions of people, not as an abstract entity but as a numerical presence requiring some measure of management, regulation, and, ultimately, mass removal. While the ACS ramped up the collection of data about Black aggregates, it hardly invented the scrutiny and policing of racialized bodies. Colonial officials in eighteenth-century New York, for instance, had mandated that "at least one lantern must be carried per three Negroes after sunset" in effort to limit "Black mobilities" (Browne 78). Patrollers, fugitive slave catchers, newspaper advertisements for runaways, and the use of branding to scar the flesh as a "biometric technology" (Browne 91) created a multidisciplinary cordon around both free and enslaved persons. But what made the ACS distinctive as a security apparatus was the scope of its mission to forever curtail the size of the total Black population in the United States.

As an algorithm for achieving national security, colonization confronted the "thick natural phenomenon" of the population at its thickest and, not un-coincidentally, Blackest points. Instead of merely seizing territory, security aspires to control the future by identifying and preventing potential future threats from being actualized. White nationalists, viewing each year's increase of the Black population with alarm, no doubt felt that time was running out. Fearful of the day when the "characters of blood at St. Domingo" would be written on American soil (Garrison 99), colonizationists strove to forestall this future and "to render the future motionless, to wrest it from its own futurity" (Hamilton 27). Looking ahead to the day some sixty years hence when "at this rate, we shall have a number of negroes larger by 4,000,000, than the present population," a July Fourth speaker in Potsdam, New York, saw a coming white genocide (*FJ*, "Extract"). The risk was that any increase in the Black population would exponentially multiply the contingency of possible outcomes from the erosion of white supremacy to outright insurrection. The dream of algorithmic data is nothing less than the fantasy of preparing for all possible events; the nightmare is not just the inability to anticipate every scenario but the impotence of being able to forestall the most destructive. Admittedly, population projections in the early 1800s fell well short of the predictive power of today's computer algorithms. Nevertheless, this older security logic shares a similar *mentalité de sécurité* (Dillon, *Biopolitics of Security* 18) as more advanced systems dealing with terabytes of data: aggregating information about a population seeks to dispel uncertainty about the future by taming contingency. If St. Domingo had exploded when the ratio of Blacks to whites on the island reached a tipping point, what possible outcomes awaited the United States when soon "slaves will possess a frightful numerical superiority over their masters?" wondered abolitionist William Jay in his 1835 critique of the colonization movement (8). A national security issue like none other, this question needed asking if a future apocalypse were to be averted.

If the sovereign rights of all white people included the right to make Blacks live elsewhere, the uncertainty immediately arose as to just how many people this plan might encompass. Any precise accounting was made difficult because it was not altogether clear who should be counted in the first place. Many who lent their voices and money to the ACS concentrated on transporting free people of color, who were maligned as a source of lurking unrest whose notions of freedom might spread to slave communities. Others rallied to colonization as a millennial mechanism for one day removing the stain of slavery from America's shores, not by abolishing bondage but by incrementally shrinking the Black population. Colonization offered a flexible strategy for managing distinct Black populations (free, enslaved, Northern, Southern) while at the same time lumping all Blacks into a single aggregate.

Yet population numbers, while at first reassuring, afforded anything but security. Statistics—the science of the state—seeks to tame the potential wildness of the people by construing them as a population. If a people cannot be counted, if they are literally incalculable, their behavior and future actions become incalculable as well. They have no known tendencies; their conduct defies predictable patterns. Efforts to count the people had gaps, and in the 1820s, as Patricia Cline Cohen argues in *A Calculating People*, what was not quantified and tabulated—"for instance, the number of slaveowners, black mortality, female illiteracy" (174)—proved just as revealing as what was recorded. The lack of statistical information about Black death reveals a lot about a society that persisted in ignoring the toll of its necropolitical practices. Black life, however, remained a biopolitical problem that white nationalists could not overlook. A Yale College professor's projection that "our colored population" will have increased from 757,178 in 1790 to 7,491,737 in 1870, as with other predictions about rates of increase, relied on the idea that statistics were essential to safeguarding the future. In *An Appeal in Favor of That Class of Americans Called Africans*, Lydia Maria Child pointed to the impossibility of controlling for such contingency on a mass scale: "There are in the United States two million of slaves, and three hundred thousand free blacks; and their numbers are increasing at the rate of seventy thousand annually." She then broke the data down into smaller units to emphasize the absurdity of colonization, observing that "while one hundred and fifty *free* blacks have been sent to Africa in a *year*, two hundred *slaves* have been born in a *day*" (134). Her calculations amplified the uncertainty inherent to biopolitical information. "How many ships, and how many millions of money, would it require" to resettle Blacks in Liberia? "How would the poor fellows subsist" once they arrived there? "What would be the result of landing several thousand destitute beings" on strange shores? Child saved the most difficult question for last: "And why *should* they be removed" (134). Her line of questioning, a mathematical exercise that concluded with a moral conundrum, revealed how the effort to conceive of a population as data inevitably overran its limits in ways that neither the practical activities nor conceptual algorithms of colonization could handle.

With each year and every projected annual population increase, the data became more overwhelming. Quite simply, what were Black people going to do? Were they going to steal, as the statistics from penitentiaries suggested to some? Were they going to become insane per the data from mental asylums? The 1840 census would demonstrate, helped along by a series of grave miscalculations and biased assumptions, that "the black population in the North suffered from insanity at a rate more than ten times greater than blacks in the South.... The further north one went, the likelier it became for blacks to be insane" (Cohen 192). Would the free population of the North disseminate insurrectionary ideas to enslaved persons in the South, as the frenzied reaction to Walker's *Appeal* alleged? Would free and unfree unite in a race war? Urgent questions like these invited but defied prediction, yet one thing for certain was that the Black population was going to keep increasing at an exponential rate. Imagine next that some percentage of this population, as the public presence of *Freedom's Journal* forcibly demonstrated, might become interconnected via weekly communication.

Jefferson's Trembling

No better expression of this constant state of alarm exists than Jefferson's famous admonition, which supporters of the ACS ritually repeated to urge action before it was too late: "I tremble for my country when I reflect that God is just: that his justice cannot sleep for ever: that *considering numbers*, nature and natural means only, a revolution of the wheel of fortune, an exchange of situation, is among possible events" (*Notes* 163).[29] This well-known warning became a staple of colonizationist rhetoric, a last-ditch plea to avert a coming racial revolution. Few have commented, however, then or now, on the degree to which Jefferson's entire meditation on white vulnerability in Query XVIII of *Notes on the State of Virginia* hinges on the mathematical sensibility of "considering numbers." Back in Query VIII ("Population. The number of its inhabitants?"), Jefferson laid out tables of data from Virginia's 1782 census to observe that white citizens barely edged enslaved persons by a ratio of 11:10, a slim margin of 296,852 whites to 270,762 slaves. At this moment, he had no trouble retaining his composure, and aside from remarking that "this blot in our country increases as fast, or faster, than the whites," he provided little commentary or judgment (*Notes* 87). But when he turned to the affective dimensions of the problem in Query XVIII and examined whites' indulgence in the "worst of passions" and the "unhappy influence" of slavery upon the region, he painted a portrait of white defenselessness, of a tremulous master class rendered vulnerable by its own domination.

Jeffersonian trembling became a widespread affective condition by the late 1820s. Who "does not tremble for the political and moral well-being of a country, that has within its bosom, a growing population" ("Fourth of July" 88)? The *African Repository* asked this question in its 1829 Fourth of July editorial, aligning colonization with the patriotic mission of white nationalists everywhere. In seeking support from Congress, the Kentucky Colonization Society conjured a gothic scenario by suggesting that Jefferson's worst fears would manifest as "the horrors of St. Domingo" soon to arise at home. "Those dreadful events foreboded by Mr. Jefferson" in the 1780s now loomed more ominously after decades of relative inaction. If Jefferson wrote at a moment "when there were only about *seven hundred thousand Blacks* in the United States, how much more forcibly will they apply to the present, when there are probably not less than *two millions and a half*?" ("Memorial" 348). Jesse Burton Harrison, who claimed to have known Jefferson personally, raised this imponderable question in his 1827 address to the Lynchburg Colonization Society. He began calmly enough by considering numbers and observing that "in 1810, there were 30,000 and in 1820 there were 37,000 free blacks in Virginia, an increase of about one fourth in ten years, which number would double itself, at that rate, in about 33 years" (196). Statistical governance soon spiraled out of control by pointing to the sway of a "corroding evil" that caused Harrison to "tremble for the danger of a disaffection spreading through their seductions."[30] Ratios and rationality, counting and calculation, made math truly terrifying for white nationalists.

An esteemed chemistry professor at Yale College fared little better when he considered the numbers. Professor Benjamin Silliman (whose name adorns a residential college at the university today) alluded to but preferred not to rehearse the scene of Jeffersonian trembling in his 1832 July Fourth address to the Connecticut Colonization Society, an organization he had cofounded. Yet his remarks made clear that Jefferson's prophecy was on everyone's mind: "Who has not heard the memorable sentiments of Mr. Jefferson uttered more than half a century ago, and which are too familiar to need recital?" he asked (170). Instead, he proposed looking objectively at the data to examine "the progressive increase of the colored population" (170). But what he discovered nearly unhinged him. With each passing decade, the future grew more uncertain, leading Silliman to foresee "the horrors of the first outburst of nocturnal massacre!" the flower of white American youth cut down by "promiscuous butchery," the atmosphere rent by "the shriek of terror and despair," and the entire landscape transformed into a "silent, bloody sepulcher" (171). Yes, he admitted, in the coming race war Blacks would suffer as well, but their biopolitical potential as a military force would mean that they would "care not for their own thousands and tens of thousands slain, for they have still new myriads to replace them" (172). Wave after wave of Black insurgents would overwhelm whites because Blacks, from a statistical point of view, were literally an "overwhelming population" that in the space of four score years, from 1790 to 1870, seemed destined to increase tenfold (171).

Silliman's math followed a logic of Malthusian displacement that viewed every Black subject taking the spot of a potential white citizen.[31] Black numbers were increasing while white people, according to Silliman, were reproducing at a "lower ratio," the two factors combining in an incipient expression of the twenty-first-century bugbear of a "white genocide." In the political arithmetic where every addition to the Black population meant one less white person, the overall net gain was +2 in favor of African Americans. Now translate this displacement to a population of thousands upon thousands. The increase

1822.]	Some of the Causes of National Anxiety.	
In 1790	Our colored population was	757,178
" 1800		1,006,921
" 1810		1,377,780
" 1820		1,771,658
" 1830		2,330,039
At the same rate of increase it will be		
In 1840		3,045,504
" 1850		4,111,430
" 1860		5,549,435
" 1870		7,491,737

FIGURE 5.2. Benjamin Silliman, "Some of the Causes of National Anxiety," adapted from a table by Mathew Carey.

of 600,000 Blacks between 1820 and 1830, according to the table in Silliman's "Some of the Causes of National Anxiety," thus also corresponds to a loss of 600,000 whites who otherwise would have been part of the republic had they not been displaced (see figure 5.2). The final tally, then, pushed the advantage to 1.2 million in favor of what Silliman's table (borrowed from Mathew Carey) possessively denominated as "our colored population." Jefferson, who mentioned a knowledge of Malthus in letters, had accepted the notion of displacement by coupling his proposal that enslaved people "be colonized" with a plan to import whites to fill the resulting vacuum (*Notes* 138). While Blacks were being sent elsewhere, American ships should be dispatched "at the same time to other parts of the world for an equal number of white inhabitants" (138). Here, an aesthetic principle of balance subtends Jefferson's political arithmetic to ensure equilibrium lest the total population lack sufficient numbers to ensure a stable racial economy.

Colonizationists sought to preserve this balance, or to put it more accurately, the population imbalance that would leave white hegemony uncontested for all time. The Rockbridge Colonization Society of Virginia argued the case emphatically: "The tendency of the scheme, and one of its objects, is to secure slaveholders, and the whole southern country, against certain evil consequences growing out of the present three-fold mixture of our population," comprised of whites, free persons of color, and enslaved people ("Address" 274). The math behind this displacement was as clear as could be. Assuming that "every black family occupies the room of a white family," the racial ratio grew more lopsided every year since the rate of increase among the "coloured population" supposedly outpaced that of whites. But with each Black household removed, a white family could take its place, doubling the net gain for the overall white population. The figures were calculated with an eye toward the upcoming decennial census: "If we colonize 1000 a year, we shall gain a relative strength of 2000. Let us remove 10,000 a year, and we gain, relatively, 20,000 each year, and 200,000 in ten years" ("Address" 276). What such "relative strength" might be needed for—whether as an estimate of white labor power in the future or as a daily reminder of the importance of white numerical superiority in ensuring public safety—was never explicitly stated. Implicitly, however, these numbers emphasized the perceived vital need of maintaining white majorities to dispel the consternation about white population decline. This worry has rarely waned: in the twenty-first century, it takes shape in the conspiracy theory of "the great replacement" and the murderous racial violence that it fuels.

Soon after the *African Repository* printed this address, it drew the attention of abolitionist William Jay, who diagnosed its fixation with security as a racial function. Relying on this documentary evidence supplied by colonizationists themselves, he faithfully presented their deportation agenda, adding only capitalization to pinpoint how the project "to SECURE slaveholders" was the central mission even though that feature was regularly downplayed in ACS communications. Jay's *Inquiry into the Character and Tendency of the American Colonization* (1835) recognized that projections about population size ("200,000 in ten years") made in the name of "domestic tranquility" forced whites to confront an ever-present risk in those regions where enslaved persons "possess a frightful numerical superiority" over whites (8). The data suggested to Jay that the most important and often only possession that enslaved people had was their own biopolitical potential.

This intuitive understanding of biopower stemmed from Jay's familiarity with the emerging field of political economy. Building on the fundamental tenet of supply and demand, Jay developed an analogy about "the man-market" that stocked and replenished Southern plantations (93). Imagine that half the sheep in the United States should be "carried out of the country" (93). Prices for sheep would in turn skyrocket. Now imagine that cholera carried off 200,000 to 300,000 enslaved persons or that colonization somehow accomplished the same. This mathematical word problem staged a mordant critique. Even in a world of hypothetical sheep, the real wolves were easy to identify. The removal or death of 200,000 slave laborers exposed colonization as a necropolitical scheme designed to strip all rights of nativity and residence from Black people. A loss of roughly 10 percent of the total Black population of two million—Jay made it clear that the intent behind colonization was nothing less than decimation—would produce a cascading effect of runaway inflation and market volatility. First destabilization: on the "man-market" the price of "human flesh would rise many per cent" whether enslaved persons were carried off by disease or colonization (93). Second destabilization: with the reduction of the Southern workforce, agricultural production would suffer, forcing many planters into bankruptcy. The next set of owners, eager to turn a profit, "immediately goes into the market to re-stock the farm" (94), sending the price of enslaved persons through the roof once more, adding to the cycle of runaway speculation and economic insecurity. Third destabilization: with slave property at a premium, holders of human assets become less inclined to manumit their slaves on the condition that they be shipped out of the country courtesy of the Colonization Society. The excess population cannot be exiled to Africa when there is no excess, only scarcity. Fourth destabilization and the final conundrum: insofar as supporters pitched colonization as a pathway to gradual abolition, their strategy obviated their goal by shrinking supply and therefore heightening demand.

Political arithmetic led to feverish conclusions. Consider how one writer for the *Christian Mirror* experienced the discomfort that "a little calculation" caused. Numbers engendered uncontrollable affect: "The present slave population in the United States, is nearly two millions; and there is an annual increase of nearly fifty thousand; and their situation is such as engenders and fosters in their bosoms the most deadly hate to our institutions and ourselves" (*FJ*, "Slavery"). Each clause heightened the sense of peril, building to an irrevocable chain of events destined to end the "same way that it was in Santo Domingo" ("Slavery"). If enslaved persons were harboring thoughts of vengeance, what was transpiring in bosoms of white folks? "I tremble at the thought," wrote this contributor to the *Christian Mirror*, channeling the nervous strains of Jeffersonian affect. Considering numbers, "we have just reason to fear," he wrote ("Slavery"). The *Yankee and Boston Literary Gazette* republished this mathematical nightmare, and before long it landed on the editor's desk at *Freedom's Journal*. Russwurm's decision to reprint it seemed to confirm what Silliman and other advocates of national security most feared: that free people of color constituted a subversive communication circuit, spreading incendiary ideas with the power to knit the Black populations of the Atlantic world together in a fearful conspiracy. In his July Fourth address titled "Some of the Causes of National Anxiety," Silliman, like others of his generation, looked at the projected rates of Black population increase and wondered aloud if "an African sceptre may not be reared and sustained" over America before long (172).

White nationalists intensified these concerns by pointing to specific locales across the slaveholding South where Blacks outnumbered whites day in and day out. David Walker was only reiterating what ACS members already knew when he blandly remarked, "In some of the West-India Islands, and over a large part of South America, there are six or eight coloured persons for one white" (71). Unlike the sublime which holds terror at a distance, the discourse of racial proportion brought terror home, highlighting instances where magnitude becomes not aesthetic but "simply terrible" and terrifying when "danger and pain press too nearly" (E. Burke). The "terror of Mississippi Valley racial-capitalism" (Johnson 84), as in other regions of the South with Black majorities, conjured up ominous visions of the Caribbean island where the Black population dwarfed the white residents: Haiti. *Freedom's Journal* delivered the foreboding prediction: "The tale of St. Domingo, with all its horrors, will be but infant's prattle" in comparison to a slave rebellion on American soil ("Extract"). Herman Melville's debilitated captain, Benito Cereno, his frame wracked "with nervous suffering" and "almost worn to a skeleton" (*Benito Cereno* 679), exhibits the full set of symptoms brought on by acute racial distress. There is reason to his madness—specifically mathematical reason since aboard the *San Dominick* he has experienced firsthand the bloody consequences of being outnumbered and overrun by Blacks. The subject who exhibited Jeffersonian trembling was reacting to racial excess, an unreconciled surfeit, that was simultaneously abstracted as a population and embodied in its Blackness. But for this specifically American variant of the sublime, there would be no transcendence, no overcoming of the vulnerability that had come to define whiteness.

The Political Economy of Reproduction and Mortality

Despite alarmist projections about the annual reproductive increase of free people of color and enslaved persons, rarely in the discourse of colonization do women and children appear in any significant way. *Freedom's Journal* typically took the male slave as representative of all enslaved persons, and when the paper did invoke women, it often hewed close to convention by rebuking women for indulging in gossip and finery.[32] Meanwhile, contributors to the *African Repository* sidestepped the indelicate question of how the master class participated in the reproduction of its labor force through rape. When Philadelphia publisher Mathew Carey pledged $100 a year for ten years to promote the settlement of Liberia, the connection between population increase and enslaved Black women's sexuality came into view but only obliquely. Looking at the "past ratio of the increase of the coloured population," Carey predicted that their numbers "will in the year 1868, amount to above 10,000,000; in 1882, to 15,000,000.... Who can regard this enormous increase without affright? Who can consider any expense too great to avert the horrible consequences, with which it is pregnant?" (271). The sexualized brutality endemic to the slave economy added to white trembling: Carey's furtive and perhaps unknowing allusion to reproductive capacity intimated the ever-present concern that in a not too distant future Black biopower was sure to become ungovernable. For the time being, however, the arithmetical language of "natural increase" sanitized how the biopolitical regime of slaveholding derived both profit and violent pleasure from the bodies of Black women.

Under this "biocapitalization of the female slave," as Ingrid Diran explains, slaveholders extracted surplus capital from female reproduction, counting each new birth as a valuable addition to their "stock" (700). Slave girls and women were "*securitized* as the promise of derivative values" (Diran 713), hedging against the planter's financial risk through the human capital that was literally derived from their bodies. In *Slavery and the Numbers Game*, a classic critique of economic historians who downplayed the vulnerability of Black women's sexuality under slavery, Herbert Gutman carefully parsed the data to reveal slave owners' deep investments in fertility and increase that allowed "the slave labor force to reproduce itself" (96). Like others of the master class, Jefferson balanced his trembling with the cruel appreciation that "enslaved black women gave birth to white wealth" (Davis 117). His relationship with Sally Hemings and the six children she bore gave him intimate knowledge of this fact. There is no getting around Adrienne Davis's point that "the political economy of slavery systematically expropriated black women's sexuality and reproductive capacity for white pleasure and profit" (105). In a January 17, 1819, letter to one of his overseers, Jefferson fused Black women's sexuality to political economy: "I consider the labor of a breeding woman as no object, and that. A child raised every 2. years is of more profit than the crop of the best labor man. in this, as in all other cases, providence has made our interests & our duties coincide perfectly" (Jefferson to Joel Yancy 42). So fortunate did white men like Jefferson consider themselves that they viewed the biopolitical power they held over enslaved women's sexuality as consonant with the hierarchical order of the universe that accorded them their privilege. Increase was a demographic factor that they tracked intimately but impassively. Jeffersonian trembling, in short, was never that distant from the sexual excitement that hinged on violence and brought economic profit. Yet only five years later, Jefferson callously suggested that because "the estimated value of the new-born infant is so low, (say twelve dollars and fifty cents) that it would probably be yielded gratis by the owner," yearly population increases might be managed by separating enslaved mothers and their children once they reach "a proper age for deportation," leaving only "the old stock [to] . . . die off in the ordinary course of nature" (Jefferson to Jared Sparks 291). Death would accomplish what colonization could not.

Around the time that Jefferson was instructing his subaltern about the providential arrangements of white husbandry, he expressed deep interest in the new science of political economy that was a forerunner to biopolitics. On January 8, 1819, a neighboring planter wrote Jefferson to thank him for sending a recently translated edition of Antoine Destutt de Tracy's *A Treatise on Political Economy*.[33] Courtesy of Joseph Milligan, a bookseller whom Jefferson frequently patronized, a dozen copies of this work had arrived in Monticello earlier that winter.[34] He confirmed that John Adams now had a copy at his home in Quincy, which he had sent along with a note explaining that the work "has been translated under his [Jefferson's] eye" (Milligan to Adams). Two years earlier, Jefferson had produced a detailed prospectus for an English translation of de Tracy's research, promoting the book as the finest specimen from "the hands of the political sect in France called the Economists," praising its distillation of "a comprehensive system on the Natural order of societies," and providing a chapter breakdown that included "of Population" as one of its main subject headings. Despite the erudite nature of Jefferson's interest in the work of a Continental *philosophe*, political economy remained an embodied discourse that in the slaveholding United States was always a "sexual political economy" (Davis 105). For men like Jefferson, the "natural" increase of population was wondrous: here was a labor force whose ability to reproduce itself was an uncontested biological fact. "Racial capitalism swung on a reproductive hinge," as Walter Johnson states ("To Remake the World"), which explains why Jefferson had no difficulty with numbers when he reduced political economy to the simple but exemplary math of the female subject isolated under patriarchy: "I consider the labor of a breeding woman . . ." But by the second decade of the nineteenth century, "considering numbers" and trembling for one's country entailed calculations of a more complex and threatening order.

With more data came more uncertainty. To be sure, for much of the nineteenth century, the white inheritors of Jefferson's social order wielded terror over the people they bought and sold, tracked and separated from kin, raped and tortured. But they also inherited Jefferson's trembling, as they realized that the very demographics and composition of that social order spelled a threat. In an ominous distortion of the American Revolutionary ethos to democratize power, terror became widely available as well, accessible to any white person sensible enough to be nervous about the unregulated biopower of the Black population. The racial fear that suffused the discourse of national security altered the vectors of terror. "Terror is not when some command and strike fear into others," according to Foucault. Instead, "there is terror when those who command tremble with fear themselves" (*Security* 201). Jefferson anticipated this recognition, but he also provided, however reluctantly, an important supplement by intuiting how central race, an overlooked category in Foucault's analysis, is to the biopolitics of fear.[35]

White trembling heightened insecurity by shifting its concerns inward, away from the physical demarcations associated with frontiers and borders. Demography could be more menacing than geography. The connection between *terrere* ("to frighten" or "to fill with fear") and *territorium* ("a place from which people are warned off") may have just as much to do with people's interiority as the geostrategic features of physical space.[36] Under the logic of American colonization, the people to be warned off, above all, were free Blacks, and white nationalists rightly concluded that grouping them into a population would make this task easier. To those afflicted with Jeffersonian trembling, fixating on the biopolitics of Black population increase became a matter of future survival. Detractors of the colonizationist movement played upon these fears: from the 500,000 free persons of color highlighted by *Freedom's Journal* to David Walker's assertion that there are "five or six hundred thousand Coloured persons" (71) in Virginia, counting people became a source of terror in its own right. For Walker, the attestation that 450,000 of Virginia's 500,000–600,000 Blacks were ready to die if a race war erupted represented one more sign that the scale was tipping toward an American Armageddon. For *Freedom's Journal*, "the principles of freedom," like Black people themselves, "are too rapid in their growth" to hope that the "drizzling process of transporting two millions of people across the Atlantic" will ebb the overwhelming tide of racial revenge on the horizon ("People of Colour. (Continued)"). Written when *Freedom's Journal* was barely a month old, this column raised the unthinkable: the arresting possibility that a population could act and behave, not as a manageable data set but as a people.

Unlike a population that acts according to what is foreseeable and probable, people do what is improbable. A population behaves according to established patterns and likely tendencies; people, in contrast, "do not really belong to the population" (Foucault, *Security* 43). To whom, then, might they belong? What if they belonged to no one other than themselves? Ultimately, it was this possibility that white nationalists identified as a high-priority security matter, spurring them into action. Or, more exactly, they moved toward reaction, throwing their dubious charity and political arithmetic behind a plan to curb, systemically diminish, and finally extirpate Blackness from the homeland.

Rates of Return

Professor Silliman's diagnosis that "national anxiety" stems from the anticipated 7,491,737 Blacks who will be inhabiting the United States by 1870, Howlett's frantic math, Benito Cereno's "occasional nervous contortions" (686), and other expressions of Jeffersonian trembling overtook white Americans who considered the numbers. Colonizationists, however, knew not to let a crisis go to waste. In the anxiety over national racial insecurity, they perceived an opportunity for expanding racial capitalism in the name of financial security.

By subdividing this population into free people of color and slaves, the colonization movement endeavored to make slavery not just sustainable but also profitable. By draining off the troublesome excess of free and emancipated Blacks, colonization promised to render bondage a stable and hence more attractive investment. Rather than diminishing slavery, the mission of the ACS "*increases the value of slaves and adds strength and security to the system of slavery*" (Garrison 74). No wonder ACS representatives selling subscriptions across the South pitched colonization as a security measure: "The successful prosecution of our scheme will remove the chief source of danger to yourselves, and enable you to hold your property in greater security," as Garrison ventriloquized the pitch made by commissioned agents (74). Multiple senses of security were wrapped up in such appeals: securing donations, ensuring financial security, securing "property" threatened by abolitionists as well as its tendency to run away, and, most of all, securing a white future endangered by the possibility of slave revolt. What was good for national security turned out to be just as salutary for the bottom line of the slaveholding economy.

Advocates promoted colonization as a sensible financial strategy for protecting planters' investments in human capital. William Segar Archer, who owned two thousand acres of prime cropland and eighty-eight slaves, offered a basic lesson in economics to make this case. With the slave population increasing daily, slaves glutted the market, lowering the value of the slaveholder's investment. Colonization discovered a solution in using the notion of Liberia to regulate supply and demand by establishing a transnational site to offload "the excess of colored population" (qtd. in Garrison 76). Economic security was at stake: the "depreciating value of the slaves" resulting from "their disproportionate multiplication" was putting white wealth in jeopardy. Such claims were not off base: historians of the global slave economy have documented how the roots of the Panic of 1837 lay in rapidly declining prices for slaves. By going all in on colonization, Archer argued, "*depreciation would be relieved and retarded at the same time*" (qtd. in Garrison 76). The plan, of course, had psychic benefits as well. Alluding to the Southampton Rebellion, "a recent and most tragical catastrophe" in his home state of Virginia, Archer reminded his audience at the annual ACS meeting that such sound fiscal principles also underwrote the public safety of the South. The combination of financial security and racial security that Archer advocated was relatively simple and straightforward. Not so the national economy's growing reliance on slave-backed securities, which, despite their status as securities, introduced tremendous amounts of risk to the national political economy.

Financial securities offered a convenient, fungible, and, above all, lucrative means of guarding against insecurity—until, of course, those same securities crashed, dragging the antebellum economy down into economic crisis. The traffic in human beings spawned a secondary market in tradable forms of debt and credit that were sold as securities throughout North America and Europe. As Walter Johnson explains, "cotton merchants required some sort of security from the planters to whom they loaned money. That security was the value of the enslaved" ("To Remake the World"). Slave-backed securities became a mainstay for controlling the movement, distribution, exchange, and even mortality of people. Speculating on the mortgages held on planters' human property offered risk-averse investors protection against financial risk. Under this form of securitization, which bundled debt and then resold that debt, investments were safeguarded and credit extended for the initial outlay of credit that enabled the purchase of seed, farming implements, and enslaved persons. Securitization paid additional dividends by ensuring that the vast majority of the U.S. Black population, its enslaved portion, never be perceived as or given the opportunity to act as people. The goal was instead to get them to behave like capital, supremely fungible and increasing in value through biofinancialization.[37] As to the vexing remainder made up by free persons of color, here's where white nationalists stepped in to offer colonization as a solution.

Colonization was charity with a vengeance, derided by critics as a scheme designed to "enhance the value and security of slave property, by removing the free blacks," in the words of William Jay, an ardent abolitionist and son of the first Chief Justice of the United States (12). Jay's observation constituted an incisive thrust: beginning in the late 1820s, banks and brokerages in North American and European financial centers devised a secondary commerce in slaves in order to unite maximum profit with minimal risk. Investors did not have to travel to the slave markets in Charleston or New Orleans to reap a profit nor did they have to traffic in slaves directly. From the trading floors of Wall Street to the Bourse de Paris, speculators bought and sold mortgages on slaves. The financialization of slavery permitted brokers to ignore the auction block and still profit, bloodlessly so it seemed, from the debts that planters accrued in purchasing slaves. The result, according to one historian of capitalism, was epochal: by aggregating mortgages held on enslaved persons into tradable securities, investors in New York, Amsterdam, London, Paris, and other metropolitan cities "changed the financial history of the Western world" (Baptist, *Half* 424).[38] Slave-backed securities provided a political economic solution to the problem of racial security. In the face of an uncertain future, slave-backed securities theoretically protected slave owners, their creditors, and investors from risk by converting slave capital into highly desirable bonds. The Panic of 1837 would provide a different conclusion, as the crash revealed how supposedly secure investments in the slave economy succumbed to unendurable levels of risk. For speculators who swore by slave-backed securities, the very financial mechanisms designed to minimize exposure actually "aggravated the financial risk" and "introduced greater insecurity into their enterprise" (Rothman 130).[39]

The slave system's reliance on slave-backed securities performed the essential function of consolidating racial hegemony. "Finance regards itself primarily as a security technology: one that seeks to secure a fickle future, tame uncertainty and insure against disaster," according to Marieke de Goede ("Financial Security" 162).[40] By investing in planters' debts incurred through the purchase of human capital—that is, by financializing the backbone of the racialized economy—speculators in return offered security for an entire social system. "The cords of credit and debt—of advance and obligation—that cinched the Atlantic economy together were anchored with the mutually defining values of land and slaves," writes Walter Johnson (*River* 86). Within the pre–Civil War world economy, the risk of planters suffering ruin from seasonal drought, potential insect infestation, or the certain depletion and death of their labor force was effectively pooled and redistributed as sellable shares. Even though actual slave bodies were not literally traded at the stock exchanges of Western metropolitan centers, such shares never transcended their racial substrate. The Citizen's Bank Faith Bond sold in Europe circulated with an exchange value that "was approximately that of a first-rate female slave in New Orleans" (Baptist, *Half* 247). While these airy transactions could never fully liquefy the sources of racial embodiment, financial securities theoretically kept risk and uncertainty at a safe distance. Could economic investment in human capital resolve the uncertainties created by the burgeoning Black population that loomed in the nation's future? Investors, colonizationists, and white nationalists all banked that it could. Speculators turned to securitization to insure debt by reselling credit extended to Southern planters as tradable securities. Favorable rates of return seemed like an ideal way to solve the problem of Black rates of increase.

The 2008 financial collapse has provided historians of slavery with a ready analogy for understanding how slave-backed securities crashed the antebellum economy in 1837. Edward Baptist compares the bundling of subprime mortgages to slave-backed securities in order to illustrate how making real property liquid greases the wheels of capitalism on a global scale. In the early 2000s, brokers who snapped up "mortgage-backed securities planned to share in streams of income generated by homebuyers' mortgage payments" (*Half* 248). Through financialization, millions of mortgages were smooshed together, repackaged, and then resold. In the 1820s–1830s, speculators likewise expected handsome returns on investment by purchasing loans that slave owners had taken out to buy their property. At the start of the financial chain, "slaves were purchased on credit and then further collateralized in pursuit of additional financing" (Beckert and Rockman 16). Credit and collateral held as promissory notes and mortgages was then offered to speculators in the form of slave-backed securities, creating a secondary traffic in slaves that "generated revenue for investors from enslavers' repayments of mortgages on enslaved people" (Baptist, *Half* 248). But unlike the millions of home mortgages resold as subprime securities in the 2000s, this set of millions was a human population.

Financial security meshed with the interests of national security in viewing the population as a valuable capital investment. Yet capital in this embodied form "would not simply rust or lie fallow. It would starve. It would steal. It would revolt," as Walter Johnson states (*River* 13). Life could be tabulated and financialized, yet that accounting of biopower not only failed to curtail the capacity of the *bios* to generate uncertainty but also introduced the very sort of financial vulnerability it was designed to remove. In the pre–Civil War economy, slave-backed securities designed to offer protection against risk actually encouraged the wild speculations and easy credit that led to the Panic of 1837. As a financial strategy for converting debt into a tradable commodity, securitization seeks to offset economic gambles, but it is also a mechanism that never fully sheds the entirety of social existence as a zone of contingency and risk. Despite the bullish optimism for mortgage- and slave-backed securities across different eras of global capital, security in each scenario unravels into insecurity in spectacular ways. Elaborating on the contemporary half of the parallel between the investment economy of the early twenty-first century and the slave economy of the 1830s, Walter Johnson in *River of Dark Dreams* describes how in the twenty-first century "overinvestment in real estate, mortgage-backed securities, 'security' technology, and defense contracting" (13) wiped out trillions of dollars in capital in a matter of months, sending the value of pension plans and retirement portfolios plummeting.[41] For the historical aspect of the analogy, Baptist tallies how slavery's speculative economy rested shakily on "the biggest pool of collateral in the United States: 2 million slaves worth over $1 billion," representing nearly "20 percent of all the wealth owned by all U.S. citizens" (*Half* 245), all of which came crashing to a halt with the Panic of 1837. Virtually all sectors of the economy became insecure: stocks suffered drastic devaluation, creditors saw assets vanish overnight, and planters struggled to pay their debts by selling their human property, while enslaved persons remained most vulnerable of all, liable to be sold and separated from kin and community by an auctioneer's gavel.[42]

Legacies

Years before the credit crisis of 1837 exploded, white nationalists had warned that burgeoning Black population numbers could create financial as well as racial instability. When John Randolph of Roanoke attended the convention of a newly founded colonization society in 1817, he took the floor to explain how sending free people of color to Africa would provide needed protections for the institution of slavery. He proceeded cautiously, advising that this "delicate question . . . ought to be left as much out of view as possible" (ACS, *View of Exertions* 9) to avoid alienating Northerners who might be hoping for a gradual solution to slavery. Randolph had little patience for celebrating altruism or other "nobler motives" that might have drawn do-gooders to this historic meeting. Instead, he signaled that slave owners like himself were eager to support any plan for "providing a retreat for this part of our population," that is, any Black person who is not already enslaved. Colonization "does not in any wise affect the question of negro slavery, but, as far it goes, must materially tend to secure the property of every master in the United States over his slaves" (ACS 9). Randolph felt the urgency, shared by every slaveholder he knew, of dealing with the "mixed and intermediate population of free negroes," which posed "one of the greatest sources of the insecurity" to white hegemony (ACS 9). He went a step further: the "insecurity" fomented by the Black population heightened the economically precarious nature of the slave system itself. Too many Black people made slavery insecure.

Randolph approached this contradiction with the principles of political economy in hand, asserting that free people of color were responsible for the "unprofitableness, of slave property." Simply by virtue of their existence within U.S. borders, free Blacks conveyed to their brethren in bondage the possibility that they, too, might be something other than property. Randolph blamed the free population for spreading "discontent," knitting together slaves in extensive and secretive communication networks, and acting as "depositories of stolen goods" (ACS 9). These offenses threatened slaveholders' profit margin, endangering the financial stability of slavery as a whole. Certainly, however, the greatest cost of all was psychological: "the care attendant on their [slaveholders'] possession" (ACS 10) of other human beings exerted a toll that could not easily be assuaged. Randolph had been feeling this way for some time prior to delivering this speech at the inaugural meeting of the ACS. In a letter of January 28, 1804, he confided in unmistakable Jeffersonian accents, "I tremble for the dreadful retribution" awaiting a nation that seemed on a course to relive the events of Saint-Domingue (qtd. in Wood 115). Should "the negroes get possession" of the lower South, he continued, Americans would have no more success in retaking Georgia or South Carolina than the French did in recovering Haiti. If this cataclysm were to happen, a substantial chunk of U.S. territory would become *territorium*, redolent with its original meaning of "a place from which [white] people are warned off."

The political economy of slavery was shadowed by a speculative affective economy: emotions may not be "property" of a subject nor does affect "reside in an object or sign" (Ahmed, "Affective Economies" 119–20), but the trembling unleashed by slavery revealed how the excessive biopower held by people defined as objects, viewed as property, and aggregated as a population imperiled the future of American whiteness. Unless men in Randolph's class took steps to "to rid our own country of a useless and pernicious, if not a dangerous portion of its population" (ACS 5), Randolph advised, the existential threat to slavery could not long be averted. The threat was not just what free people of color posed *to* slavery; the calculations bound up with the biopolitics of increase also illuminated the threat *of* slavery. Randolph's plea anticipated how in/security forced racial capitalism to confront the contingencies that had multiplied with the financialization of Black population growth. From the outset, as the Fourth of July addresses and other sources examined in this chapter suggest, the colonization movement was never able to resolve whether its approach to security through political economy and population management removed insecurity or heightened it.

Colonization had received Randolph's influential support early on because of the movement's potential to stabilize and secure slavery well into the future. His participation in the ACS left long legacies, two of which invite brief comment. Upon his death, Randolph manumitted the 383 enslaved individuals on Roanoke plantation, attesting in an 1821 will: "I give and bequeath to all my slaves their freedom, heartily regretting that I have been the owner of one." The will was challenged but upheld in court. Bequeathed $8,000 for the purchase of land, the manumitted persons made their way northward to Ohio where tracts had been acquired for their resettlement.[43] But "the good white citizens of that community, mostly of Teutonic stock, were terrified," according to the sardonic assessment of a local historian, who in 1965 researched the varying fortunes of the migrants (Hill 182). Whites in Mercer County, Ohio, actively opposed the newcomers, resolving to "resist the settlement of blacks and mulattoes in this country to the full extent of our means, the bayonet not excepted" (Ohio History Connection). The white chaperone accompanying the emancipated Randolph slaves on their journey northward "offered to place one thousand dollars in the hands of any person as security for the good behavior of his charges" (Hill 182). His offer was rejected.

A second legacy provides the subject matter of the next chapter, which describes how Black newspapers and pamphlets tapped into "revolutionary biopower" (Hacking 292) by refiguring the population arithmetic that fed the political and financial motives behind securitization. As part of this investment in political arithmetic, David Walker would have occasion in his "appeal to the coloured citizens of the world" to return to John Randolph's words.

6

Creating White Insecurity

FROM DAVID WALKER'S *APPEAL*
TO THE *LIBERIA HERALD*

NO MATTER HOW PROPHETICALLY Fourth of July orators spoke of a near-total removal of Blacks from U.S. shores at some millennial day, colonization as a strategy for securing the population proceeded by fits and starts. Free people of color, the initial and persistent target of the American Colonization Society, more than resented the exertions of white people whose philanthropy rested on a program of Black exile. Anti-colonization efforts became a focal point of Black organizing and print culture by the 1820s. Early on in its two-and-a-half-year run, John Russwurm and Samuel Cornish's *Freedom's Journal* stressed the infeasibility of an experiment designed to "dispose of 30,000 Blacks in a year" ("People of Colour"), the minimum number thought to be required for keeping the African American population from growing any larger given statistical rates of increase. Along with other flashes of protest such as James Forten's *Letters from a Man of Colour* and David Walker's *Appeal*, *Freedom's Journal* recognized that white nationalists' fear of increase was itself increasing. After *Freedom's Journal* folded in March 1829, Walker, who had acted as an authorized agent for the paper, intensified this line of provocation by drawing what must have been unwelcome attention to regions of the South where sizable Black majorities caused whites to "quake and tremble" (71). With some deliberate prodding, this fear of increase could be aggravated and amplified, as defiant contributors to a widening Black public sphere discerned. In their hands, biopolitical estimates of Blackness were converted into rhetorical and statistical ammunition to undercut and dismantle the racially homogeneous future that white nationalists endeavored to secure.

The biostatistical findings that set Jefferson and other white nationalists trembling inspired a very different set of affects among the participants in Black print culture. Jefferson would have no better nor more acerbic interlocutor than Walker, who identified *Notes on the State of Virginia* as a virulent source code for American racism. When Walker acknowledged that "a much greater philosopher the world never afforded" (31) than Jefferson, he confronted the formidable problem of overcoming the enduring discriminatory pattern established by the founding father's pronouncements about Blacks and their marginal place in the national future. Every Black parent had the duty of procuring Jefferson's book, Walker advised, so that their children could learn to refute its arguments about racial difference and inferiority. Walker led the way by echoing Jefferson's infamous prophecy, "I tremble for my country when I reflect that God is just," but then veered sharply to claim absolute negation as a sublime and revolutionary ethos: "But when I reflect that God is just, and that millions of my wretched brethren would meet death with glory—yea, more, would plunge into the very mouths of cannons and be torn into particles as minute as the atoms which compose the elements of the earth, in preference to a mean submission to the lash of tyrants, I am with streaming eyes, compelled to shrink back into nothingness" (32–33). If Jefferson had been obsessed with "considering numbers," Walker promised to give him more than his fill. In an effort to restore his affective equilibrium, Jefferson had expressed the belief in *Notes* that "change" was "already perceptible" and that a bloodless solution to the Africanist presence that would not require the "extirpation" of slave owners might lie on the national horizon (163). But Walker's own consideration of numbers, the increase by "millions of my wretched brethren" in the half century following Jefferson's predictions, indicated his impatience with the hazy timeline for "total emancipation" that Jefferson had laid out in 1781. He instead described the fixed resolve of Blacks, who, given the enormity of slavery, were prepared to brave total annihilation if such a drastic course proved the only way to topple injustice.

In an era when the American passion for counting and statistics powered an early form of algorithmic governmentality, Walker committed to an altogether different calculus, one based on "nothingness," a prototypical expression of Afro-pessimism. Contemplating the infinitude of matter and the moment of its ultimate obliteration, he wrested none of the recuperative energy that typically graces the subject's encounter with the sublime.[1] "Nothingness" is a protest at once mathematical and ontological, emptying out the foundations of both numbers and existence. Above all, it represents a refusal to surrender one's body and being to biopolitical calculation. How can "nothingness" be counted? More than mere negation, this moment of provocation fits with Walker's rhetoric that both vacates and acknowledges "black collective being" in Stephen Best's reading (9). When Walker avows, "For what is the use of living, when in fact I am dead" (81), he is not voicing resignation but rather an intention to withhold life from an extractive system of racial capitalism that, among other things, gave men like Jefferson the time and opportunity to fret over and philosophize about all the contingencies bearing upon the racial future of the United States. Walker's own declaration is opposed to life only insofar as Black life becomes the property, quite literally, of biopolitics. His words offset another revered document, as he circles back to Jefferson one last time, specifically the assertions to life and liberty found in a "*declaration made July, 4, 1776*" (84).[2] He quotes Jefferson at length, pausing only when he reaches the assertion that people have the right "to throw off such government, and to provide new guards for their future security." At this point, he erupts, "see your Declaration Americans!!!" (85). Walker then continues, "Hear your language further! ☞" pointing readers once more to the exact same sentence that ends the previous passage he has just quoted, closing once again with "future security" (85).

If security tries to tame the future, using biopolitical information to pin down and predict "aleatory events that occur within a population" (Foucault, "*Society*" 246), "nothingness" renders that project forever incomplete and always uncertain, in a word, insecure. This chapter, however, begins at the opposite end of the spectrum by examining what it meant for Blacks to have something—property—instead of nothing.

A Municipal Fine for Being Black

In the political fiction invented by social contract theorists, the desire to safeguard the fruits of one's labor from predation impelled people to consent to sovereign rule in exchange for protection. Slavery, of course, contradicted this fundamental precept by transforming persons into property, in effect, dispossessing some people of personhood while adding to the property of others. True, real estate and other forms of property provided Northern Blacks some small buffer against discriminatory practices such as laws that made property ownership a prerequisite of voting. Yet as James Forten argued in his pamphlet, *Letters from a Man of Colour, on a Late Bill before the Senate of Pennsylvania* (1813), even free persons of color who held property could not count on their successful accumulation of capital to guarantee their safety. Their vulnerability encompassed more than the familiar disregard for Black property rights since, as Forten perceived, free people of color were put at risk by the property they owned. As early as the War of 1812 when whites started worrying about the prospect of large numbers of fugitives from slavery using the wartime chaos to seek refuge in Northern cities, Black-owned property was transformed from an asset into a source of insecurity.

Fifteen years after the date of their original publication, *Freedom's Journal* serialized and reprinted Forten's *Letters* across several issues in spring 1828. Despite the time lapse and changed circumstances, the letters had become newly relevant at a moment when a different national security initiative—colonization—was offloading even greater risk onto African Americans.[3] In one respect, not much had changed from the original context of Forten's protest in 1813 when celebrations of the Fourth of July drew crowds of drunken whites acting like "the destroying Hyena or the avaricious Wolf" (8). In Forten's view, legislative efforts to restrict Black people's movements and to levy specific taxes on Black-owned property, despite having the aura of democratic officialdom, exhibited the same racist force of the mob. But from Cornish and Russwurm's perspective in 1828, what had changed was the ubiquity of racist predation. The everyday rituals of white supremacy, they charged, targeted Black people not just on national holidays but every single day of the year. While the colonization movement might have appeared to be more beneficent and humane than the anti-Black surveillance measures proposed in the Pennsylvania Assembly that sparked Forten's outrage, it intensified the protocols of population management. Forten's analysis of the anxiety created by the crisis over Black refugees provided valuable insights that would later serve *Freedom's Journal* in responding to the various mandates and lures of exile held out by the colonization movement. By drawing a straight line between the fear of Black refugees in 1813 and the colonization campaign to make African Americans into exiles, Forten's letters in their original appearance and then in their republication in *Freedom's Journal* in 1828 exposed how security racialized and criminalized a population.

As Forten surveyed a tense situation in Philadelphia in 1813, he warned that the city fathers were gearing up to "commence the reign of terror over others" (4) in reaction to their apprehensions that Black refugees would soon be streaming in from war-torn regions. Aiming to curtail the migration of Blacks into the state, the Pennsylvania House of Representatives proposed a bill that explicitly made border security into a matter of racial surveillance. Alarmed that the commotion created by the war with Britain was encouraging fugitives and refugees to pour into the city of brotherly love, white citizens called for registering Blacks in what now looks like an early version of a national database. Although the bill never became law, white Philadelphians could not be accused of being halfhearted about their racism; as historian Gary Nash reports, "five times from 1805 to 1814 the legislature debated bills to seal the state off from incoming black migrants or to fasten a special tax on black householders for the support of indigents of their race" (180–81). The bill that motivated Forten to pen a series of public letters marshaled biopolitical data to create an air of imminent crisis. According to the petition delivered to the Pennsylvania legislature, "the number of people of color on record" residing within Philadelphia "amounts to 9762" (Pennsylvania General Assembly 417). At this scale, the population constituted "the largest free Black community in the United States" at the time (Nash 102). The official account was likely prone to underreporting, leaving white inhabitants guessing at the true extent of Philadelphia's Black population.

Far from providing reassurance, the known data cited by the petitioners fed into worries about all the Blacks who could not be counted. What white Philadelphians knew for sure—the census figures showing that there were nearly 10,000 Blacks living in the city—only heightened their sense of insecurity over what they did not know, in this case, all those whom they could not pin down or track. The bill's backers hypothesized that in contrast to the precise number of Black residents in Philadelphia known and accounted for, "there are about 4000 runaway negroes there who are not on record" (Pennsylvania General Assembly 417). Estimates that some unknown number of fugitives were avoiding detection in the city's poorer areas made swift legislative action urgent lest "the emigration of people of colour into the commonwealth of Pennsylvania" (216) chip away at white hegemony. Ultimately, though, white numerical superiority in Philadelphia was never in jeopardy.

Still, the potential flood of fugitives exposed that charity had its limits and, moreover, that those limits were tested once wealth and property seemed at risk. White wealth appeared contingent—and potentially less secure—if it was going to be requisitioned, taxed, or otherwise endangered to care for a refugee population. To forestall such a crisis, a merchant named Jacob Mitchell and Colonel Lewis Rush of the Pennsylvania militia introduced a bill to address any uncertainty about who was going to pay to support an influx of refugees with no assets (indeed, these people were themselves viewed as self-stolen and liberated assets) and few employment prospects. The two assemblymen claimed that enacting racial profiling measures in the city would solve the crisis before it ever began. Their proposal for white security relied on a two-step operation that combined surveillance with the stipulation that Philadelphia's Black residents post bonds—that is, some form of security—as collateral against any drain upon resources that the newcomers might pose. The first move was to register the Black population, ascertaining their addresses, condition, and number. The second was to hold Black wealth as insurance against the conduct of fugitives who used the chaos created by the recent war as an opportunity to escape racial bondage.[4] Arguing that anything less than complete knowledge would be insufficient, Mitchell and Rush joined forces in the Pennsylvania House to urge that "provision may be made to oblige them all"— that is, African Americans—"to be registered" (Pennsylvania General Assembly 417). The total approach made security a matter of population: every single Black person, including those already counted in the previous census, was to be entered into what amounted to a citywide database. With this information, city officials would be able to make one group of Blacks, free people of color, responsible for the welfare for another, fugitives from slavery. Given that the plan stipulated that "a tax may be levied upon them for the support of their own poor" (417), the registry would no doubt prove instrumental in determining whom to tax and how much—and to exempt white resources altogether from being in any way diminished by the charitable effort to relocate the refugees. "The commonwealth of Pennsylvania" that was ritualistically invoked in the language of Mitchell and Rush's bill, it turned out, was only available for some.

Confronted with the prospect of racist surveillance being written into law, Forten protested the registry from his position as a successful capitalist whose sail-making business had earned him wealth and renown. He addressed the petition before the Pennsylvania legislature by rejecting the proposed mandate that free people of color put up collateral for any expenses or damages created by a wave of Black war refugees. The quantifiable amount of white paranoia—the 9,762 Blacks known to be living in the city plus approximately 4,000 runaways—created a vaguely statistical probability that bad behavior would erupt and charitable resources soon be overwhelmed. In response to Mitchell and Rush, who had constructed people of Forten's color and class as a "them" upon whom "a tax may be levied," Forten sought to reclaim a sense of agency by exposing the incoherence of the proposed security measures. "Many of us are men of property, for the security of which, we have hitherto looked to the laws of our blessed state," he declared in the pamphlet's first letter (2).

Were this bill to pass, however, "our property is jeopardized" and held as security against whatever expenses were required to support newly arrived and indigent Black refugees.

Forten recognized the tax for what it was: a municipal fine for being Black. The legal seizure of Black property owners' assets seemed consistent with unfeeling and unfair laws, already on the books, to send fugitives back to slavery. The injustice of such anti-Blackness was steeped in contradiction: property "which years of honest industry have accumulated" (1), the very sort of capital that served as a sign of social respectability and financial stability, now exposed successful Blacks to legal predation. The implicit terms of the social contract that bind people to the commonwealth, Forten recognized, were being suspended not simply to withhold protections to Black property owners but to actively discriminate against Black men of means and seize their assets. Forten's *Letters from a Man of Colour* pinpointed how the bill would convert Black-owned capital into a form of debt that was like no other: this liability was incurred prior to and independent of any actions committed by the property holders themselves. Black Philadelphians' only stigma was owning property in the first place. In effect, the owner of a successful business in maritime stores, to use Forten himself as an example, would be held accountable for the conduct of others precisely because he enjoyed financial security. The contradiction that Forten perceived made sense only in the alchemy of racism: security really was insecurity. Assets, "the security of which" the commonwealth's legal structure was bound to protect, became the very thing that at once exposed individual "men of property" to penalties preemptively and justified the biopolitical supervision of an entire community.

The indemnity held against an emergent Black middle class appeared to whites as an act of justifiable prudence, a security precaution proposed in the face of anticipated demographic shifts that would increase the size of the city's Black population. City and state officials sought to offload the burden created by the war's upheaval onto a successful Black middle class that they no doubt resented. Fears about increased crime and poverty did more than heighten white insecurity: in the uncertain wartime landscape, whites responded to a potential refugee crisis by making Blacks bear the price of white apprehensions. In the city of brotherly love, influential whites like Mitchell and Rush sought to regulate Black sociality by transmuting shared ties into collective precarity. The result was that affective bonds that members of the Black community might have felt for their less fortunate brethren were perverted into a liability.

Four years after the initial publication of *Letters from a Man of Colour* and soon after the ACS was founded with the express mission to find an "asylum" for free and emancipated persons "on the coast of Africa, or some other place, not within any of the states or territorial governments of the United States" (ACS, *View of Exertions* 4), Forten joined forces with Russell Parrott to oppose this campaign of soft exile. In *Resolutions and Remonstrances of the People of Colour Against Colonization to the Coast of Africa* (1818), addressed to the "humane and benevolent Inhabitants" (45) of Philadelphia, these two pillars of the city's free Black community argued that colonization generated as much vulnerability as feelings of safety.[5] Moreover, they asserted, the resulting vulnerability that colonization produced was unevenly apportioned among the city's white and Black residents. Colonization, they felt, endangered the cords of affection that tied so many Black people to their enslaved brethren in the South and that these "cords, which now connect them with us, will be stretched by the distance to which their ends will be carried, until they break" (46). Forten and Parrott detected the same invidious logic that had characterized proposals to surveil Black people and single out their wealth for taxation: a deliberate strategy to weaken fraternal feeling. Born out of a mass meeting, their pamphlet itself memorialized the communal ties endangered by colonization.

Forten and Parrott wrote with a keen sense of masculine indebtedness to the "wives and children whom we had left in servitude" (46). Rescuing loved ones from slavery was hard enough from north of the Mason-Dixon Line without contending with this new hurdle of humanitarian reform thrown up by white nationalists. Theirs was a debt of kinship that could never be discharged from across the Atlantic should the ACS deliver on its proposals. With every African American person transported to "the burning plains of Guinea" (47), the intergenerational trauma of the slave trade would be reawakened, making what was collective memory into a fresh injury. "All the heart-rending agonies which were endured by our forefathers when they were dragged into bondage from Africa will be again renewed, and with increased anguish" (47), making husbands into widowers and children into orphans.

Likely one of the first instances of refuting the political arithmetic behind white nationalism, *Resolutions and Remonstrances* exposed how racialized forms of enumeration underwrote national security. Colonization pretended to be an enlightened approach for curtailing the threat of Black biopower: "Diminished in numbers, the slave population of the southern states, which by its magnitude alarms its proprietors, will be easily secured," Forten and Parrott charged (47).[6] Troublemakers and malcontents "will be sent to the colony; and the tame and submissive will be retained" (47) to work harder and suffer even more. How large might this class of ungovernable and unruly subjects be? Forten and Parrott did not hazard a guess, but they did sketch its qualitative dimensions by asserting that those individuals "who thus may become dangerous to the quiet of their masters" were equal to "those among their bondmen who feel that they should be free" (47). If this grouping were only a tiny fraction of the overall enslaved population, small enough to be shipped off on an annual basis, then colonizationists were probably on the right track. Transporting a few hundred outspoken free people of color would provide the "means to assure safety and submission" of the slave population (47). But Forten and Parrott hinted at another scenario: if the number were greater, say a much larger figure approaching the size of the overall aggregate, then neither colonization nor slavery could be viewed as sustainable. "Southern masters will colonize only those whom it may be dangerous to keep among them," they predicted (47). What if the "dangerous" included nearly everyone? In this question lay the grandest hopes and deepest fears of colonization, its urgency, and its utter failure.

Fire! Fire!!

White Philadelphians' efforts to regulate the local Black population were soon eclipsed by the establishment of the ACS and its plans to implement colonization across the nation at large. A far more ambitious undertaking than discouraging Black migrants from fleeing to one Northern city, mass deportation required vaster resources as well as more ominous rhetoric. As one colonizationist put it, any rational person looking "into futurity" would "behold an appalling scene—in less than one hundred years, (a short time, we would hope, in the life of this republic,) 16,000,000 of blacks" (Polk 77). For some fearful observers, it might already have been too late to prevent this future: "if something is not done to avert the threatened evil . . . if something is not done, as sure as the decree of fate, the hour will arrive, which some prophetic voice seems already to foretell . . . *thine end shall come!*" (Peabody 13). A looming destiny for the nation, as William Peabody warned in his 1828 Fourth of July address, was presaged by "the tremendous example of Hayti" (13) set to repeat itself on U.S. shores.

The solution of exiling suspected troublemakers, the "bondmen who feel that they should be free," to recall Forten and Parrott's phrase, became less viable the more the price for slaves was predicted to rise. Abolitionist William

Jay discerned that as the ACS succeeded in expelling formerly enslaved persons, it actually created a disincentive for slave owners to manumit their slaves and send them to Liberia. A bookish analogy explained the contradictory political economy of colonization: "The idea of abolishing slavery, by increasing the demand for slaves, is about as wise, as would be a plan for lessening the circulation of infidel books, by raising a fund for their purchase" (Jay 93). The end result of white America's affective obsession with racialized security was that the slave population, like a library of licentious books, became its own repository of dangerous musings and fancies.

"Circulation," whether of books or Black people, proved disquieting for those who held slaves as well as for those who did not; through no other capacity than their own existence and movement, Blacks, like immoral books, increased in danger and value simultaneously. This was the threat of print circulation as Black circulation, a threat that materialized each week in the pages of *Freedom's Journal*. Census data used to predict future behavior signified quite differently in the hands of the paper's two Black editors. By repeating numbers whites already knew too well, they recirculated data as terror. The "statistical enthusiasm" (Hacking 281) that seized white Americans became a source of dread; in the columns of *Freedom's Journal*, the racial arithmetic for estimating Black biopower did not fit neatly into the protocols of the colonization algorithm. Much of the original content in this first African American newspaper covered Black gatherings, Black parades, Black church congregations, Black philanthropic meetings, the entire sum of which suggested a different calculus, one invested with the stirrings of voice and agency, that would not simply be counted. So, while the weekly content of *Freedom's Journal* detailed the dangers Northern Blacks faced from kidnappers who would sell free people into slavery or the travails of economic precarity afflicting the community as a whole, it also sought to make vulnerability more equitable by apportioning a share of insecurity to their white neighbors. Each week stories about arson, Black people parading through New York City streets, and, of course, reports of Black population increase gave *Freedom's Journal* the wherewithal to create insecurity.

Mixing original news stories and reprinted items, *Freedom's Journal* warned of dangers that must have seemed bizarre to readers. "Attempt of an Eagle to Devour a Boy" told of a seven-year-old farm child who valiantly defended himself with a sickle to ward off a raptor whose talons could have "lacerated him dreadfully" and whose beak "would have torn out his eyes." Harvesting implements could quickly turn deadly. A farmhand showing off his skill at reaping delivered an "accidental cut of a scythe" that caused "a coloured man" to bleed out ("Summary" 3). By midsummer, scythe use was common enough that this same July issue also reported the case of a laborer who attacked his employer and "nearly cut him in two" and was still at large at the time of printing ("Summary" 7). Fall brought no respite from calamity, and the October 5 paper reported freak accidents such as being struck by lightning or the deaths of an Ohio man and his two sons after they descended into a well and were overcome by carbonic gas. If only they had exercised proper caution and first lowered a lit candle to check for the presence of suffocating fumes, the editors opined. Assembled into a weekly column, the incidents piled up to remind readers of the contingencies that rendered daily existence fragile and uncertain.

Freedom's Journal also supplied a steady stream of advisories detailing more everyday dangers familiar to Black residents of Northern cities. Houses of prostitution, gambling dens, and the easy flow of liquor made the urban landscape treacherous for free people of color trying to gain respectability. The threat of "man-stealing" ("Notice") could only be partially counteracted by collective efforts for self-defense and the vigilance of neighborhood organizations such as the Protecting Society of Philadelphia that the editors championed. The newspaper reminded readers that, unlike the slip of scythe or other accident, racial peril remained a constant feature of life in the North. Colonization embodied this threat in institutional form. Although the ACS did not pose a forceful threat equal to kidnapping, it manifested a persistent and unsettling presence across much of *Freedom's Journal*'s two-and-a-half-year run. While *Freedom's Journal*'s position on Liberia would end in a shocking about-face, for much of its existence it met colonization with a range of reactions: from cautious interest about life in Africa to polite refusal to outright defiance.

By and large, though, the bulk of the coverage that the paper devoted to colonization rejected this program of philanthropic exile for its anti-Black agenda. Still, the editors often moved carefully, not wanting to alienate influential whites in New York and elsewhere. Cornish and Russwurm reprinted columns from the *African Repository* more than any other source, giving ample space to historical essays about African civilization, letters reporting on conditions in Liberia, and arguments both for and against colonization. White writers authored some original content for *Freedom's Journal*, turning to a nascent Black press in hopes of rallying African American support for the colonization cause.[7] The editors proved adept at reframing and taking control over white-authored content. In a series of columns taken from diplomat Alexander Hill Everett's *America: Or, a General Survey of the Political Situation of the Several Powers of the Western Continent* (1827), they arranged the excerpts so that the final installment culminated with a commentary on the futility of deportation and exile. Everett, who had published his own biopolitical treatise, *New Thoughts on Population*, a year earlier, proved useful in making the case that African colonization represented a clunky and ineffective form of population management. "When we consider that the natural increase of that takes place among the slaves, amounting to not less than thirty or forty thousand a year, and that the [colonization] society have not yet made arrangements for transporting annually to Africa more than three or four hundred persons," the undertaking seemed hopeless ("European Colonies"). "Honest zeal and generous philanthropy" should really be seen for what it was: "a great positive evil" that "keeps up in the public mind an impression, that the situation of the slaves can be violently and suddenly altered for the better, by this expedient of emigration" ("European Colonies").

Freedom's Journal paired Everett's remarks with a text from "the late lamented, RUSSEL PARROT [sic] of Philadelphia" that explained why so many whites were committed to an impractical scheme that experts in political economy like Everett deemed misleading and futile.[8] For Parrott, the question never was how to scientifically prune "an overgrown population" whose size defied wholesale repatriation. Instead, he perceived how "the frightful amount" of this population "is studiously concealed ... [in] Gothic darkness" ("From the Union"): the millions of persons held in bondage was shocking, but "frightful" here also pinpoints the "source of uneasiness" that whites experienced as they looked at the political arithmetic. Feeling outnumbered, even though they were not, whites rushed to pass a series of anti-Black laws across the South. Why else would Virginia make it illegal to manumit slaves unless there was concern about adding to the numbers of free Blacks? Why else would the Carolinas prohibit religious gatherings of free and enslaved people unless numbers were themselves the problem? Seized by "fearful and dreadful forebodings," white people, in Parrott's view, were grasping at the straws of colonization for a sense of security no matter how "chimerical" it might have been ("From the Union").

Freedom's Journal essayed week after week to inculcate Black respectability and decorum, but it also was insouciant and sly enough to caution readers, white as well as Black, that a security algorithm could neither predict nor control all conflagrations of instability.[9] Drawing on political arithmetic and then projecting those statistics into the future, the paper showed how inadequate white nationalists' efforts were in keeping pace with a people whose numbers were increasing exponentially. While *Freedom's Journal* generally strove to maintain good relations with potential white allies and benefactors, it also knew how to quicken the affective vulnerabilities of a slaveholding republic by literally adding to the sum of white fears. As the contributor "Investigator" asked in the pages of *Freedom's Journal*, "Is this not a gross encroachment upon the rights of from four to five hundred thousand coloured citizens?" ("Colonization Society. No. 1"). Somewhat fuzzy on the exact figure, the author cut the sample size another way by asserting that "there is not one out of every ten thousand" Black persons from Maine to the Gulf Coast who would consent to expatriation. What "Investigator" knew for sure was that the white men such as Henry Clay, Bushrod Washington, and other dignitaries backing colonization were numerically insignificant in comparison. Their math was even shakier, off by a factor of one hundred: "our population will have increased five hundred thousand, before the Society will have removed five thousand." "Investigator's" calculations revealed a knack for using biopolitical statistics to instill insecurity among whites.

Warning signs flashed forth from virtually every issue of *Freedom's Journal*. Reports of fire and rumors of arson appeared without stop alongside columns decrying racial prejudice and the horrors of slavery. Suspected links among fire, arson, and slave insurrection had long kept whites on edge, as Jill Lepore's history about a rash of fires in colonial-era New York City suggests. Often no more than a single sentence, the notice of fires in the pages of *Freedom's Journal* was hardly remarkable in an era of hay barns, clapboard houses, and open flames. Then again, that everydayness was precisely occasion for trembling. A fire in New Orleans near a downtown theater destroyed many of the buildings surrounding a public square (May 18, 1827, 2). A tavern burned to the ground, claiming a seven-year-old girl as its victim (May 4, 1827, 3). Flames consumed a home along with 100 bushels of corn in Johnstown, New York (June 15, 1827, 3). A "calamitous fire" in a narrow street with wooden frame buildings "spread with the rapidity of lightning" ("Destructive Fire!"). At what point in the future might one of these instances spark a wider conflagration that swept across the nation? All in all, some 200 instances of fire received mention across 102 issues of *Freedom's Journal*.

Each blaze was hardly significant on its own, yet the aggregate held more portentous meanings. The editors had no hesitation about reprinting the words of one July Fourth speaker, who regretted that "even now they [Southerners] cannot hear the midnight cry of fire unaccompanied with agonizing apprehensions" ("Extract"). Taking precautions against fire required confronting what so many were loath to recognize, namely, that fire fueled racialized insecurity—not just in some abstract sense but in the vivid possibility that Blacks might take advantage of commotion and confusion created by smoke and flames to begin murdering whites. Cornish and Russwurm let readers draw their own incendiary conclusions when they republished a column from a Southern paper that regarded Blacks as a combustible presence: "Our slave population has been aptly characterized . . . as 'a volcano in full operation,'" burning with an inextinguishable "inward flame" and eating away at "the beauty of our political system" from the inside ("From the Alexandria Gazette"). Weekly reports of fire fused this metaphor to everyday reality, and this issue's weekly compilation of events included more mentions of fire from Johnstown, New York, to Mobile, Alabama. A state of high alert kept Southern cities in constant agitation so that "when aroused by the alarm of fire; instead of proceeding to the scene of conflagration and lending their assistance to extinguish it, the militia fly to their arms and patrole [*sic*] the streets to prevent an insurrection of the slaves," according to the reprinted article. Cornish and Russwurm's original source was the Benevolent Society of Alexandria for Ameliorating and Improving the Condition of the People of Colour, whose report directly linked the size of the Black population to the explosive situation in the South. Pulling data from the 1820 federal census, the report's authors presented a table showing that the more than one million enslaved persons in Virginia, Georgia, Alabama, Mississippi, Louisiana, and the Carolinas needed to be counterbalanced with exactly 1,181,044 whites "to guard the slaves in time of war." The surplus remainder of the white population—18 percent of the total—left small room for error. Faced with these statistics, the authors reached no resolution other than to end with terror and trembling, falling back on the well-worn Jeffersonian admonition about divine justice and the imminence of slave rebellion.

Black Parades, Besieged Whites

Henry Clay nonetheless sounded a note of confidence in 1827 when he trumpeted the work of the American Colonization Society at its annual meeting: "I shall proceed to show, by reference to indisputable statistical details and calculations, that it is within the compass of reasonable human means" to "eradicate every cause of alarm or solicitude from the breasts of the most timid" of his fellow citizens (*Speech of the Hon. Henry Clay* 7). For as little as $120,000 per year, 6,000 free people of color could be shipped to Liberia, at once cutting into the rate of Black population increase and creating "a vacuum in society," which "by all the laws of population" would be filled by children of "the European race" (7).

When "A Man of Colour" reported on Clay's speech for *Freedom's Journal*, he registered consternation. "It should be no small matter of concern to the free people of colour" that the ACS leadership was planning "to get effectually rid of the free people" ("Original Communication"). White fear, this correspondent perceived, was being offloaded onto Blacks through a campaign of soft terror. Particularly concerning was Clay's testimonial that some Colored Conventions were themselves passing motions in favor of colonization. Clay's address concluded with an appendix of the proceedings from a meeting of African Americans in Baltimore, who avowed, "if *you* have every reason to wish for our removal, how much greater are our inducements to remove!" (6). The resolution supposedly attested to the willingness of Maryland's sizable community of free people to consent to their own exile in accordance with white wishes. But, according to "A Man of Colour," this testimonial had been hotly contested on the convention floor with more than two-thirds of the attendees dissenting. In an effort to set the record straight, he invoked a different set of numbers from a different urban center, the 3,000 people, consisting of Philadelphia's "most respectable people of colour" (37) who had gathered to protest colonization.[10] In the demographic discourse of ratios and exponential population increases, the writer effectively halved Clay's plan to export 6,000 Blacks annually, throwing off the razor-thin margins that were crucial to the Colonization Society's projections. And, perhaps most importantly, by affirming the respectability of this group of African Americans opposed to colonization, "A Man of Colour" disaggregated a population that Clay had lumped together in order to present these grievances and, indeed, present itself as a people and not as a statistical aggregate.

Nothing better than a parade offered visible manifestation of a people. Starting in 1827, African Americans in New York marched annually to commemorate the state's abolition of slavery, the last Northeastern state to do so. For Emancipation Day festivities on July 4, 1827, "Black men took to the streets, celebrating in a parade the likes of which New Yorkers had never seen," writes Carla Peterson (72). By legislative edict, all enslaved persons in New York born after July 4, 1799, would be declared free twenty-eight years later, July 4, 1827. In the intervening years, the number of free people of color in New York City increased threefold, from 3,500 to 10,368 in 1820.[11] Close to 10 percent of New York State's African American population took part in the procession. The parade route added to the shock of the spectacle: "The parade's organizers picked a particularly bold starting point, as St. John's [Park] anchored one of New York's richest white neighborhoods," Benjamin Fagan surmises (36). Curiously, despite its assertions about providing a communications network for 500,000 free people of colour, *Freedom's Journal* took a mostly dim view of these mass gatherings. Then again, Cornish and Russwurm's critique might have been expected all along: any public event that featured rousing speeches, invited alcohol consumption, and encouraged boisterous behavior was sure to worry editors who regularly ran columns with headlines that railed against "Grog Shops" and advised "Propriety of Conduct." Voicing "our protest against all public processions," Cornish and Russwurm explained their reluctance to back any event that might alienate "many warm friends in this city," that is, white allies who might feel unnerved by the public spectacle of Black throngs marching and acting in unison ("New-York"). Their frequent scolding of working-class exuberance left little room to support an event that might tarnish, if only by association, the reputation of the city's more prosperous African American residents.

As early as April of that year, *Freedom's Journal* began calling for restraint on the Fourth of July by printing the resolves of "a very large and respectable number of the People of Colour" who agreed to "abstain from all procession in the public streets on that day" ("Meeting"). Rather than undercut the significance of Emancipation Day by encouraging public displays that might test the bounds of propriety, a Committee of Arrangements planned a more decorous event, one guided by "discriminating taste," that would relocate the celebration from the public streets to a meeting hall decorated with uplifting banners promoting temperance and other virtues ("Abolition"). Somewhat grudgingly and after the fact, Cornish and Russwurm acknowledged that an unauthorized parade—that is, without the endorsement of *Freedom's Journal*—had taken place on July 5 and drew an estimated two thousand people of color celebrating the abolition of slavery in New York.[12] "Not having been present, we can say nothing of its merits" ("Abolition"), the editors sniffed, although they did pause to commend the marchers for observing order and decorum throughout the day.

Cornish and Russwurm modified their position on parades and processions once a defamatory article in the city's white press questioned the rights of Black people to gather in public at all. A week in advance of the expected parade, the editor of the *Morning Chronicle*, Mordecai Noah, ran a column that essentially functioned as a security advisory, warning white New Yorkers that "the grand coloured Jubilee" planned for Emancipation Day posed a danger to public safety.[13] So keenly did Noah anticipate feeling "threatened on or about the day which is now near at hand"—the Fourth of July—that he regretted that New York had ever freed its slaves in the first place. If nothing else, Noah was skilled in his racism. He aptly perceived that the unpredictability of Black biopower constituted a security risk. The fateful day was nearing, according to Noah, when "this part of our population," amounting to "some 12 to 15,000 individuals," would be freed and would then descend on New York City, swelling the city's ranks of criminals and paupers. Noah's repeated reference to "our" Blacks reads as something like a last-ditch bid to assert control and ownership. Sometimes a possessive adjective really is all about possession. Noah supplied a gratuitous flourish, predicting that in addition to the crime reports and charity rolls, New York would also have to add to its "*dandy* register" to accommodate the stereotypes peopling his fantastic vision.

More worrisome still, Noah predicted that any civic celebration would draw African Americans to the city from across the state. This "immediate accession to our population" would clog the streets and thoroughfares with loud and uncouth visitors, who would soon be challenging white entitlements to public space. New Yorkers would be "thrust from the side walks" by Black "thousands" ready to "dispute our possession of Broadway, Bowery, and Park" ("Emancipation of Slaves"). In Noah's eyes, the exponential increase of the Black population through reproduction and birth that colonizationists projected was bad enough. Now with Emancipation Day in New York State nearing, an ill-considered legislative edict signed into law by a previous generation was about to upset the ratio of whites to free Blacks. Armed with advance warning of "this Jubilee nonsense," white residents had scant but still time enough to consult their slaveholding neighbors in the South for solutions. The *Morning Chronicle* advised that the best way to treat free people of color was to treat them like slaves. "In no part of the Southern states . . . a public *festival* of this sort would by no means be permitted" ("Emancipation") lest a population flex its biopower by materializing and acting in concert. Barring this ability to exercise control over African American public life, the only foreseeable prospect for the immediate future was insecurity: "we are at a loss to know what results other than a pernicious nature" might ensue from the free population suddenly increasing its ranks through the manumission of all enslaved persons in the state.

Freedom's Journal responded to this nervous tirade by turning the biopolitical tables on Noah in a personal and intimate way. A cluster of articles following the Fourth of July controversy put the *Morning Chronicle*'s editor in the public crosshairs by hinting at rumors about his louche sexual habits and remarking upon his failure to add to the white population through lawful procreation of his own. Dubbing Noah "the bachelor," the writer, most likely Russwurm, castigated Noah for "prostituting his learning, wit, and talents" to slander and misrepresent Black New Yorkers ("Major Noah's 'Negroes'"). The accusation embroiled Noah in more than figurative prostitution. Not only was this unmarried man "for ever harping on Broadway, negroes, prostitutes, &c" and spinning a chain of unflattering associations. Russwurm aimed the salacious innuendo at Noah to imply nothing so much as the idea that Noah delighted in prostitutes. Observing that "streets and places of amusement are nightly crowded" with white "Blackguards, prostitutes, &c.," Russwurm feigned incredulity: "We wonder the bachelor has never seen them," which was no doubt to insinuate that Noah saw—and perhaps visited—these unsavory types all the time. Respectable African American readers of *Freedom's Journal*, he continued, needed to be protected from the likes of Noah. Family men, anxious to safeguard their "wives and daughters" from a white bachelor always mentioning prostitutes, should beware the *Morning Chronicle*'s editor. "Nor should we trust Noah, had we daughters with a dowry of fifty or a hundred thousand," quipped Russwurm. Noah's tendency to see women as sexualized commodities might just impel him to put aside his anti-Black prejudice if he thought he could gain some financial advantage through racial mixing. Russwurm's rejoinder trapped this white editorial rival in his own bachelorhood, undone by his lack of virility, and discredited by his penchant for delivering an "unmanly and slanderous attack on the coloured population of this city" ("Major Noah's 'Negroes'").

Freedom's Journal had cleared the way for this line of attack with whispers about Noah's failure to participate in the rituals of heterosexual procreation. In the previous week's issue, a writer capped off his rebuke of Noah by touching what must have been a sore spot: "I am not covetous of sitting at the table of Mr. N—, to hold by his arm in the streets,—to marry his daughter, should he ever have one—nor sleep in his bed—neither should I think myself honoured in the possession of all these favors" ("Mordecai").[14] This cagey thrust raised the hobgoblin of amalgamation but then just as quickly backed away from the insinuation by dispelling the notion that the author wanted anything to do with Noah's bed. Long before talk of a "white genocide" entered mainstream discourse with the Trump presidency, *Freedom's Journal* exploited fears about white purity and population decline caused by racial mixing and low fertility rates.[15] With (U.S.) Independence Day and (African American) Emancipation Day folded into one another, the celebration of freedom became a theater of white anxiety. The swelling of New York's African American population, the mass of Black marchers in the streets, the suggestions about the dissolute sexuality of certain white men, and, finally, the cracks about Noah's childlessness all fed into the disquietude that resulted from, to invoke Jefferson's phrase once more, the supposedly rational activity of "considering numbers."

No wonder that Noah, consumed by such statistical dread, viewed the social landscape "through the '*camera obscura*' of prejudice" ("Mordecai"), distorting reality so that the white procurers and prostitutes of Broadway became Black. Two decades before Karl Marx in "The German Ideology" famously invoked the camera obscura to analogize how capitalist ideology flipped material reality upside down, *Freedom's Journal* here turned to this imaging technology to explain how white masculine insecurity exaggerated the putatively criminal, rude, and boisterous elements of free people of color in both number and kind. Noah's allegations about Black rowdies must have rankled Cornish and Russwurm, who saw their journalistic venture as a means of inculcating the virtues of respectability and industriousness among their readership. In contrast to Noah's blinkered view, the portrait they painted corrected the inverted reality created by Noah's racism: theirs was a critique that did not shy away from hinting at how implied connections among prostitution, bachelorhood, and white male sexuality resulted in the *de*crease of the white population.

The public tussle between Cornish and Russwurm's *Freedom's Journal* and Mordecai Noah's *Morning Chronicle* boiled over into subsequent issues. On September 7, 1827, *Freedom's Journal* ran a lengthy column by "Wilberforce" that questioned whether the tactic of insinuating a sexual union with Noah's nonexistent legal daughter might alienate potential white allies. Imagine what would happen "if this number of your paper were to penetrate to one of those large farms in the South"? Adopting the pen name of the famous British abolitionist to signal his general support of abolition as well as his whiteness, Wilberforce used *Freedom's Journal* to express concern that if a newspaper column featuring the irreverent suggestion that a Black man wanted to marry Noah's daughter made its way to the plantation South, it would prompt swift reprisals that would worsen the slave's condition. Suppose a "poor slave is beginning to read the bible" when his master peruses this particular issue. Would not the fearful owner "at once tear the blessed treasure from his trembling hands, for fear that *such matter* would next be put into their hands?" ("Wilberforce" 102). To adapt a slaveholder's warning that Frederick Douglass presented in his *Narrative*, if one were to give an enslaved person a Bible, the next thing he or she might be reading would be *Freedom's Journal*. Wilberforce asked, "Will it do any good to prove to them that they *deserve white wives*" (102)? Would not the editors' decision to publish such insouciant content cause "unmingled injury"? For this white critic offering friendly but unsolicited advice about rhetorical strategy to a Black newspaper, the only thing that encouragement of racial mingling, even if only an ironic thrust, will create is "unmingled" reprisals—that is, pure violence—against Black people. In a column signed "Junior Editor," Russwurm responded that "Wilberforce" had "put a wrong construction, on the meaning of our respected correspondent" who "has no desire for a white wife, as he has long formed an union with one of his own colour" ("Junior Editor"). With a final jab that contrasted Noah's failure to participate in a respectable sexual union, Russwurm highlighted a portrait of Black heteronormativity, often itself an intimate precondition of Black increase.

Any reader who had followed *Freedom's Journal* from its start might have presumed that having copies reach the South had been the editors' ambition all along. As Cornish and Russwurm announced in their inaugural address to the public, "It is our earnest wish to make our Journal a medium of intercourse between our brethren in the different states of this great confederacy" ("To Our Patrons"). Their declaration confirmed the dangers that John Randolph had predicted at the first meeting of the ACS that "free negroes" constituted "one of the greatest sources of the insecurity" because of their ability to serve as communication relays for their enslaved comrades. The sheer existence of a Black press intensified this security threat. When was a "confederacy" not also a network or a conspiracy waiting to strike? "Black activists regarded print, rather than oratory, as promising to link together the disparate and scattered African American communities of the early Republic," as Levine states (*Dislocating* 71). Assessing their progress at the end of their first year of publication, Cornish and Russwurm looked back on their decision to open this relay, what they called "a channel of public communication," and establish a Black communication network. The implicit question was: how far might their signal reach and who would tune in whether by reading or through secondhand circulation? The untested editors had faced daunting challenges of time, resources, and opposition. They nonetheless asked, "Could we hesitate one moment?" ("Our Own Concerns" 163).

At a time when the ability of the ACS to emancipate at most a few hundred enslaved persons per year represented an approach to abolition so gradual as to leave slavery virtually untouched, the idea of an African American publication circulating with any speed or range was cause for white consternation. In an original contribution to *Freedom's Journal* fashioned as a slaveholder's soliloquy, "Aristides" showed why: the author's satire undercut the precautions that the plantation owner took in order to purchase his and his family's safety. By preventing his human property from reading or communicating with free people color—a twin potential materialized in *Freedom's Journal*— the master thinks, "I may possibly live in sfaety [sic], and enjoy the sweet satisfaction of sleeping under the anodynes of swords and pisto s [sic]." Asking himself, "will not these free people of colour communicate this knowledge to my slaves," the slave owner turns to colonization as a security measure. By contributing a modest sum to the ACS, no more than the price of one or two slaves, the master thinks to rid the Black population of its undesirable elements. This simple calculation settles the moral bargain as well. Physical safety need not come at the cost of economic security: rather than "hazard the loss of the whole" through insurrection, a modest investment to support colonization will diminish the meddlesome presence of free Blacks (Aristides 114–15). The column closed with Aristides dropping the slaveholder's persona and reasserting his own voice to warn "the coloured freeman" of the threat posed by colonization, "a *scheme*, as *barbarous* as it is *cunning*." Through its sheer existence as what Cornish and Russwurm in their inaugural issue had called a "public channel" ("To Our Patrons") linking different segments of the Black population, *Freedom's Journal*, even if at times its messaging courted white allies and chided African Americans in the urban North for excessive displays or lively behavior, could do nothing other than promote white insecurity.

Each week *Freedom's Journal* encouraged opportunities for advancement by running advertisements for adult evening classes offered at the New York African Mutual Instruction Society, outlining curricula for Black youth to receive a "good English education," including the study of Latin and natural philosophy, at the Academy in Morris Alley, and advertising rooms to let in a reputable boardinghouse owned by Scipio C. Augustus ("Academy"). Such notices promoted more than these particular services: *Freedom's Journal* through its commercial sections was cultivating a larger image of African Americans' interest in education, business, and respectability. One recurring advertisement offered "*New and Second Handed Clothing*" and promised to clean "Woollen Clothing in the neatest manner, and on the most reasonable terms" ("Clothing"). A threat to white security nonetheless lay in this public notice of politeness: the proprietor (who better to uphold a notion of propriety?) of this clothing store at No. 42 Brattle Street, Boston, was the radical Black abolitionist David Walker.[16]

The Calculations of David Walker's *Appeal*

Walker's Appeal, in Four Articles, Together with a Preamble, to the Colored Citizens of the World smuggles an affective charge into the formal structure of an Enlightenment-era legal proof. Laid out like the U.S. Constitution as a series of "articles" with a "preamble" and referring to Jefferson and the Declaration of Independence multiple times, Walker adopts the legal structure of an official petition to a higher court. But he makes his appeal not to white institutions but to a divine tribunal that will one day dispense vengeance and retribution. The pamphlet challenges the racialized rationale behind national security while also stoking fears about the revolutionary potential of Black biopower. Its rhetoric of racial Armageddon feeds white insecurity at an existential level. Even so, Walker asserts that it is Blacks who are afflicted by "a perpetual source of terror and dismay" (4). The terror that whites wage against Blacks is characterized by "such incomprehensible magnitude" and is "so impenetrable" that it imbues American racism with gothic dread (3–4). Like Clara Wieland struggling to express her inexpressible horror, Walker confronts the impossibility of conveying the immensity of racial injustice: "Oh Heaven! I am full!!! I can hardly move my pen!!!" (25). As we saw in the discussion of *Wieland* in chapter 4, terror often rebounds on the scene of writing itself. For even taking the risk to broach this topic, Walker predicts that he will be murdered, pilloried as an example "to strike terror into others" and make them "the more secure in wretchedness" (25–26). Putting its author's personal safety on the line, the *Appeal* upends the conventional justification of security as antithesis of terror. Security is instead nothing short of a campaign of white terror; security does not defend against terror but requires—and even invites—it.

Walker's *Appeal* challenged the racialized view that saw Black exile on a mass scale as a necessary component of national security. With the exception of kidnapping, nothing made its author and other members of the free Black community feel more vulnerable than colonization. Taking direct aim at Secretary of State Clay for his reassurances to Southerners that colonization societies had no desire to interfere with slavery, Walker condemned any social policy that sought to drive a wedge between free and enslaved Blacks. As quoted in the *Appeal*, Clay described free people of color as a contagion infecting their enslaved compatriots with "*bad habits*," namely their belief that they "certainly *ought* and *must* be FREE" (52). Lest this dangerous truth spread, colonizationists desired "to fix a plan to get those of the coloured people, who are said to be free, away" from their brothers and sisters in chains; the goal was to quarantine the enslaved population and render it "more secure in ignorance and wretchedness" (52).

White security demanded Black deprivation, a tortuous and torturing logic that Walker found most fully expressed in John Randolph's speech at the first convention of the ACS in 1816 where Clay presided as chairman. At least two versions of Randolph's remarks circulated, and instead of drawing from the authorized proceedings of this historic meeting, *A View of Exertions Lately Made for the Purpose of Colonizing the Free People of Colour, in the United States, in Africa, or Elsewhere* (discussed in the previous chapter's examination of Randolph's position), Walker worked with the more emotional and gothic version contained in Jesse Torrey's *A Portraiture of Domestic Slavery . . . and, A Project of a Colonial Asylum for Free Persons of Colour* (1817). Both texts present Randolph's argument that the sizable population of free Blacks poses a danger to the slave system. The two versions of the speech similarly rehearse the rationale used to justify the ambitious plan to uproot free people of color, all in order to stabilize slavery by literally unsettling a population. The shorter version published in *View of Exertions*, which circulated with the support of the ACS, argues that colonization "must materially tend to secure the property of every master in the United States over his slaves" (9). The free population constitutes "one of the greatest sources of the insecurity," a chronic source of ideological contagion that stems from the very existence of Black freedom, but, thankfully, as Randolph explained in this version of his remarks, colonization could strengthen slavery and resolve the contradiction by stripping African Americans of agency by regarding most as property and the small remainder as nuisances to be exiled elsewhere.

Walker's *Appeal*, in contrast, pulls back the curtain on white trembling by turning to Dr. Torrey's account of the speech to get a look at the inner workings of fear. The version of Randolph who appears in these remarks seems much closer to being unhinged, overwrought by the dangers closing in on slaveholders from all sides: "The great slave-holder, Mr. R. said, was frequently a mere sentry at his own door" (62). The more human capital that the plantation owner has, the greater his and his family's physical peril. Property holding does not make the problem of Black freedom or potential agency go away. For any white Southerner, burdened by these daily worries, the specter of free Black people often seemed a "greater bug-bear" (61) than slaveholding itself. As with the speaker who takes the rostrum in the version circulated by the ACS, the Randolph who speaks in Walker's *Appeal* wastes no time with pretending to be motivated by conscience. Not only does colonization pose no threat to bondage, but, according to Randolph's blunt avowal, it actually shores up the slave system by providing a safe and socially responsible outlet for manumission. Colonization, he predicts, will "prove one of the greatest securities to enable the master to keep in possession his own property" (62). The arrangement increases social stability throughout the slaveholding South by protecting slave owners' investments. Liberia was hardly the ameliorative solution to racial bondage that supporters with antislavery sentiments sometimes claimed: coerced exile instead stabilized slavery as a national fixture through the biopolitical management of people.

In Walker's analysis, the colonization society that whites founded in the name of national security begins to look a lot like a terrorist organization. Practicing "a politics of textual (re)circulation" and "underscoring the printed or textualized dimensions of his response to the ACS" (Levine, *Dislocating* 99), Walker reframed Randolph's speech to his advantage. His pamphlet quotes the statesman from Roanoke plantation verbatim and without a break save one brief interpolation: "this description of people, [referring to us half free ones] were pointed out as a great evil" (61). Walker interrupts at the moment when free Blacks are imagined as a security threat. Accused of exerting a baleful influence on the slave population, free Blacks find that white vulnerability places their families, homes, and status as Americans in jeopardy. As Randolph had acknowledged, the colonization society emerged from fear. Garrison's *Liberator* put the case bluntly, charging that the "*true motive*" behind the ACS was "terror lest that blacks should rise to avenge their accumulated wrongs" (10). Walker is more cutting still: colonization allows whites to export their terror. Black insecurity, the liminal condition of being "half free," arises from the Jeffersonian trembling of the slaveholder as he stands guard in his own house, afraid of his own lawful property.

Walker disputes the math that white nationalists used as fodder for their argument about a widespread Black menace. Instead of enumerating Blacks, why not count up the numbers of white people who have oppressed, tortured, and murdered fellow human beings with darker skin for hundreds of years? "How many thousand souls have the blacks murdered in cold blood" compared to white people engaged in the transatlantic slave trade, he asks. No precise answer was forthcoming: how could one begin to account for and quantify the inhumanity of enslavement? A footnote extends this line of questioning: "How many millions souls of the human family have the blacks beat nearly to death, to keep them from learning to read the Word of God, and from writing" (68)? This counterfactual thrust demands that any such scrutiny be directed at white violence instead. Despite the impossibility of calculating such infinite violence, Walker turned the political arithmetic of "considering numbers" into something of a resource for insurrection. He divides the 335,000 "coloured people" in Jamaica by the total number of whites on the island, 15,000. The result, an astounding ratio of 22:1—"22 coloured persons for one white!!!!!!!" (72)—disaggregates the white population, stranding this lone individual on a mathematical island, cut off from family and other sources of solidarity. The *Appeal* aims to sever and isolate white people from political community much as enslavement and colonization are doing to African Americans. Such lopsided ratios should alarm any rational white person. The *Appeal* includes a newspaper report of a slave coffle in Kentucky that used its numerical superiority to overpower three white men leading the group. Sixty people overpowered the two slave drivers and the wagoner: the odds were stacked 20:1 in their favor and, were it not for a bit of bad luck, they would not have been recaptured. One of the injured drivers "deceived" the fugitives by pretending to be dead and escaped with the help of a "*servile woman*" (28). Walker restrains neither his dismay nor his gendered contempt: "I declare, the actions of this black woman are really insupportable" (28). But the Black men are also to blame—and not just in this one incident—for not realizing that they often outnumber whites and for not pressing their numerical advantage. In the aftermath of the small-scale rebellion in Kentucky, the recaptured slaves "will have to suffer as much for the two [white men] whom they secured, as if they had put one hundred to death" (29). Political arithmetic always had the potential to lose proportion and become a lethal matter.

To kill is security at its most extreme, an enactment of the necropolitical insight that the "biophysical elimination" of an enemy, in the words of Achille Mbembe, "strengthen[s] my potential to life and security" ("Necropolitics" 18).[17] Were Blacks to make such calculations, Walker understood, it would strike terror in the hearts of white Americans. To resist the vulnerabilities that Randolph and other colonizationists mandated for Black people, Walker's math shows that security for African Americans can be achieved, at least rhetorically, by exploiting arithmetical ratios of Blacks to whites. By inverting ratios, Walker counts—and looks to count on—Black male biopower:

> It is just the way with black men—eight white men can frighten fifty of them; whereas, if you can only get courage into the blacks, I do declare it, that one good black man can put to death six white men; and I give it as a fact, let twelve black men get well armed for battle, and they will kill and put to flight fifty whites. The reason is, the blacks, once you get them started, they glory in death. (29)

Walker upends the math that supports notions of Black docility and cowardice, but just as significant are the connections he makes among ratios, rationality, and the exercise of reason. Whether it is one, eight, or twelve freedom fighters, the varying numbers in this word problem make it hard to quantify and keep track of Black revolutionary potential. Walker's use of political arithmetic introduces uncertainty—just how many Black rebels might there be?—into the Southern security equation. Beyond proving that Black people are endowed with reason (after all, having to make repeated demonstrations of this fact soon grows wearisome), Walker offers a set of calculations to counter the rational arguments that Jefferson, Clay, Randolph, and other eminent white statesmen used to enumerate and thus regulate Black life in the United States.

Without question, accounting ledgers, the financialization of slave mortgages, and censuses along with the algorithms of the colonization movement all functioned as biopolitical tools put to the service of settler colonialism and plantation capitalism. No wonder that algorithms are easily racialized in ways reminiscent of the Code Noir (McKittrick 115). Yet quantification, like other aspects of political arithmetic, can be seized as an "antiracist tool," as Molly Farrell suggests in her reading of Absalom Jones and Richard Allen's defense of Black Philadelphians after the yellow fever epidemic of 1793 ("Data as Poetry" 1050). Walker's diligence in "considering numbers" rivals Jeffersonian calculations by turning biopolitical data into an "*infopolitical*" resource for contesting the math of political inclusion and exclusion (MacLellan 915). Looking at how Canadian colonialism seeks to incorporate Native people as exclusions within the liberal state, Matthew MacLellan argues that an "*Indigenous infopolitics*" offers alternative ways of counting that lead to "political empowerment and resistance" (924). While attestations of agency and resistance found in critical discourse can sometimes take on a predictable or schematic cast, it is equally the case that biopolitics are not simply repressive.[18] As a profoundly mathematical text, Walker's *Appeal* deploys anew the raw material of information whose sum total becomes the production of white insecurity.

Walker's calculations insinuate that Blacks in the United States could and should be calculating. No better evidence of this possibility exists than Walker's *Appeal* itself, a pamphlet designed to sow vulnerability across the South. Its circulation, as Peter Hinks has shown, prompted authorities to fear links of all kinds: between its publication and recent fires, between slave literacy and insurrection, and among Black people themselves.[19] Its language dared white readers to ignore what they already knew: their centuries-long campaign of terror now imperiled the security of their nation's future. "I tell you Americans!"

Walker declares, "that unless you speedily alter your course, *you* and your *Country are gone!!!!!!*" (45). Although white Americans may have had their eyes closed and ears plugged ("Hear it Americans!!" he implores), the *Appeal* attempts to puncture this bubble of false tranquility. Walker enlists scripture, mathematical rationality, and arresting typographical effects as part of this urgent effort, but ultimately, he presents the material existence of the *Appeal* itself as a threat that can be neither assuaged nor overlooked.[20] "Now I ask the Americans to see the fearful terror they labor under for fear that my brethren will get my Book and read it," as Walker imagined the radical specter of a Black readership (45). Even if "the quick reaction of the authorities readily stopped the work from ever threatening the fundamental security of any Southern locale" (Hinks xv), the psychological toll on white peace of mind, impossible to measure, cannot be discounted as anything less than alarming. The affective toll of white insecurity could only be partially allayed by burning pamphlets, doubling patrols, or increasing slave surveillance.

By encouraging African Americans to procure his pamphlet and strike fear into the hearts of white Americans, Walker delivered a masterstroke by demonstrating that reading itself can be terrifying. If security tries to remove contingency from the future, then the safe bet for Walker in 1830 was that others assuredly "will get my Book" in the days to come.

The Political Balance of the Globe and the *Liberia Herald*

Despite sowing the seeds of cultural nationalism and fostering African American communication networks, it seemed that Black print culture did not provide Russwurm, after he became sole editor of *Freedom's Journal*, with enough reassurance or support to continue his labors. The newspaper folded shortly before the appearance of the first edition of Walker's *Appeal*, and by the end of 1829, Russwurm sailed to West Africa, becoming one of the more than 15,000 African Americans who eventually left the United States to colonize Liberia.[21]

Russwurm's sudden change infuriated his associates at the time and continues to puzzle scholars even now. "Any colored man" who supports colonization "should be considered a traitor to his brethren, and discarded by every respectable man of colour," wrote his former coeditor Cornish. When Walker used these same words for his *Appeal*, there could be little doubt that Russwurm remained the target. Given *Freedom Journal's* campaign to remind free Blacks about the social and political importance of upright public decorum, the jab about respectability must have stung Russwurm. Critics, both then and now, have expressed surprise over his decision to join forces with a deportation movement that the columns of *Freedom's Journal* had so consistently denounced. "What triggered this apparently sudden change of heart is not at all clear," writes Winston James in his comprehensive and even-handed biography of Russwurm (45). James surmises that perhaps this accomplished African American leader, the third Black person to receive a degree from a U.S. college, reached a breaking point when he realized that American racism was insurmountable. Perhaps Russwurm himself drew a distinction between self-chosen emigration and colonization.[22] Others did not: Blacks in Philadelphia at the time burnt the editor in effigy for his pro-colonization position (Beyan 34). But in the pages of *Freedom's Journal*, Russwurm wondered that anyone was surprised. On February 14, 1829, with the flourish of the editorial "we," Russwurm announced to readers that while the paper had "always been in direct opposition to the plan of colonizing the coast of Africa," the moment to shift course had come and "that our views are materially changed. We have always said, that when convinced of our error, we should hasten to acknowledge it— *that period has now arrived* . . . we come out from this examination, a decided supporter of the ACS" ("Liberia" 362).

In 1829, as Russwurm surveyed the situation of African Americans, the prospects for internal migration now seemed bleaker than when Forten had protested the plan to create a registry for Black inhabitants during the War of 1812. As *Freedom's Journal* reported in March 1829, Ohio and other states were on the verge of closing their borders to Black migrants. If manumitted persons had few safe havens after leaving the South and if free persons of color could strive for social respectability but be denied the opportunity to enter and buy cheap land in western states, then Russwurm perhaps concluded that more welcoming shores lay elsewhere. Anyone looking at the obvious fact that African Americans were living in "a land in which we cannot enjoy the privileges of citizen" would reach a similar conclusion, he suggested in the next week's issue ("Freedom's Journal" 370). Europe could not be viewed as a viable option, as that continent was "already overburdened with a starving population" ("Liberia" 362). Where to turn in the face of this grim recognition that the United States was inhospitable to Black life and likely to remain so?

Dispatches received at the newspaper's office in lower Manhattan helped convince Russwurm of his decision. On the same page sounding an alarm bell that several free states were debating laws to close their borders to free people of color, *Freedom's Journal* featured observations from a Pennsylvania newspaper detailing and contrasting the populations of Asia, Africa, Oceania, and the Americas culled from the research of an Italian demographer. Printed on a single sheet in French and organized into a grid shaded blue, purple, green, and pink, "Balance Politique du Globe en 1828" by the Italian demographer Adriano Balbi supplied the *Philadelphia Evening Post* with comparative biopolitical data about the religion, wealth, geography, and population size of the world's regions and peoples (see figure 6.1). The data appealed to Russwurm, who no doubt was feeling battered by his compatriots' adverse reaction to the announcement that he was emigrating to Liberia. Estimates that placed "the whole population of the whole globe . . . at 737 millions" lent greater context to the travails of 500,000 free people of color and the sufferings of more than two million enslaved persons ("Political Balance"). With the global population inching toward one billion people, these figures illustrated the plight faced by African Americans. Where in a crowded world could people with no rights find security and tranquility?

Certainly not Ohio or other free states, which, as Russwurm reported in a column adjacent to this biopolitical overview, were devising laws to restrict the entry of Black migrants and fugitives. Suppose that Virginia emancipated all its slaves. By existing statute, all free Blacks would be obliged to leave the state and, as Russwurm assumes, neighboring states in the North would act defensively by "forbidding the emigration of free persons of colour into their limits" ("Colonization"). Little over a year later, Russwurm, having become editor of the *Liberia Herald*, would declare that his apprehensions had been justified. *Freedom's Journal* had folded, but Russwurm now found that as an African colonist the *Liberia Herald* gave him a platform to announce that Ohio had indeed enacted and that Indiana was on the brink of passing "laws which we predicted some months ago" to bar Black emigrants. Likening himself to a seasoned sailor who sees the signs of a coming tempest and trims his sails, Russwurm stated that in light of growing oppression in the United States he was right to act courageously by emigrating to Liberia "in pursuit of Freedom" ("Island of Fernando Po"). The population statistics from Balbi's "Balance Politique du Globe" that he had weighed the previous year in the final issues of *Freedom's Journal* pushed his deliberations beyond U.S. borders. If Europe teems with "228 millions of population" and if Asia is bursting with "590 millions of inhabitants," Africa with "60 millions of population" appears as the rational choice. True, the Americas boast fewer people than these other continents, but among the territories of the New World "the United States hold the first rank in population . . . being stated at 11,600,900" ("Political Balance . . . concluded").

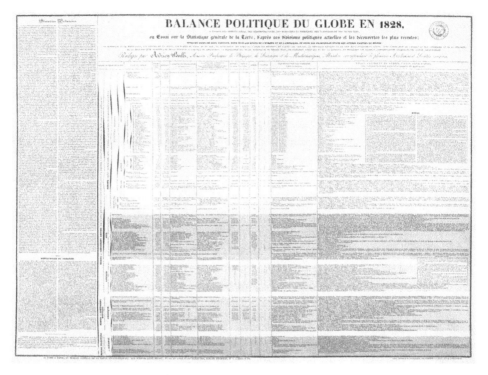

FIGURE 6.1. Adriano Balbi, "Balance Politique du Globe en 1828."

In Russwurm's final analysis, the first had indeed become the last, that is, the last place on earth where Blacks could find refuge.

Once settled in Liberia, Russwurm continued to rely on biopolitical information to defend his decision and to assert that the infant colony rested on stable foundations. Perhaps the most important calculation and prediction to make about a population was what percentage might die. As the editor of the *Liberia Herald* who resurrected the paper after a short-lived run that had ended four years earlier, Russwurm became intensely interested in one particular aspect of population statistics—mortality figures. Looking to counter widely held beliefs that disease, malnutrition, and an unhealthy climate made African colonization a death sentence for exiles, he made his case by comparing the fortunes of his new home to the dismal news received from the settlement on the island of Fernando Po (now Bioko) in the Gulf of Guinea.[23] Estimating what percentage of the population might die was crucial to establishing a permanent foothold for Black émigrés to Liberia. According to the intelligence that the *Liberia Herald* received, only three of forty-three British marines on the island had survived the ravages of tropical illness and "but one solitary individual" of twenty-three mechanics remained alive. The naval commander stationed at Fernando Po displayed an incipient understanding of actuarial science by giving "orders that *fifteen graves* should be kept open all the time!" ("Island of Fernando Po" 6). In contrast, Liberia offered a salubrious climate that encouraged trade, industry, and education.[24] The *Liberia Herald* added a poetic flourish to this public relations campaign for settlement by invoking Lydia Huntley Sigourney's colonization tribute timed for July Fourth. Addressed to ocean breezes that "swept the breadth of that fragrant land" and "the breath of spice bud" ("Poetry") that perfumed the colony, Liberia in her poetic portrait hardly appeared as a fetid zone of miasma. But on Fernando Po, where "so great was the mortality, at one time, that the bare recollection and mention of it, is enough to chill one's blood" ("Island of Fernando Po" 7), the environment itself seemed suffused by a gothic horror that rendered everyone vulnerable to disease and death.[25]

A healthy population of colonists in Liberia demanded a biopolitical regimen similar to what Russwurm had endorsed in one of his last actions as editor of *Freedom's Journal*. The final issue presented articles for governing the colony, observing the need for "public morals" and regulations to ensure "the security, and title of public or individual property."[26] None of these governmental mandates, however, had a chance of success without enforcement to ensure the health and well-being of its people. Article XII of the "Plan of Civil Government for the Colony of Liberia" thus called for the appointment of health commissioners to determine which cases should receive "medical attention" and to "report nuisances to the public health" ("Plan"). Once in Liberia, Russwurm defended the settlement's governance by charging that "Mr. Garrison of the Liberator" ("Mortality") had seriously misrepresented the situation in describing the mortality rates of recent emigrants. Russwurm had it on good authority from the colony's physician that only two emigrants from the recently docked *Volador* had succumbed to illness. Yet he also would have had to acknowledge that the editorship of the *Liberia Herald* opened up only after the previous person tapped for the position died upon arrival. Even if tropical diseases shortened life spans, the editorial voice of the *Liberia Herald* opined (in an article reprinted in the Kentucky *Western Luminary*) that although "we may not live to the age of three score and ten in Africa," an abbreviated existence with "the full rights of a citizen" is preferable to extended life under American inequality ("Liberia" 3). Such "accelerated death" (LaFleur and Schuller 607) associated with the biopolitical management of race would be more protracted in Russwurm's case, and he survived long enough to preside over "West's Africa's, and probably the continent's, first black newspaper" (James 61) before becoming the first Black governor of Maryland in Liberia in 1836 after colonizationists in Maryland split from the main body of the ACS. His tenure as editor was rocky, and many colonists found his close alliance with the white colonial governor objectionable to the point where a mob of enraged readers gathered in protest at the offices of the *Liberia Herald*.[27]

For former allies in the United States who remained dismayed and mystified by Russwurm's "treachery," the sorry state of the *Liberia Herald* itself provided tangible proof that unhealthy conditions awaited anyone foolhardy enough to believe the reports circulated by the ACS. Copies of the paper that made their way back to the United States were so blemished and soggy that they appeared as "miasmatic material texts," to cite Adam Lewis's apt phrasing (120). The *Emancipator*, an abolitionist newspaper from New York, reported that issues of the *Liberia Herald* it received were "so stained with the dampness of the climate, as to be scarcely legible" and gave off "a smell like grass which has been for months soaking in water" that the unwholesome nature of the colony—and no doubt colonization, too—could be readily inferred (qtd. in Lewis 120). Antislavery periodicals that emerged in the wake of *Freedom's Journal*'s demise "emphasized the poor quality of the *Liberia Herald* as a way to galvanize their anticolonization stance" (Lewis 118).[28] Sigourney's "On the Publication of the Liberia Herald" that celebrated Russwurm's latest experiment in bringing the illumination of print culture to "that dark, deserted land" could offer no rejoinder to imputations about out-of-control death rates among Liberian colonists. Nor could her poem evade the complications of stripping the colonists of their American past. The first verse begins by casting the *Liberia Herald* as a missionary returning with scientific knowledge, which for "so long" had been "expatriate from thy native sphere," to the continent. Science in the abstract, not U.S.-born Blacks and their accumulated lived historical existence, becomes the exile returning to its African home. Whatever degree of alienation that African colonization might have represented for Black Americans, the "resurrection" (350)—Sigourney's term—of imported print cultures in Africa compensates for the exiles' sacrifice of birthplace, longevity, and ultimately life itself.

Sigourney's poetic displacements were nothing compared to the actual dispossession of Indigenous peoples by African American colonists. Glowing reports that "most of the settlers appear to be rapidly acquiring property"

("Washington, February 10, 1832") could only come at the expense of the land's native inhabitants. Seizing land through treaties brokered by ACS representatives or at gunpoint, "the newly independent black settler-colonists, in turn, promptly disenfranchised those very West Africans" (Kazanjian, *Brink* 54). Under Russwurm's editorship, the *Liberia Herald* kept close watch on regional conflicts to assess the threat level posed by neighboring tribes. The April 6, 1830, issue featured a pair of articles, "Native War to Leeward" and "Native War at the Windward," making it seem that the colony was hemmed in on two sides. Replete with gruesome details about the mass killings of infants and children whose bodies floated down the Mesurado River to Monrovia, such intelligence made the defensive precautions undertaken by the colony—stocking up on arms, drilling the militia, appealing to Western naval powers for support—seem like sensible policy. The effects of colonial violence would simmer for generations, erupting at the end of the twentieth century in civil wars that claimed the lives of hundreds of thousands of Liberians.

A healthy population might be necessary for war. The future of Liberia depended on achieving numbers stable enough to withstand the ravages brought on by the violence of settler colonialism. Having biopolitical information about potential enemies—their size, proximity to Monrovia, demeanor of neighboring tribes—was regarded as even more necessary for security. A scrapbook with the handwritten title, "Liberia," held by the Schomburg Center for Research in Black Culture, includes a map that would have provided a useful overview for rendering the landscape in biopolitical terms.[29] Stitched together with extracts from an 1832 issue of the *Liberia Herald*, a contemporaneous map displays the locations of the fort, weapons magazine, and defensive positions (see figure 6.2). It also supplies an ethnobiopolitical key to the region's tribal inhabitants. The Veys (now the Vai people) "are an active, warlike, & proud people: population 12,000 to 15,000." The Dey/Dei tribe gave less cause for alarm, characterized as "an indolent and inoffensive people: population 6000 to 8000." The Bassa people, estimated to number 125,000 strong, occupy a land that "rivals, in fertility, any part of the African coast." As an artifact of biopower, the "Colony of Liberia" map found alongside the *Liberia Herald* in the scrapbook forms part of what Amos Beyan sees as the disastrous legacy of Russwurm's policies and attitudes in Liberia, first as newspaper editor and then as colonial governor.[30] Beyan asserts that Russwurm's commercial dealings with neighboring tribes indirectly supported the slave trade and that he did not protest racial hierarchies that accorded light-skinned Blacks preferential treatment because "he was among the chief beneficiaries of such a system" (56).[31]

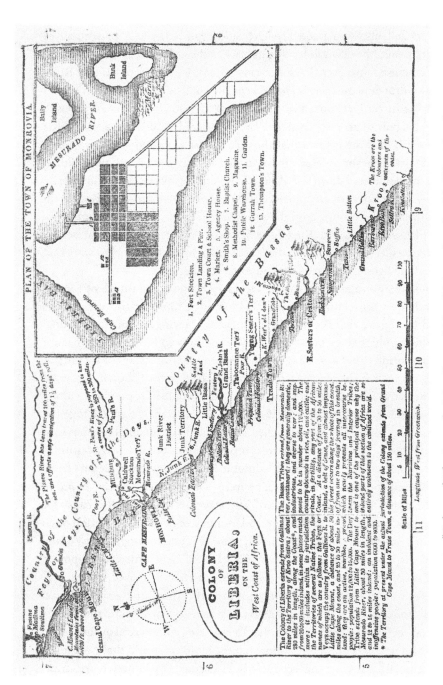

FIGURE 6.2. "Colony of Liberia, on the West Coast of Africa." *Liberia*. Scrapbook held by Schomburg Center for Research in Black Culture, New York.

The ultimate consequences of such thinking would not be fully accounted until the end of the twentieth century and the First and Second Liberian Civil Wars. In Beyan's judgment, settler colonists such as Russwurm should be counted "among the sources of Liberia's social and political disorders that tragically led to the deaths of more than 250,000 Liberians from 1980 through 2003" (121). The history of the American colonization of Liberia was not the first instance nor would it be the last of U.S. national security destabilizing other parts of the globe.

"Who Is There to Mourn?"

Like Walker who played on Jefferson's fears about a growing Black population in a white republic, Russwurm, now settled on the west coast of Africa, also engaged Jefferson. In June 1830, the editor of the *Liberia Herald* republished the speech of Logan, the Cayuga orator, that Jefferson had translated, romanticized, and included in *Notes on the State of Virginia*. In the wake of settler colonial violence, Logan ponders his existence as a population of one. But in the context of the *Liberia Herald*, with its monthly tally of colonists' deaths, Logan's mourning about extinction pressed that much more closely: Russwurm's recirculation of Jefferson's quotation of Logan today cannot be read without tragic irony. At the time, however, the reappearance of Jefferson's Logan in Africa failed to create affective understandings that might have seeded amity instead of violence between African American settler colonialists and indigenous Africans. Even though the American colonization movement, according to Brandon Mills, looked to policies of Native American removal as both a precedent and plan for Black colonization, few at the time seemed willing to consider what these connections might have meant in transnational contexts.[32]

In the pages of the *Liberia Herald* in 1830, Logan presented a figure of sympathetic identification for the exiles who had left behind all they knew in the United States. The white enactment of necropolitical measures in the name of security might well have resonated for African Americans who had been nudged, convinced, or pressured to emigrate to a tropical climate where sickness and death ran high. Yet what did it mean to reprint this celebrated example of "native" eloquence at a time when African American colonists to Liberia were relying on force and coercion in their dealings with African "natives"? The colonists, now Americo-Liberians, "shared the same race and skin color of those they wished to dominate" (Gershoni 99). Logan recounts how, despite having been "the friend of white men," settlers murdered his entire family, "sparing not even my women and children" (Jefferson, *Notes* 253). Extermination is population security at its most absolute. The tragic contexts of an armed militia, land seizure, and frontier violence surrounding Logan's oratory must also have created uncomfortable parallels for African American exiles who settled West Africa. The figure of the sole surviving Native person underpins romanticized narratives of extinction—what Jonathan Elmer has called the "Logan effect" (119). Courtesy first of Jefferson in Virginia and then Russwurm in Liberia, the transatlantic recirculation of Logan's speech fuses a new cycle of settler colonialism to a legacy of American displacement and genocide. Caught somewhere in the middle are Black exiles, their population construed as a security threat to the white republic but once in Africa threatened by its own mortality. In either case, the math worked out the same: with his bloodline destroyed, Logan asked, "Who is there to mourn for Logan?—Not one" (*Notes* 254). This finality of zero brings counting to a close. With "not one" person to enumerate, population security is achieved at last.

EPILOGUE

What Comes after Security?

WHAT COMES AFTER SECURITY? At a moment when security has grown to encompass spheres and events far beyond its original remit in social contract theory, it no doubt seems fruitless to ponder the remote possibility that security could be something other than a source of continuous vulnerability. Precaution and national preparedness now encroach upon the economy, public health, the weather and climate, and the environment, as "seemingly disparate types of events—ranging from terrorist attacks, to hurricanes and earthquakes, to epidemics—have been brought into the same framework of 'security threats'" (Lakoff 247). Not long after his imprisonment in Nuremburg by U.S. occupying forces at the end of World War II, Carl Schmitt registered how conditions were ripe for this emergence of a totalizing security regime: "There is nothing which is not somehow related to the state" ("Strong State" 218). Despite his role as a theorist of the Nazi state, Schmitt made this pronouncement with decided ambivalence because he felt that liberalism's overextension into nonpolitical realms had weakened state sovereignty. He perceived how biopolitical measures, whose early emanations are examined in the chapters of this book, had become indispensable elements of liberalism's political order. Nothing falls outside of the state, which has become *total in a purely quantitative sense* (218), absorbing all aspects of life, including those that lie beyond the political realm, in ways that overextend and dilute sovereign power.

Implicit in this dissent from quantitative liberal democracy is Schmitt's frustration with the abandonment of government in a qualitative sense, which in former times had allowed for the exercise of "genuine power" ("Strong State" 223), a position that should give us as much pause today as it did in 1945. Any attempt to read Schmitt's critique of the "remarkable indiscriminate quantitative *expansion of the state* in all directions" (219) as a defense of democratic humanism runs into serious trouble. As Agamben reminds us, Schmitt had more than a passing flirtation with Nazism and his ideas about sovereignty's origins in the state of exception where *homo sacer* could be killed became the rule in the concentration camp. If it is true that "today it is not the city but rather the camp that is the fundamental biopolitical paradigm of the West" (*Homo Sacer* 181), then it becomes necessary to accept that security has emerged as the political goal that justifies seeing the imminence of threat everywhere, indeed, in seeing "life itself... [as] an open system, nonlinear and exponentially chaotic" (Mbembe, "Thoughts on the Planetary") that must be made quantitative, calculable, and predictable. The figure of *homo securus* described in this book's introduction represents the summation of this attitude: at one moment inviting the extension of surveillance, enumeration, and other forms of quantification, the subject of security at the next moment experiences vulnerability over the fact that so many facets of life are deemed insecure and in need of securitization.

The problem with security, according to International Relations professor Ole Wæver, is that it does not know "where to stop," more often than not squeezing multisided conflicts and complex crises into militarized frameworks. Nowhere does this tendency have more pronounced effects than in approaches to environmental problems, which securitization treats with "'us vs. them' thinking" that is ill-equipped for the planetary scale of climate change. Security, because it tends to view "threats as coming from outside a state's own borders," encourages nations to minimize their "own contributions to environmental problems" (Wæver 64) while laying blame and responsibility elsewhere. Likewise, treating population flows as a security issue has similar effects, leading to perceptions of migrants and refugees as a "them" whose experiences and culture are inherently antagonistic to the values of the homeland.[1] In these contexts where security has become quantitatively unending—which is part of what Benjamin was describing with the assertion that "the 'state of emergency' in which we live is not the exception but the rule"—it becomes difficult to imagine alternatives. While I agree with Grewal that "if there is work to be done, it is to ensure that authoritarian security regimes lose their power" (31), thinking about what comes after security is a formidable task, perhaps one that outstrips our capacity and our imaginations. The challenge of prying political and social life apart from securitization looks even more difficult with the recognition that conservatives, not to mention hawkish reactionaries, are generally regarded as the best custodians of national security. By monopolizing the war on terror, the right has enjoyed considerable success in ramping up national security spending, installing domestic surveillance programs with unparalleled reach and incredible technological sophistication, and at the same time building feudal border walls while impeding action on the existential dangers of climate change. Now that security, like so many other issues from gun control to reproductive rights, has fallen prey to partisanship, the possibilities for transformative change have grown only slimmer.[2]

There remains to examine, however, a strange twist of intellectual and literary history, which at the very least suggests that the expansion of security legitimated by the continuous state of emergency might not be as totalizing as it seems. This history takes us back one last time to Schmitt, whose 1938 book on Hobbes, as we saw in this book's introduction, adduced the maxim *extra civitatem securitas*, no security outside the state. Armed with this principle, the Leviathan becomes the sole sovereign and "functions as an irresistible instrument of quietude" (46). Such tranquility echoes with the original meanings of *se-cura*, of being without care, an attitude that also borders on care-lessness. But in 1945, while working on a disclaimer that would distance himself from that text, he signed the note, "Honestly your good friend Benito Cereno" (qtd. in Sollors 406).[3] The identification with Melville's doomed captain fits into Schmitt's ongoing and complex fascination with Melville's 1853 novella that scholars such as Werner Sollors and Thomas Beebee have examined. His relationship to the story was personal as well as allegorical, perhaps a roundabout way to justify his actions after having been "an innocent hostage taken by Babo-as-Hitler and his black SS mutineers" (Sollors 420). Or was the reference to the role he was now forced to play under the U.S. occupation of postwar Germany? The first performance stretches the limits of our credulity, as "Schmitt unlike Benito Cereno, had indeed been an accomplice, a dinner guest at the table of henchmen" (Sollors 420). The second readily becomes allegorical, as the story of a captain controlled by slave rebels serves as a point for reflection examining "the consequences of the destruction of national sovereignty and of the dethroning of elites by the masses" (Beebee 117). In either case, the significance of Melville's story for this former theorist of the National Socialist state most likely lay in its status as a preeminent narrative of security and terror.

By the historical Amasa Delano's own account, his lack of concern (*se-cura*) kept him safe while aboard the *Tryal*, unable to perceive that he was walking among Black rebels and not Black slaves.[4] Melville absorbs Delano's ease into a tableau of population increase, a "pleasant sort of sunny sight" (704) that his romantic racialism associates with Black motherhood. The sight of Black reproduction adding to unspecified Black numbers does not seem to alarm the American captain, or rather, he stumbles over himself to allay the fears that do arise. Even after taking an informal census of the "clamorous throng of whites and blacks, but the latter outnumbering the former more than could have been expected" (676), he exhibits few symptoms of the Jeffersonian trembling that plagued his countrymen. The halting narrative he hears from Don Benito is all about racial ratios, explaining how storms and scurvy decimated the white crew. Above all, what makes Delano feel secure is the performance of the padlocked and chained Atufal. White masculinity has nothing to fear from what Melville in a very different context called "the power of blackness": the excess of biopolitical data that is in plain sight on the decks of the *San Dominick* creates no cause for alarm in the bit of security theater orchestrated by Babo because the symbology of a lone captive absorbs all of Delano's attention. To invoke Schmitt once more, the American's feelings of security function as "an irresistible instrument of quietude" that heightens not just his own danger but that of his ship and crew.

After the rebels are executed and order restored, Delano regains a sense of security that once again renders him complacent and careless. As many readers have pointed out, his final bit of encouragement to forget what has happened just as "yon bright sun has forgotten it all, and the blue sea, and the blue sky; these have turned over new leaves" (754) amounts to a supreme act of obfuscation, a willful displacement of historical events onto the phenomena of the natural world. Yet the gauzy state of nature that Delano prefers to the material conditions of transatlantic slavery represents an altogether different ideological landscape than either Hobbes or Locke imagined. For men like Delano, there is no more powerful display of the imperial state's sovereignty than the spectacle of Babo's head affixed to a pike in the public square. Such a reading, however, cannot gainsay the unappeasable threat that others have detected in "that hive of subtlety" (755) that stares back at onlookers. Delano achieves this sense of well-being by embracing the imperative of security to leave nothing to the imagination and to settle on single meanings. "What has cast such a shadow upon you?" he asks Benito Cereno, who simply responds, "The negro" (754). Does he mean the individualized case of Babo, or do dread and despair arise from "the negro" as an uncountable, unaccountable mass category, a population that is sure to harbor other rebels and just as sure to unsettle the presumed security of whiteness? Delano does not inquire further: "There was no more conversation that day." Ultimately, security rejects uncertainty and shuts down interpretation. As Delano exemplifies, security is not about knowing more; it is an attitude about knowing less.

For the American captain, nothing comes after security. Conversation ends, investigations wrap up, and executions reach their brutal finality. That's where Delano ends up, but not *The Piazza Tales*, the collection containing *Benito Cereno*, which has three more stories to offer. To adopt an approach that is both literal and literary, what immediately comes after *Benito Cereno* as a security coda is "The Lightning-Rod Man," a whimsical sort of tale lacking both the length and gravitas of the preceding novella. Nonetheless, for all its lighthearted irony in discussing mortal danger and divine judgment, "The Lightning-Rod Man" presents a rare interruption in the affective feedback loop between security and insecurity.

Amid a tempestuous electrical storm, a stranger shows up at the door of the unnamed narrator. Part huckster and part evangelist, the seller of lightning rods seeks to convince his mark that he stands in imminent danger from the impossible-to-predict "zig-zag irradiations" shooting down from the heavens (756). What algorithms or other tools might offset or at least predict a lightning bolt's erratic path? His pitch might be likened to an advertisement for a home security system with the threat of damnation thrown into the mix. Nowhere is safe to stand: not the carpet, not the oak floorboards, and certainly not beside one's fellow man, all of which are described as excellent conductors of electricity. The narrator pleads, "Pray, will you tell me where and how one may be safe in a time like this?" (760). His question serves equally as well at this juncture of my argument: given the ways that security transformed the state of nature into physical space of the frontier (chapter 3), the ways that information about terror becomes sublime (chapter 4), and the ways that security is woven into whiteness and Black exile (chapters 5 and 6), one also may very well wonder if space exists to imagine forms of political and social existence that do not have safety as their ultimate horizon. The genius of Melville's story is that his interlocutor realizes over the course of his telling that he has asked the wrong question. Not "where and how one may be safe" but *why* one needs to pursue safety at the expense of all other values.

"The Lightning-Rod Man" dramatizes how security is misrecognized as the antidote to terror instead of its source. Bolts of lightning, the salesman is forced to admit, have struck the very structures where his copper rods have been installed. Nor do attempts to turn to religion for safety or salvation work any better, as a "servant girl [was] struck at her bed-side with a rosary in her hand; the beads being metal" (758). Security proves elusive when the very measures taken to ensure safety attract and require exposure to risk. Most insidious of all, this religious hawker, something of an avatar for the shape-shifter at the center of Melville's *The Confidence-Man*, makes the rejection of fellow feeling a precondition of security. Rugs are conductors of current as are wet clothes, windows, chimneys, walls, barns, and farm animals. But it seems that the best—and most dangerous—conductors are people themselves. To a mindset that sees contingency everywhere in the form of "irregular" (756) thunderbolts that can strike at any moment with no predictable pattern, there is no such thing as collective security. There is instead only individual danger. Melville's narrator is incredulous, "Do I dream? Man avoid man? and in danger-time, too" (761). The possibility of security as a source of collective striving is perverted into a source of individualized risk. So thoroughly securitized has society become that there is no society, only individual calculations of exposure and precaution.

The lightning-rod man's would-be customer does his best to dissent from the state of constant emergency that he is asked to buy into. Melville's skeptic intuits that security goes hand in hand with blind obedience, sensing that consent is often more accurately an irrevocable contract under which, as Schmitt outlines, "whoever searches for his security with another one becomes subject to that other one" (*Leviathan* 49). The language of this contract, we might note, is slippery: the subject does not actually need to receive safety and protection to be obligated; simply desiring security is enough to be bound to another. Like the rabbit in Locke's story of the social contract where pursuit alone converts prey into property (chapter 3), the subject becomes bound by security for the sake of security. Melville's narrator refuses to enter the contractual relation that buying a lightning-rod represents because the exchange would also require him to accept fear as the basis for social relations overall. Perhaps he believes with Mark Neocleous that "to be free, we must renounce security" ("Securitati Perpetuae" 27), but whatever the case, the narrator acts decisively, snapping the huckster's rod in two and throwing him out of the house. De-securitization requires a similar break, the refusal to accept the normalization of the state of emergency that otherwise legitimates an exceptional politics. It thus entails moving beyond "the Schmittean rendering of the political significance of existential insecurities" (Huysmans 143), which is to say that de-securitization is at core an affective response that does not buy into the fear of contingency so that other horizons for politics beyond security may emerge.

Yet the question remains, what follows the renunciation of security, were such defiance possible? After tossing the lightning-rod man from his front door, Melville's narrator has little success in establishing alternate coordinates for social connection and political community: in "spite of my dissuasive talk of him to my neighbors, the Lightning-rod man still dwells in the land . . . and drives a brave trade with the fears of man" (763). Whatever the narrator's resistance to this atmospheric security regime, which, like many others, relies on manipulating a quivering humanity to create perceived needs that can only be satisfied by commodity consumption, his objections fail to convince anyone else about the possibility of life after security. In structural terms, despite coming after *Benito Cereno*, the exemplar of nineteenth-century American literature that marks the coincidence of security and racialized insecurity in unparalleled fashion, "The Lightning-Rod Man" remains trapped in the cycle of vulnerability that has driven American politics since at least as long as Ben Franklin's dictum about "liberty" and "temporary safety" first stirred audiences.

I do not pretend to envision what Melville could not. If there is a politics and a literature beyond security, it might be glimpsed only at the end of an attenuated chain of reference: in Agamben's reading of Benjamin's reading of Kafka's reading of what may come after law has been loosened from the sovereign state of exception. "Just as children play with disused objects," so, too, one day humanity might adapt and rework the notion of legal authority that departs from canonical or accepted meanings. Only this sort of "play"—though Agamben also describes the practice as "study"—will "free them [people] from it [the law] for good" (*Homo Sacer* 64). But any new use of law also "has been contaminated by law" and therefore "must also be freed from its own value." This conundrum points to the impossibility of security: the task that remains is to arrive at a conceptual and affective orientation where being secure with and among others can be freed from the conceptual and affective armature of security.

ACKNOWLEDGMENTS

I HAD BEEN WRITING a very different book. After a short but sullen excursion into Ayn Rand as part of an effort to understand the ideological and cultural shifts that had led up to the presidential election of 2016, it was difficult to muster the enthusiasm to tackle much more of the same. That pursuit was, of course, shortsighted in its view that the twenty-first-century ascendancy of an energetic and reactionary populism was somehow exceptional. But one insight that I did take with me as I began thinking about security was that governance often relies on fantasies of vulnerability. This notion on its own, however, was hardly enough to sustain the engagements with political theory, surveillance studies, algorithms, information theory, and literary history that are a part of this book. For that support, I was fortunate enough to have the encouragement and intellectual camaraderie of friends and colleagues. They gave me the confidence to abandon my previous (and lugubrious) investigations and to think about security in its many forms from the national to the personal.

Rachel Adams, Monique Allewaert, Colleen Glenney Boggs, Michael Boyden, Lisa Cooper, Julia Dauer, Wai Chee Dimock, Ramzi Fawaz, Danuta Fjellestad, Susan Gillman, Sara Guyer, Ron Harris, Donatella Izzo, Caroline Levine, Donald Pease, Michael Rothberg, Xiomara Santamarina, Sean Teuton, Anja Wanner, David Watson, Edlie Wong, and David Zimmerman have every day reminded me of the challenges and joys of thinking, writing, and teaching. Susan Stanford Friedman brought my attention to Nathaniel Hawthorne's "Sights from a Steeple," a suggestion that helped me add nuance to the American timeline of security and surveillance. A pathbreaking scholar, she is deeply missed by her colleagues. The late Jeffrey Steele pointed me to the passages in Walter Benjamin's *The Arcades Project* that touch on James Fenimore Cooper. Laila Amine, Anna Brickhouse, Paul Downes, David Glimp, and Yogita Goyal read drafts of articles and chapters, providing feedback on those portions that inevitably made the whole better. Johannes Voelz, whose excellent book on insecurity precedes mine, has been an ideal interlocutor. I am grateful to him for convening at Goethe University an international community of scholars and inviting my participation. A final first draft of the manuscript was sent to Elisa Tamarkin and Colleen Boggs, who each offered deft suggestions that showed me where I might expand and intensify aspects of my argument. Bob Levine has listened to and commented on this project at every turn: his knowledge and acumen have been instrumental to this book and, indeed, to my career as a whole since we first met at the annual conference of the American Studies Association in Kansas City in 1996.

Much of the writing of this book coincided with taking on administrative roles, first as department chair and then as director of the Center for the Humanities at the University of Wisconsin-Madison. I scarcely could have survived without the constant support of Marrion Ladd, Megan Massino, Spring Sherrod, and Melissa Ulbricht. Throughout this time, Susan Zaeske, Associate Dean of the Humanities, has been a wonderful teammate, as we've worked together to hire a cohort of new colleagues and launch new initiatives centered on public engagement.

Archival holdings at the John Hay Library at Brown University, the New York Public Library, and the Schomburg Center for Research in Black Culture have enhanced my findings. The librarians and staff at these institutions have been generous with their knowledge, time, and expertise. Tolu Akinwole, Alesia Alexander, Johs Rasmussen, and Kyle Smith provided research support in tracking down and confirming hard-to-find sources. I wish to thank the Dorothy Draheim Fund at UW-Madison, which enabled me to visit these archives and to secure this research support. Jenn Backer brought her keen eyes to the manuscript in its final stages. Generous support from a National Endowment for the Humanities fellowship enabled me to complete the research and writing necessary for turning a manuscript into a book.

Portions of this book appeared previously as journal articles and book chapters. In addition to be being grateful for these opportunities to share my research, I have benefited immensely from the feedback of editors and anonymous peer reviewers. Gordon Hutner published an early version of chapter 3 and parts of chapter 6 in *American Literary History*, but that's only the tip of the iceberg since for years he has been a limitless source of professional advice, knowledge, and good practical wisdom about writing and editing. "Security and the Informational Sublime," which later became chapter 4, appeared in *REAL: Yearbook of Research in English and American Literature* 35 (2019) as part of a special issue titled "The Aesthetics of Security" edited by Winfried Fluck, Rieke Jordan, and Johannes Voelz. The *Journal of American Studies* 56, no. 3 (2022) published "Jeffersonian Trembling: The Racial Origins of National

Security," and I appreciate the help of Sinéad Moynihan as part of that process. Finally, Bert Emerson and Greg Laski, editors of *Democracies in America: Keywords for the 19th Century and Today*, created a project that enabled me to explore the lasting relevance of Benjamin Franklin's formulations about liberty and security. The manuscript was in good hands with Ali Parrington, who helped prepare the final pages. Above all, I am grateful to Anne Savarese at Princeton University Press for her confidence in the project and her help in bringing this book to completion.

    Maya Castronovo and Julian Castronovo continually help me to see, listen to, and experience the world in new ways. For years, they've been faster than me, and now I also appreciate how they've grown to be quicker, sharper, and more intuitive with art, media, and ideas. Of course, I'm always still catching up to Leslie Bow: best friend and confidante for the long run.

NOTES

Introduction

1. Woodward presents his argument as a competing claim to Frederick Jackson Turner's frontier thesis. Free security could be considered as important as free land in the development of American ideology. He writes: "if the influence of free land may be considered significant in the shaping of American character and national history," then the comparative security of the United States during much of nineteenth century must be seen as equally significant (5).

2. Hobbes learned the importance of preventing internal discord from his translation of Thucydides, whose *History of the Peloponnesian War* chronicled how civil war hastened the fall of the Athenian empire. See Arends 263–64, 275.

3. This governmental report also emphasizes that "the implications of climate change on national security are not all beyond U.S. borders—they pose risks here at home" ("National Security Implications" 3) in ways that presume national solidarity as necessary for meeting external threats.

4. The edited collection *Insecurity* (2022) begins with Richard Grusin observing, "The 2020 presidential election was declared by Trump's own appointed election security officials in the Department of Homeland Security's Cybersecurity and Infrastructure Security Agency to have been the 'most secure in American history'" (vii).

5. The essential distinction between friend and enemy that Schmitt adduces hinges upon the initial effort "to create tranquility, security, and order and thereby establish the normal situation" (*Concept of the Political* 46). As we'll see, when an emergency or crisis becomes the normative state of affairs, constant and continuing security is normalized as well.

6. Benjamin's exhortation to counter the state of emergency by "bring[ing] about a real state of emergency" (*Illuminations* 257) has grown increasingly more difficult, as the suspension of law and emergency measures have become routine (see Agamben, *State of Exception* 6–7).

7. Agamben derives these conclusions by drawing on examples of postrevolutionary France, neutral Switzerland, and 1930s Germany (*State of Exception* 11–16).

8. See also Brightman, who identifies a "psychology of insecurity that underlies American geopolitical strategy" (9). She sees this pathology manifested in military power that is prioritized over diplomacy or economic actions such as sanctions. Nonetheless, it is important to examine how these other modes of achieving national security are coordinated with military potential and actions.

9. According to Neocleous, use of "insecurity" emerged only recently in political theoretical discourse as an effect of bourgeois modernity. Prior to that, the key term conjoined with "security" was not "insecurity" but "fear." See Neocleous, "Securitati Perpetuae" (4–9).

10. Schmitt's relationship to the Nazi Reich was complex, to say the least. Arendt describes Schmitt as a "convinced Nazi" (qtd. in Wolin 426) while Bendersky reads Schmitt's engagement with Hobbes as a covert attempt to distance himself from the Nationalist Sociality Party. Schwab may be the most forgiving, concluding in part from his conversations with Schmitt that he was "an anti-Nazi who toiled to prevent Hitler from acquiring power; a friend and teacher of Marxists and Jews" (xiii). It is difficult to reconcile this view with Schmitt's assertions that Jewish theorists and philosophers, especially Moses Mendelssohn, were guilty of "castrating a leviathan that had been full of vitality" (*Leviathan* 70).

11. The states of emergency and exception are aligned concepts that Agamben draws from Benjamin and Schmitt, respectively. Most important is his reminder that "one must not forget here that both Benjamin and Schmitt had before them a state—the Nazi Reich—in which the state of exception proclaimed in 1933 had never been repealed" (*State of Exception* 57).

12. See, for instance, Gray's work on digital surveillance and constitutional rights to privacy and Hochman's work on wiretapping, crime, and national security.

13. With thanks to Johannes Voelz for this insight.

14. Lakoff makes a persuasive case that the transition from insurance in the nineteenth century to preparedness in the twentieth century represents a significant development in security culture. Where insurance seeks "to collectivize individual risk" through public health measures or social security programs, "preparedness does not seek to prevent the occurrence of the disastrous event but rather assumes that the event will happen" (250, 253).

15. Careful readers will have noticed that this chronological plan is already out of sequence since Cooper's novel is written after Brown's but that *Wieland* is set historically just after the Seven Years' War and before *The Pioneers*. "Anachronic" is not the same thing as "anachronistic." Nagel and Wood prefer the former as a term with less baggage than the latter, which assumes that "every event and every object has its proper location within objective and linear time" (13). Anachronic approaches and queer temporalities, as Freeman writes, offer possibilities for "using the past differently: neither as an example that the present must follow, nor as a golden time to return to, but as a means of politically reframing the present and what seem like its imperatives" ("Synchronic/Anachronic" 137). Castronovo ("Fact, Faction, Anachronism") discusses the role that anachronistic thinking can play in opening up ossified facts to new interpretation.

16. Freeman's work represents an insightful example of the temporal turn in criticism. Here, I'm drawing on her formulation, "Time, then, is not only of the essence; it actually produces 'essences'—well-rested bodies, controlled orgasms, and so on" ("Introduction" 160).

17. De Grazia associates anachronism with "insurrectionary tactics" (31), a point that is borne out by Insko's study of how U.S. abolitionism relied on radical historiographies.

18. Nagel and Wood also bring Valéry to bear on their discussion on methods such as anachrony that rely on discontinuity (11). Their work led me to Valéry, who then led me to Poincaré.

Chapter 1

1. For pushback against the "neorealist assumptions" of Security Studies, see Dalby (22) and Peoples and Vaughn-Williams (9). Their critiques fit with the emergence of critical security studies, which argues for more varied disciplinary approaches beyond the state-focused and implicit military tenor of International Relations.

2. The contingent nature of aesthetics is a consistent feature in philosophical commentary. Dewey's *Art as Experience*, for example, concludes with this sentence: "Art is a mode of prediction not found in charts and statistics, and it insinuates possibilities of human relations not to be found in rule and precept, admonition and administration" (349).

3. Schneier, for instance, makes a distinction between security reality and "security theater" that implicitly dismisses aesthetic considerations as mere show (*Beyond Fear* 38).

4. The insight about the reversible connection between academic discipline and punitive disciplining has been widely made, and Michael Walzer's early observation of this point is one of the most acute (205).

5. Bigo and Tsoukala observe that International Relations has a "monopoly on the meanings of security" (6) and instead argue for interdisciplinary approaches. They include law, sociology, and psychology but make no mention of art, aesthetics, or literature.

6. The goal of human security, however, can be perverted and hijacked by authoritarian practices of the "human-security state," as Amar shows in his case studies of Brazil and Egypt (5–17).

7. A sense of home, for instance, depends on viewing others as strangers. "The home does not secure identity by expelling strangers, but requires those strangers" (Ahmed, "Home and Away" 340) to set the boundary between the safe and familiar and the foreign and threatening. In *Fear: The History of a Political Idea*, Robin writes, "Convinced that we lack moral or political principles to bind us together, we savor the experience of being afraid . . . for only fear, we believe, can turn us from isolated men and women into a united people" (3). Fear by this reading is thus not a private emotion but the grounding of a political sensibility.

8. The increase in the corporate privatization of security has been widely studied along with its ability to act as a governing force "alongside other entities such as national governments, supranational authorities, and NGOs" (Johnston 47).

9. Writing about passwords and other computer security precautions, Lennon argues that "every new security enhancement produces a new security risk by presenting attackers with new means and opportunities for technically (and nontechnically) compromising any given system or class of systems" (*Passwords* 6).

10. Paying for security introduces problems that can prove destabilizing to sovereign powers. See Glimp's study of Renaissance England where "the effort to fund security itself becomes the threat, a harm that makes people feel attacked, vulnerable, less secure."

11. For fuller treatment of "slow media" in this context and its relevance to contemporary political discourse, see Castronovo ("Information Warfare").

12. For an important argument about the relation of information to literary aesthetics, see Lee, who explores the range of affects from despair to delight created by their convergence.

13. Thanks to Lee Edelman for discussing this example with me. What counts as suspicious often implies a perspective rooted in whiteness that exercises suspicion toward persons of color, especially Black and Muslim men (Hanhardt 215).

14. Adams writes, "philosophers of care claim that persons are bound together by shared vulnerability and interdependence" (248). It is important to remember, as Adams and others point out, that vulnerability is not often shared equally and is experienced asymmetrically. See also Edwards, who looks to Black women's literature for forms of care—"unsecured, insecure forms of safety" (30)—that can counter state security regimes.

15. See the chapters in *Vulnerability in Resistance*, especially the contributions by Butler, Gambetti, Hirsch, and Sabsay.

16. See the *New York Times* op-ed that President George W. Bush published on the one-year anniversary of 9/11 with the headline, "Securing Freedom's Triumph."

17. See *The Birth of Biopolitics*, especially the lecture of January 24, 1979 (66).

18. De Goede contends that the national imperatives behind the "finance-security assemblage" (*Speculative Security* xxix) come powerfully into play with the tracking of everyday financial transactions that supposedly have connections to terrorist organizations.

19. The temporal reach of security and surveillance encompasses the past as well as the future. In its ruling in *Carpenter v. United States* (discussed a bit more in chapter 4), the U.S. Supreme Court expressed concern that cell-site records containing GPS locations empower the government with "near perfect surveillance and allow it to travel back in time to retrace a person's whereabouts" (2).

20. See also Zuboff's notion of surveillance capitalism and how it restricts "our right to the future tense," transforming people as subjects into objects (337). Zuboff is focused on the corporate structures of social media giants such as Facebook. But these concerns are not the end result of technology but their enabling condition. Surveillance is a subset, a particularly effective mode of power/knowledge, of security. See, for instance, how Voelz examines the temporal aspects of total security where "a future fully brought under control would turn into a *fait accompli*" (*Poetics* 12).

21. Levy describes this cycle of risk-taking and risk-management (40). The mutiny aboard the *Creole* (also the subject of a novella by Frederick Douglass) is for Levy an exemplary case to examine the financialization of risk in the Atlantic slave world. See 21–59.

22. An additional layer of affective complexity can be seen in the video of Rumsfeld's performance of these remarks. Even as the transcription might express frustration, Rumsfeld's visible buoyancy at this stage of the press conference is noteworthy. I would suggest that this eagerness comes from the continuing justification for the militarization of security that "unknown knowns" supplies. So pleased was Rumsfeld with this phrasing that it inspired the title of his memoir, *Known and Unknown*.

23. For a fascinating and speculative link between the profile in seventeenth-century art and statistical and racial profiling in later centuries, see Amoore (132–37). On the secondary nature of Black pain in comparison to white injury, see King (13–18) and also Yao's discussion of how feelings were weighted unequally within nineteenth-century biopolitical regimes (32–33).

24. Thomson in 1759 documented these and other practices that led to the "Iniquity of the Walk" (44).

25. Even though "the white people" emerged as a group identity during the violent conflicts of the 1750s and afterward, it was hardly the coherent identity that it is now. At various points, Quakers, Catholics, and Moravians were viewed as threats to white interests on the frontier. According to Silver, "the singularity at the heart of Indian war was that when faced with attack, Europeans would fall out among themselves further, looking inward at a supposedly Indian-tainted elite for traces of guilt instead of outward at more obvious enemies" (99). For a contrasting view, see Griffin, who begins his account of stadial notions of race in early America by noting that "Puritans and adventurers had employed the language of racial subordination" (13) in tandem with violence toward the Indigenous peoples they encountered. But it may have been that the racial designation of whiteness mattered most. Griffin thus implies that racial

affinity took precedence over notions of essential racial difference: "While they [settlers] claimed to talk as 'white people,' they did not view Indians as an alien race and did not refer to Indians by their physical features" (65).

26. See the *New York Times* series, "One Nation, Tracked," especially Thompson and Warzel's reporting in "Twelve Million Phones, One Data Set, Zero Privacy."

Chapter 2

1. Or, alternatively, "I protect, therefore I obligate" in Hal Foster's gloss on Schmitt's phrasing as a motto for homeland security.

2. The historical context does not neatly line up with the theoretical one in this instance. It would be a mistake to see that Franklin established a state of exception around "skulking murderers" because he never considered Indians as part of the legal order in the first place. Declaring marauders as enemies is not the same thing as cordoning them off in a state of exception. It is important to remember that the state of exception is not simply equitable to lawlessness. Instead, the exception to the legal order and the protections it provides remain bound up with the juridical function of the state. The exception is "defined by the oxymoron *ecstasy-belonging*" that both binds and abandons the subject to the law (Agamben, *State of Exception* 35).

3. For precursors to Franklin's efforts plus consideration of the Caribbean contexts behind biopolitical statistics in the Americas, see Farrell. On the importance of Franklin's *Observations* to the origins of population studies, especially Malthus, see Hodgson, "Malthus' *Essay on Population*."

4. As Griffin explains, the area of west of the Appalachians Line was constructed as a Hobbesian wild zone where "new settlers west of the [Proclamation] line ... confronted direct threats to their lives, liberty, and property on a regular basis" (63).

5. The new tally leads Bird to conclude that Federalists were "far more serious and more determined ... to criminalize dissent and to suppress the opposition press and party than has been recognized" (7).

6. In 1920, Eugene V. Debs ran for the presidency from the Atlanta Federal Penitentiary where he had been sentenced for sedition.

7. Even more curious was that in addition to giving these weighted instructions to the jury, Paterson seemed little disposed to allow Lyon to mount a defense. Paterson was set to let the jury begin its deliberations when, as Lyon wrote, "I interrupted him with an inquiry into the cause why I should not be heard; he politely sat down and directed me to proceed" (Wharton 340).

8. Camps were set up and local jails were used for detention in the Hawaiian Islands. See https://www.nps.gov/hono/index.htm and https://www.hawaiiinternment.org/students/internment-camps-hawai'i for more of this history.

9. See Mills on proposals to settle lands acquired through the Louisiana Purchase with Black colonists (21–22).

10. See the website "Yale, Slavery & Abolition," http://www.yaleslavery.org/TownGown/coloniz.html.

11. This second column also provided an opportunity to take another crack at craniology by turning its questionable analytics on white people: "Methinks, slave-holders must be somewhat lacking in their crania, to dream even of being able to keep in the nineteenth century, nearly *two millions* of their beings enslaved!" (Mordecai 91).

Chapter 3

1. Elmer develops this point with more nuance, positing that in Locke and Hobbes "the state of nature is what we might call an *empirical myth*" (11). For additional discussion, see Faber on the imagined correlations between the American frontier and the Lockean state of nature.

2. Griffin describes traveler accounts that presented lands west of the Appalachians as the real-world complement to the state of nature (31–32). Settlers applied "a theoretical concept of time to a place" by transposing Hobbesian ideas to the American continent (22). See also Aravamudan, who states that "colonial America served an interpretative occasion, historical example, and mythical construct for Hobbes" (43). Moreover, as Feng has posited, the Hobbesian social contract enabled and justified settler colonialism by associating aggression and savagery in the state of nature with nonwhite inhabitants of the New World. In contrast to Hobbes, Locke distinguished the state of nature from the state of war. The latter in Locke's mind presupposed a society that had the potential to provide a common judge, but for Hobbes there would be "constant warre" without such an authority. Locke's state of nature is less cruel and anarchic than Hobbes's; for more on this point, see Mack (23–24).

3. Faludi posits the American security myth as an enduring narrative that aligns contemporary responses to terrorism with "our earliest national experience" (*Terror Dream* 215) in ways that set up implicit but tenuous connections that obscure the violence that American "victims" of terrorism historically waged against Indigenous people. She also critiques such comparisons, citing a local newspaper column that likened an episode from King William's War to the attacks of 9/11. Referring to the story of Hannah Dunston, who in 1697 was taken captive, the article that Faludi quotes declares, "Let's be honest here. What was done to her by the Abenaki Indians, if done today by Islamic militants, would be called terror" (251). For similar language, slightly modulated by the use of scare quotes, see Gaddis comparing 9/11 and "concerns about security" created by nineteenth-century Indian attack: "The 'terrorists' of that day [the 1800s] caused Americans on the frontier to fear for their lives. Today's terrorists provoke similar anxieties, but the frontier can now be anywhere" (86).

4. Thomas reminds us that the Lockean state of nature that fosters "Natty's forest freedom" is itself "a man-made construct" conducive to the individualist ethos of a newly powerful capitalist order (41).

5. In thinking about the reach of government surveillance, it is important to remember that in the United States, video and other forms of electronic surveillance require the coordination and cooperation of private companies unlike in the UK where "public funds" and "public oversights" are part of public safety discourse (Monahan 5). At the most basic level, then, the sheer fact that the success of programs like Stellarwind depended upon the cooperation of telecommunications companies shows how surveillance in the United States is more than a government apparatus.

6. Amy Kaplan provides a similar assessment: "The language of security has been colonizing every arena and idiom of daily life and political culture, globally and locally, socially and psychically, from domestic to national spheres, home to the homeland, city to battlefield, prison to gated community, airport to the internet, Wall Street to immigration detention centers" (16).

7. It is important to acknowledge that Hobbes does not align with the contractual logic of liberalism. In this regard, see Paul Downes's use of Hobbes's thinking in "an attempt to think about what a postliberal and countercapitalist democratic sovereignty might look like" (3).

8. Like the exhortation "See Something, Say Something," this Homeland Security script encourages racial and ethnic profiling. Such campaigns reanimate the violent assumptions that fueled lynching as a vigilante measure to protect the safety of white women (Hanhardt 215).

9. For a representative view that opposes traditional notions of privacy and civil rights to surveillance, see Parenti (210–11). Notions of the subject as a private individual under security effectively work against Beck's idea that risk society can lead to "a reawakening solidarity based on *shared* and *admitted* oppression" (*Risk* 125). Nevertheless, it remains important to consider the "revolutionary potentials" (125) that he and others envision. As an alternative to fetishized notions of privacy, advocates of post-liberal conceptions of privacy suggest that privacy entails a social capacity. See, for example, Cheney-Lippold (205–24).

10. For more on this idea, see Castronovo (*Propaganda 1776* 29–56).

11. The theoretical push to discover property within the state of nature dates back to medieval claims that "*Dominium* did not appear when the laws allowed appropriation and exchange; it had been present from the beginning of time, even when appropriation and exchange were unnecessary" (Tuck 29). The result was that private property itself could be construed as natural (see Tuck 28). Of course, what is natural has long been the product of a cultural economic order. In his reading of natural law in *The Pioneers*, Thomas observes, "the Lockean state of nature might owe its formulation to the capitalist economic system gaining ascendancy in Locke's day" (41).

12. On this point, see Cheyfitz, "Savage Law" and *Poetics of Imperialism* (48–49).

13. Cheyfitz provides a deft examination of how the notion of property dispossesses Native Americans ("Savage Law" 121–25).

14. "Gifts" and notions of racial inheritance warrant a longer discussion that is usefully aided by Levine's "Temporality, Race, and Empire." Thought to be a mixed-race individual, Edwards is revealed to be white at the end of the novel. His claim to property lies in his whiteness.

15. The claim is made by James Fenimore Cooper (the novelist's namesake) in his 1897 introduction to Cooper's *A Guide in the Wilderness*. Subsequent commentators have expressed doubt whether William Cooper was murdered at all or if he died from natural causes. See A. Taylor 364.

16. Cooper acutely understood the dual senses of "title." While working on *The Pioneers*, he was continually mortgaging and remortgaging real estate property. See Franklin 335–66.

17. For more on the U.S. survey and its reverberations into the nineteenth century, see Goddard.

18. "Collecting it all" requires an array of sophisticated resources, both technological and legal, as Nakashima and Warrick report. See also chapter 3 of Greenwald's *No Place to Hide*, titled "Collect It All."

19. As Nelson underscores, Natty's use of "wasty ways" entails a critique of "civil law's support of possessive individualism" as well as a complaint about the wanton depletion of natural resources (103).

20. See Gray 8. For a similar argument in the terms of technological freedom, see Schneier, *Data and Goliath* 7.

21. See, for instance, Birchall's notion of a "datatariat" that would redraw the boundaries of political subjectivity by allowing for equitable access and by promoting collectivity over individualism (43–44). Murison ends her study of nineteenth-century privacy by seeking to rescue privacy from "an apolitical quietism" and to imagine its "renewal" for the twenty-first century (218).

Chapter 4

1. Dillon offers a slightly different formulation: "Politics, government and rule are problematised in terms of the infinite government of finite things. The infinity of finite things knows no eschatology in the traditional sense of an ending to time combined with the advent of a different, a better, time to come" (*Biopolitics of Security* 7). While I agree with Dillon's contention that surveillance seeks a total account of individuals and other finite entities, it's also the case that security is simultaneously driven and frustrated by its incomplete knowledge of an inexhaustible supply of data.

2. For Potolsky, the national security sublime produces "a sense of resignation or bewilderment at such encounters [with an immense state apparatus] rather than the traditional feeling of elevation and transcendence" (34).

3. Burke agrees about the need for distance and security when experiencing the sublime: "terror is a passion which always produces delight when it does not press too closely" (42).

4. The conspiracies and deceptive rhetoric that animate Brown's novels, as critics have shown, insinuate that the atmosphere of early American republicanism was prone to dark misgivings. See Levine (*Conspiracy and Romance*), Sizemore, and Looby. Galluzzo ties sublime terror in *Wieland* to mentions of the Seven Years' War and connotations of Jacobin radicalism. See also Cahill on the "aesthetic state" in *Wieland* (196–99). Gordon Wood views conspiracy as a contrasting tendency to the age's pretensions to enlightenment (17).

5. In letters to his family, Brown wrote about safety, as the yellow fever epidemic approached New York. On August 25, 1793, he reassured his brother James that his "abode is far enough from the seat of the disease" to provide "the utmost security" (Dunlap 4). In a follow-up from September 4, Brown chides James for his susceptibility, not to yellow fever but to print by believing the worst about the epidemic: "When did you learn to rely upon rumor news-paper information?" (Dunlap 4).

6. In addition to textual sources, sculpture reanimates Cicero in the form of a bust copied from an archaeological treasure unearthed from some Roman ruins. Clara's story about the sculpture's provenance reminds us that the humanities professor at best can often only *profess*, that is, claim as fact what may be only supposition and interpretation. The scavenger who sells Wieland a bust of Cicero "professed to have copied this piece from an antique dug up with his own hands in the environs of Modena" (22). Neither the Roman orator's text nor the bust can escape doubts about their "purity."

7. If "Brown embraces the problematic and inescapable need for creating narrative explanations" (P. Gilmore 119), the storytelling required by these narratives creates another set of problems whose dimensions are communicative and philosophical.

8. For a critique of such technological determinism that sees print as inherently progressive, see Warner (5–7). An additional problem is the assumption that "technology has an ontological status prior to culture" (Warner 5), as though print is an external force that pushes "culture" in the abstract toward Enlightenment values and practices.

9. As Gleick observes, "From the point of view of the cryptologist, a secrecy system is almost identical with a noisy communication system" (216). One tries to hide a message within noise while the other attempts to filter out the noise that impedes meaning.

10. For more extensive explanation of the mathematical aspects of Shannon's theory, see Paulson.

11. For more on Weaver's adjustments to Shannon, see Schweighauser 8–9.

12. Wieland falls into the error that worried Locke: "Only we must be sure that it be a divine revelation, and that we understand it right: else we shall expose ourselves to all the extravagancy of enthusiasm, and all the error of wrong principles, if we have faith and assurance in what is not divine revelation" (*Essay* 520). For Wieland, "enthusiasm" becomes the murder of his family.

13. While culture "wants to erase all traces of mediation" (Bolter and Grusin 5), there is also a countervailing tendency to proliferate its media. This double movement of culture to erase and multiply its media constitutes for Bolter and Grusin the logic of remediation.

14. What's more, Luhmann also sees the rise of the eighteenth-century novel as an effect of mass media, specifically in the conjunction of modern journalism and the printing press (*Reality* 55).

15. See Barnard on how "this misreading-effect" has been perpetuated.

16. Contrast the doubling of digital and print texts with the effort to resolve and unify Brown's characters by using digital means. A 2003 article in *Literary and Linguistic Computing* applied "stylometric techniques" and "multivariate analysis" to *Wieland* and *Memoirs of Carwin* in order to show that the voice of Carwin is consistent across both texts (Stewart 129). The goal is that "statistical evidence" about sentence length and word choice will demonstrate that "Brown has created a narrator with a distinctive voice" (129). The implicit aim is to bring wholeness and unity to Brown's characterization, a sort of transcendent vision of authorship in control of its fictional universe. Such authority, based on the consistency of information, I am suggesting, is conceptually elusive.

17. For a critique that questions the usefulness of digital searching, see Da's argument that core components of digital humanities provide little that is "operationalizable" in the sense of "the NSA keeping track of terrorist webs on social media by investigating up to three nodes of connection" (632). Knowing what other books readers of Junot Díaz's *The Brief Wondrous Life of Oscar Wao* also bought on Amazon.com, to use Da's example, gives scant information that we can act upon, say, to build a critical interpretation.

Chapter 5

1. "Even such persons as William Lloyd Garrison were heard delivering Fourth of July colonization orations," notes Sweet (260). Garrison would break with the colonization movement and his *Thoughts on African Colonization* (more on this text below) offers a trenchant critique of the crusade.

2. The ACS counted on broad support from American churches in presenting their case to the public. As Sweet writes, "What can only be termed a massive propaganda blitz was aimed at the clergy. Colonization auxiliaries dispatched collection agents into the fields to persuade ecclesiastical bodies and local clergymen to transform Independence Day celebrations into rites applauding the merits of colonization. Sermon topics, statistics, colonization arguments and even itinerant evangelists for colonization were provided local churches for the occasion" (260). As Jordan Alexander Stein demonstrates, the colonization mission relied on a particular notion of Christian teleology in which Liberia as a "nation, necessarily, serves divine ends" ("A Christian Nation" 866).

3. In light of these concerted public efforts to tackle the "problem" of the U.S. Black population, Armstrong and Tennenhouse seem to be overstating their case in arguing that novelistic

narrative "was the means of bringing the problem of population from the background squarely into the foreground of the novel" (679). In their reading, *Uncle Tom's Cabin* draws from the captivity narrative to "test the liberal fantasy of a government that could deal with the problem of population one individual at a time" (679). As the incidence of pro-colonization Fourth of July addresses shows, population was already a prominent and racialized concern that defied individual metrics. Across multitudinous pamphlets, reports, and critiques associated with colonization, population was only rarely approached on an individual scale. The challenge as well as the millennial payoff of colonization was its supposed capacity for dealing with population en masse.

4. Foucault defines biopower as "the set of mechanisms through which the basic biological features of the human species became the object of a political strategy, or a general strategy of power" (*Security* 1). The approach is two-pronged, involving, on the one hand, discipline, which "is exercised on the bodies of individuals" and security, which "is exercised over a whole population" (11). Security identifies the population as a principal concern for biopolitics. As LaFleur and Schuller explain, within biopolitical thinking, population "denotes a biological phenomenon subject to and thus best administered through its own processes, such as rates of mortality, birth, illness, wealth generation, and income distribution" (606).

5. The scholarship on Jefferson's ideas about race is copious. For a treatment that examines his specific views on race and colonization, see Saillant. For Saillant, Enlightenment ideas may have initially fueled support for colonization, "but colonization in Liberia helped to create a new idea of liberty that broke sharply with enlightened ideas and values" (262) by sacrificing notions of universalism to market ideas about trade between separate peoples.

6. See the Library of Congress online exhibit, "The African-American Mosaic," https://www.loc.gov/exhibits/african/afam004.html.

7. There is some range to the historical span for tabulating the numbers of people colonized through ACS efforts, which produces varying counts. "In its century of operations, the Colonization Society oversaw the removal of 15,385 blacks to Liberia," according to Castiglia (192). Stopping the tally at the start of the Civil War, Guyatt states, "around 10,000 blacks, fewer than 1 percent of those in the United States in 1820, were removed to Liberia between 1820 and 1860" (987). Power-Greene writes, "Although Liberia did inspire nearly 13,000 African Americans to leave the United States to settle there between the founding of the colony and the Civil War, this represented less than 3 percent of the total free black population in the United States during that time" (xviii).

8. Totaro and Ninno associate the dominance of the algorithm as a mode of modern thinking with the social dominance of cultural hegemony (32).

9. For an examination of vexed intersections between Blackness and data regimes later in the nineteenth century and into the twentieth, see Womack.

10. See Perry on the reproductive anxieties behind white supremacists' invocation of "white genocide." Not only do "white genocide" and "replacement theory" fuel racial anxiety; these bogus conspiracy theories also justify murderous violence on a mass scale as shootings in Christchurch, New Zealand, and Buffalo, New York, demonstrate.

11. Horsman notes that those who boasted their "pure" descent from white stock were "prepared to accept only a few of the inhabitants of the Spanish West and Southwest as white" (276). But, as Roediger argues, for many working-class people, the stigmatization of Blackness and its

entanglement with class identity helped solidify their hold upon whiteness, which otherwise might have been tenuous at times.

12. Then again, the proximity of figures such as Steve Bannon, Stephen Miller, and others to the Trump presidential administration, not to mention media outlets such as Breitbart News and Fox News, indicates that white nationalism has made substantial inroads from the margins toward the center of acceptable discourse. Giroux contends that white supremacy has become normalized through the militarization of domestic spaces.

13. See Anderson (32), who describes how the census and other forms of "data analysis became increasingly common and of interest to Americans" (23) in the first decades of the nineteenth century.

14. That leader arose in 1831 in the shape of Nat Turner, proving from one perspective at least that colonizationists had been right to fuse biostatistical data to national security. The copy of this address that I consulted at the John Hay Library at Brown University has no publication information or author. Mills identifies Congregationalist minister Leonard Bacon as the author of these sensational comparisons.

15. In quantifying the number of African Americans, the adherents of political arithmetic evaluated any positive gain in Black population as a negative net effect. The math was at core contradictory, but it most certainly fit with what McKittrick views as "the breathless numbers, the absolutely economic, the mathematics of the unliving" (17) that so often defined Blackness.

16. While African Americans opposed colonization plans spearheaded by *white* organizations, African Americans since the late eighteenth century had shown interest in emigrating to places such as Trinidad, Jamaica, Saint Domingue, and Barbados. Haitian president Henri Christophe made "several attempts to resettle black emigrants of the U.S. in Haiti" (S. Young 96). The ACS quickly moved to squelch suggestions about Haiti as a potential destination for African American colonists (Mills 59–61) because the idea competed with its own plans and also because "many of its southern slaveholding members strongly objected to the expansion of a black national power so close to the American mainland" (Horton and Horton 1294). Such rifts exemplified fundamental differences between voluntary Black emigration and white plans to colonize Africa with African Americans. "The key issue here was black agency," something that the ACS absolutely failed to acknowledge (Power-Greene 7). The ACS was tone deaf when it came to listening to the objections of African Americans or inviting their participation in meaningful ways. The ACS never understood the distinction "between black-initiated emigration and white-sponsored colonization" (S. Young 107). See also Bacon on the distinction that *Freedom's Journal* made between compelled colonization and voluntary emigration (182). Horton and Horton argue that attitudes toward colonization were largely generational (178–79, 191). As African-born Blacks were superseded by U.S.-born Blacks, remaining in the United States and working to achieve civil rights and promote abolition became a preferred strategy to emigration and colonization. Paul Cuffee, Prince Hall, James Forten, Phillis Wheatley, and Olaudah Equiano were among those in the late eighteenth and early nineteenth centuries who supported Black emigration before the formation of the ACS. Horton and Horton also make the case that African American criticism of the ACS varied by geography: "The primary strength of the American Colonization Society among blacks was in the upper South, particularly in Baltimore and Richmond" where opportunities were more scarce than in Northern urban centers (189).

Power-Greene notes that Black women's views on colonization are underrepresented in archives and provides discussion of Maria Stewart, Sarah Mapps Douglass, and Mary Ann Shadd Cary.

17. Allen continued that if "Liberia were annexed, it would be the most vulnerable part of the United States" (10). On the other hand, if Liberia were left unprotected, there would be no need to worry about European powers swooping in with imperialist designs since "the surest defence of Liberia is her weakness. No powerful nations would wage war against a people too feeble to make even a show of resistance" (10). See Mills's *The World Colonization Made* on how white ideas about Black resettlement fit with the ambitions of empire. As Finley made the point in his 1816 pamphlet that led to the formation of the ACS, "Most nations have had their colonies. Greece and Rome planted many which grew and flourished, and which, as they grew, added strength and lustre to the mother country" (1). But for a persuasive and contrasting view that argues that the hopes for Liberia rested on projecting its status as a racially separate Christian nation and not a colonial possession, see Stein, "A Christian Nation."

18. Governmentality is exercised not only through formal governmental structures but also maintained across a "constellation of objects, people, technologies, and apparatuses interconnected within a circulatory system of state and population" (Randell-Moon and Tippet x). As Schuller argues, biopolitical dictates flow through "private institutions of sentiment" (21).

19. *Freedom's Journal* reported in 1828 that a Senate committee on foreign relations had investigated colonization and determined the costs to be prohibitive. While the transportation costs for sending the annual increase among the free people of color would amount to just $700,000 per year, it could cost as much as $5,700,000 to remove the annual increase of the slave population. The Senate committee estimated the cost of removing the entire slave population at $190,000,000 (*FJ*, "Colonization Society").

20. Guyatt describes how the ACS brought together "northerners who were offended by the persistence of slavery in the United States and who fretted about racial mixing in America's cities and southerners who doubted slavery's long-term viability and shared the northern discomfort with a large free black population" (994). Castiglia identifies an overlooked strain of colonization discourse that viewed white prejudice as intractable and ineradicable. If whites could not overcome their racism, then the only solution, according to Robert Finley and other early members of the ACS, was to remove an unfortunate people whose presence motivated discrimination (see Castiglia 207).

21. Writers and editors operated with an awareness that African American print culture would be read and likely archived by whites and white institutions. On this point, see Peterson's observation that Cornish and Russwurm supplied the African Free School in New York City with free copies because they recognized that a "white-run institution, would be better to preserve the school's history than their peripatetic newspaper offices" (68). Moreover, as Cohen and Stein argue, the notion of "print culture"—as opposed to simply "print"—expands to "unintended readers" and "publics that may not yet recognize themselves as such" (7). Knowing that *Freedom's Journal* "would likely find its way into the hands of white readers . . . Cornish and Russwurm included numerous accounts of upright black behavior" (Fagan 23). The concept of fluid and flexible print terrain is essential to understanding the history of Black print culture. In turn, Black print culture nurtured an adaptable sense of community that was responsive to "the shifting contingencies of African American life" (Ernest 281). Russwurm became sole editor after Cornish stepped away from the daily management of the paper in September 1827. Even

though the partnership of Cornish and Russwurm dissolved before the paper was less than a year old, the weekly section with rate and subscription information continued to list Cornish as an authorized agent for the paper, joining agents in Philadelphia, Providence, Canada, England, and Haiti. Cornish also regularly advertised in the back pages of the paper "TWO THOUSAND Acres of excellent LAND" for sale to anyone who would see the land settled by "coloured famers" (May 9, 1828, 7). Before it ceased publication in March 1829, *Freedom's Journal* "had a total of 38 authorized agents from four countries, including a number from the southern states" (Levine, *Dislocating* 94). Because Cornish resigned the editorship in September 1827, well before Russwurm's support of colonization, "it appears unlikely, then, that Russwurm and Cornish's editorial partnership dissolved over colonization," argues Bacon (56). James views the strained partnership of the two as a matter of different dispositions between the "conservative" Cornish and the "hothead" Russwurm (41).

22. Fagan connects this expanded sense of nationalism and related ideas of "chosenness" to the function and mission of nineteenth-century Black newspapers (6–10).

23. Colored Conventions also aggregated data in ways that linked demography to civic engagement (see Patterson). Later in the century, W.E.B. Du Bois assembled data portraits that connected infographics to social justice (see Battle-Baptiste and Rusert).

24. Scholars estimate that 700–800 people subscribed to the paper (see Fagan 24; Bacon 51) at a cost of $3 per year, $2.50 if "paid at the time of subscribing" (*FJ*, "Proposal"). Readers and listeners likely far outnumbered subscribers. As McHenry suggests, "Even if verifiable circulation figures were available they would be unreliable as indicators of the number of *Freedom's Journal*'s readers, as placement in reading rooms and the sharing of copies among whole congregations and associations as well as between friends and neighbors distinguishes the newspaper's actual readership from its list of subscribers" (89).

25. The secret congress that meets in *Imperium in Imperio* debates several options, including emigrating to the African Congo Free State, seizing Texas and Louisiana for a Black republic, and working from within the United States to secure equality. In all cases, the participants recognize the biopolitical potential invested in the "lives of over seven million five hundred thousand people" (129).

26. The status of a population as a political agent is at best murky. "A population does not come to the bargaining table, and it does not become a political problem through intersubjective disagreements," writes Dillon (*Biopolitics of Security* 164).

27. Foucault's history is predominantly European. For a critique, see Mbembe ("Necropolitics"), who examines the coordination of biopower, the plantation system, and colonialism, and Weheliye, who argues that "biopolitics discourse not only misconstrues how profoundly race and racism shape the modern idea of the human, it also overlooks or perfunctorily writes off theorizations of race, subjection, and humanity found in black and ethnic studies, allowing bare life and biopolitics discourse to imagine an indivisible biological substance anterior to racialization" (4). For a study of "political arithmetic" and "population tracking" in the colonial contexts of British settlements in the New World, see Farrell ("Witch Hunts" 653).

28. As "a datum that depends on a series of variables" (Foucault, *Security* 71), the population tasks the science of government with pinning down the variables of living and dying so that projections about the future can be made. Mining population data can yield answers to any number of known unknowns that the discourse of security tries to resolve. Which street corners

are most likely to be hubs of criminal activity? Which borrowers are most likely to default on mortgages? Which neighborhood's residents are most likely to have shorter life expectancy? Questions like these are routinely overlaid with racial assumptions that prepackage the answers so that stricter policing or unfavorable lending rates to minority borrowers appear as inevitable. LaFleur and Schuller express this argument in historical terms: "While beliefs about the significance of racial difference—or, as eighteenth-century naturalists tended to describe it, 'human variety'—differed greatly across time and space, the separation, categorization, and hierarchization of human life into racial taxa extended the reach of biopower in the early Americas in ways that would have wide-ranging consequences for Black and Native peoples, in particular" (608).

29. Emphasis added. As Guyatt describes Jefferson's thinking, colonization would bring about a "double emancipation" (991) by rescuing whites from Blacks while freeing Blacks from slavery. Kazanjian identifies Jeffersonian colonization as a numerical and statistical solution to an otherwise intractable national problem. Approaching "colonization as a form of racial governmentality" (Kazanjian, *Colonizing Trick* 93), early supporters conceived of colonization not simply as a deportation scheme but as a millennial mission to disseminate Christianity and U.S. political ideals among Africans. Jefferson's remarks were instrumental in popularizing the notion of colonization (Mills 10).

30. A Virginia lawyer with moderate antislavery feelings, Harrison's participation in the ACS illustrates the organization's ability to appeal to slavery's critics as well its defenders.

31. See Hodgson on how ideas about Malthusian displacement played into proslavery and abolitionist debates over slavery. Describing the "Malthus effect" as a type of "genopolitics" bound up with international security, Dean argues that "we need to address Foucault's failure to address Malthus's contribution" (20).

32. Bacon provides an overview of *Freedom's Journal* perspectives on women's public and private roles. The newspaper was adamant in its support of female education.

33. For more on Jefferson's long-standing interest in statistics and "settler colonial biopolitics," see Dikant.

34. Milligan also reported that a traveling book agent had success in selling *Political Economy* in other Virginia locales.

35. Jeffersonian trembling partly fills the "lacunae of racism as an object of knowledge" that Weheliye (57) discerns in Foucault's account of biopower. Slave masters' iron sway was threatened by the power they wielded so cruelly; the beneficiaries of racial supremacy experienced the effects of the dread and fear they had sought to instill in others.

36. For the link between terror and territory in critical geography, see Elden xxx.

37. In the secondary market of credit, mortgages, and slave-backed securities, biocapitalization evolved into biofinancialization. That is, capital reproduced itself not merely through biological reproduction but also through complex instruments for trading debt rather than simple commodity production.

38. The "creation of innovative financial tools," Baptist argues, allowed "more and more of the Western world ... to invest directly in slavery's expansion" (*Half* xxviii). On the prevalence of the use of slave mortgages as security for loans during the antebellum era, see Bonnie Martin. It was not just banks that were party to these financial dealings. "Churches in the Charleston area were second only to banks among the institutions that accepted human collateral" in lending out money (Martin 845–46). An important difference exists between slave-backed securities

and slave mortgages. Securities are a more complex financial instrument, representing the agglomeration of multiple slave mortgages that are then sold off in uniform chunks as bonds.

39. As critics since Marx have contended, capitalism itself generates insecurity. Where the idea of security dates back to the *securitas* of the classical era, insecurity only emerges with the advent of capitalism. See Neocleous ("Securitati Perpetuae" 4) as well as Astra Taylor, who dubs capitalism an "insecurity machine."

40. De Goede makes the case that financial security should be understood as an indispensable component of national security ("Financial Security" 161–63). National security becomes wrapped up in the larger process of securitization through which debts, loans, and credit "are repackaged and resold in the financial markets—thus, turned into tradeable securities" (163). Securitization dates back to the Renaissance expansion of capitalism when the loans and credit that fueled investment and speculation were backed by securities that could be paid in specie or, in a rare dramatic instance, a pound of flesh.

41. "By the spring of 2009, the International Monetary Fund was estimating that over $50 trillion in asset values worldwide . . . had been destroyed" (Harvey 6).

42. As the 1837 crash destabilized slave-backed securities, the situation of slaves on whom mortgages were held and resold became precarious. As Rothman explains in the context of the Mississippi Valley, "Just as slaves and slavery had sat at the core of Mississippi's economy before the crash, many white Mississippians now turned to their enslaved property to stave off financial disaster. Bearing the brunt of their owners' failures, thousands of slaves who had already lost families and communities through forced migration to the southwest disappeared back into the cash nexus as planters tried stanching losses by selling off their most valuable remaining assets, along with their land and their livestock" (137).

43. Why Africa no longer appeared to Randolph as a possibility—logistically impractical? too expensive?—is not known. The choice to settle in western Ohio appears to have been made by William Leigh, a friend who survived after Randolph's death. For more discussion of Randolph's changing attitudes toward colonization and the frosty reception of former slaves of Roanoke plantation in Ohio, see L. Hill and also Wood. On the role that colonization discourse played in fueling vehement opposition to Black immigrants to the Midwest, see Mills 119–28.

Chapter 6

1. The prototypical American example of an encounter with the sublime that releases tension can be found in Jefferson. Standing atop Virginia's Natural Bridge, he confronts the "intolerable" and drops to all fours, crushed to the earth. But Jefferson is able to rally himself in a familiar philosophical turnabout: "It is impossible for the emotions, arising from the sublime, to be felt beyond what they are here: so beautiful an arch, so elevated, so light, and springing, as it were, up to heaven" (*Notes* 25). His composure restored, Jefferson finds satisfaction by mentioning the economic productive capacities of the stream that the arch spans. Flowing in even the driest months, the water has sufficient power "to turn a grist-mill" (25).

2. Only the words, not the numbers, are italicized at this juncture in the *Appeal*, perhaps because the printers had italic type for letters but not numbers.

3. Forten had been privately receptive to the ACS but kept silent on seeing the tide of Black public opinion arrayed against colonization (Horton and Horton 188–89).

4. Even before the War of 1812, Philadelphia had a reputation as a haven for runaways. See Nash's chapter on Philadelphia as a "city of refuge."

5. Forten and Parrott's pamphlet grew out of a mass meeting of Black Philadelphians in 1817. Opposition to colonization was part of the docket at such protests and remained a prominent concern at Black conventions in the 1830s. For more, see Power-Greene 51–52.

6. Forten and Parrott's analysis continued to resonate throughout the colonization debate for decades. Garrison quoted these sentences in *Thoughts on African Colonization* (part II, p. 12).

7. Bacon suggests such articles "created specifically to persuade African Americans" should be viewed distinctly from "the numerous sermons and tracts written by white colonizationists for other white readers" (18).

8. A short notice mentioning that "Mr. Russwurm . . . is on a tour to the Eastward" and that readers should "pardon any deficiency in the present number" (July 27, 1827) suggests that Cornish might have functioned as the sole editor for this issue.

9. McHenry states that *Freedom's Journal* and other early Black newspapers "were a means of assuming a quality of respectability . . . as both polite and political gesture" (86).

10. Public protests and meetings against the efforts of the ACS unified African Americans, as Bacon notes. Colonization spurred the "first widespread use of mass meetings" among African Americans, according to Lerone Bennett (qtd. in Bacon 22–23).

11. See Harris 117. As the free Black population swelled, so did white anxieties. Newspapers contributed to the myth of Black criminality, reinforcing "the idea of the Black urban presence as dangerous if not carefully managed" (Harris 113). Yet given the influx of European immigrants to New York, the overall ratio of African Americans to whites in the city actually decreased with each decade. See Hirsch 415, but also exercise caution since this source adopts an apologist perspective and, by and large, excuses limitations on Black voting.

12. Marching the day after the Fourth of July served a critical function. "The fact that the promises of the Fourth of July had not yet been fully realized led many to propose that commemorations should take place on July 5 instead" (Bacon 89). Sweet comments that postponing celebrations until July 5 allowed African Americans to "symbolically express their alienation from the promises of July 4." Moreover, by not taking to streets and public spaces on July 4, they could minimize contact with "the drunken wrath of Fourth of July white mobs" (259). Participation in these parades ebbed by the 1830s, as public processions fused with radical abolitionism. But, as Harris argues, this development was also accompanied by attempts to regulate Black public presence: "Increasingly, public celebrations of emancipation and black equality were led by the radical abolitionists, who limited the participation of the masses in favor of controlled celebrations that extolled moral reform and antislavery sentiments in more conservative fashion" (128).

13. In keeping with its practice of recontextualizing white print discourse, *Freedom's Journal* seized and reprinted this screed in order to refute it.

14. The writer of this piece signed himself "Mordecai," challenging the editor on the appropriateness of his namesake from the Book of Esther.

15. Noah's hold on normative whiteness might have been tenuous at times. His Jewishness has been cited as a reason for his removal as the U.S. consul to Tunis. *Freedom's Journal* attempted to appeal to cross-racial feelings by imploring Noah "to remember that the nation from which he sprang, has been long held, in the utmost contempt in most parts of the world; and

that in sympathizing with his own house, he would cherish a fellow-feeling for us" ("Mordecai").

16. Before helping to subsidize the paper with his advertising business, Walker had backed this publishing venture. Hinks reports that nearly a month before the first issue appeared "a meeting had been held at Walker's house to consider 'giving aid and support to the Freedom's Journal'" (75). Walker's observation in the *Appeal* that "the American preachers . . . have newspapers and monthly periodicals, which they receive in continual succession" stressed the necessity and importance of developing a Black press as a counterforce (45).

17. Whether Walker is making a distinction between violence or the threat of violence is an issue that echoes scholarly debates over Walker's attitude toward interracial politics. Hinks detects an "undercurrent of necessary conciliation in the *Appeal*" (249) that Levine disputes (*Dislocating* 102).

18. Agamben's tendency to ontologize Foucault's historical account of biopolitics is relevant to this point. See Koopman (97).

19. Describing how "tyrants and false Christians" restricted the movements of Reverend Richard Allen, bishop of the African Methodist Episcopal Church, prohibiting him from traveling to the South, Walker anticipates the circulation bans issued on his own pamphlet. For more on the circulation history of the *Appeal*, see Hinks 116–72 and Levine, *Dislocating* 67–118.

20. For more on the fascinating history of Walker's "radical typography," see Dinius.

21. Not long after Russwurm suspended publication of *Freedom's Journal*, his former editorial partner, Cornish, filled the void by starting *The Rights of All*. In terms of longevity, this paper met with less success, lasting less than a year.

22. See Bacon for this suggestion, who notes the tension between opposition to colonization and support for the missionary efforts of African Americans who emigrated to Liberia (182).

23. Writing from Liberia to his half brother, Francis Edward, on March 31, 1831, Russwurm sought to correct the record: "The reports you see published in the U.S. are much exaggerated about its unhealthiness" (qtd. in James 231). Notwithstanding this assertion, mortality in the colony was "devastating" (83), according to McDaniel's demographic analysis.

24. Russwurm had not always been so sanguine about Liberian prospects. In the columns of *Freedom's Journal*, "Veritas" stated that "the biil [*sic*] of mortality at the Colony of Africa, exceeds anything of the kind" and attested that he had the names of recent exiles from Virginia "who have perished" ("Colonization Society" 192).

25. Associations among climate, disease, and race have a long history. For a recent examination, see Allewaert.

26. I retain the italicized letter "u" as it appeared in the original article in the *Liberia Herald* as tangible evidence of printing practices. One surmise is that the printer's case was low on certain letters in normal font.

27. Beyan describes Russwurm's travails as editor, including his lack of support for freedom of the press (70–79).

28. Meanwhile, supporters of the ACS charged that "narratives of Liberian mortality were sensationalized and exaggerated by colonization critics" (Lewis 116). Private views might have disclosed more honest assessments. Joseph Dailey, Russwurm's partner in selling tobacco, pork, and other staple goods, made the grim observation that recent immigrants "continue to die. . . . The sight of coffins and their tenants are so common and deaths so numerous . . . that one loses

those impressions of awe and solemnity of feeling with which the sight of a corpse has inspired one in America" (Beyan 81). The mortality rate in Monrovia may have been higher than other West African settlements such as Maryland in Liberia, a colony of which Russwurm became governor in 1836, where techniques for treating malaria and other sicknesses had more success.

29. The inclusion of this map in a scrapbook of materials about Liberia indicates how it combined with other facets of colonization discourse. Mills identifies the map as the work of A. Finley from 1830.

30. Historical judgments of Russwurm have often been severe, treating him as "a Black Benedict Arnold" (James 108) or as a tragic figure whose "mulatto privilege" allowed him to behave as "virtually white" (S. Young 92, 109). James's examination of the historical misperceptions surrounding Russwurm is instructive (108–12).

31. Nonetheless Russwurm felt that the presence of a newspaper in West Africa would help provide evidence about the continuation of the international slave trade, which remained in practice even though it had been outlawed in 1807. From the Liberian coast, it was easy to "witness the daily passage of slavers up & down the coast; & see what many of our citizens have, hundreds of their fellowmen, actually in chains, on board; he would then begin to think that the traffic was far from being discontinued" (March 6, 1830, reprinted in James 220).

32. For more on the connections between Native American removal and colonization, see Mills, chapter 3.

Epilogue

1. Huysmans describes the expansion of security thinking to issues of migration and contends that "defining environmental problems from a security perspective is in some cases outright counter-productive" (126).

2. Rojecki argues that the "right holds a structural advantage based on strength of group identification and belief coherence in the politics of insecurity" (211). Edwards offers detailed readings of how Black women have been constructed as domestic security threats even as they are also enlisted as representatives of the U.S. security state.

3. Beebee describes the note that Schmitt sought to have appended to future editions of *The Leviathan* as a *Waschzettel*, originally meaning a laundry list but evolving to signify a more general list of items. For books, a *Waschzettel* would be a one- to two-page insert or flyer to promote a book. Given the context of the U.S. postwar occupation of Germany, it seems, as Anja Wanner suggested to me, that Schmitt might be using the word to "to refer to some kind of fake/ironic/meta advertising."

4. According to the account provided by the prototype of Melville's clueless captain, "It was to my great advantage, that, on this occasion, the temperament of my mind was unusually pleasant. The apparent sufferings of those about me had softened my feelings into sympathy; or, doubtless my interference with some of their transactions would have cost me my life" (Delano 323).

WORKS CITED

ACLU v. Clapper. 804 F.3d 617 (2d Cir. 2015). http://pdfserver.amlaw.com/nlj/NSA_ca2_20150507.pdf.

Adams, Rachel. "Modernism's Cares: Reading For and With." In *The Oxford Handbook of Twentieth-Century American Literature*, edited by Leslie Bow and Russ Castronovo, 246–63. New York: Oxford University Press, 2023.

"Address of the Rockbridge Col. Society." *African Repository and Colonial Journal* 4 (1828–29): 273–81.

"The African-American Mosaic." Online exhibition. Library of Congress. https://www.loc.gov/exhibits/african/afam004.html.

Agamben, Giorgio. *Homo Sacer: Sovereign Power and Bare Life*. Stanford: Stanford University Press, 1998.

———. "Security and Terror." Translated by Carolin Emcke. *Theory & Event* 5, no. 4 (2001): 1–4.

———. *State of Exception*. Translated by Kevin Attell. Chicago: University of Chicago Press, 2005.

Ahmed, Sara. "Affective Economies." *Social Text* 22, no. 2 (Summer 2004): 117–39. https://muse.jhu.edu/article/55780.

———. *The Cultural Politics of Emotion*. Edinburgh: Edinburgh University Press, 2004.

———. "Home and Away: Narratives of Migration and Estrangement." *International Journal of Cultural Studies* 2, no. 3 (December 1999): 329–47.

———. "A Phenomenology of Whiteness." *Feminist Theory* 8, no. 2 (August 2007): 149–68.

Ahuja, Neel. *Biosecurities: Disease Interventions, Empire, and the Government of Species*. Durham: Duke University Press, 2016.

Alexander, Michelle. *The New Jim Crow: Mass Incarceration in the Age of Colorblindness*. Rev. ed. New York: New Press, 2012.

Allen, William H. *The Elevation of a Race and the Redemption of a Continent: An Address Delivered before the American Colonization Society, January 15, 1878*. Washington, DC, 1878.

Allewaert, Monique. *Ariel's Ecology: Plantations, Personhood, and Colonialism in the American Tropics*. Minneapolis: University of Minnesota Press, 2013.

Allington, Daniel, Sarah Brouillette, and David Golumbia. "Neoliberal Tools (and Archives): A Political History of Digital Humanities." *Los Angeles Review of Books*, May 1, 2016. https://lareviewofbooks.org/article/neoliberal-tools-archives-political-history-digital-humanities/.

Amar, Paul. *The Security Archipelago: Human-Security States, Sexuality Politics, and the End of Neoliberalism*. Durham: Duke University Press, 2013.

"America's Private Sector Army." *The Week*, January 8, 2015. https://theweek.com/articles/451720/americas-private-sector-army.

American Colonization Society (ACS). *Review of the Reports of the American Colonization Society*. John Hay Library, Metcalf Collection, vol. 451, Brown University.

———. *A View of Exertions Lately Made for the Purpose of Colonizing the Free People of Colour, in the United States, in Africa, or Elsewhere*. Washington, DC: Printed by Jonathan Elliot, 1817.

American State Papers: Post Office Department. Edited by Walter Lowrie and Walter S. Franklin. Washington, DC: Gales and Seaton, 1832–61.

Ames, Fisher. *The Works of Fisher Ames: With a Selection of His Speeches and Correspondence*. Vol. 1. Boston: Little, Brown, 1854.

Amoore, Louise. *The Politics of Possibility: Risk and Security beyond Probability*. Durham: Duke University Press, 2013.

Anderson, Margo J. *The American Census: A Social History*. 2nd ed. New Haven: Yale University Press, 2015.

Anker, Elisabeth. "The Liberalism of Horror." *Social Science Research* 81, no. 4 (Winter 2014): 795–823.

Aravamudan, Srinivas. "Hobbes and America." In *The Postcolonial Enlightenment: Eighteenth-Century Colonialism and Postcolonial Theory*, edited by Daniel Carey and Lynn Festa, 37–70. New York: Oxford University Press, 2009.

Arends, J. Frederik M. "From Homer to Hobbes and Beyond—Aspects of 'Security' in the European Tradition." In *Globalization and Environmental Challenges: Reconceptualizing Security in the 21st Century*, edited by Hans Günter Brauch, Úrsula Oswald Spring, Czeslaw Mesjasz, John Grin, Pál Dunay, Navnita Chadha Behera, Béchir Chourou, Patricia Kameri-Mbote, and P. H. Liotta, 263–77. Berlin: Springer, 2008.

Arendt, Hannah. "What Is Freedom?" In *Between Past and Future: Six Exercises in Political Thought*, 143–71. New York: Viking, 1961.

Aristides. "Slavery." *Freedom's Journal*, September 28, 1827, 114–15.

Armstrong, Nancy, and Warren Montag. "The Figure in the Carpet." *PMLA* 132, no. 3 (May 2017): 613–19.

Armstrong, Nancy, and Leonard Tennenhouse. "The Problem of Population and the Form of the American Novel." *American Literary History* 20, no. 4 (Winter 2008): 667–85.

Arneil, Barbara. *John Locke and America: The Defence of English Colonialism*. New York: Oxford University Press, 1996.

Assange, Julian. "Who Should Own the Internet?" *New York Times*, December 4, 2014. https://www.nytimes.com/2014/12/04/opinion/julian-assange-on-living-in-a-surveillance-society.html.

Bacon, Jacqueline. *Freedom's Journal: The First African-American Newspaper*. Lanham, MD: Lexington Books, 2007.

Balbi, Adriano. *Balance Politique du Globe en 1828 . . . ou essai sur la statistique générale de la terre . . . .* Paris: Imprimerie de Decourchant, 1828. http://objects.library.uu.nl/reader/viewer.php?obj=1874-380411&pagenum=1&lan=en.

Baptist, Edward E. *The Half Has Never Been Told: Slavery and the Making of American Capitalism*. New York: Basic Books, 2014.

———. "Toxic Debt, Liar Loans, Collateralized and Securitized Human Beings, and the Panic of 1837." In *Capitalism Takes Command: The Social Transformation of Nineteenth-Century*

America, edited by Michael Zakim and Gary J. Kornblith, 69–92. Chicago: University of Chicago Press, 2011.

Barnard, Philip. "*Clara Howard; in a Series of Letters.*" In *The Oxford Handbook to Charles Brockden Brown*, edited by Philip Barnard, 123–38. New York: Oxford University Press, 2019.

Battle-Baptiste, Whitney, and Britt Rusert. Introduction to *W.E.B. Du Bois's Data Portraits: Visualizing Black America: The Color Line at the Turn of the Twentieth Century*, edited by Whitney Battle-Baptiste and Britt Rusert, 7–22. New York: Princeton Architectural Press, 2018.

Beck, Ulrich. *Risk Society: Towards a New Modernity*. Translated by Mark Ritter. London: Sage, 1992.

———. "The Terrorist Threat: World Risk Society Revisited." *Theory, Culture & Society* 19, no. 4 (August 2002): 39–55.

Beckert, Sven, and Seth Rothman. "Slavery's Capitalism." In *Slavery's Capitalism Book: A New History of American Economic Development*, edited by Sven Beckert and Seth Rockman, 1–27. Philadelphia: University of Pennsylvania Press, 2016.

Thomas O. Beebee. "Carl Schmitt's Myth of Benito Cereno." *Seminar: A Journal of Germanic Studies* 42, no. 2 (2006): 114–34.

"Ben Franklin's Famous 'Liberty, Safety' Quote Lost Its Context in 21st Century." *All Things Considered*, National Public Radio, March 2, 2015. https://www.npr.org/2015/03/02/390245038/ben-franklins-famous-liberty-safety-quote-lost-its-context-in-21st-century.

Bendersky, Joseph W. *Carl Schmitt: Theorist for the Reich*. Princeton: Princeton University Press, 1983.

Benjamin, Walter. *The Arcades Project*. Translated by Howard Eiland and Kevin McLaughlin. Cambridge, MA: Harvard University Press, 2002.

———. *Illuminations*. Translated by Harry Zohn. New York: Schocken, 1968.

Berki, R. N. *Security and Society: Reflections on Law, Order and Politics*. New York: St. Martin's, 1986.

Berlant, Lauren. *Cruel Optimism*. Durham: Duke University Press, 2011.

Berman, Russell A., and Johannes Voelz. "Introduction." *Telos* 170 (Spring 2015): 3–6.

Best, Stephen. *None Like Us: Blackness, Belonging, Aesthetic Life*. Durham: Duke University Press, 2018.

Beyan, Amos J. *African American Settlements in West Africa: John Brown Russwurm and the American Civilizing Efforts*. New York: Palgrave Macmillan, 2005.

Bigo, Didier. "Globalized (In)security: The Field and the Ban-Opticon." In *Terror, Insecurity, and Liberty: Illiberal Practices of Liberal Regimes after 9/11*, edited by Didier Bigo and Anastassia Tsoukala, 10–48. New York: Routledge, 2008.

Bigo, Didier, and Anastassia Tsoukala. "Understanding (In)security." In *Terror, Insecurity, and Liberty: Illiberal Practices of Liberal Regimes after 9/11*, edited by Didier Bigo and Anastassia Tsoukala, 1–9. New York: Routledge, 2008.

Bilbija, Marina. "'Dear Anglo': Scrambling the Signs of Anglo-Modernity from New York to Lagos." *American Literary History* 32, no. 4 (Winter 2020): 645–67.

Birchall, Clare. "Aesthetics of the Secret." *New Formations* 83, no. 3 (Winter 2014): 25–46.

Bird, Wendell. *Criminal Dissent: Prosecutions under the Alien and Sedition Acts of 1798*. Cambridge, MA: Harvard University Press, 2020.

Bolter, Jay David, and Richard Grusin. *Remediation: Understanding New Media*. Cambridge, MA: MIT Press, 1999.

Brennan, Timothy. "The Digital-Humanities Bust." *Chronicle of Higher Education*, October 15, 2017.
Brightman, Carol. *Total Insecurity: The Myth of American Omnipotence*. London: Verso, 2004.
Brown, Charles Brockden. *Arthur Mervyn, or Memoirs of the Year 1793*. Kent, OH: Kent State University Press, 1980.
———. *Clara Howard*. In *The Novels and Related Works of Charles Brockden Brown: Bicentennial Edition*. Vol. 5. Kent, OH: Kent State University Press, 1986.
———. *Wieland* and *Memoirs of Carwin, the Biloquist*. Edited by Emory Elliott. New York: Oxford University Press, 2009.
Browne, Simone. *Dark Matters: On the Surveillance of Blackness*. Durham: Duke University Press, 2015.
Building Security Services and Systems. "Recent Growth in the Private Security Industry." Building Security Services and Systems blog. https://www.buildingsecurity.com/recent-private-security-growth/#:~:text=The%20U.S.%20security%20industry%20has,heading%20to%20non%2DIT%20sources.
Burke, Anthony. "Aporias of Insecurity." *Alternatives: Global, Local, Political* 27, no. 1 (January–March 2002): 1–27.
Burke, Edmund. *A Philosophical Enquiry into the Origin of Our Ideas of the Sublime and Beautiful*. New York: Oxford University Press, 1998.
Butler, Judith. *Bodies That Matter: On the Discursive Limits of "Sex."* New York: Routledge, 1993.
———. *The Force of Nonviolence: An Ethico-Political Bind*. London: Verso, 2020.
———. "Rethinking Vulnerability and Resistance." In *Vulnerability in Resistance*, edited by Judith Butler, Zeynep Gambetti, and Leticia Sabsay, 12–27. Durham: Duke University Press, 2016.
Butler, Judith, Zeynep Gambetti, and Leticia Sabsay. *Vulnerability in Resistance*. Durham: Duke University Press, 2016.
Cahill, Edward. *Liberty of the Imagination: Aesthetic Theory, Literary Form, and Politics in the Early United States*. Philadelphia: University of Pennsylvania Press, 2012.
Carey, Mathew. "Letter from Matthew Carey, Esq. of Philadelphia." *African Repository and Colonial Journal* 4 (1829): 270–72.
Carpenter, Zoë. "Librarians versus the NSA." *The Nation*, May 25, 2015. https://www.thenation.com/article/archive/librarians-versus-nsa/.
Carpenter v. United States. 138 S. Ct. 2206 (2018). https://supreme.justia.com/cases/federal/us/585/16-402/#tab-opinion-3919270.
Castiglia, Christopher. "Pedagogical Discipline and the Creation of White Citizenship: John Witherspoon, Robert Finley, and the Colonization Society." *Early American Literature* 33, no. 2 (1998): 192–214.
Castronovo, Russ. "Facts, Faction, Anachronism." *PMLA* 134, no. 5 (October 2019): 1143–49.
———. "Information Warfare and Slow Media: Loyalism and the Lesson of Revolutionary Failure." *American Literature* 89, no. 4 (December 2017): 821–49.
———. *Propaganda 1776: Secrets, Leaks, and Revolutionary Communications in Early America*. New York: Oxford University Press, 2018.
Cheney-Lippold, John. *We Are Data: Algorithms and the Making of Our Digital Selves*. New York: New York University Press, 2017.

Chertoff, Michael. "War v. Crime: Breaking the Chains of the Old Security Paradigm." In *Confronting Terror: 9/11 and the Future of American National Security*, edited by Dean Reuter and John Yoo, 51–64. New York: Encounter Books, 2011.

Cheyfitz, Eric. *The Poetics of Imperialism: Translation and Colonization from* The Tempest *to* Tarzan. Philadelphia: University of Pennsylvania Press, 1991.

———. "Savage Law: The Plot against American Indians in *Johnson and Graham's Lessee v. M'Intosh* and *The Pioneers*." In *The Cultures of United States Imperialism*, edited by Amy Kaplan and Donald E. Pease, 109–28. Durham: Duke University Press, 1994.

Child, Lydia Maria. *An Appeal in Favor of That Class of Americans Called Africans*. Boston: Allen and Ticknor, 1833.

Clay, Henry. *Speech of the Hon. Henry Clay, Before the American Colonization Society, in the Hall of the House of Representatives, Jan. 20, 1827*. Washington, DC: Columbian Office, 1827.

Clough, Patricia Ticineto, and Craig Willse. "Introduction: Beyond Biopolitics: The Governance of Life and Death." In *Beyond Biopolitics: Essays on the Governance of Life and Death*, edited by Patricia Ticineto Clough and Craig Willse, 1–16. Durham: Duke University Press, 2011.

Coates, Ta-Nehisi. *Between the World and Me*. New York: Spiegel and Grau, 2015.

Cohen, Patricia Cline. *A Calculating People: The Spread of Numeracy in Early America*. New York: Routledge, 1999.

Cohen, Lara Langer, and Jordan Alexander Stein. "Introduction: Early African American Print Culture." In *Early African American Print Culture*, edited by Lara Langer Cohen and Jordan Alexander Stein, 1–16. Philadelphia: University of Pennsylvania Press, 2014.

Coleridge, Samuel Taylor. *Coleridge's Lectures on Shakspeare [sic] and Other Old Poets and Dramatists*. London: J. M. Dent, 1907.

Collins, Graham P. "Claude E. Shannon: Founder of Information Theory." *Scientific American*, October 14, 2002. https://www.scientificamerican.com/article/claude-e-shannon-founder/.

Conrad, Joseph. *The Secret Agent*. New York: Oxford University Press, 2004.

Cooper, James Fenimore. *The Crater or Vulcan's Peak*. Cambridge, MA: Harvard University Press, 1962.

———. *The Deerslayer*. New York: Oxford University Press, 1993.

———. *The Pathfinder; or, The Inland Sea*. New York: Hurd and Houghton, 1871.

———. *The Pioneers*. New York: Penguin, 1988.

Cooper, William. *A Guide in the Wilderness; or the History of the First Settlement in the Western Counties of New York, with useful Instructions to Future Settlers. In a series of letters addressed by Judge Cooper, of Coopers-Town, to William Sampson, Barrister, of New York*. Dublin: Gilbert and Hodges, 1810.

Craig, Hugh. "Stylistic Analysis and Authorship Studies." In *A Companion to Digital Humanities*, edited by Susan Schreibman, Ray Siemens, and John Unsworth, 273–88. Oxford: Blackwell, 2004.

Crawford, Adam. "Policing and Security as 'Club Goods': The New Enclosures?" In *Democracy, Society and the Governance of Security*, edited by Jennifer Wood and Benoît Dupont, 111–38. Cambridge: Cambridge University Press, 2006.

Crawford, Neta C. "A Security Regime among Democracies: Cooperation among Iroquois Nations." *International Organization* 48, no. 3 (Summer 1994): 345–85.

Da, Nan Z. "The Computational Case against Computational Literary Studies." *Critical Inquiry* 45, no. 3 (Spring 2019): 601–39.
Daily National Intelligencer. "Philadelphia, Nov. 21." November 24, 1825, 3.
Dalby, Simon. "Contesting an Essential Concept: Reading the Dilemmas in Contemporary Security Discourse." In *Critical Security Studies: Concepts and Cases*, edited by Keith Krause and Michael C. Williams, 3–31. Minneapolis: University of Minnesota Press, 1997.
Davis, Adrienne. "'Don't Let Nobody Bother Yo' Principle': The Sexual Economy of American Slavery." In *Sister Circle: Black Women and Work*, edited by Sharon Harley and the Black Women and Work Collective, 103–27. New Brunswick, NJ: Rutgers University Press, 2002.
Dean, Mitchell. "The Malthus Effect: Population and the Liberal Government of Life." *Economy and Society* 44, no. 1 (February 2015): 18–39.
"Defense Department Briefing." C-SPAN, February 12, 2002. Video, 44:12. https://www.c-span.org/video/?168646-1/defense-department-briefing.
De Goede, Marieke. "Financial Security." *Finance and Society* 3, no. 2 (2017): 159–72.
———. *Speculative Security: The Politics of Pursuing Terrorist Monies*. Minneapolis: University of Minnesota Press, 2012.
de Grazia, Margreta. "Anachronism." In *Cultural Reformations: Medieval and Renaissance in Literary History*, edited by Brian Cummings and James Simpson, 12–32. New York: Oxford University Press, 2010.
Delano, Amasa. *Narrative of voyages and travels in the northern and southern hemispheres: Comprising three voyages round the world; together with a voyage of survey and discovery, in the Pacific Ocean and oriental islands*. Boston: E. G. House, 1817.
DeLillo, Don. *Cosmopolis*. New York: Scribner, 2003.
Deloria, Philip J. "The Stories We Tell: American Indians and American Historical Narratives." Lecture at the Center for the Humanities, University of Wisconsin-Madison, March 10, 2021.
Dewey, John. *Art as Experience*. New York: Capricorn Books, 1958.
Dickinson, Baxter. *Sermon, Delivered at Springfield, Mass., July 4th, 1829, Before the Auxiliary Colonization Society of Hampden County*. Springfield, MA: S. Bowles, 1829.
Dikant, Thomas. "Settler Colonial Statistics: Jefferson, Biopolitics, and *Notes on the State of Virginia*." *Early American Literature* 54, no. 1 (January 2019): 69–96.
Dillon, Michael. *Biopolitics of Security: A Political Analytic of Finitude*. London: Routledge, 2015.
———. *Politics of Security: Towards a Political Philosophy of Continental Thought*. New York: Routledge, 1996.
Dinius, Marcy J. "'Look!! Look!!! at This!!!!': The Radical Typography of David Walker's *Appeal*." *PMLA* 126, no. 1 (January 2011): 55–72.
Diran, Ingrid. "Scenes of Speculation: Harriet Jacobs and the Biopolitics of Human Capital." *American Quarterly* 71, no. 3 (2019): 697–718. https://doi.org/10.1353/aq.2019.0050.
Doctorow, Cory. *Little Brother*. New York: Tom Doherty, 2008.
Domestic Surveillance Directorate. "About the Domestic Surveillance Directorate." https://nsa.gov1.info/about/index.html.
Downes, Paul. *Hobbes, Sovereignty, and Early American Literature*. Cambridge: Cambridge University Press, 2015.
Drucker, Johanna. "Humanities Approaches to Graphical Display." *Digital Humanities Quarterly* 5, no. 1 (2011).

Dunlap, William. *Memoirs of Charles Brockden Brown, the American Novelist. Author of Wieland, Ormond, Arthur Mervyn, &c. with Selections from His Original Letters, and Miscellaneous Writings*. London: Henry Colburn, 1822.

Edwards, Erica R. *The Other Side of Terror: Black Women and the Culture of US Empire*. New York: New York University Press, 2021.

Eggers, Dave. *The Circle*. New York: Knopf, 2013.

Elden, Stuart. *Terror and Territory: The Spatial Extent of Sovereignty*. Minneapolis: University of Minnesota Press, 2009.

Electronic Freedom Foundation. "Surveillance Drones." https://www.eff.org/issues/surveillance-drones/.

Elliott, Emory. Introduction to *Wieland* and *Memoirs of Carwin, the Biloquist*, by Charles Brockden Brown, vii–xxx. Edited by Emory Elliott. New York: Oxford University Press, 2009.

Elmer, Jonathan. *On Lingering and Being Last: Race and Sovereignty in the New World*. New York: Fordham University Press, 2008.

Emerson, R. Guy. "Vigilant Subjects, Risky Objects: 'If You See Something, Say Something.'" *Theory & Event* 25, no. 3 (July 2022): 614–38.

Ericson, Richard V. "The Division of Expert Knowledge in Policing and Security." *British Journal of Sociology* 45, no. 2 (June 1994): 149–75. https://doi.org/10.2307/591490.

Ernest, John. *Liberation Historiography: African American Writers and the Challenge of History, 1794–1861*. Chapel Hill: University of North Carolina Press, 2004.

Examination of Thomas C. Brown, A Free Colored Citizen of S. Carolina as to the Actual State of Things in Liberia in the Years 1833 and 1834, at the Chatham Street Chapel, May 9th and 10th, 1834. New York: S. W. Benedict, 1834.

Faber, Michael J. "The American Frontier as State of Nature." *World Affairs* 181, no. 1 (Spring 2018): 22–41.

Fagan, Benjamin. *The Black Newspaper and the Chosen Nation*. Athens: University of Georgia Press, 2016.

Faludi, Susan. "America's Guardian Myths." *New York Times*, September 7, 2007.

———. *The Terror Dream: Myth and Misogyny in an Insecure America*. New York: Picador, 2008.

Farrell, Molly. "Data as Poetry in Cowper's Statistical 'Effusions.'" *English Literary History* 87, no. 4 (Winter 2020): 1025–54.

———. "Witch Hunts and Census Conflicts: Becoming a Population in Colonial Massachusetts." *American Quarterly* 71, no. 3 (September 2019): 653–74.

Feng, Janice. "Domesticating Political Resistance: Rhetoric, Time, and (the Limits of) Settler Sovereignty in Thomas Hobbes's *Leviathan*." *Theory & Event* 25, no. 1 (January 2022): 4–24.

Ferguson, Robert A. *The American Enlightenment, 1750–1820*. Cambridge, MA: Harvard University Press, 1997.

Fiedler, Leslie. *Love and Death in the American Novel*. Funks Grove, IL: Dalkey Archive Press, 2003.

The Fifteenth Annual Report of the American Society for Colonizing the Free People of Colour in the United States. With an Appendix. Washington, DC, 1832.

Finley, Robert. *Thoughts on the Colonization of Free Blacks*. Washington, DC, 1816. https://credo.library.umass.edu/view/full/murb003-i319.

Finn, Ed. *What Algorithms Want: Imagination in the Age of Computing*. Cambridge, MA: MIT Press, 2017.

Fliegelman, Jay. *Prodigals and Pilgrims: The American Revolution against Patriarchal Authority, 1750–1800*. Cambridge: Cambridge University Press, 1982.

Forten, James. *Letters from a Man of Colour, on a Late Bill before the Senate of Pennsylvania*. Pennsylvania, 1813.

Forten, James, and Russell Parrott. "To the humane and benevolent Inhabitants of the city and county of Philadelphia." In *Witness for Freedom: African American on Race, Slavery, and Emancipation*, edited by C. Peter Ripley, 30–32. Chapel Hill: University of North Carolina Press, 1993.

Foster, Frances Smith. "A Narrative of the Interesting Origins and (Somewhat) Surprising Developments of African-American Print Culture." *American Literary History* 17, no. 4 (Winter 2005): 714–40.

Foster, Hal. "I Am the Decider." *London Review of Books* 33, no. 6 (March 17, 2011). https://www.lrb.co.uk/the-paper/v33/n06/hal-foster/i-am-the-decider.

Foucault, Michel. *The Birth of Biopolitics: Lectures at the Collège de France, 1978–1979*. Translated by Graham Burchell. Picador: New York, 2008.

———. *Discipline and Punish: The Birth of the Prison*. Translated by Alan Sheridan. New York: Vintage, 1979.

———. *The History of Sexuality*. Translated by Robert Hurley. New York: Vintage, 1985.

———. *Naissance de la Biopolitique. Cours au Collège de France (1978–1979)*. Paris: Éditions du Seuil/Gallimard, 2004.

———. "Omnes et Singulatim: Towards a Criticism of 'Political Reason.'" The Tanner Lectures on Human Values. Delivered at Stanford University, October 10 and 16, 1979. https://tannerlectures.utah.edu/_resources/documents/a-to-z/f/foucault81.pdf.

———. *Security, Territory, Population: Lectures at the Collège de France, 1977–78*. Translated by Graham Burchell. New York: Picador, 2007.

———. *"Society Must Be Defended": Lectures at the Collège de France, 1975–1976*. Translated by David Macey. New York: Picador, 2003.

"Fourth of July." *African Repository and Colonial Journal* 5 (1829–30): 87–91.

Franklin, Benjamin. Benjamin Franklin to Joseph Priestley, October 3, 1775, extract. *Founders Online*, National Archives. Published in *The Papers of Benjamin Franklin*, vol. 22, *March 23, 1775, through October 27, 1776*, edited by William B. Willcox, 217–18. New Haven: Yale University Press, 1982. https://founders.archives.gov/documents/Franklin/01-22-02-0137.

———. *An Historical Review of the Constitution and Government of Pennsylvania*. New York: Arno Press, 1972.

———. *The Interest of Great Britain Considered. Founders Online*, https://founders.archives.gov/documents/Franklin/01-09-02-0029.

———. "Objections to Barclay's Draft Articles of February 16." *Founders Online*, https://founders.archives.gov/documents/Franklin/01-21-02-0269.

———. "Observations Concerning the Increase of Mankind, 1751." *Founders Online*, National Archives. Published in *The Papers of Benjamin Franklin*, vol. 4, *July 1, 1750, through June 30, 1753*, edited by Leonard W. Labaree, 225–34. New Haven: Yale University Press, 1961. https://founders.archives.gov/documents/Franklin/01-04-02-0080.

Franklin, Wayne. *James Fenimore Cooper: The Early Years*. New Haven: Yale University Press, 2007.

Freedom's Journal. 1827–29.

———. "Abolition of Slavery." July 6, 1827, 67.

———. "Academy." September 9, 1828, 199.

———. "Attempt of an Eagle to Devour a Boy." October 12, 1827, 123.

———. "Clothing." November 21, 1828, 270.

———. "Colonization." March 14, 1829, 394.

———. "Colonization Society." February 29, 1828, 192.

———. "Colonization Society." May 30, 1828, 74.

———. "Colonization Society. No. 1." September 7, 1827, 102.

———. "Destructive Fire!" February 22, 1828, 191.

———. "Emancipation of Slaves." June 29, 1827, 63.

———. "European Colonies in America. (Concluded)." July 27, 1827, 73.

———. "Extract from an Address, delivered in Potsdam, N.Y., July 4th, 1826, by the Rev. O. P. Hoyt, Pastor of the Presbyterian Church in that town." May 18, 1827, 37.

———. "For the Freedom's Journal." September 27, 1827, 102.

———. "From the Alexandria Gazette. Views of the Benevolent Society of Alexandria for ameliorating and improving the condition of the People of Colour. No. IV. On the Political Tendency of Slavery in the United States." June 15, 1827, 53.

———. "Major Noah's 'Negroes.'" August 24, 1827, 95.

———. "Meeting of the People of Colour." April 27, 1827, 26.

———. "New-York. March 30." March 30, 1827, 10.

———. "Notice." April 25, 1828, 39.

———. "Original Communication. For the Freedom's Journal." May 18, 1827, 38.

———. "Our Own Concerns." December 21, 1827, 162–63.

———. "People of Colour." March 30, 1827, 9.

———. "People of Colour. (Continued)." April 13, 1827, 17.

———. "Plan of Civil Government for the Colony of Liberia." March 28, 1829, 405–6.

———. "Political Balance of the Globe in 1828." March 14, 1829, 394.

———. "Political Balance of the Globe in 1828 concluded." March 21, 1829, 400.

———. "Proposal for Publishing The FREEDOM'S JOURNAL. Prospectus." March 16, 1827, 1.

———. "Slavery." January 31, 1829, 344.

———. "Summary." July 27, 1827, 3.

———. "Summary." July 27, 1827, 7.

———. "To Our Patrons." March 16, 1827, 1.

———. "To the Senior Editor." August 10, 1827, 86–87.

Freeman, Elizabeth. "Introduction." *GLQ* 13, nos. 2–3 (2007): 159–76.

———. "Synchronic/Anachronic." In *A Vocabulary of the Present*, edited by Joel Burges and Amy J. Elias, 129–43. New York: New York University Press, 2016.

Friedman, Benjamin H. "Managing Fear: The Politics of Homeland Security." *Political Science Quarterly* 126, no. 1 (2011): 77–105.

Freud, Sigmund. "Character and Anal Eroticism." In *The Freud Reader*, edited by Peter Gay, 293–97. New York: Norton, 1995.

———. *Three Essays on the Theory of Sexuality* (1905). *The Standard Edition of the Complete Psychological Works of Sigmund Freud*. Vol. VII (1901–1905): *A Case of Hysteria, Three Essays on Sexuality and Other Works*, 123–246. Translated by James Strachey. London: Hogarth Press and the Institute for Psycho-Analysis, 1953–74.

———. *The Uncanny*. Translated by David McLintock. London: Penguin Books, 2003.

Gaddis, John Lewis. *Surprise, Security, and the American Experience*. Cambridge, MA: Harvard University Press, 2004.

Galli, Carlo. *Political Spaces and Global War*. Minneapolis: University of Minnesota Press, 2010.

Galluzzo, Anthony. "Charles Brockden Brown's *Wieland* and the Aesthetics of Terror: Revolution, Reaction, and the Radical Enlightenment in Early American Letters." *Eighteenth-Century Studies* 42, no. 2 (Winter 2009): 255–71.

Garrison, William Lloyd. *Thoughts on African Colonization, or an Impartial Exhibition of the Doctrines, Principles and Purposes of the American Colonization Society. Together with the Resolutions, Addresses and Remonstrances of the Free People of Color*. Boston: Garrison and Knapp, 1832. http://www.gutenberg.org/files/31178/31178-h/31178-h.htm.

Geoghegan, Bernard. "Information." In *Digital Keywords: A Vocabulary of Information Society and Culture*, edited by Benjamin Peters, 173–83. Princeton: Princeton University Press, 2016.

George, Larry N. "American Insecurities and the Ontopolitics of U.S. Pharmacotic Wars." In *The Geopolitics of American Insecurity: Terror, Power and Foreign Policy*, edited by François Debrix and Mark J. Lacy, 34–53. London: Routledge, 2009.

Gershoni, Yekutiel. *Black Colonialism: The Americo-Liberian Scramble for the Hinterland*. Boulder, CO: Westview, 1985.

Gilmore, Michael T. "Charles Brockden Brown." In *The Cambridge History of American Literature*. Vol. 1, *1590–1820*, edited by Sacvan Bercovitch, 644–60. Cambridge: Cambridge University Press, 1994.

Gilmore, Paul. "Charles Brocken Brown's Romance and the Limits of Science and History." *English Literary History* 84, no. 1 (Spring 2017): 117–42.

Gilmore, Ruth Wilson. *Golden Gulag: Prisons, Surplus, Crisis, and Opposition in Globalizing California*. Berkeley: University of California Press, 2007.

———. "Race and Globalization." In *Geographies of Global Change: Remapping the World*, edited by R. J. Johnston, Peter J. Taylor, and Michael J. Watts, 261–74. 2nd ed. Malden, MA: Blackwell, 2002.

Giroux, Henry A. "White Nationalism, Armed Culture and State Violence in the Age of Donald Trump." *Philosophy and Social Criticism* 43, no. 9 (2017): 887–910.

Gitelman, Lisa. *Always Already New: Media, History, and the Data of Culture*. Cambridge, MA: MIT Press, 2006.

Gleick, James. *The Information: A History, a Theory, a Flood*. New York: Pantheon, 2011.

Glimp, David. "Security Dilemmas: Fiscal Policy and the Limits of Sovereignty in Renaissance English Literature." 2023. University of Colorado-Boulder, book ms.

Goddard, Todd. "A Property in the Horizon: Placelessness in Nineteenth-Century American Literature and Culture." PhD diss., University of Wisconsin-Madison, 2013.

Grady, James. *Six Days of the Condor*. New York: Norton, 1974.

Gray, David. *The Fourth Amendment in the Age of Surveillance*. Cambridge: Cambridge University Press, 2017.

Greenwald, Glenn. "Edward Snowden and the Secrets of the National Security State." Lecture at the University of Utah, Salt Lake City, April 7, 2015.

———. *No Place to Hide: Edward Snowden, the NSA, and the U.S. Surveillance State*. New York: Metropolitan Books, 2014.

Grewal, Inderpal. *Saving the Security State: Exceptional Citizens in Twenty-First-Century America*. Durham: Duke University Press, 2017.

Griffin, Patrick. *American Leviathan: Empire, Nation, and Revolutionary Frontier*. New York: Hill and Wang, 2007.

Griggs, Sutton E. *Imperium in Imperio*. New York: Modern Library, 2003.

Grusin, Richard. Introduction to *Insecurity*, edited by Richard Grusin, vii–xix. Minneapolis: University of Minnesota Press, 2022.

Gutman, Herbert G. *Slavery and the Numbers Game: A Critique of Time on the Cross*. Urbana: University of Illinois Press, 1975.

Guyatt, Nicholas. "'The Outskirts of Our Happiness': Race and the Lure of Colonization in the Early Republic." *Journal of American History* 95, no. 4 (March 2009): 986–1011.

Hacking, Ian. "Biopower and the Avalanche of Printed Numbers." *Humanities and Society* 5, nos. 3–4 (1982): 279–95.

Hall, Harrison. *Illustrations from The Spy, The Pioneers, and the Waverley Novels. With Explanatory and Critical Remarks*. Philadelphia: C. Alexander, 1828.

Hamilton, Alexander, James Madison, and John Jay. *The Federalist Papers*. New York: Mentor, 1961.

Hamilton, John T. *Security: Politics, Humanity, and the Philology of Care*. Princeton: Princeton University Press, 1993.

Hanhardt, Christina B. "Safe." In *Keywords for American Cultural Studies*, edited by Bruce Burgett and Glenn Hendler, 213–17. 3rd ed. New York: New York University Press, 2020.

Harris, Cheryl I. "Whiteness as Property." *Harvard Law Review* 106, no. 8 (1993): 1707–91. https://doi.org/10.2307/1341787.

Harris, Leslie M. *In the Shadow of Slavery: African Americans in New York City, 1626–1863*. Chicago: University of Chicago Press, 2003.

Harrison, Jesse Burton. "The Colonization Society vindicated to Virginia, In a discourse delivered before the Lynchburg Colonization Society, at its anniversary, in July, 1827." *African Repository and Colonial Journal* 4 (1828–29): 193–208.

Hartz, Louis. *The Liberal Tradition in America*. New York: Harcourt Brace, 1991.

Harvey, David. *The Enigma of Capital and the Crises of Capitalism*. New York: Oxford University Press, 2010.

Hawthorne, Nathaniel. "Sights from a Steeple." In *Tales and Sketches. Including Twice-Told Tales, Mosses from an Old Manse, and The Snow Image; A Wonder Book for Girls and Boys; Tanglewood Tales for Girls and Boys; Being a Second Wonder Book*, 42–48. New York: Library of America, 1982.

Hayles, N. Katherine. *How We Became Posthuman: Virtual Bodies in Cybernetics, Literature, and Informatics*. Chicago: University of Chicago Press, 1999.

Heater, W. B. W. B. Heater to Henry L. Stimson, Secretary of War, cc to Sec. Frank Knox, Sec. Harold Ickes, Attorney General Francis Biddle, November 1, 1942. Japanese Relocation and Internment Files, box 1, file 4, University of Hawaiʻi at Manoa.

Herz, John H. "Idealist Internationalism and the Security Dilemma." *World Politics* 2, no. 2 (January 1950): 157–80.

Hewitt, Elizabeth. "Romanticism of Numbers: Hamilton, Jefferson, and the Sublime." *American Literary History* 31, no. 4 (Winter 2019): 619–38.

Hill, Kashmir. "The Secretive Company That Might End Privacy as We Know It." *New York Times*, February 10, 2020.

Hill, Leonard U. "John Randolph's Freed Slaves Settle in Western Ohio." *Cincinnati Historical Bulletin* 23, no. 2 (1965): 179–87.

Hinks, Peter P. *To Awaken My Afflicted Brethren: David Walker and the Problem of Slave Resistance*. University Park: Penn State University Press, 1997.

Hirsch, Leo H., Jr. "The Free Negro in New York." *Journal of Negro History* 16, no. 4 (October 1931): 415–53.

Hirsch, Marianne. "Vulnerable Times." In *Vulnerability in Resistance*, edited by Judith Butler, Zeynep Gambetti, and Leticia Sabsay, 76–96. Durham: Duke University Press, 2016.

Hobbes, Thomas. *The Elements of Law: Natural and Politic* [1640]. Edited by Ferdinand Tönnies. Oxford: James Thornton, 1888. https://www.google.com/books/edition/The_Elements_of _Law/3hDSyx3tymIC?hl=en&gbpv=0.

———. *Leviathan*. Cambridge: Cambridge University Press, 1996.

Hochman, Brian. *The Listeners: A History of Wiretapping in the United States*. Cambridge, MA: Harvard University Press, 2022.

Hodgson, Dennis. "Malthus' *Essay on Population* and the American Debate over Slavery." *Comparative Studies in Society and History* 51, no. 4 (October 2009): 742–70.

Hole, Jeffrey. "Correlatives of Liberalism: Melville's Managers and the Microphysics of Security." *Telos* 170 (Spring 2015): 131–48.

Homer. *The Iliad*. Translated by William Cowper. Edited by Robert Southey. New York: D. Appleton, 1860. https://ia802704.us.archive.org/33/items/theiliadofhomer16452gut /16452-h/16452-h.htm.

Honig, Bonnie. *Emergency Politics: Paradox, Law, Democracy*. Princeton: Princeton University Press, 2009.

Horsman, Reginald. *Race and Manifest Destiny: The Origins of Racial Anglo-Saxonism*. Cambridge, MA: Harvard University Press, 1986.

Horton, James Oliver, and Lois E. Horton. *In Hope of Liberty: Culture, Community, and Protest among Northern Free Blacks, 1700–1860*. New York: Oxford University Press, 1997.

Howlett, Henan. *An Address on Slavery, and Against Immediate Emancipation; with a Plan of Their Being Gradually Emancipated & Colonized, in 32 Years*. New York: S. B. White, 1834.

Huysmans, Jef. *The Politics of Insecurity: Fear, Migration, and Asylum in the EU*. London: Routledge, 2006.

Insko, Jeffrey. *History, Abolition, and the Ever-Present Now in Antebellum American Writing*. New York: Oxford University Press, 2018.

James, Winston. *The Struggles of John Brown Russwurm: The Life and Writings of a Pan-Africanist Pioneer, 1799–1851*. New York: New York University Press, 2010.

Jay, William. *An Inquiry into the Character and Tendency of the American Colonization and American Anti-Slavery Societies*. 4th ed. New York: R. G. Williams, for the American Antislavery Society, 1837.

Jefferson, Thomas. *Notes on the State of Virginia*. Chapel Hill: University of North Carolina Press, 2011.

———. Thomas Jefferson to Jared Sparks, February 4, 1824. In *The Writings of Thomas Jefferson*, edited by Paul Leicester Ford, vol. 10, 290–93. New York: G. P. Putnam, 1899.

———. Thomas Jefferson to Joel Yancy, January 17, 1819. In *Thomas Jefferson's Farm Book with Commentary and Relevant Extracts from Other Writings*, edited by Edwin Morris Betts, 42. Princeton: Princeton University Press, 1953.

Johnson, Hildegard Binder. *Order Upon the Land: The U.S. Rectangular Land Survey and the Upper Mississippi Country*. New York: Oxford University Press, 1976.

Johnson, Jessica Marie. "Markup Bodies: Black [Life] Studies and Slavery [Death] Studies at the Digital Crossroads." *Social Text* 36, no. 4 (December 2018): 57–79.

Johnson, Walter. *River of Dark Dreams: Slavery and Empire in the Cotton Kingdom*. Cambridge, MA: Harvard University Press, 2013.

———. "To Remake the World: Slavery, Racial Capitalism, and Justice." *Boston Review*, February 20, 2018.

Johnston, Les. "Transnational Security Governance." In *Democracy, Society and the Governance of Security*, edited by Jennifer Wood and Benoît Dupont, 33–51. Cambridge: Cambridge University Press, 2006.

Junior Editor. "Wilberforce." *Freedom's Journal*, September 7, 1827, 103.

Kahn, David. *The Codebreakers: The Story of Secret Writing*. New York: Macmillan, 1967.

Kant, Immanuel. *The Critique of Judgement*. Translated by J. H. Bernard. New York: Hafner, 1951.

Kaplan, Amy. "In the Name of Security." *Review of International American Studies* 3, nos. 3–4 (Summer–Fall 2009): 15–24.

Kazanjian, David. *The Brink of Freedom: Improvising Life in the Nineteenth-Century Atlantic World*. Durham: Duke University Press, 2016.

———. *The Colonizing Trick: National Culture and Imperial Citizenship in Early America*. Minneapolis: University of Minnesota Press, 2003.

King, Debra Walker. *African Americans and the Culture of Pain*. Charlottesville: University of Virginia Press, 2008.

Kirell, Andrew. "Reagan Aide: Trump's Critics Are the Real Xenophobes." *Daily Beast*, April 13, 2017. https://www.thedailybeast.com/reagan-aide-trumps-critics-are-the-real-xenophobes.

Knickmeyer, Ellen. "Study Says Nearly Half of Defense Spending for 9/11 Wars Went to Private Contractors." *PBS NewsHour*, September 13, 2021.

Koopman, Colin. "Michel Foucault's Critical Empiricism Today: Concepts and Analysis in the Critique of Biopower and Infopower." In *Foucault Now: Current Perspectives in Foucault Studies*, edited by James D. Faubion, 88–111. Malden, MA: Polity, 2014.

Kopec, Andrew. "The Digital Humanities, Inc.: Literary Criticism and the Fate of a Profession." *PMLA* 131, no. 2 (March 2016): 324–39.

Krause, Keith, and Michael C. Williams. *Critical Security Studies: Concepts and Cases*. Minneapolis: University of Minnesota Press, 1997.

LaFleur, Greta, and Kyla Schuller. "Introduction: Technologies of Life and Architectures of Death in Early America." *American Quarterly* 71, no. 3 (September 2019): 603–24.

Lakoff, Andrew. "Preparing for the Next National Emergency." *Public Culture* 19, no. 2 (2007): 247–71.

Laporte, Dominique. *History of Shit*. Translated by Nadia Benabid and Rodolphe el-Khoury. Cambridge, MA: MIT Press, 2000.

Lee, Maurice. *Overwhelmed: Literature, Aesthetics, and the Nineteenth-Century Information Revolution*. Princeton: Princeton University Press, 2019.

Lemay, J. A. Leo. *The Life of Benjamin Franklin*. 3 vols. Philadelphia: University of Pennsylvania Press, 2006.

Lennon, Brian. "The Digital Humanities and National Security." *differences* 25, no. 1 (Spring 2014): 132–55.

———. *Passwords: Philology, Security, Authentication*. Cambridge, MA: Harvard University Press, 2018.

Lepler, Jessica M. *The Many Panics of 1837: People, Politics, and the Creation of a Transatlantic Financial Crisis*. Cambridge: Cambridge University Press, 2013.

Lepore, Jill. *New York Burning: Liberty, Slavery, and Conspiracy in Eighteenth-Century Manhattan*. New York: Vintage Books, 2006.

Levine, Robert S. *Conspiracy and Romance: Studies in Brockden Brown, Cooper, Hawthorne, and Melville*. Cambridge: Cambridge University Press, 1989.

———. *Dislocating Race and Nation: Episodes in Nineteenth-Century American Literary Nationalism*. Chapel Hill: University of North Carolina Press, 2008.

———. "Temporality, Race, and Empire in Cooper's *The Deerslayer*: The Beginning of the End." In *The Oxford Handbook of Nineteenth-Century American Literature*, edited by Russ Castronovo, 163–78. New York: Oxford University Press, 2012.

Levy, Jonathan. *Freaks of Fortune: The Emerging World of Capitalism and Risk in America*. Cambridge, MA: Harvard University Press, 2012.

Lewis, Adam. "'A Traitor to His Brethren'? John Brown Russwurm and the *Liberia Herald*." *American Periodicals* 25, no. 2 (2015): 112–23.

The Liberator. "Liberia Herald—John B. Russwurm." February 25, 1832, 282–83.

Liberia Herald. "Island of Fernando Po—Liberia." April 6, 1830, 6–7.

———. "Mortality of the Emigrants, per Volador of Baltimore." December 22, 1831, 39.

———. "Poetry." April 22, 1831, 6.

Litwack, Leon. *North of Slavery: The Negro in the Free States, 1790–1860*. Chicago: University of Chicago Press, 1961.

Loader, Ian, and Neil Walker. *Civilizing Security*. Cambridge: Cambridge University Press, 2007.

———. "Necessary Virtues: The Legitimate Place of the State in the Production of Security." In *Democracy, Society and the Governance of Security*, edited by Jennifer Wood and Benoît Dupont, 165–95. Cambridge: Cambridge University Press, 2006.

Locke, John. *An Essay Concerning Human Understanding*. Monee, IL: WLC Books, 2009.

———. *Second Treatise of Government*. Indianapolis: Hackett, 1980.

Looby, Christopher. *Voicing America: Language, Literary Form, and the Origins of the United States*. Chicago: University of Chicago Press, 1996.

Luhmann, Niklas. "How Can the Mind Participate in Communication?" In *Materialities of Communication*, edited by Hans Ulrich Gumbrecht and K. Ludwig Pfeiffer, translated by William Whobrey, 371–88. Stanford: Stanford University Press, 1994.

———. *The Reality of Mass Media*. Translated by Kathleen Cross. Stanford: Stanford University Press, 2000.

Mack, Eric. *John Locke*. New York: Bloomsbury Academic, 2013.

MacLellan, Matthew. "Indigenous Infopolitics: Biopolitics as Resistance to White Paper Liberalism in Canada." *Theory & Event* 21, no. 4 (October 2018): 914–36.

Mandel, Emily St. John. *Station Eleven*. New York: Knopf, 2014.

Mangrum, Benjamin. "Aggregation, Public Criticism, and the History of Reading Big Data." *PMLA* 133, no. 5 (October 2018): 1207–24.

Margolis, Stacey. "Network Theory circa 1800: Charles Brockden Brown's *Arthur Mervyn*." *Novel* 45, no. 3 (Fall 2012): 343–67.

Maryland Journal and the Baltimore Advertiser. "New-York, March 6." March 13, 1775.

———. "New-York, March 16." March 29, 1775.

Masco, Joseph. *Theater of Operations: National Security Affect from the Cold War to the War on Terror*. Durham: Duke University Press, 2014.

Massumi, Brian. "National Enterprise Emergency: Steps toward an Ecology of Powers." *Theory, Culture & Society* 26, no. 6 (2009): 153–85.

Martin, Bonnie. "Slavery's Invisible Engine: Mortgaging Human Property." *Journal of Southern History* 76, no. 4 (November 2010): 817–66.

Martin, Randy. "From the Race War to the War on Terror." In *Beyond Biopolitics: Essays on the Governance of Life and Death*, edited by Patricia Ticineto Clough and Craig Willse, 258–74. Durham: Duke University Press, 2011.

Marx, Gary T. "Surveillance and Society." In *Encyclopedia of Social Theory*, edited by George Ritzer, 2:816–21. Thousand Oaks, CA: Sage, 2005. http://web.mit.edu/gtmarx/www/surandsoc.html.

Mazzone, Jason. "The Security Constitution." *UCLA Law Review* 53, no. 1 (October 2005): 29–152.

Mbembe, Achille. "Necropolitics." Translated by Libby Meintjes. *Public Culture* 15, no. 1 (Winter 2003): 11–40.

———. "Thoughts on the Planetary: An Interview with Achille Mbembe." By Torbjørn Tumyr Nilsen. *New Frame*, September 5, 2019. https://www.newframe.com/thoughts-on-the-planetary-an-interview-with-achille-mbembe/.

McCarthy, Anne C. "Reading the Red Bull Sublime." *PMLA* 132, no. 3 (May 2017): 543–57.

McCloy, James. Letter of November 17, 1942. Japanese Internment and Relocation Files, box 1, University of Hawai'i at Manoa.

McCrum, Robert. "The 100 Best Nonfiction Books: No. 90—An Essay Concerning Human Understanding by John Locke (1689)." *The Guardian*, March 23, 2017. https://www.theguardian.com/books/2017/oct/23/essay-concerning-human-understanding-1689-by-john-locke-no-90-100-best-nonfiction.

McDaniel, Antonio. *Swing Low, Sweet Chariot: The Mortality Cost of Colonizing Liberia in the Nineteenth Century*. Chicago: University of Chicago Press, 1995.

McFate, Sean. "Mercenaries and War: Understanding Private Armies Today." National Defense University Press, December 4, 2019. https://ndupress.ndu.edu/Media/News/Article/2031922/mercenaries-and-war-understanding-private-armies-today/.

McHenry, Elizabeth. *Forgotten Readers: Recovering the Lost History of African American Literary Societies*. Durham: Duke University Press, 2002.

McKittrick, Katherine. *Dear Science and Other Stories*. Durham: Duke University Press, 2021.

Melville, Herman. *Benito Cereno*. In *Pierre or, The Ambiguities; Israel Potter: His Fifty Years of Exile; The Piazza Tales; The Confidence-Man: His Masquerade; Uncollected Prose; Billy Budd, Sailor (An Inside Narrative)*. New York: Library of America, 1984.

———. "The Lightning-Rod Man." In *Pierre or, The Ambiguities; Israel Potter: His Fifty Years of Exile; The Piazza Tales; The Confidence-Man: His Masquerade; Uncollected Prose; Billy Budd, Sailor (An Inside Narrative)*. New York: Library of America, 1984.

"Memorial of the Kentucky Colonization Society." *African Repository and Colonial Journal* 5 (1829–30): 347–49.

Michel, Jean-Baptiste, Yuan Kui Shen, Aviva Presser Aiden, Adrian Veres, Matthew K. Gray, The Google Books Team, Joseph P. Pickett, et al. "Quantitative Analysis of Culture Using Millions of Digitized Books." *Science* 331, no. 6014 (January 14, 2011): 176–82.

Milligan, Joseph. Letter to John Adams, November 30, 1818. *Founders Online*, National Archives, https://founders.archives.gov/documents/Adams/99-02-02-7033.

Mills, Brandon. *The World Colonization Made: The Racial Geography of Early American Empire*. Philadelphia: University of Pennsylvania Press, 2020.

Mishra, Vijay. *The Gothic Sublime*. Albany: State University of New York Press, 1994.

Mitchell, W. J. T. *What Do Pictures Want? The Lives and Loves of Images*. Chicago: University of Chicago Press, 2005.

Monahan, Torin. "Questioning Surveillance and Security." In *Surveillance and Security: Technological Politics and Power in Everyday Life*, edited by Torin Monahan, 1–26. New York: Routledge, 2006.

Mordecai. "Original Communications." *Freedom's Journal*, August 17, 1827, 90.

Morris, David B. "Gothic Sublimity." *New Literary History* 16, no. 2 (Winter 1985): 299–319.

Mosco, Vincent. *The Digital Sublime: Myth, Power, and Cyberspace*. Cambridge, MA: MIT Press, 2004.

Murison, Justine S. *Faith in Exposure: Privacy and Secularism in the Nineteenth-Century United States*. Philadelphia: University of Pennsylvania Press, 2023.

Mythen, Gabe. *Ulrich Beck: A Critical Introduction to the Risk Society*. London: Pluto Press, 2004.

Nagel, Alexander, and Christopher Wood. *Anachronic Renaissance*. New York: Zone Books, 2010.

Nakashima, Ellen, and Joby Warrick. "For NSA Chief, Terrorist Threat Drives Passion to 'Collect It All.'" *Washington Post*, July 14, 2013. https://www.washingtonpost.com/world/national-security/for-nsa-chief-terrorist-threat-drives-passion-to-collect-it-all/2013/07/14/3d26ef80-ea49-11e2-a301-ea5a8116d211_story.html.

Nash, Gary. *Forging Freedom: The Formation of Philadelphia's Black Community, 1720–1840*. Cambridge, MA: Harvard University Press, 1988.

National Advocate. "Bethell Meeting." November 23, 1825, 2.

National Archives. "Louisiana Purchase Treaty (1803)." Milestone Documents. https://www.archives.gov/milestone-documents/louisiana-purchase-treaty.

National Gazette. "Distressing Occurrence." November 24, 1825, 3.

National Nuclear Security Administration. "Planetary Defense." https://www.energy.gov/nnsa/planetary-defense.

"The National Security Implications of a Changing Climate." White House report, May 2015. https://obamawhitehouse.archives.gov/sites/default/files/docs/National_Security_Implications_of_Changing_Climate_Final_051915.pdf.

Nelson, Dana D. *Commons Democracy: Reading the Politics of Participation in the Early United States*. New York: Fordham University Press, 2016.
Neocleous, Mark. *Critique of Security*. Montreal: McGill-Queen's University Press, 2008.
———. "Securitati Perpetuae: Death, Fear, and the History of Insecurity." In *Insecurity*, edited by Richard Grusin, 1–30. Minneapolis: University of Minnesota Press, 2022.
New York Times. "The Government Uses 'Near Perfect Surveillance' Data on Americans." Editorial, February 7, 2020.
Ohio History Connection. "The Arrival of the Randolph Freedpeople." Ohio History Connection Blogroll, March 8, 2017. https://www.ohiohistory.org/the-arrival-of-the-randolph-freedpeople/.
Oliver, William Bourn. *An address, delivered at Springfield, before the Hampden colonization society, July 4th, 1828*. Springfield: S. Bowles, 1828.
O'Neil, Cathy. *Weapons of Math Destruction: How Big Data Increases Inequality and Threatens Democracy*. New York: Crown, 2016.
Paik, A. Naomi. "Deadly Entanglements: U.S. Imperialism and Perils of Privatizing Security." In *Insecurity*, edited by Richard Grusin, 65–93. Minneapolis: University of Minnesota Press, 2022.
Paine, Thomas. *Common Sense*. Philadelphia: W. and T. Bradford, 1776. http://www.gutenberg.org/files/147/147-h/147-h.htm.
Parenti, Christian. *The Soft Cage: Surveillance in America from Slavery to the War on Terror*. New York: Basic Books, 2003.
Parker, Arthur C. *The Constitution of the Five Nations or The Iroquois Book of the Great Law*. Albany: New York State Museum Bulletin, 1916. https://play.google.com/books/reader?id=b3E_AQAAMAAJ&pg=GBS.PA6&hl=en.
Parkinson, Robert. *The Common Cause: Creating Race and Nation in the American Revolution*. Chapel Hill: University of North Carolina Press, 2016.
Parrott, Russell. "From the Union by Russel [sic] Parrott of Philadelphia." *Freedom's Journal*, July 27, 1827, 73.
Patterson, Sarah Lynn. "As the True Guardians of Our Interests: The Ethos of Black Leadership and Demography at Antebellum Colored Conventions." In *The Colored Conventions Movement: Black Organizing in the Nineteenth Century*, edited by Sarah Lynn Patterson, 221–29. Chapel Hill: University of North Carolina Press, 2021.
Paulson, William R. *The Noise of Culture: Literary Texts in a World of Information*. Ithaca: Cornell University Press, 1988.
Peabody, William Bourn Oliver. "An address, delivered at Springfield, before the Hampden colonization society, July 4th, 1828." Springfield: S. Bowles, 1828.
Pease, Donald. "Sublime Politics." In *The American Sublime*, edited by Mary Arensberg, 21–50. Albany: State University of New York Press, 1986.
Pennsylvania Assembly. "Pennsylvania Assembly: Reply to the Governor, 11 November 1755." *Founders Online*, National Archives. Published in *The Papers of Benjamin Franklin*, vol. 6, *April 1, 1755, through September 30, 1756*, edited by Leonard W. Labaree, 238–43. New Haven: Yale University Press, 1963. https://founders.archives.gov/documents/Franklin/01-06-02-0107.
Pennsylvania General Assembly, House of Representatives. *Journal of the Pennsylvania House of Representatives* 23 (1812–13). Harrisburg: Printed by J. Peacock, 1813.

Peoples, Columba, and Nick Vaughan-Williams. *Critical Security Studies: An Introduction.* 2nd ed. New York: Routledge, 2015.

Perry, Barbara. "'White Genocide': White Supremacists and the Politics of Reproduction." In *Home-Grown Hate: Gender and Organized Racism*, edited by Abby L. Ferber, 71–91. London: Routledge, 2004.

Peterson, Carla. *Black Gotham: A Family History of African-Americans in Nineteenth-Century New York City.* New Haven: Yale University Press, 2011.

Poincaré, Henri. *Science and Hypothesis.* New York: Walter Scott Publishing, 1907.

Polk, Josiah F. "Mr. Polk's Report." *African Repository and Colonial Journal* 6 (1830–31): 71–80.

Potolsky, Matthew. *The National Security Sublime: On the Aesthetics of Government Secrecy.* New York: Routledge, 2017.

Power-Greene, Ousmane K. *Against Wind and Tide: The African American Struggle against the Colonization Movement.* New York: New York University Press, 2014.

Puar, Jasbir. *Terrorist Assemblages: Homonationalism in Queer Times.* Durham: Duke University Press, 2007.

Pugliese, Joseph. "Death by Metadata: The Bioinformationalisation of Life and the Transliteration to Flesh." In *Security, Race, Biopower: Essays on Technology and Corporeality*, edited by Holly Randell-Moon and Ryan Tippet, 3–20. New York: Palgrave Macmillan, 2016.

Pynchon, Thomas. *Bleeding Edge.* New York: Penguin, 2013.

Rancière, Jacques. "The Concept of Anachronism and the Historian's Truth." Translated by Noel Fitzpatrick and Tim Stott. *In/Print* 3, no. 1, art. 3 (2015). https://arrow.tudublin.ie/inp/vol3/iss1/3/.

Randell-Moon, Holly, and Ryan Tippet. Introduction to *Security, Race, Biopower: Essays on Technology and Corporeality*, edited by Holly Randell-Moon and Ryan Tippet, v–xxvi. New York: Palgrave Macmillan, 2016.

Reese, David M. *Letters to the Hon. William Jay, Being a Reply to His "Inquiry into the American Colonization and American Anti-Slavery Societies."* New York: Leavitt, Lord, 1835.

Resolutions and Remonstrances of the People of Colour Against Colonization to the Coast of Africa. Philadelphia, 1818.

Ringe, Donald A. *American Gothic: Imagination and Reason in 19th-Century Fiction.* Lexington: University of Kentucky Press, 1982.

Roberts, Siân Silyn. *Gothic Subjects: The Transformation of Individualism in American Fiction, 1790–1861.* Philadelphia: University of Pennsylvania Press, 2014.

Robin, Corey. *Fear: The History of a Political Idea.* New York: Oxford University Press, 2004.

Roediger, David. *The Wages of Whiteness: Race and the Making of the American Working Class.* New York: Verso, 1991.

Rohy, Valerie. *Anachronism and Its Others: Sexuality, Race, and Temporality.* Albany: State University of New York Press, 2009.

Rojecki, Andrew. *America and the Politics of Insecurity.* Baltimore: Johns Hopkins University Press, 2016.

Rosen, David, and Aaron Santesso. *The Watchman in Pieces: Surveillance, Literature, and Liberal Personhood.* New Haven: Yale University Press, 2013.

Rothman, Joshua D. "The Contours of Cotton Capitalism: Speculation, Slavery, and Economic Panic in Mississippi, 1832–1841." In *Slavery's Capitalism: A New History of American Economic*

Development, edited by Sven Beckert and Seth Rockman, 122–45. Philadelphia: University of Pennsylvania Press, 2016.

Rothschild, Emma. "What Is Security?" *Daedalus* 124, no. 3 (Summer 1995): 53–98.

Rouvroy, Antoinette. "Algorithmic Governmentality and the Death of Politics." *Green European Journal*, March 27, 2020. https://www.greeneuropeanjournal.eu/algorithmic-governmentality-and-the-death-of-politics/.

———. "The End(s) of Critique: Data Behaviourism versus Due Process." In *Privacy, Due Process and the Computational Turn: The Philosophy of Law Meets the Philosophy of Technology*, edited by Mireille Hildebrandt and Katja de Vries, 143–67. New York: Routledge, 2015.

Rowe, John Carlos. *Literary Culture and U.S. Imperialism: From the Revolution to World War II*. New York: Oxford University Press, 2000.

Ruggles, David. *The "Extinguisher" Extinguished! or David M. Reese, M.D. "Used Up." By David Ruggles, a Man of Color. Together with Some Remarks upon a Late Production, Entitled "An Address on Slavery and Against Immediate Emancipation with a Plan of their Being Gradually Emancipated and Colonized in Thirty-two Years." By Heman Howlett*. New York: David Ruggles, 1834.

Rumsfeld, Donald H. "Transforming the Military." *Foreign Affairs* 81, no. 3 (May/June 2002): 20–32.

Russwurm, John B. "Freedom's Journal." *Freedom's Journal*, February 21, 1829, 370.

———. "Liberia." *Freedom's Journal*, February 14, 1829, 362.

Saillant, John. "The American Enlightenment in Africa: Jefferson's Colonizationism and Black Virginians' Migration to Liberia, 1776–1840." *Eighteenth-Century Studies* 31, no. 3 (Spring 1998): 261–82.

Saxton, Alexander. *The Rise and Fall of the White Republic: Class Politics and Mass Culture in Nineteenth-Century America*. London: Verso, 1990.

Schiller, Friedrich. "Of the Sublime: Toward the Further Elaboration of Some Kantian Ideas." Translated by Daniel Platt. The Schiller Institute. https://archive.schillerinstitute.com/transl/trans_of_sublime.html.

———. "On the Sublime." In *Aesthetical and Philosophical Essays*. https://www.gutenberg.org/files/6798/6798-h/6798-h.htm#link2H_4_0033.

Schmitt, Carl. *The Concept of the Political*. Translated by George Schwab. Expanded ed. Chicago: University of Chicago Press, 2007.

———. *The Leviathan in the State Theory of Thomas Hobbes: Meaning and Failure of a Political Symbol*. Translated by George Schwab and Ema Hilfstein. Westport, CT: Greenwood Press, 1996.

———. "Strong State and Sound Economy: An Address to Business Leaders." In Renato Cristi, *Carl Schmitt and Authoritarian Liberalism: Strong State, Free Economy*, 212–32. Cardiff: University of Wales Press, 1998.

Schneier, Bruce. *Beyond Fear: Thinking Sensibly about Security in an Uncertain World*. New York: Copernicus Books, 2006.

———. *Data and Goliath: The Hidden Battles to Collect Your Data and Control Your World*. New York: Norton, 2015.

Schuller, Kyla. *The Biopolitics of Feeling: Race, Sex, and Science in the Nineteenth Century*. Durham: Duke University Press, 2017.

Schwab, George. Introduction to Carl Schmitt, *The Leviathan in the State Theory of Thomas Hobbes: Meaning and Failure of a Political Symbol*, translated by George Schwab and Ema Hilfstein, xi–xxxi. Westport, CT: Greenwood Press, 1996.

Schweighauser, Philipp. *The Noises of American Literature, 1890–1985*. Gainesville: University of Florida Press, 2006.

Sedgwick, Eve Kosofsky. *The Coherence of Gothic Conventions*. New York: Methuen, 1986.

Selectmen of Plymouth County. "To His Excellency Thomas Gage, Esq." *Maryland Journal and the Baltimore Advertiser*, March 13, 1775.

Seltzer, Mark. "Saying Makes It So: Language and Event in Brown's 'Wieland.'" *Early American Literature* 13, no. 1 (1978): 81–91. http://www.jstor.org/stable/25070867.

Semple, Lorenzo Jr., and David Rayfiel. Screenplay for *Three Days of the Condor*. 1975. https://www.awesomefilm.com/script/ThreeDaysoftheCondor.pdf.

Seventh Annual Report of the American Society for Colonizing the Free People of Colour of the United States. Within an Appendix. Washington, DC: Davis and Force, 1824.

Shannon, Claude E., and Warren Weaver. *The Mathematical Theory of Communication*. Urbana: University of Illinois Press, 1964.

Shklar, Judith N. "The Liberalism of Fear." In *Liberalism and the Moral Life*, edited by Nancy L. Rosenblum, 21–38. Cambridge, MA: Harvard University Press, 2013.

Sigourney, Lydia Huntley. "On the Publication of the Liberia Herald." *African Repository and Colonial Journal* 6, no. 11 (1831): 350–51.

Silliman, Benjamin. "Some of the Causes of National Anxiety." *African Repository and Colonial Journal* 8 (1832–33): 161–78.

Silver, Peter. *Our Savage Neighbors: How Indian War Transformed Early America*. New York: Norton, 2008.

Sizemore, Michelle. *American Enchantment: Rituals of the People in the Post-Revolutionary World*. New York: Oxford University Press, 2017.

Smith, James Morton. *Freedom's Fetters: The Alien and Sedition Law and American Civil Liberties*. Ithaca: Cornell University Press, 1956.

Sollors, Werner. "'Better to Die by Them than for Them': Carl Schmitt Reads 'Benito Cereno.'" *Critical Inquiry* 46 (Winter 2020): 401–20.

Soni, Jimmy, and Rob Goodman. *A Mind at Play: How Claude Shannon Invented the Information Age*. New York: Simon and Schuster, 2017.

Sparks, Earl Sylvester. *History and Theory of Agricultural Credit in the United States*. New York: Thomas Y. Crowell, 1932.

Spero, Patrick. *Frontier Country: The Politics of War in Early Pennsylvania*. Philadelphia: University of Pennsylvania Press, 2016.

Stanley, Jay, and Barry Steinhardt. *Bigger Monster, Weaker Chains: The Growth of an American Surveillance Society*. New York: American Civil Liberties Union, January 15, 2003. http://www.ratical.org/ratville/CAH/BMWC.html.

Stein, Jordan Alexander. "American Literary History and Queer Temporalities." *American Literary History* 25, no. 4 (December 2013): 855–69.

———. "'A Christian Nation Calls for Its Wandering Children': Life, Liberty, Liberia." *American Literary History* 19, no. 4 (Winter 2007): 849–73.

Stewart, Larry L. "Charles Brockden Brown: Quantitative Analysis and Literary Interpretation." *Literary and Linguistic Computing* 18, no. 2 (2003): 129–38.

Sweet, Leonard I. "The Fourth of July and Black Americans in the Nineteenth Century: Northern Leadership Opinion within the Context of the Black Experience." *Journal of Negro History* 61, no. 3 (July 1976): 256–75.

Tambling, Jeremy. *On Anachronism*. Manchester: Manchester University Press, 2010.

Taylor, Alan. *William Cooper's Town: Power and Persuasion on the Frontier of the Early American Republic*. New York: Knopf, 1995.

Taylor, Astra. "The Insecurity Machine." *Logic* 10 (May 4, 2020).

Thomas, Brook. *Cross-Examinations of Law and Literature: Cooper, Hawthorne, Stowe, and Melville*. Cambridge: Cambridge University Press, 1987.

Thompson, Stuart A., and Charlie Warzel. "Twelve Million Phones, One Data Set, Zero Privacy." *New York Times*, December 19, 2019. https://www.nytimes.com/interactive/2019/12/19/opinion/location-tracking-cell-phone.html.

Thomson, Charles. *An Enquiry into the Causes of the Alienation of the Delaware and Shawanese Indians from the British Interest: and into the Measures Taken for Recovering their friendship... Together with the Remarkable Journal of Christian French*. London: J. Wilkie, 1759. https://archive.org/details/McGillLibrary-104415-150.

Tilly, Charles. "War Making and State Making as Organized Crime." In *Bringing the State Back In*, edited by Peter B. Evans, Dietrich Rueschemeyer, and Theda Skocpol, 169–91. Cambridge: Cambridge University Press, 1985.

Torrey, Jesse. *A Portraiture of Domestic Slavery, in the United States: With Reflections on the Practicability of Restoring the Moral Rights of the Slave, Without Impairing the Legal Privileges of the Possessor; and, A Project of a Colonial Asylum for Free Persons of Colour: Including Memoirs of Facts on the Interior Traffic in Slaves, and, on Kidnapping*. Philadelphia: John Bioren, printer, 1817.

Totaro, Paolo, and Domenico Ninno. "The Concept of Algorithm as an Interpretative Key of Modern Rationality." *Theory, Culture, & Society* 31, no. 4 (2014): 29–49.

Treverton, Gregory F. *Intelligence for an Age of Terror*. Cambridge: Cambridge University Press, 2009.

Tsoukala, Anastassia. "Democracy in the Light of Security: British and French Political Discourses on Domestic Counter-Terrorism Policies." *Political Studies* 54, no. 3 (2006): 607–27.

Tuck, Richard. *Natural Rights Theories: Their Origin and Development*. Cambridge: Cambridge University Press, 1979.

Tyson, Job R. *A Discourse Before the Young Men's Colonization Society of Pennsylvania: Delivered October 24, 1834, In St. Paul's Church, Philadelphia*. Philadelphia: Printed for the Society, 1834.

United Nations General Assembly. Resolution 66/290, Follow-up to Paragraph 143 on Human Security of the 2005 World Summit Outcome, A/RES/66/290, September 10, 2012. https://digitallibrary.un.org/record/737105?ln=en.

United Nations Trust Fund for Human Security. "What Is Human Security?" https://www.un.org/humansecurity/what-is-human-security/.

United States Department of Homeland Security. "If You See Something, Say Something." Radio: Protect Your Every Day Public Service Announcement. January 26, 2015.

Valéry, Paul. *Introduction to the Method of Leonardo Da Vinci*. Translated by Thomas McGreevy. London: John Rodker, 1929.

Vareschi, Mark. *Everywhere and Nowhere: Anonymity and Mediation in Eighteenth-Century Britain*. Minneapolis: University of Minnesota Press, 2018.

Virginia Gazette. "Williamsburg, April 22." April 22, 1775.

Voelz, Johannes. *The Poetics of Insecurity: American Fiction and the Use of Threat.* Cambridge: Cambridge University Press, 2017.

———. "Security Theory." In *The City in American Literature,* edited by Kevin McNamara, 283–311. New York: Cambridge University Press, 2021.

Wæver, Ole. "Security and Desecuritization." In *On Security,* edited by Ronnie Lipschutz, 46–86. New York: Columbia University Press, 1995.

Walker, David. *Walker's Appeal, in Four Articles; Together with a Preamble, to the Colored Citizens of the World, But in Particular, and Very Especially, to Those of The United States of America, Written in Boston, State of Massachusetts, September 28, 1829. Third and Last Edition, with Additional Notes, Corrections, Etc.* Boston: David Walker, 1830.

Walker, R. B. J. "The Subject of Security." In *Critical Security Studies: Concepts and Cases,* edited by Keith Krause and Michael C. Williams, 61–81. Minneapolis: University of Minnesota Press, 1997.

Walzer, Michael. *The Company of Critics: Social Criticism and Political Commitment in the Twentieth Century.* Rev. ed. New York: Basic Books, 2002.

Warner, Michael. *The Letters of the Republic: Publication and the Public Sphere in Eighteenth-Century America.* Cambridge, MA: Harvard University Press, 1990.

Warren, Samuel D., and Louis D. Brandeis. "The Right to Privacy." *Harvard Law Review* 4, no. 5 (December 1890): 193–220.

"Washington, February 10, 1832, letter from William Abels." *Schomburg Center Scrapbooks: Liberia.* Schomburg Center for Research in Black Culture, New York Public Library.

Watts, Steven. *The Romance of Real Life: Charles Brockden Brown and the Origins of American Culture.* Baltimore: Johns Hopkins University Press, 1994.

Weheliye, Alexander G. *Habeas Viscus: Racializing Assemblages, Biopolitics, and Black Feminist Theories of the Human.* Durham: Duke University Press, 2014.

Weiskel, Thomas. *The Romantic Sublime: Studies in the Structure and Psychology of Transcendence.* Baltimore: Johns Hopkins University Press, 1976.

Western Luminary. "Liberia: From the *Liberia Herald.*" May 1, 1833, 3.

Wharton, Francis. *State Trials of the United States During the Administrations of Washington and Adams. With References, Historical and Professional, and Preliminary Notes on the Politics of the Times.* Philadelphia: Cary and Hart, 1849.

Wheeler, Tom. "How the Republicans Sold Your Privacy to Internet Providers." *New York Times,* March 29, 2017.

Whittlesey, Elisha. *An Address, Delivered before the Tallmadge Colonization Society, on the Fourth July, 1833.* Ravenna: Office of the Ohio Star, 1833.

Wilberforce. "For the Freedom's Journal." *Freedom's Journal,* September 7, 1827, 101–2.

Wilkens, Matthew. "Canons, Close Reading, and the Evolution of Method." In *Debates in the Digital Humanities,* edited by Matthew K. Gold, 249–58. Minneapolis: University of Minnesota Press, 2012.

Williams, Michael C., and Keith Krause. "Preface: Toward Critical Security Studies." In *Critical Security Studies: Concepts and Cases,* edited by Keith Krause and Michael C. Williams, vii–xxi. Minneapolis: University of Minnesota Press, 1997.

Wolin, Richard. "Carl Schmitt: The Conservative Revolutionary Habitus and the Aesthetics of Horror." *Political Theory* 20, no. 3 (August 1992): 424–47.

Womack, Autumn. *The Matter of Black Living: The Aesthetic Experiment of Racial Data, 1880–1930*. Chicago: University of Chicago Press, 2022.

Wood, Gordon S. "Rhetoric and Reality in the American Revolution." *William and Mary Quarterly*, 3rd ser., 23, no. 1 (January 1966): 3–32.

Wood, Nicholas. "John Randolph of Roanoke and the Politics of Slavery in the Early Republic." *Virginia Magazine of History and Biography* 120, no. 2 (Summer 2012): 106–43.

Woodward, C. Vann. "The Age of Reinterpretation." *American Historical Review* 66, no. 1 (October 1960): 1–19.

Yale, Calvin. *A sermon, Delivered before the Vermont Colonization Society, at Montpelier, October 17, 1827*. Montpelier, VT: E. P. Walton, 1827.

Yao, Xine. *Disaffected: The Cultural Politics of Unfeeling in Nineteenth-Century America*. Durham: Duke University Press, 2021.

Young, Iris Marion. "The Logic of Masculinist Protection: Reflections on the Current Security State." *Signs* 29, no. 1 (2003): 1–25.

Young, Sandra Sandiford. "John Brown Russwurm's Dilemma: Citizenship Emigration." In *Prophets of Protest: Reconsidering the History of American Abolitionism*, edited by Timothy Patrick McCarthy and John Stauffer, 90–113. New York: New Press, 2006.

Zeskind, Leonard. *Blood and Politics: The History of the White Nationalist Movement from the Margins to the Mainstream*. New York: Farrar, Straus and Giroux, 2009.

Zuboff, Shoshana. *The Age of Surveillance Capitalism: The Fight for a Human Future at the New Frontier of Power*. New York: Public Affairs, 2019.

INDEX

Page numbers in italics indicate illustrations.

abolitionism, 165, 169, 181, 211–13; Emancipation Day and, 207–11, 256n12; Garrison and, 186; Howlett on, 170; Insko on, 242n17; Jay on, 175, 180, 188, 201–2. *See also* slavery

ACLU v. Clapper (2015), 85

Adams, John, 69–72, 184

Adams, Rachel, 243n14

aesthetics, 21; affect and, 21–22, 68, 119; Freud and, 28; of information, 120–25, 135; security and, 21–23. *See also* sublime

affect, 2–3, 6–8, 16, 31, 43, 93, 99, 235; aesthetics and, 21–22, 68, 119; Ahmed on, 6, 191; Freud on, 98; of Jefferson, 155–56, 177, 181; of Rumsfeld, 244n22; terror and, 83, 120; vulnerability and, 10, 86, 129, 150, 159, 205

African Repository and Colonial Journal, 163–64, 180, 203

Agamben, Giorgio, 6–8, 61, 241nn6–7, 257n18; on depoliticization, 39; on legal authority, 235; on Schmitt, 229–30

agency, 34–36, 51–54

Ahmed, Sara, 43, 51, 156

Ahuja, Neel, 47

Alexander, Janet, 95

Alexander, Keith, 107

Alexander, Michelle, 4

algorithms, 48, 55; and bulk data, 89–90; of colonization, 202; of governmentality, 157–58, 161–62, 194; of social media, 32, 47, 52

Alien and Sedition Acts (1798), 68–72

Allen, Richard, 218

Allen, William H., 164, 252n17

Al-Qaeda, 3, 117

Amar, Paul, 13–14

American Civil Liberties Union (ACLU), 29, 85, 88

American Colonization Society (ACS), 4, 74–76, 155–57; Blacks resettled by, 250n7; church support of, 249n2; Clay on, 206–7; disbanding of, 157; establishment of, 72, 167; Forten on, 200–201; Garrison on, 186, 216; Jay on, 201–2; local chapters of, 153–55, 177–79; membership of, 165, 252n20; mission of, 200; opponents of, 163; during Reconstruction, 164–65; Russwurm on, 193, 219–20; as security apparatus, 174. *See also* colonization schemes; Liberia

American Enlightenment (1750–1820), 132

Ames, Fisher, 69–70

amnesia, "structural," 143

Amoore, Louise, 93

anachronism, 14–15, 242n15

Anderson, Margo J., 251n13

Anker, Elisabeth, 8, 86, 90, 91

Annales school of history, 14–15

anti-Semitism, 242n10, 256n15

Aravamudan, Srinivas, 246n2

Archer, William Segar, 186–87

Arends, J. Frederik M., 13

Arendt, Hannah, 13, 36–40

Aristotle's *Poetics*, 117

INDEX

Armstrong, Nancy, 249n3
Arneil, Barbara, 101–2
Arnold, Matthew, 32
arson rumors, 205–6
asphaleia ("security"), 41
Assange, Julian, 89
Atta, Mohamed, 82
Auxiliary Colonization Society, 161

Bacon, Jacqueline, 256n7, 256n12
Balbi, Adriano, 221–22, 222
Balzac, Honoré de, 82
Bannon, Steve, 251n12
Baptist, Edward, 189, 254n38
Barlow, Joel, 70
Bassa people, 225, 226
Beck, Ulrich, 3, 33; on risk, 11, 86–87; on terrorism, 92
Beebee, Thomas, 231, 258n5
Benjamin, Walter, 83, 116; on Balzac, 82; on Cooper, 81–82; on detective fiction, 81–82, 88; Kafka and, 235; on state of emergency, 5, 34–35, 230, 241n6
Berlant, Lauren, 93
Berlin, Isaiah, 39
Beyan, Amos, 225–27
Bigo, Didier, 61
biometrics, 51–52, 88
biopolitics, 6–7, 37–38, 90–91, 195; Agamben on, 257n18; Dillon on, 37, 38, 119, 248n1; of fear, 185; of increased population, 172–76; of security, 37, 38, 248n1; statistics for, 154–64, 166–67
biopower, 38, 51, 68, 155–56; Black, 160–61, 170, 183, 200, 202, 209, 214; definition of, 250n4; Noah on, 209; racism and, 254n35; "revolutionary," 192; Walker on, 185, 217–18
Birchall, Clare, 94–95
Black festivals, 207–11
Black-Indian alliances, 66–68, 72, 162
Black Lives Matter, 51
Black print culture, 194, 203, 212, 224, 248n8, 253n21, 256n9

Blackwater Corporation (Academi), 44–45
Brandeis, Louis D., 86, 88
Brightman, Carol, 30, 241n8
Brown, Charles Brockden, 8, 16; Gilmore on, 127, 132; Locke and, 126, 130–32, 143, 249n12; Rowe on, 128; Walker and, 214
Brown, Charles Brockden, works of: *Arthur Mervyn*, 126; *Clara Howard*, 148–51; *Edgar Huntly*, 126; *Memoirs of Carwin*, 25, 43, 137–41, 144–45; *Ormond*, 126; *Wieland*, 12, 28, 126–35, 137–44, 151
Brown, Wendy, 8
Browne, Simone, 50, 158, 168
bulk data, 89–90, 118–19
Burke, Anthony, 26, 30, 89
Burke, Edmund, 70, 141, 152; on Locke, 29, 138; on sublime, 120, 121; on terror, 182
Bush, George W., 1, 5, 244n16
Butler, Judith, 8–10, 40

Canadian colonialism, 218
captivity narratives, 82, 250n3
Carey, Mathew, 179, 182–83
Carpenter v. United States (2018), 85, 86, 88, 244n19
Cary, Mary Ann Shadd, 252n16
Castiglia, Christopher, 250n7, 252n20
Cato Institute, 29
cell phones, 88, 135–36
census, 153, 156, 168–70, 174, 251n13; of 1820, 161, 206; of 1840, 176; *Freedom's Journal* and, 202; Jefferson and, 177
Charlottesville rally (2017), 159
Chertoff, Michael, 95, 118
Cheyfitz, Eric, 101, 104
Child, Lydia Maria, 176
Cicero, 128–29, 135, 148
Citizen's Bank Faith Bond, 189
Clay, Henry, 159, 165, 205–7
Coates, Ta-Nehisi, 4
Code Noir, 218
Cohen, Patricia Cline, 175, 176
Cold War, 22, 27, 55; spy novels of, 117–18
Coleridge, Samuel Taylor, 14

colonialism: Canadian, 218; Enlightenment and, 250n5; settler, 29, 33, 48–50, 57, 61, 83, 109–10, 225, 228; slavery and, 33, 49, 67; social contract and, 246n2
colonization schemes, 153–64, 175–76, 187–93, 200–201; abolition versus, 169; algorithms of, 202; Black-initiated plans of, 251n16; cost of, 164–65, 206, 252n19; Jay on, 180–81; Jefferson on, 254n29; Walker on, 163–64, 215–16. *See also* American Colonization Society
communication: gothic theory of, 134, 137–47, *140*; mathematical theory of, 135–36, 139, 142
Connecticut Colonization Society, 178
Conrad, Joseph, 6
Constitution (US), 53–54; Fourth Amendment to, 53, 94, 105–6, 112; Hamilton on, 91–93; Protection Clause of, 71; social contract and, 36–37
Cooper, James Fenimore, 83–84, 99–107; Benjamin on, 81–82; Locke and, 99–100; on slavery, 84, 102
Cooper, James Fenimore, works of: *The Crater*, 35–36; *The Deerslayer*, 84, 107; *Last of the Mohicans*, 81, 83–84; *The Pathfinder*, 115; *The Prairie*, 84, 110. See also *Pioneers*
Cooper, William, 102–3, 106
Coppola, Francis Ford, 26
Cornish, Samuel E., 193, 257n21; on Emancipation Day festivities, 208–12; as founder of *Freedom's Journal*, 75, 167–70; Russwurm and, 206, 219, 253n21
coronavirus pandemic, 35, 51
Cowper, William, 9
Crawford, Adam, 49
Crawford, Neta, 65, 66
critical security studies, 20, 242n1
cryptography, 134, 248n9
Cuban Missile Crisis, 5
Cuffee, Paul, 251n16
Custis, George Washington Parke, 160
cyberterrorism, 3

data brokers, 85
Davis, Adrienne, 183
Day, Jeremiah, 75
Declaration of Independence, 50, 63–64, 195, 214
de Goede, Marieke, 42, 244n18, 255n40
de Grazia, Margreta, 242n17
Dei people, 225, 226
Dekanahwideh (Indigenous leader), 65
Delano, Amasa, 231–32
Delaware people, 49, 58–59, 64–65. *See also* Indigenous peoples
DeLillo, Don, 32
Deloria, Philip, 67
de Man, Paul, 136
Department of Homeland Security (DHS), 19, 29, 93–95
Destutt de Tracy, Antoine, 184
detective fiction, 81–82, 88
Dickinson, Baxter, 154, 161
Digital Humanities, 149, 249nn16–17
Dillon, Michael, 27, 44; on biopolitics, 37, 38, 119, 248n1
Diran, Ingrid, 183
disaster movies, 20, 91–92
disinformation, 30, 31, 251n12
Doctorow, Cory, 95–97
Domestic Surveillance Directorate, 95, 96
Douglass, Frederick, 211, 244n21
Douglass, Sarah Mapps, 252n16
Downes, Paul, 34
Du Bois, W.E.B., 253n23
Dumas, Alexandre, 81
Dunlap, William, 148
Dunston, Hannah, 246n3

earnest money, 43
economic crisis: of 1837, 76–77, 187, 188, 190; of 2008, 23, 189, 255n41
Edwards, Erica R., 13, 258n2
Elden, Stuart, 108
Electronic Freedom Foundation, 97–98
Elliott, Emory, 149
Elmer, Jonathan, 228

286 INDEX

Emancipation Day festivities, 207–11, 256n12
Emerson, R. Guy, 33
Enlightenment, 84, 120, 138; American, 132; colonization and, 250n5; gothic fiction and, 48; Jefferson and, 156; Kant on, 125, 133; Locke on, 130–32; Mosco on, 125; print culture and, 248n8; Walker and, 214
entropy, 134, 141
Equiano, Olaudah, 251n16
Era of Good Feelings, 166
Everett, Alexander Hill, 203–4
Everett, Edward, 165

Fagan, Benjamin, 208
fake news, 30, 31, 251n12
Faludi, Susan, 82–83, 246n3
Farrell, Molly, 218
fear: Beck on, 86–87; biopolitics of, 185; Foucault on, 90–91; "futurity" of, 43; Hobbes on, 24–25; Locke on, 87, 90–92; security and, 23–25, 86–87, 90, 124; Shklar on, 86; vulnerability and, 9–10, 15. *See also* terror
Federalist Papers, The, 91–93
FedEx Corporation, 44
feminism. *See* gender issues
Feng, Janice, 246n2
Ferguson, Robert A., 132
Fernando Po (Bioko Island), 221–23
Fiedler, Leslie, 126, 149
Finley, Robert, 72, 73, 252n17, 252n20
Forten, James, 193, 195–201, 220, 251n16
Foster, Frances Smith, 168
Foucault, Michel, 185, 253n27, 254n31; Agamben and, 257n18; algorithms and, 48, 55, 157–58, 161–62; on biopolitics, 37, 90–91, 195; on biopower, 51, 250n4; on discipline, 21–22, 104, 125; on governmentality, 172–73; on liberalism, 38, 90–91; on statistics, 154, 158, 162–63
Fourth of July: parades on, 196, 207–9, 256n12; speeches on, 153–56, 161–62, 174, 178, 192, 249n1, 250n3
Franklin, Benjamin, 235; Hobbes and, 57–58; on Indigenous peoples, 61–63; on population growth, 43, 62, 68, 156; on security versus freedom, 56–62, 81, 87, 90; on slavery, 62; on whiteness, 62–63
freedom: Arendt on, 13, 36–40; Berlin on, 39; Brown on, 128; Foucault on, 38; Franklin on, 56–62, 81, 87, 90; Locke on, 83; Milton on, 43–44; positive/negative, 39; security and, 36–39, 84; Shannon on, 47, 152
Freedom's Journal, 11, 155, 158; archives of, 252n21; circulation of, 253n24; Cornish at, 74–75, 167–70; Forten and, 196; on Liberia, 203; Russwurm at, 75, 167–70, 223; shutdown of, 170, 193, 219
free people of color, 50, 72, 73; Code Noir and, 218; colonization schemes for, 163–64, 166–67, 186, 190–91; Emancipation Day festivities and, 207–11; white nationalism and, 153–58, 173–74
French Revolution, 72–73, 106, 108–9
Freud, Sigmund, 97–99; aesthetics and, 28; gothic fiction and, 126; on uncanny, 28, 82

Gaddis, Lewis, 2, 246n3
Gage, Thomas, 66–67
Galli, Carlo, 7
Galluzzo, Anthony, 142
Garrison, William Lloyd, 72, 155; on American Colonization Society, 186, 216; on colonization schemes, 187, 249n1; Russwurm on, 223
gender issues, 13, 33, 170, 182–83, 243n14
genocide: of Indigenous peoples, 29, 48, 82–83; white fears of, 14, 159, 174, 178, 250n10
George III of Great Britain, 64
Gershoni, Yekutiel, 227–28
Gervinus, Georg Gottfried, 28
Gilmore, Michael, 127, 132
Gilmore, Ruth Wilson, 27, 159
Giroux, Henry A., 251n12
Gitelman, Lisa, 143, 145–46
Gleick, James, 134, 141–42, 248n9
gothic fiction, 48, 115–17, 125–34; Fiedler on, 126; Freud and, 127; Sedgwick on, 125–27
gothic humanities, 147–52

gothic theory of communication, 134, 137–47, 140
governmentality, 172–73, 252n18; algorithms of, 157–58, 161–62, 194
Grady, James, 10–11, 48
Greenwald, Glenn, 96, 98, 108, 109, 112–13
Grewal, Inderpal, 7, 13, 230; on "logic of vigilantism," 33; on "securitization of everyday life," 52
Griffin, Patrick, 244n25, 246n2
Griggs, Sutton, 169
Griswold, Roger, 70
Grusin, Richard, 241n4
Gutman, Herbert, 183
Guyatt, Nicholas, 250n7, 252n20, 254n29

Haiti, 162, 174, 177, 181, 182, 191; Black emigration to, 251n16
Hall, Prince, 251n16
Hamilton, Alexander, 91–93, 106
Hamilton, John, 26, 39
Harris, Cheryl, 49
Harrison, Jesse Burton, 177–78
Hartz, Louis, 83
Haudenosaunee, 65. *See also* Indigenous peoples
Hawthorne, Nathaniel, 76–77
Hayden, Michael, 33
Hayles, N. Katherine, 142, 143
Hemings, Sally, 183
Henri Christophe of Haiti, 251n16
Herz, John, 27
Hinks, Peter, 218
Hirsch, Marianne, 9
Hitchcock, Alfred, 26
Hobbes, Thomas, 2, 7, 41; Anker on, 90, 91; Downes on, 34; Franklin and, 57–58; Locke on, 90; Schiller and, 24; Schmitt on, 7–8, 231, 234; on social contract, 36–37; on state of nature, 83, 91, 246n2; on sublime, 24–25; Thucydides and, 241n2
Hobbes, Thomas, works of: *Elements of Law*, 24–25, 41; *Leviathan*, 24–25, 41, 57, 90

Homeland Security. *See* Department of Homeland Security
Homer, 9, 41
homo sacer, 6–7, 230, 235
homo securus, 7–10, 230
Honig, Bonnie, 34, 35
Horsman, Reginald, 160, 250n11
Howlett, Henan, 170–72, 171, 174, 186
Hurricane Katrina (2005), 5
Hussein, Saddam, 46
Huysmans, Jef, 234, 258n1

Indigenous peoples, 58–59, 227–28; Black alliances with, 66–68, 72, 162; Canadian, 218; Franklin on, 61–63; genocide of, 29, 48, 82–83; Iroquois Constitution and, 65–66; Liberian, 224–27, 226; treaties with, 49, 64–65
individualism, 34; Fourth Amendment on, 94; Thomas on, 246n4
information, 30–34; aesthetics of, 120–25, 135; Benjamin on, 116; misinformation and, 3, 30–34, 140, 251n12; storytelling and, 117–20, 125; theories of, 134–37, 136, 137, 139, 142–43
informational sublime, 115–18
insecurity: financial forms of, 42–43, 45, 76–77, 187–91, 199; generated from security, 25–28, 50, 109; information and, 30–33, 67; profitability of, 44–46; psychology of, 30; racial, 51, 64, 73, 164, 168–70, 186, 188. *See also* security
Insko, Jeffrey, 242n17
Iraq, 46–47
Iroquois Confederacy, 64–66
ISIS (Islamic State of Iraq and Syria), 3, 117

Jamaica, 217, 251n16
James, Henry, 142
James, Winston, 220
January 6th coup (2021), 31
Japanese American internment camps, 71–72
Jay, William, 175, 180–81, 188, 201–2

Jefferson, Thomas, 16, 153–56, 177–86, 191; affect of, 155–56, 177, 181; on colonization schemes, 72–73, 254n29; Davis on, 183; Declaration of Independence and, 50, 63–64, 195, 214; on Logan, 227–28; Louisiana Purchase and, 72–73; on multiracial society, 8, 43; *Notes on the State of Virginia*, 50, 177, 194, 227–28; on slavery, 124, 177; on sublime, 123–24, 255n1; as surveyor, 106–7; Turner and, 50; Walker on, 50, 194–95, 214
Jim Crow laws, 3–4. *See also* racism
Johnson, Ben, 14
Johnson, Samuel, 106
Johnson, Walter, 184, 187–90
Jones, Absalom, 218

Kafka, Franz, 235
Kahn, David, 31
Kant, Immanuel, 120–25, 133
Kaplan, Amy, 246n6
Kazanjian, David, 254n29
Kentucky Colonization Society, 177
Key, Francis Scott, 165
King Philip's War (1675–76), 30

LaFleur, Greta, 250n4, 254n28
Lakoff, Andrew, 13, 20, 229, 242n14
Land Ordinance of 1785 (US), 106–7
Laporte, Dominique, 97, 112
Lee, Maurice, 8, 31, 121
Leigh, William, 255n43
Lenape. *See* Delaware people
Lepler, Jessica, 76–77
Lepore, Jill, 205
Levine, Robert S., 113, 247n14, 248n4; *Dislocating the Nation*, 73, 212, 216, 253n21, 257n17, 257n19
Levy, Jonathan, 45–46, 244n21
Lewis, Adam, 224
Lewis, Sinclair, 71
liberalism, 86, 90; Foucault on, 38, 90; Hobbes and, 90; Locke and, 57; Neocleous on, 38, 84; technologies of, 84–95. *See also* neoliberalism

Liberator, The, 155
Liberia, 74, 158, 203, 219–27; Allen on, 164, 252n17; Child on, 176; civil wars in, 225, 227; Clay on, 206–7; emigration to, 250n7; Garrison on, 187; map of, 226; mortality rates in, 257n28, 257nn23–24; Walker on, 163, 216. *See also* American Colonization Society
Liberia Herald, 158, 221–25, 257n27, 258n31
Litwack, Leon, 166
Loader, Ian, 36, 119
Locke, John, 101–2; Brown and, 126, 130–32, 143, 249n12; Burke on, 29, 138; on equality, 83, 92; on fear, 87, 90–92; Franklin and, 57; on freedom, 94, 132; on Hobbes, 90; Luhmann on, 143; on property, 98–102; on social contract, 83, 234; on state of nature, 83, 86, 90, 91, 246n2
Locke, John, works of: *An Essay Concerning Human Understanding*, 92, 94, 130–32, 138, 143, 145; *Second Treatise of Government*, 83, 86–87, 98–99, 101–2
Logan (Indigenous leader), 227–28
logarithms, 134–35
Louisiana Purchase, 72–73
Luhmann, Niklas, 32–33, 143, 145–47, 152
Lynchburg Colonization Society, 177–78
lynching, 50, 247n8
Lyon, Matthew, 69–71

MacLellan, Matthew, 218
Malthus, Thomas, 178, 254n30
malware, 24, 149–50, *150*
Mandel, Emily St. John, 35–36
Margolis, Stacey, 130, 146
Marshall, John, 165
Marx, Gary T., 111
Masco, Joseph, 13–14, 26, 39
Maslow, Abraham, 19–21
Massumi, Brian, 154, 158
Mbembe, Achille, 217, 253n27
McCarthy, Anne C., 117
McCarthyism, 69
McHenry, Elizabeth, 253n24, 256n9

McKittrick, Katherine, 158, 251n15
Melville, Herman, works of: *Benito Cereno*, 182, 186, 231–33, 235; *The Confidence-Man*, 233–34; "The Lightning-Rod Man," 233–35
Mendelssohn, Moses, 242n10
metadata, 85–86, 107
Miller, Stephen, 251n12
Milligan, Joseph, 184
Mills, Brandon, 227
Milton, John, 24, 43–44
Mishra, Vijay, 125
misinformation, 3, 30–34, 140, 251n12
Mitchell, Jacob, 197–98
Mitchell, W.J.T., 150
Morris, David B., 125
Morris, Robert Hunter, 58–60
Mosco, Vincent, 125
Mother Bethel African Methodist Episcopal Church, 73–74

Nagel, Alexander, 14–15, 242n18
Napoleon Bonaparte, 72–73
Nash, Gary, 166, 197
National Security Agency (NSA), 16, 19, 116; Assange on, 89; metadata and, 107; Schneier on, 85; social media and, 32; surveillance programs of, 26, 85
natural disasters, 5, 20, 91–92
Neocleous, Mark, 7, 22, 234; on insecurity, 241n9; on liberalism, 38, 84; on "security fetishism," 89; on "technique of security," 84
neoliberalism, 7, 13, 52, 56, 157. *See also* liberalism
Newtonian physics, 131
Nietzsche, Friedrich, 39
Noah, Mordecai, 74, 208–12, 256n15
NSA. *See* National Security Agency
nuclear weapons, 23, 27

Operation Enduring Freedom, 6
Operation Infinite Justice, 6
Orwell, George, 96

Paine, Thomas, 1, 130
Panic of 1837, 76–77, 187, 188, 190
Parker, Arthur Caswell, 65–66
Parkinson, Robert, 67–68
Parrott, Russell, 169–70, 172, 200–201, 204
passenger pigeons, 109–11, 115
Paterson, William, 70–71
Paulson, William, 136
Peabody, William Bourn Oliver, 201
Penn, William, 65
people of color. *See* free people of color
Perry, Barbara, 250n10
Peterson, Carla, 207
Philadelphia, 73–74, 203; Black residents of, 196–99, 218, 220, 256n4
Pioneers, The (Cooper), 11, 12, 48, 103–14; frontispiece to, 103–4, *105*; privacy in, 84, 86, 103–7, 112–14; security in, 29, 90
Poe, Edgar Allan, 28
Poincaré, Henri, 15
political balance of the globe, 221–22, *222*
Polk, Josiah F., 201
Pollack, Sydney, 11, 26
postal service, 44, 50
Potolsky, Matthew, 118, 248n2
Power-Greene, Ousemane K., 250n7
Priestley, Joseph, 68
print culture, 203, 212, 224, 248n8, 253n21, 256n9
prison system, 3–4, 27, 169, 246n6
privacy, 85–86; Assange on, 89; constitutional notions of, 16; Cooper on, 84; Doctorow on, 97; human rights and, 112–13; photography and, 88; property and, 49–50, 85–87, 106, 111–13; security versus, 94–95
property: Cooper on, 84, 99–102; Locke on, 98–102; privacy and, 49–50, 85–87, 106, 111–13; security and, 84, 91, 103–4; special tax on, 195–201
Protecting Society of Philadelphia, 203
Puar, Jasbir, 13

QAnon, 31

racial insecurity, 51, 64, 73, 164, 168–70, 186, 188
racial profiling, 48, 198
racism, 3–4, 50, 73–74; biopower and, 254n35; definition of, 27, 159; of Franklin, 62–63; lynching and, 50, 247n8; nationalism and, 153–58; security and, 22, 27
Radcliffe, Ann, 127
Rand Corporation, 29
Randolph, John, 159, 190–92, 212, 215–17, 255n43
"replacement theory," 159, 250n10. *See also* whiteness
Roberts, Siân Silyn, 132
Rockbridge (VA) Colonization Society, 179
Roediger, David, 160, 250n11
Rojecki, Andrew, 258n2
Romanticism, 143–44
Roosevelt, Franklin D., 56, 71–72
Rosen, David, 89–90, 106
Rothman, Joshua D., 255n42
Rothschild, Emma, 46
Rousseau, Jean-Jacques, 83
Rouvroy, Antoinette, 42, 47, 157–58, 162
Rowe, John Carlos, 128
Rowlandson, Mary, 30, 82
Ruggles, David, 170–72
Rumsfeld, Donald, 10, 32, 46–47; affect of, 244n22
Rush, Lewis, 197–99
Russwurm, John Brown, 193, 219–27, 257nn23–24, 258n28; Cornish and, 206, 219, 253n21; on Emancipation Day festivities, 208–12; at *Freedom's Journal*, 75, 167–70, 223; on Garrison, 223; legacy of, 258n30; at *Liberia Herald*, 221–27, 257n27, 258n31

Saillant, John, 156
Saint-Domingue (Santo Domingo). *See* Haiti
Santesso, Aaron, 89–90, 106
Saxton, Alexander, 51

Schiller, Friedrich von: Hobbes and, 24; on sublime, 120, 123, 124
Schmitt, Carl, 3, 57–58, 229–30; anti-Semitism of, 242n10; on friend/enemy distinction, 5, 241n5; on Hobbes, 7–8, 231, 234
Schneier, Bruce, 12, 85
Schuller, Kyla, 51, 250n4, 252n18
Scott, Tony, 26
Securitas Corporation, 26
security, 21–23; agency and, 34–36, 51–54; collective striving toward, 34–36; contradiction of, 19–21; etymology of, 25–26, 39, 41; fear and, 23–25, 86–87, 90; freedom and, 36–39, 84, 128; information needed for, 30–34; insecurity generated from, 5, 7, 20, 25–28, 35, 50, 109, 119; interpretation of data and, 46–48; property and, 84, 91, 103–4; as protection racket, 37; racism and, 27; Schiller on, 123; social contract and, 12–13, 89; terror and, 28–30; time and, 41–45, 63–66, 157, 161–62, 174, 194, 244n19, 244n20. *See also* insecurity
security studies, 20, 242n1
Sedgwick, Eve Kosofsky, 125–27
Seltzer, Mark, 144
September 11th attacks (2001), 2; Faludi on, 82, 83, 246n3; homeland security after, 28–29, 118; Masco on, 13; privacy after, 85
settler colonialism, 29, 33, 48–50, 57, 61, 83, 109–10, 225, 228. *See also* colonialism
Seven Years' War (1756–63), 57, 81, 248n4
Shakespeare, William, 25, 45
Shannon, Claude E., 8, 47; information theory of, 134–37, *136*, 139, 142–43
Shawnee, 58–59
Shays' Rebellion (1786–87), 53
Shklar, Judith N., 8, 86, 90
Sierra Leone, 72
Sigourney, Lydia Huntley, 223, 224
Silliman, Benjamin, 75–76, 178–79, *179*, 181, 186
Silver, Peter, 49, 244n25
Sioux, 110

slave-backed securities, 42, 45, 48–49, 76–77, 187–90, 254nn37–38; de Goede on, 255n40; Rothman on, 255n42
slave patrols, 4, 50, 67, 158
slave rebellions, 40; Indian alliances with, 66–68, 72; Nat Turner and, 50, 187, 251n14
slavery, 33, 73–74, 181–83, 202; Code Noir and, 218; colonialism and, 33, 49, 67; Cooper on, 84, 102; Franklin on, 62; Howlett on, 170; Jefferson on, 124, 177; prison system and, 3–4; Torrey on, 215; War of 1812 and, 196. *See also* abolitionism
slave trade, 45, 200; Beyan on, 225; Russwurm on, 258n31; Walker on, 216
smallpox, 63
Smith, James Morton, 68–69
Snowden, Edward, 26, 89, 91, 96–97, 112
social contract, 36–37; colonialism and, 246n2; Locke on, 83, 234; origin story of, 82–83; Rousseau on, 83; security and, 12–13, 89
social media: algorithms of, 32, 47, 52; Assange on, 89; disinformation on, 31; surveillance of, 42–43
Socrates, 144
Sollors, Werner, 231
Southampton Rebellion (1831), 187
Spero, Patrick, 49
spy novels, 117–18
state of emergency, 5–6, 67; Benjamin on, 5, 34–35, 230, 242n11
state of exception, 13, 61, 64, 230, 242n11, 245n2; Agamben on, 6–8, 235
state of nature: Hamilton on, 91–93; Hobbes on, 83, 91, 246n2; Locke on, 83, 86, 90, 91, 246n2
static (noise), 135–37, *136*, *137*, 140, 248n9
statistics: biopolitical, 154–64, 166–67; physiocrats and, 172
Stein, Jordan Alexander, 249n2
Stellarwind surveillance program, 85, 246n5
Stewart, Maria, 252n16
storytelling, 117–20, 125
Stowe, Harriet Beecher, 77, 250n3

sublime, 13, 21, 120–25; Burke on, 120, 121; definition of, 120; "digital," 125; "gothic," 125; Hobbes on, 24–25; informational, 114–18; Jefferson on, 123–24, 255n1; Kant on, 120–24; "mathematical," 122; Mishra on, 125; Schiller on, 120, 123, 124. *See also* aesthetics
summum bonum/malum, 90
Sun Microsystems, 89
surveillance, 26–27; Assange on, 89; Cooper on, 84, 86, 103–7; etymology of, 106; literature and, 89–90; "racializing" of, 50, 168; racial profiling and, 48; social media and, 42–43; software for, 85, 89, 96, 246n5; surveying and, 106–7
Sweet, Leonard I., 249n2, 256n12

Tallmadge Colonization Society, 153–54
Tambling, Jeremy, 15
Taylor, Alan, 103
Tennenhouse, Leonard, 249n3
terror, 84, 138, 182; affect and, 83, 120; Beck on, 92; Faludi on, 82–83, 246n3; Foucault on, 185; informational sublime and, 115–17; "poetry" of, 82; of "racial apocalypse," 161; security and, 28–30, 124; state of nature and, 83; unspeakable, 125–34. *See also* fear; "war on terror"
thermodynamics, 134, 141
Thomas, Brook, 246n4
Thomas, George, 64–65
Thucydides, 241n2
Tilly, Charles, 37
Torrey, Jesse, 215
Toussaint Louverture, 162
Treverton, Gregory, 117–19
Trump, Donald, 31, 72, 210, 241n4, 251n12
Tsoukala, Anastassia, 40
Turing, Alan, 134, 142
Turner, Frederick Jackson, 241n1
Turner, Nat, 50, 187, 251n14

uncanny, 28, 82, 93–94, 127
United Nations, 24, 36
"Unite the Right" movement, 159

USA PATRIOT Act (2001), 28–29, 118
Utah Data Center, 96

vacuum domicillium, 87, 101–3
Vai people, 225, 226
Valéry, Paul, 15–16
Vermont Colonization Society, 155
vigilantism, 30, 33, 50, 247n8
Voelz, Johannes, 22–23, 34
voting rights, 166, 195–96, 256n11
vulnerability, 9–10, 13, 26; affect and, 10, 86, 129, 150, 159, 205; information and, 33; reading and, 10–11; white nationalism and, 159–60; whiteness and, 49–51, 155–56

Wæver, Ole, 230
Walker, David, 8, 50, 182, 213, 257n16; *Appeal . . . to the Colored Citizens of the World*, 158, 193–95, 214–19, 257n167; on biopower, 185, 217–18; on colonization schemes, 163–64, 215–16; on Jefferson, 50, 194–95, 214; on Randolph, 215–17
Walker, Neil, 36, 119
Walking Purchase, 49, 64–65
Walpole, Horace, 127
Warner, Michael, 248n8
War of 1812, 1–2, 153, 196, 220
"war on terror," 28–29, 44, 53, 230–31; Faludi on, 82, 83; Masco on, 26; Treverton on, 117. *See also* terror
Warren, Samuel D., 86, 88

Washington, Bushrod, 165, 205
Washington, George, 69, 106
Watts, Steven, 149
Weaver, Warren, 135–37, 137, 142
Weber, Max, 34
Weheliye, Alexander, 160, 253n27, 254n35
Wells-Barnett, Ida B., 50
western movies, 82
Wheatley, Phillis, 251n16
Wheeler, Tom, 88–89
"white genocide" fears, 14, 159, 174, 178, 250n10
white nationalism, 153–60, 193–94
whiteness, 22, 27, 76–77; Ahmed on, 51, 156; class distinctions and, 250n11; Franklin on, 62–63; identity and, 16, 48–51; "replacement theory" and, 159, 250n10; voting rights and, 166, 195–96, 256n11; vulnerability and, 49–51, 155–56; Weheliye on, 160
Whittlesey, Elisha, 153–54
wilderness/wasteland, 86–87; Cooper on, 83–84, 99–103; Locke on, 86–87, 101–2
Woodward, C. Vann, 1–2, 4, 241n1

Yale, Calvin, 155
yellow fever, 63, 218, 248n5

Zeskind, Leonard, 159
Zuboff, Shoshana, 42, 244n20

A NOTE ON THE TYPE

This book has been composed in Arno, an Old-style serif typeface in the classic Venetian tradition, designed by Robert Slimbach at Adobe.